Current Trends and Best Practices of Pedagogical Content Knowledge (PCK)

Nazli Ruya Taskin Bedizel
Balikesir University, Turkey

Vice President of Editorial	Melissa Wagner
Managing Editor of Acquisitions	Mikaela Felty
Managing Editor of Book Development	Jocelynn Hessler
Production Manager	Mike Brehm
Cover Design	Phillip Shickler

Published in the United States of America by
IGI Global Scientific Publishing
701 East Chocolate Avenue
Hershey, PA, 17033, USA
Tel: 717-533-8845
Fax: 717-533-8661
Website: https://www.igi-global.com E-mail: cust@igi-global.com

Copyright © 2025 by IGI Global Scientific Publishing. All rights reserved. No part of this publication may be reproduced, stored or distributed in any form or by any means, electronic or mechanical, including photocopying, without written permission from the publisher.
Product or company names used in this set are for identification purposes only. Inclusion of the names of the products or companies does not indicate a claim of ownership by IGI Global Scientific Publishing of the trademark or registered trademark.

Library of Congress Cataloging-in-Publication Data

Names: Bedizel, Nazli Ruya Taskin, 1985- editor.
Title: Current trends and best practices of pedagogical content knowledge (PCK) / Edited by Nazli Ruya Taskin Bedizel.
Other titles: Research on the nature and development of pedagogical content knowledge (PCK)
Description: Hershey, PA : IGI Global, [2025] | Includes bibliographical references and index. | Summary: "This book compiles a collection of research articles that explore the multifaceted aspects of PCK, aiming to provide valuable insights and practical examples for educators, researchers, and professionals involved in teacher education programs"-- Provided by publisher.
Identifiers: LCCN 2024038894 (print) | LCCN 2024038895 (ebook) | ISBN 9798369306550 (hardcover) | ISBN 9798369347195 (paperback) | ISBN 9798369306567 (ebook)
Subjects: LCSH: Pedagogical content knowledge--Research. | Educators--Effect of technological innovations on. | Teachers--Training of. | Culturally relevant pedagogy--Research.
Classification: LCC LB1028.3 .H3555539 2024 (print) | LCC LB1028.3 (ebook) | DDC 371.33--dc23/eng/20240916
LC record available at https://lccn.loc.gov/2024038894
LC ebook record available at https://lccn.loc.gov/2024038895

British Cataloguing in Publication Data
A Cataloguing in Publication record for this book is available from the British Library.

All work contributed to this book is new, previously-unpublished material.
The views expressed in this book are those of the authors, but not necessarily of the publisher.
This book contains information sourced from authentic and highly regarded references, with reasonable efforts made to ensure the reliability of the data and information presented. The authors, editors, and publisher believe the information in this book to be accurate and true as of the date of publication. Every effort has been made to trace and credit the copyright holders of all materials included. However, the authors, editors, and publisher cannot assume responsibility for the validity of all materials or the consequences of their use. Should any

Table of Contents

Preface xv

Acknowledgment xxii

Chapter 1
Developing and Applying PCK in Diverse Subjects: Best Practices for
Mathematics, Science, Social Sciences, and Language Arts 1
    R. Vettriselvan, Academy of Maritime Education and Training, India
    Deepa Rajesh, Academy of Maritime Education and Training, India
    S. Subhashini, PSGR Krishnammal College for Women, India
    K. Gajalakshmi, PSGR Krishnammal College for Women, India
    R. Sakthivel, DMI-St.Eugene University, Zambia

Chapter 2
Examining the Diverse Sources Influencing the Development of Pedagogical
Content Knowledge (PCK) Among Educators in Various Educational Settings 31
    Jamila Khurshid, University of Poonch, Rawalakot, Pakistan
    Nabila Khurshid, Comsats University, Islamabad, Pakistan
    Nyela Ashraf, University of Poonch, Rawalakot, Pakistan
    Arslan Arshad, Alhamd University, Islamabad, Pakistan

Chapter 3
Leveraging Learning Progressions to Enhance Pedagogical Content
Knowledge in Science Education 41
    Sam Ramaila, University of Johannesburg, South Africa

Chapter 4
Phronesis as a Pathway for the Nature and Development of Pedagogical
Content Knowledge (PCK): Seeing Through Indigenous Gnoseology 89
    Jahid Siraz Chowdhury, Universiti Malaya, Malaysia
    Zulkarnain A. Hatta, Lincoln University Collge, Malaysia
    Sneha Singh, University of Auckland, New Zealand

Chapter 5
Harnessing Pedagogical Content Knowledge for Cross-Disciplinary
Innovation in Engineering 119

*H. Kareemullah, Department of Electronics and Instrumentation
Engineering, B.S.A. Crescent Institute of Science and Technology,
Chennai, India*

*M. D. Mohan Gift, Department of Mechanical Engineering, Grace
College of Engineering, Tuticorin, India*

*R. Bhaskaran, Department of Information Technology, PSNA College of
Engineering and Technology, Dindigul, India*

*T. Santhana Krishnan, Department of Electrical and Electronics
Engineering, Rajalakshmi Engineering College, Thandalam, India*

*S. Senthil kumar, Department of Electrical and Electronics Engineering,
New Prince Shri Bhavani College of Engineering and Technology,
Chennai, India*

Chapter 6
Mapping the Growth of Pedagogical Content Knowledge Across Teaching
Careers 151

*Thangjam Ravichandra, Department of Finance and Accounts, Alliance
School of Business, Alliance University, Bengaluru, India*

*M. Mariappan, Department of Civil Engineering, Dr. Mahalingam
College of Engineering and Technology, Pollachi, India*

*C. V. Padmaja, Department of English, GITAM University,
Visakhapatnam, India*

*Narasinga Rao Barnikana, Department of English, National Law
Institute University, Bhopal, India*

*T. Saravanan, Department of Electronics and Communication
Engineering, New Prince Shri Bhavani College of Engineering and
Technology, Chennai, India*

*Sampath Boopathi, Department of Mechanical Engineering,
Muthayammal Engineering College, Namakkal, India*

Chapter 7
Developing Science Pedagogical Content Knowledge (PCK) Among
Preservice and Novice Elementary Teachers 183

Sandy White Watson, University of Louisiana at Monroe, USA

Chapter 8
Current Trends and Best Practices of How In-Service Teachers Can Develop and Apply PCK in Social Sciences 213
    Deepak Maun, O.P. Jindal Global University, India
    Parth Sharma, University of Petroleum and Energy Studies, India
    Ta Huy Hung, Vietnam National University, Vietnam

Chapter 9
Unlocking Ms. Inaoka's PCK: A Case of Grammar Instruction in a Japanese Junior High School 237
    Kunitaro Mizuno, Kobe Women's University, Japan

Chapter 10
A System Thinking Approach to Pre-Service Teachers' Formation: An Epistemological Perspective From Europe and USA 263
    Francesco Maiorana, IIS G. B. Vaccarini Catania, Italy
    Andrew P. Csizmadia, Newman University, UK
    Gretchen M. Richards, Independent Researcher, USA
    Giusy Cristaldi, IIS Concetto Marchesi Mascalucia, Italy
    Janet L. Bavonese, Jacksonville University, USA

Chapter 11
Challenges and Innovations in Developing PCK Among Pre-Service Teachers 291
    Xuan-Hoa Nghiem, Vietnam National University, Vietnam
    Dhanashree Tharkude, Dr. Vishwanath Karad MIT World Peace University, India
    Neeti Goyal, University of Petroleum and Energy Studies, Dehradun, India
    Ajay Chandel, Lovely Professional University, India
    Shashank Mittal, O.P. Jindal Global University, India

Chapter 12
Training Teachers in Pedagogical Content Knowledge: A Bridging Method Between University and School 319
    Pasquale Gallo, University Magna Grecia Catanzaro, Italy
    Rosa Iaquinta, Independent Researcher, Italy

Chapter 13
Pedagogical Content Knowledge (PCK) and Assessment Practices: Teachers' PCK and Their Assessment Practices and Their Influences on Student Learning Outcomes 345

    Mohit Yadav, O.P. Jindal Global University, India
    Ashutosh Pandey, FORE School of Management, India
    Ajay Chandel, Lovely Professional University, India
    Ta Huy Hung, Vietnam National University, Hanoi, Vietnam

Compilation of References 369

About the Contributors 429

Index 435

Detailed Table of Contents

Preface xv

Acknowledgment xxii

Chapter 1
Developing and Applying PCK in Diverse Subjects: Best Practices for
Mathematics, Science, Social Sciences, and Language Arts 1
    R. Vettriselvan, Academy of Maritime Education and Training, India
    Deepa Rajesh, Academy of Maritime Education and Training, India
    S. Subhashini, PSGR Krishnammal College for Women, India
    K. Gajalakshmi, PSGR Krishnammal College for Women, India
    R. Sakthivel, DMI-St.Eugene University, Zambia

This chapter explores how in-service teachers can effectively develop and apply Pedagogical Content Knowledge (PCK) across various subjects—mathematics, science, social sciences, and language arts. PCK, which merges subject matter expertise with tailored teaching strategies, is crucial for enhancing educational outcomes. The chapter reviews current trends and best practices in PCK development, offering practical approaches for integrating effective pedagogical techniques with subject-specific content. It provides actionable insights into how educators can adapt their methods to address the unique challenges of each discipline, thus improving instructional practices and student engagement. By focusing on innovative strategies and real-world applications, this chapter serves as a comprehensive guide for teachers aiming to refine their PCK and elevate their teaching effectiveness.

Chapter 2
Examining the Diverse Sources Influencing the Development of Pedagogical
Content Knowledge (PCK) Among Educators in Various Educational Settings   31
    Jamila Khurshid, University of Poonch, Rawalakot, Pakistan
    Nabila Khurshid, Comsats University, Islamabad, Pakistan
    Nyela Ashraf, University of Poonch, Rawalakot, Pakistan
    Arslan Arshad, Alhamd University, Islamabad, Pakistan

This comprehensive study delves into the intricate web of diverse sources that influence the development of Pedagogical Content Knowledge (PCK) among educators in a multitude of educational settings. By exploring the impact of factors such as teacher education programs, classroom experiences, professional development workshops, specialized content knowledge, mentorship programs, and technology integration, this research aims to provide a holistic understanding of how educators acquire, refine, and apply their PCK. Through an in-depth analysis of these multifaceted sources, this study seeks to shed light on the complex interplay between different influences on PCK development and their implications for enhancing teaching practices and fostering effective student learning outcomes.

Chapter 3
Leveraging Learning Progressions to Enhance Pedagogical Content
Knowledge in Science Education 41
 Sam Ramaila, University of Johannesburg, South Africa

This chapter explores how learning progressions can enhance Pedagogical Content Knowledge (PCK) in science education. By providing a structured sequence of concepts and skills, learning progressions help educators align teaching strategies with students' cognitive development. This alignment offers deeper insights into student understanding and engagement with scientific concepts, improving PCK. The chapter examines the theoretical foundations of learning progressions and PCK, discusses strategies for integrating progressions into classroom practice, and uses case studies to show how they aid in addressing misconceptions, scaffolding learning, and promoting conceptual understanding. It emphasizes the importance of learning progressions in refining PCK and improving science education, ultimately preparing students for advanced inquiry and problem-solving.

Chapter 4
Phronesis as a Pathway for the Nature and Development of Pedagogical
Content Knowledge (PCK): Seeing Through Indigenous Gnoseology................. 89
 Jahid Siraz Chowdhury, Universiti Malaya, Malaysia
 Zulkarnain A. Hatta, Lincoln University Collge, Malaysia
 Sneha Singh, University of Auckland, New Zealand

This chapter examines the relationship between Indigenous Science and the new Western Baconian History of Philosophy of Science. It focuses on the Durkheimian Sociology of Knowledge and the connection between knowledge production and democracy. It rejects the notion that knowledge is merely labor and reflects Aristotle's stance that knowledge benefits societies. In critiquing the qualitative-quantitative dichotomy in the social sciences, this article reveals its deceptive nature, departing from empirical data analysis. This chapter explores the function of social science as a transition between the pre-colonial and post-colonial eras. Reconstructing a colonial history that marginalized non-Western thinkers and proposes a synthesis of Aristotelian Gnoseology, Indigenous Holism, Al-Farabian volunteerism, Patanjali's mind-body-spiritual odyssey, and Buddha's enlightenment, this chapter synthesis gives rise to Indigenous Gnosticism, which guides social scientists to contribute to human welfare and intellectual happiness while grounding their assertions in philosophical rigor.

Chapter 5
Harnessing Pedagogical Content Knowledge for Cross-Disciplinary Innovation in Engineering 119
    H. Kareemullah, Department of Electronics and Instrumentation Engineering, B.S.A. Crescent Institute of Science and Technology, Chennai, India
    M. D. Mohan Gift, Department of Mechanical Engineering, Grace College of Engineering, Tuticorin, India
    R. Bhaskaran, Department of Information Technology, PSNA College of Engineering and Technology, Dindigul, India
    T. Santhana Krishnan, Department of Electrical and Electronics Engineering, Rajalakshmi Engineering College, Thandalam, India
    S. Senthil kumar, Department of Electrical and Electronics Engineering, New Prince Shri Bhavani College of Engineering and Technology, Chennai, India

The chapter will present the integration of PCK toward the fostering of cross-disciplinary innovation within engineering. Being itself the composite of content expertise with effective teaching strategies, PCK acts as the main ingredient in developing holistic approaches to education that transcend traditional boundaries. On the basis of PCK, educators will be able to design curricula that enhance not only disciplinary-based understanding but also interdisciplinary collaboration. The chapter shares cases on how PCK-driven approaches to engineering education will let learners solve complex problems creatively and think innovatively about a wide range of contexts. It also provides strategies for embedding PCK in engineering programs through collaborative projects, interdisciplinary workshops, and experiential learning opportunities.

Chapter 6
Mapping the Growth of Pedagogical Content Knowledge Across Teaching
Careers 151
    Thangjam Ravichandra, Department of Finance and Accounts, Alliance
        School of Business, Alliance University, Bengaluru, India
    M. Mariappan, Department of Civil Engineering, Dr. Mahalingam
        College of Engineering and Technology, Pollachi, India
    C. V. Padmaja, Department of English, GITAM University,
        Visakhapatnam, India
    Narasinga Rao Barnikana, Department of English, National Law
        Institute University, Bhopal, India
    T. Saravanan, Department of Electronics and Communication
        Engineering, New Prince Shri Bhavani College of Engineering and
        Technology, Chennai, India
    Sampath Boopathi, Department of Mechanical Engineering,
        Muthayammal Engineering College, Namakkal, India

This chapter of the book presents how pedagogical content knowledge among teachers undergoes changes throughout their careers. The authors try to trace how this kind of expertise develops and finally impacts teaching practices. By analyzing data on a longitudinal basis, case studies will be made in order to realize how PCK develops among teachers from the initial VET stage into the entire life career history of a teacher, mainly focusing on key factors that might lead to its development. It discusses how professional development, reflective practice, and classroom experience work to improve PCK and how these are changed with the changes in educational contexts and student needs. The chapter provides insights into the mechanisms by which PCK deepens, offering practical recommendations for educators and policymakers in supporting ongoing professional growth. It thus illuminates the dynamics of teaching expertise and its implications for teacher education and the quality of instruction.

Chapter 7
Developing Science Pedagogical Content Knowledge (PCK) Among
Preservice and Novice Elementary Teachers 183
    Sandy White Watson, University of Louisiana at Monroe, USA

In this chapter, the author focuses on elementary-level practicing and pre-service teachers' development of pedagogical content knowledge (PCK), beginning with the state of U.S. students' science performance, and science instruction in elementary school settings. The historical development of studies related to teachers' knowledge forms (content, pedagogical, and pedagogical content) are explored individually, along with an investigation of models of PCK, PCK specific to teaching science, and studies on strategies for facilitating PCK development among elementary teacher candidates and in-service teachers.

Chapter 8
Current Trends and Best Practices of How In-Service Teachers Can Develop and Apply PCK in Social Sciences 213
    Deepak Maun, O.P. Jindal Global University, India
    Parth Sharma, University of Petroleum and Energy Studies, India
    Ta Huy Hung, Vietnam National University, Vietnam

Pedagogical Content Knowledge (PCK) is pivotal in advancing social sciences education by combining deep subject expertise with effective teaching practices. This paper explores current trends and best practices in developing and applying PCK, such as project-based learning, flipped classrooms, and service learning. It examines challenges including limited professional development, inadequate resources, and resistance to change, and identifies future directions such as leveraging advanced technology, fostering interdisciplinary approaches, and expanding community partnerships. By addressing these barriers and embracing emerging opportunities, educators can enhance instructional quality and student engagement. This study highlights the importance of continuous refinement and adaptation in teaching strategies to meet diverse student needs and prepare them for a dynamic world.

Chapter 9
Unlocking Ms. Inaoka's PCK: A Case of Grammar Instruction in a Japanese Junior High School.. 237
    Kunitaro Mizuno, Kobe Women's University, Japan

This paper explores the integration of Pedagogical Content Knowledge (PCK) in pre-service English teacher education in Japan. It focuses on the design and delivery of a course using PCK to enhance the preparation of future English teachers. The study centers on an introductory lesson on the "be going to" form by Ms. Inaoka, a renowned teacher, to illustrate the practical application of PCK. Through the analysis of video recordings and a collaborative online platform, students engage with and reflect on teaching strategies, enhancing their understanding of PCK. The paper also discusses the Pedagogical Reasoning and Action model proposed by Shulman, which outlines the transformation process through which teachers develop PCK, emphasizing comprehension, transformation, and instruction. This study contributes to the understanding of how theory and practice are integrated in teacher education and how effective pedagogical strategies are developed through the lens of PCK, thus preparing teachers to be more responsive and effective in diverse classroom settings.

Chapter 10
A System Thinking Approach to Pre-Service Teachers' Formation: An
Epistemological Perspective From Europe and USA 263
    Francesco Maiorana, IIS G. B. Vaccarini Catania, Italy
    Andrew P. Csizmadia, Newman University, UK
    Gretchen M. Richards, Independent Researcher, USA
    Giusy Cristaldi, IIS Concetto Marchesi Mascalucia, Italy
    Janet L. Bavonese, Jacksonville University, USA

It is acknowledged that it is necessary to introduce computing for a quality education starting from primary education. This can be accomplished by empowering pre-service teachers to become confident in teaching computing. The work will review the literature and compare teacher pre-service formation (PSF) activities in each author's country with an overview of the respective continents. Drawn from direct field experiences, this work will present, discuss, compare, and draw conclusions and best practices, through the lens of system thinking, on the complex process of pre-service computing teacher transformation. Similarities are acknowledged, while differences in approaches are highlighted. Using the lens of systems thinking, a review of research and theory to examine pre-service teacher (PST) formation will include Technological Pedagogical Content Knowledge (TPCK) in the realm of science, technology, engineering, arts, and mathematics (STEAM). Celia (Computer Educators Learning Inclusive Actor) will represent the teaching candidates' professional pathways in each country.

Chapter 11
Challenges and Innovations in Developing PCK Among Pre-Service
Teachers 291
    Xuan-Hoa Nghiem, Vietnam National University, Vietnam
    Dhanashree Tharkude, Dr. Vishwanath Karad MIT World Peace
       University, India
    Neeti Goyal, University of Petroleum and Energy Studies, Dehradun,
       India
    Ajay Chandel, Lovely Professional University, India
    Shashank Mittal, O.P. Jindal Global University, India

This chapter explores the development of Pedagogical Content Knowledge (PCK) among pre-service teachers, highlighting the challenges and innovations that shape their growth. Through detailed case studies, including the integration of technology, differentiated instruction, and culturally responsive teaching, the chapter examines effective strategies and the role of mentorship in enhancing PCK. It identifies common themes such as the importance of adapting teaching methods to diverse learner needs and the impact of reflective practice. Future directions emphasize the need for incorporating advanced technologies, data-driven instruction, and social-emotional learning into PCK frameworks. The chapter concludes by underscoring the significance of ongoing innovation and support in teacher preparation to improve educational outcomes.

Chapter 12
Training Teachers in Pedagogical Content Knowledge: A Bridging Method Between University and School 319
    Pasquale Gallo, University Magna Grecia Catanzaro, Italy
    Rosa Iaquinta, Independent Researcher, Italy

The teaching needs expressed by new generations require teachers to have various skills: pedagogical, didactic, communicative and design. The work is the result of an experimental project conducted in the academic field, which involved two teachers with extensive professional experience both as teachers in schools and universities. The interest of the research was to demonstrate the validity of Shulman's PCK method through classroom instruction and, at the same time, to promote in future teachers the ability to assess, through direct experience, the importance of the design and implementation of teaching and the significant role of the choice of didactic method.

Chapter 13
Pedagogical Content Knowledge (PCK) and Assessment Practices: Teachers' PCK and Their Assessment Practices and Their Influences on Student Learning Outcomes 345
    Mohit Yadav, O.P. Jindal Global University, India
    Ashutosh Pandey, FORE School of Management, India
    Ajay Chandel, Lovely Professional University, India
    Ta Huy Hung, Vietnam National University, Hanoi, Vietnam

This study explores the impact of Pedagogical Content Knowledge (PCK) on assessment practices and their subsequent influence on student learning outcomes. Through case studies of three educators—Ms. Sarah Thompson at Lincoln Middle School, Mr. David Martinez at Crestwood High School, and Ms. Emily Chen at Brookfield Elementary School—the research examines how deep subject matter expertise and pedagogical strategies shape both formative and summative assessments. The findings reveal that effective integration of PCK into assessment practices enhances student performance, engagement, and feedback quality. Despite these insights, the study acknowledges limitations such as context-specific findings and qualitative data reliance, suggesting the need for further research across diverse settings and methodologies. The study highlights the importance of PCK in creating equitable and effective assessments and provides implications for educational practice, professional development, and policy.

Compilation of References 369

About the Contributors 429

Index 435

Preface

In the realm of education, the process of imparting knowledge goes beyond simply delivering content—it involves an intricate understanding of how to convey that content in a way that ensures deep and meaningful learning. Teachers must not only be experts in their subject areas but also be skilled in the art of teaching those subjects effectively. The concept of Pedagogical Content Knowledge (PCK) encapsulates this challenge, serving as a bridge between subject matter expertise and instructional strategies that foster student comprehension and engagement. As educational practices continue to evolve in the face of technological advancements, the need for a comprehensive and adaptable guide to PCK has never been more urgent.

The book *Nature and Development of Pedagogical Content Knowledge (PCK)* stands as a crucial resource for educators, researchers, and policymakers who seek to understand and cultivate this vital form of tacit knowledge. This handbook presents a robust collection of research that delves into the nature of PCK, its historical roots, and the challenges educators face in developing it. It also offers forward-looking insights into how PCK can be enhanced and applied across various disciplines, including mathematics, science, social sciences, and language arts education. With the educational landscape constantly shifting, this work serves as both a theoretical framework and a practical guide to navigating the complexities of modern teaching.

This volume is not just an exploration of PCK in its traditional forms but also an invitation to reimagine its future. As the integration of technology into classrooms continues to grow, understanding the evolving role of PCK is essential for shaping teaching practices that are both innovative and effective. The contributions within this book address the pressing issues of how to assess and measure PCK, the cross-disciplinary applications of this knowledge, and the trajectories it will follow as education adapts to new challenges. By examining historical foundations, best practices, and current challenges, this handbook aims to equip educators with the tools they need to foster meaningful learning experiences in the classroom.

CHAPTER OVERVIEW

This handbook encompasses a wide range of topics essential to the understanding and development of Pedagogical Content Knowledge (PCK). In addition to examining the core principles of PCK, several chapters explore the best practices for in-service teachers, providing actionable strategies for immediate classroom application. Cross-disciplinary applications of PCK are discussed, revealing how the principles of PCK can be tailored to different subject areas, while also examining the role of learning progressions as frameworks for instructional design. Historical and theoretical foundations of PCK are explored, offering a deep dive into its evolution over time, while lessons learned from lesson studies provide real-world examples of PCK in action. The book also considers how PCK can be assessed and measured, helping educators develop ways to gauge their own teaching effectiveness. Finally, the trajectories of PCK are discussed, offering a forward-thinking perspective on how PCK will continue to develop in response to the ever-changing educational landscape.

Chapter 1. Developing and Applying PCK in Diverse Subjects: Best Practices for Mathematics, Science, Social Sciences, and Language Arts

Vettriselvan R., Rajesh, D., Subhashini, S., Gajalakshmi, K., Sakthivel, R.

In this chapter, the author explores how in-service teachers can effectively develop and apply Pedagogical Content Knowledge (PCK) across four core disciplines—mathematics, science, social sciences, and language arts. The chapter reviews best practices for integrating pedagogical strategies with subject-specific content, offering practical insights for teachers. By examining the unique challenges faced by educators in each field, the chapter provides actionable recommendations for enhancing teaching effectiveness and improving student engagement. The discussion includes innovative strategies and real-world applications that help teachers refine their PCK in diverse educational settings.

Chapter 2. Examining the Diverse Sources Influencing the Development of Pedagogical Content Knowledge (PCK) Among Educators in Various Educational Settings

Jamila Khurshid, Nabila Khurshid, Nyela Ashraf, Arslan Arshad

This study explores the various sources shaping the development of Pedagogical Content Knowledge (PCK) among educators across different educational contexts. It examines the impact of teacher education programs, classroom experiences, professional development workshops, mentorship, and technology integration on educators' PCK. By investigating how these factors interact, the chapter offers a comprehensive understanding of how teachers acquire, refine, and apply PCK, with the goal of enhancing teaching practices and improving student learning outcomes.

Chapter 3. Leveraging Learning Progressions to Enhance Pedagogical Content Knowledge in Science Education

Sam Ramaila

This chapter discusses how learning progressions—sequences of concepts and skills—can enhance Pedagogical Content Knowledge (PCK) in science education. By aligning teaching strategies with students' cognitive development, learning progressions provide insights into student understanding, helping educators refine their PCK. The chapter covers theoretical foundations, strategies for integrating progressions into practice, and case studies demonstrating how learning progressions can address misconceptions and promote conceptual understanding in science classrooms.

Chapter 4. Phronesis as Pathway for the Nature and Development of Pedagogical Content Knowledge (PCK): Seeing Through Indigenous Gnoseology

Jahid Siraz Chowdhury, Zulkarnain A. Hatta, Sneha Singh

This chapter explores the relationship between Indigenous Science and Western philosophy, particularly the Durkheimian Sociology of Knowledge. It critiques the qualitative-quantitative dichotomy in social sciences and proposes a synthesis of Indigenous Gnoseology and Western philosophical traditions. The chapter emphasizes the role of social science as a bridge between pre-colonial and post-colonial thought and advocates for a more inclusive, philosophical approach to knowledge development and its applications in social science.

Chapter 5. Harnessing Pedagogical Content Knowledge for Cross-Disciplinary Innovation in Engineering

H. Kareemullah, M. D. Mohan Gift, R. Bhaskaran, T. Santhana Krishnan, S. Senthil Kumar

This chapter explores how Pedagogical Content Knowledge (PCK) can foster cross-disciplinary innovation in engineering education. PCK, combining content expertise and effective teaching methods, supports the development of curricula that promote both discipline-specific knowledge and interdisciplinary collaboration. The chapter highlights case studies that demonstrate how PCK-based approaches help students solve complex problems creatively and collaborate across disciplines, and it offers strategies for embedding PCK in engineering programs through collaborative projects and experiential learning.

Chapter 6. Mapping the Growth of Pedagogical Content Knowledge Across Teaching Careers

Thangjam Ravichandra, M. Mariappan, C. V. Padmaja, Narasinga Rao Barnikana, T. Saravanan, Sampath Boopathi

This chapter traces the evolution of Pedagogical Content Knowledge (PCK) over the course of a teaching career. By analyzing longitudinal data and case studies, the authors explore how teachers' PCK develops from initial training through to their professional careers. The chapter focuses on the role of professional development, reflective practice, and classroom experience in shaping PCK and offers insights into how these elements change with educational contexts and student needs, providing practical recommendations for fostering ongoing teacher development.

Chapter 7. Developing Science Pedagogical Content Knowledge (PCK) Among Pre-service and Novice Elementary Teachers

Sandy White Watson

Focusing on elementary-level teachers, this chapter examines the development of Pedagogical Content Knowledge (PCK) specific to teaching science. The author reviews the state of science education in U.S. elementary schools and explores the historical development of PCK models in science instruction. By analyzing strategies for fostering PCK in pre-service and novice teachers, the chapter highlights the importance of subject-specific knowledge and effective teaching practices. It also discusses approaches for developing science-related PCK through targeted teacher preparation programs and ongoing professional development.

Chapter 8. Current Trends and Best Practices of How In-Service Teachers Can Develop and Apply PCK in Social Sciences

Deepak Maun, Parth Sharma, Ta Hung

This chapter delves into the development and application of Pedagogical Content Knowledge (PCK) within social sciences education. The authors examine current trends such as project-based learning, flipped classrooms, and service learning, as well as the challenges teachers face, such as limited professional development opportunities and resistance to change. The chapter also explores future directions for enhancing PCK in social sciences, including the integration of technology, interdisciplinary approaches, and community partnerships. By addressing barriers and embracing emerging opportunities, the chapter offers a comprehensive guide to improving instructional practices in social sciences education.

Chapter 9. Unlocking Ms. Inaoka's PCK: A Case of Grammar Instruction in Japanese Junior High School

Kunitaro Mizuno

This paper examines the application of Pedagogical Content Knowledge (PCK) in pre-service English teacher education in Japan, focusing on an introductory grammar lesson by Ms. Inaoka. Through video analysis and reflective practice, the study highlights how PCK is used in the design and delivery of effective lessons. It discusses Shulman's Pedagogical Reasoning and Action model, which explains how teachers develop and apply PCK, providing insights into the integration of theory and practice in teacher education.

Chapter 10. A System Thinking Approach to Pre-service Teachers' Formation: An Epistemological Perspective from Europe and USA

Francesco Maiorana, Andrew P. Csizmadia, Gretchen M. Richards, Giusy Cristaldi, Janet L. Bavonese

This chapter examines the process of pre-service teacher formation (PSF) with a focus on integrating computing education into early stages of learning. The authors adopt a systems thinking approach to review pre-service teacher activities across Europe and the USA, comparing these practices while drawing conclusions on best practices. Emphasizing the importance of a well-rounded teacher preparation framework, the chapter includes an analysis of how Technological Pedagogical Content Knowledge (TPCK) fits within the broader context of STEAM (Science, Technology, Engineering, Arts, Mathematics) education. Through cross-national comparisons and field experiences, the chapter offers insights into the transformation of pre-service teachers into capable computing educators.

Chapter 11. Challenges and Innovations in Developing PCK Among Pre-Service Teachers

Xuan-Hoa Nghiem, Dhanashree Tharkude, Neeti Goyal, Ajay Chandel, Shashank Mittal

This chapter explores the challenges and innovative strategies in developing Pedagogical Content Knowledge (PCK) among pre-service teachers. Drawing on case studies that incorporate technology, differentiated instruction, and culturally responsive teaching, the chapter discusses methods for enhancing PCK. The authors identify key factors such as mentorship, reflective practice, and adapting teaching methods to diverse student needs. Looking ahead, they argue for the inclusion of advanced technologies, data-driven instruction, and social-emotional learning in PCK frameworks to further improve teacher preparation and educational outcomes.

Chapter 12. Training Teachers in Pedagogical Content Knowledge: A Bridging Method Between University and School

Pasquale Gallo, Rosa Iaquinta

This chapter discusses a project aimed at demonstrating the effectiveness of Shulman's Pedagogical Content Knowledge (PCK) model in teacher training. It highlights how teachers with experience in both school and university settings can apply PCK methods in classroom instruction. The chapter explores how the model helps future teachers understand the importance of instructional design, teaching methods, and the practical application of PCK, emphasizing the value of experiential learning in bridging university and school contexts.

Chapter 13. Pedagogical Content Knowledge (PCK) and Assessment Practices: Teachers' PCK and Their Assessment Practices, and Its Influences on Student Learning Outcomes

Mohit Yadav, Ashutosh Pandey, Ajay Chandel, Ta Huy Hung

This chapter investigates the relationship between Pedagogical Content Knowledge (PCK) and assessment practices. Through case studies of teachers, the research examines how teachers' deep subject knowledge and teaching strategies influence both formative and summative assessments, and their impact on student learning outcomes. The chapter highlights the role of PCK in creating equitable assessments and offers implications for teacher education, professional development, and educational practice.

CONCLUSION

As we look toward the future of education, it is evident that Pedagogical Content Knowledge (PCK) will remain a cornerstone in shaping effective teaching and learning strategies. The Handbook of Research on the Nature and Development of Pedagogical Content Knowledge (PCK) serves as an invaluable resource for educators, researchers, and policymakers alike. By delving into the complex dimensions of PCK, this handbook provides essential insights and practical tools for addressing the challenges of contemporary education. Its thorough exploration of theoretical foundations, practical applications, and future directions equips educators with a robust framework to refine teaching practices and enhance student learning experiences worldwide. Through the development of PCK, educators can foster transformative education, laying the groundwork for a brighter future in teaching for generations to come.

Nazli Ruya Taskin Bedizel
Balikesir University, Turkey

Acknowledgment

I would like to express my deepest gratitude to Prof. Dr. Canan Nakiboğlu for introducing me to the captivating field of PCK during my doctoral studies. My heartfelt thanks go to my esteemed supervisors, Dr. Osman Yildirim, for being an outstanding teacher, and to Prof. Dr. Sami Özgür, for his unwavering guidance and support throughout my PhD journey centered on PCK.

Chapter 1
Developing and Applying PCK in Diverse Subjects:
Best Practices for Mathematics, Science, Social Sciences, and Language Arts

R. Vettriselvan
 https://orcid.org/0000-0002-1324-136X
Academy of Maritime Education and Training, India

Deepa Rajesh
 https://orcid.org/0009-0008-9743-4791
Academy of Maritime Education and Training, India

S. Subhashini
PSGR Krishnammal College for Women, India

K. Gajalakshmi
PSGR Krishnammal College for Women, India

R. Sakthivel
 https://orcid.org/0000-0001-9518-0064
DMI-St.Eugene University, Zambia

ABSTRACT

This chapter explores how in-service teachers can effectively develop and apply Pedagogical Content Knowledge (PCK) across various subjects—mathematics, science, social sciences, and language arts. PCK, which merges subject matter expertise with tailored teaching strategies, is crucial for enhancing educational out-

comes. The chapter reviews current trends and best practices in PCK development, offering practical approaches for integrating effective pedagogical techniques with subject-specific content. It provides actionable insights into how educators can adapt their methods to address the unique challenges of each discipline, thus improving instructional practices and student engagement. By focusing on innovative strategies and real-world applications, this chapter serves as a comprehensive guide for teachers aiming to refine their PCK and elevate their teaching effectiveness.

INTRODUCTION

Pedagogical Content Knowledge (PCK) is a well-established concept in education that plays a crucial role in bridging the gap between subject matter expertise and effective teaching strategies. Initially introduced by Lee Shulman in 1987, PCK has since evolved to represent the intersection of deep content knowledge and pedagogy, enabling educators to convey complex concepts in ways that are accessible and engaging to students. This integration is not only about what teachers know but how they adapt and present their knowledge to foster understanding among diverse learners (Shulman, 1987; Park & Oliver, 2008). PCK continues to be a key element in educational research, with evidence highlighting its significance in improving teaching practices and student outcomes. Teachers with well-developed PCK are more adept at anticipating student misconceptions, selecting appropriate instructional methods, and modifying their approaches based on student needs. In mathematics education, for instance, PCK enables teachers to break down abstract concepts and use concrete tools and representations to facilitate student understanding. Research underscores how PCK supports mathematics educators in choosing the best methods to teach topics like algebra or geometry, making abstract ideas more tangible (Depaepe, Verschaffel, & Kelchtermans, 2013; Hill, Ball, & Schilling, 2008). Similarly, in science education, PCK is essential for designing lessons that not only convey scientific knowledge but also engage students in scientific inquiry and critical thinking. Science educators with strong PCK incorporate hands-on experiments and real-world applications, helping students grasp the relevance of science in everyday life (Kind, 2015; Van Driel & Berry, 2012).

In social sciences, PCK involves navigating the interdisciplinary nature of the content, where teachers connect historical, geographical, and political topics to current societal issues. This approach requires content expertise and pedagogical skills that encourage critical thinking and analytical discussion. Studies highlight how teachers use PCK to tailor instruction to students' cultural and societal backgrounds, making the material more relatable and impactful (Van Driel, Berry, & Meirink, 2014; Carter, 2021). In language arts, teachers must integrate PCK to help students develop core literacy skills reading, writing, speaking, and listening—while also fostering a connection to literature and communication. Recent findings show that language arts educators effectively use PCK to engage diverse learners by designing culturally responsive lessons that help students develop both linguistic proficiency and critical engagement with texts (Brass & Webb, 2015; Williams, 2020). The development of PCK is influenced by a range of factors, including teacher education programs, continuous professional development, and reflective teaching practices. Teacher education programs now place an increased emphasis on integrating content knowledge with pedagogical training, preparing future educators to teach effectively across various disciplines. However, PCK is not static; it continues to evolve as teachers gain experience and adapt to changing educational environments. Ongoing professional development and reflective practice are crucial for refining PCK, enabling teachers to keep pace with new research, curriculum changes, and student needs (Evans, 2019; Darling-Hammond, 2020). Pedagogical Content Knowledge remains a vital component of effective teaching across disciplines such as mathematics, science, social sciences, and language arts. Through the integration of deep content knowledge and targeted pedagogical strategies, teachers can enhance both instructional quality and student engagement. This chapter explores contemporary approaches to PCK development, offering practical strategies for teachers to refine their pedagogical skills and improve learning outcomes in diverse classroom settings.

Purpose of the Chapter

The primary purpose of this chapter is to explore the role of Pedagogical Content Knowledge (PCK) in enhancing teaching practices across various subject areas, including mathematics, science, social sciences, and language arts. By examining how teachers integrate their content expertise with pedagogical strategies, the chapter aims to provide educators with a deeper understanding of how to improve student learning outcomes. This chapter will also focus on practical applications of PCK, offering strategies that educators can implement to address common instructional challenges and better support diverse learners. This chapter does not claim to introduce "innovative" or entirely new concepts; instead, it builds on well-established educational theories and frameworks that have demonstrated efficacy over time. While trends in education such as technology integration and culturally responsive teaching are discussed, these ideas are presented with an emphasis on their proven impact rather than as recent developments. The goal is to offer evidence-based insights and practical examples that can help teachers refine their teaching methods, ensuring they meet contemporary classroom needs without overstating the novelty of the concepts. Additionally, the chapter will outline the boundaries of PCK's applicability, acknowledging that while it provides a powerful framework for improving instruction, it is not a panacea. The discussion will be grounded in empirical research and include limitations, thus offering a balanced perspective on how teachers can adapt PCK to their unique educational contexts. The ultimate aim is to help educators develop a reflective and research-informed approach to teaching, fostering both professional growth and improved student engagement.

Understanding Pedagogical Content Knowledge (PCK)

Pedagogical Content Knowledge (PCK) is a well-established concept that bridges content knowledge and effective teaching methods. Introduced by Lee Shulman, PCK emphasizes the integration of subject-specific knowledge with pedagogical expertise, allowing teachers to transform complex subject matter into comprehensible lessons for students. It involves a combination of understanding the subject, the learning process, and the best ways to teach a specific topic (Shulman, 1986). Over time, the importance of PCK has been recognized as critical to effective teaching across disciplines, particularly in making content accessible and engaging for diverse learners.

Core Components of Pedagogical Content Knowledge (PCK)

Content Knowledge

Content knowledge refers to a teacher's deep understanding of the subject matter, which includes more than just facts and definitions. It involves recognizing the structure of the discipline, the essential concepts, and the relationships between them (Kind, 2021). For example, in mathematics education, this means understanding not just how to perform calculations but also the reasoning behind mathematical principles. In science education, content knowledge encompasses the nature of scientific inquiry and the underlying principles governing scientific concepts (Gess-Newsome & Carlson, 2020). Teachers with strong content knowledge can explain topics in ways that resonate with students and can adjust their explanations to address common misconceptions and challenges.

Pedagogical Knowledge

Pedagogical knowledge involves the strategies, methods, and techniques for effective teaching. It covers classroom management, lesson planning, differentiation, and assessment strategies. Pedagogical expertise allows teachers to present content in a way that promotes engagement and comprehension (Koehler & Mishra, 2009). A teacher with strong pedagogical knowledge can scaffold lessons, facilitate group work, and employ technology to support learning. This is particularly important in addressing the diverse needs of students in a classroom, enabling teachers to tailor their instruction to accommodate different learning styles and capabilities (Schneider & Plasman, 2021).

Curricular Knowledge

Curricular knowledge is the understanding of the structure and goals of the curriculum, including how to sequence learning and select appropriate instructional materials. Teachers with robust curricular knowledge are aware of how the content fits within broader educational standards and goals (Gess-Newsome & Carlson, 2020). For example, in social studies, this knowledge enables teachers to connect historical events with contemporary issues, making learning more relevant and meaningful for students. Additionally, curricular knowledge helps teachers select the most appropriate resources and materials to support learning objectives, ensuring students are meeting educational goals. The three components content knowledge, pedagogical knowledge, and curricular knowledge are interdependent and work synergistically to enhance teaching effectiveness. For instance, a teacher's content knowledge informs their pedagogical strategies, guiding decisions on how to present material and address student misconceptions. Pedagogical knowledge helps teachers plan lessons and activities that align with the curriculum, ensuring that learning objectives are met. Moreover, curricular knowledge ensures that instruction is cohesive and that learning builds progressively over time (Depaepe, Verschaffel, & Kelchtermans, 2013). The integration of these elements is crucial for developing a deep understanding of the content among students and promoting long-term academic success.

Distinguishing PCK from General Pedagogical Knowledge

While Pedagogical Content Knowledge (PCK) shares commonalities with general pedagogical knowledge, it stands out by focusing on the intersection of content and pedagogy within specific disciplines. General pedagogical knowledge involves strategies and techniques that are broadly applicable across subjects, such as classroom management, fostering student motivation, and utilizing formative assessments (Ball, Thames, & Phelps, 2008). These skills are necessary for creating a conducive learning environment, but they are not tied to any specific content. For example, strategies like maintaining a positive classroom climate or using formative assessment are broadly useful across disciplines. In contrast, PCK combines these general strategies with content-specific knowledge to create more effective teaching methods. PCK enables teachers to tailor their instructional approaches to the particular demands of their subject area. For instance, while general pedagogical knowledge might inform a teacher's use of group work, PCK would help determine which group activities best support learning a specific mathematical concept or scientific principle (Kind, 2021). Thus, PCK is deeply tied to the content being taught, requiring an integration of subject matter expertise with teaching strategies to address student misconceptions and promote understanding (Magnusson, Krajcik, & Borko, 1999).

PCK IN MATHEMATICS EDUCATION

Pedagogical Content Knowledge (PCK) in mathematics education plays a vital role in helping teachers bridge the gap between complex mathematical content and effective teaching methods. Mathematics presents unique challenges, including its abstract nature and the need for problem-solving, making specialized teaching approaches crucial. Teachers with well-developed PCK are better equipped to meet these challenges by aligning their instructional methods with the specific needs of both their students and the mathematical content.

Unique Challenges in Teaching Mathematics

Mathematics education presents unique challenges due to its abstract and cumulative nature. Unlike other subjects, where learning can be exploratory, mathematics demands a sequential understanding of concepts. Students often struggle with abstract ideas, such as variables and functions, which are not easily related to everyday experiences (Boaler, 2016). Furthermore, students frequently encounter difficulties with multi-step problem-solving, as they may lose track of the logical progression required to reach a solution (Kilpatrick, Swafford, & Findell, 2001). Teachers must be adept at breaking down these abstract ideas into more accessible forms and identifying common misconceptions that students may hold.

Additionally, fostering positive attitudes towards mathematics is essential, as many students view the subject as intimidating or difficult. Research indicates that students' attitudes towards mathematics can significantly affect their performance and engagement (Di Martino & Zan, 2010). Therefore, teachers need to employ strategies that not only build mathematical understanding but also boost student confidence and motivation.

Strategies for Developing and Applying PCK in Mathematics

To address these challenges, mathematics educators must develop and apply PCK through specific strategies, such as employing multiple representations and fostering problem-solving skills.

Using Multiple Representations:

One key strategy is using multiple representations to present mathematical concepts. This involves using visual, symbolic, and numerical representations to illustrate concepts like linear equations, which can be represented through graphs, tables, or equations. By providing different perspectives, teachers help students grasp abstract concepts more deeply and recognize the connections between them (Ainsworth, 2006). This approach also accommodates different learning styles, making mathematical ideas more accessible.

Fostering Problem-Solving and Critical Thinking Skills:

Another vital aspect of PCK in mathematics is the development of students' problem-solving and critical thinking skills. Instead of focusing solely on procedural skills, teachers should emphasize the reasoning behind mathematical operations and encourage students to apply these operations in various contexts (Schoenfeld, 2013). Teachers can foster critical thinking through inquiry-based learning, where students explore mathematical problems, formulate hypotheses, and test their ideas. This approach enhances students' deeper understanding of mathematical concepts and prepares them for unfamiliar challenges.

Case Studies and Examples of Effective PCK in Mathematics Classrooms

There are numerous examples of effective PCK in mathematics education. For instance, incorporating real-world applications, such as using budgeting exercises to teach mathematical concepts, helps make abstract ideas more tangible and relatable to students (Boaler, 2016). Case studies have demonstrated that when teachers integrate real-life examples into their lessons, students are more engaged and show a better understanding of complex mathematical ideas. Moreover, formative assessment strategies, where teachers continuously assess students' understanding and adjust instruction accordingly, are essential for ensuring all students progress effectively. By employing formative assessments, teachers can provide immediate feedback and modify their teaching strategies to address areas where students struggle (Black & Wiliam, 2009).

Best Practices and Practical Approaches

Effective practices in mathematics education combine content knowledge, pedagogical strategies, and attention to student needs. Practical approaches include collaborative learning, where students work together to solve problems, and the integration of technology, such as dynamic geometry software, to help students visualize mathematical concepts (Pierce & Stacey, 2010). Furthermore, ongoing professional development is essential for teachers to stay updated on the latest teaching methods and refine their PCK continuously (Desimone, 2009).

PCK IN SCIENCE EDUCATION

Pedagogical Content Knowledge (PCK) in science education is crucial for bridging the gap between scientific content and effective teaching strategies. Given the complexity of scientific concepts and processes, teachers need a deep understanding of both content and pedagogy to make science accessible, engaging, and relevant for students (Kind, 2021).

Content and Pedagogical Challenges in Science Teaching

Science education presents unique challenges due to its abstract nature and specialized terminology. Concepts like energy, force, and molecular structures are often difficult for students to grasp because they are not directly observable and can be counterintuitive (Taber, 2013). Teachers must identify these challenges and employ strategies to simplify complex ideas. Furthermore, integrating the scientific method and inquiry-based learning into lessons is essential for helping students think and act like scientists, promoting critical thinking and discovery (Bybee, 2014).

Inquiry-Based Learning and the Scientific Method as PCK Strategies

Inquiry-based learning and the scientific method are key PCK strategies in science education. Inquiry-based learning encourages students to engage in the process of scientific investigation, fostering deeper understanding and critical thinking (Bell, Smetana, & Binns, 2005). Teachers must guide students through the scientific method—observation, hypothesis formation, experimentation, and conclusion—while showing its real-world applications (Windschitl, Thompson, & Braaten, 2008).

Integrating Experiments and Real-World Applications

Incorporating experiments and real-world applications enhances students' understanding and engagement. Hands-on experiments allow students to observe scientific principles directly, reinforcing their learning (Hofstein & Lunetta, 2004). Connecting lessons to real-world issues, like climate change or biodiversity, increases relevance and student interest (Yager, 2015).

Examples of Successful PCK Implementation

Effective PCK implementation in science classrooms has shown improved student outcomes, particularly through inquiry-based learning (Minner, Levy, & Century, 2010). Additionally, technology-enhanced simulations provide valuable virtual lab experiences when physical experiments aren't feasible, helping students visualize complex processes (Rutten, van Joolingen, & van der Veen, 2012).

Enhancing PCK in Science

Enhancing PCK requires ongoing professional development, collaboration, and reflective teaching. Professional development programs help educators stay updated with new teaching methods and scientific advancements (Capps, Crawford, & Constas, 2012). Collaboration with peers allows for sharing best practices, while reflective teaching ensures continuous improvement of teaching strategies (Schön, 2017).

PCK IN SOCIAL SCIENCES EDUCATION

Pedagogical Content Knowledge (PCK) in social sciences is crucial due to the interdisciplinary nature of the subject, covering areas like history, geography, and political science. Teachers need to master content while applying appropriate pedagogical strategies tailored to the complexities of each discipline (Banks & Banks, 2019).

Addressing the Interdisciplinary Nature of Social Sciences

Social sciences require an integrated approach, blending various disciplines to show how social, political, and economic factors interact (Banks & Banks, 2019). Teachers must develop a PCK framework that connects these fields while addressing abstract, value-laden concepts like democracy and justice, requiring sensitive teaching approaches (Barton & Levstik, 2015).

Pedagogical Strategies for Teaching Complex Social Concepts

To teach complex social concepts, educators should move beyond memorization to strategies like case studies, which allow students to apply theoretical knowledge to real-world scenarios (Shaver, 2020). Role-playing and simulations further enhance understanding by providing firsthand experiences of social dynamics (Hess, 2009).

Encouraging Critical Thinking and Discussion-Based Learning

Critical thinking and discussion-based learning are essential for engaging with social phenomena. Teachers must foster an environment where students can debate respectfully and critically analyze issues from different perspectives (VanSledright, 2013). PCK helps guide these discussions, ensuring educational and productive outcomes (Wineburg, 2018).

Integrating Historical Context and Current Events

Integrating history and current events helps students connect the past to the present, deepening their understanding of contemporary social issues (Barton & Levstik, 2015). By incorporating real-time events, teachers can enhance engagement and prepare students to be informed societal participants (Journell, 2016).

Best Practices for Developing and Applying PCK in Social Sciences

Ongoing professional development and reflective practice are key to effective PCK in social sciences. Teachers should stay updated on research and collaborate with peers to refine strategies and improve instruction (National Council for the Social Studies, 2017).

PCK IN LANGUAGE ARTS EDUCATION

Pedagogical Content Knowledge (PCK) in language arts is vital for effectively teaching the multifaceted components of reading, writing, speaking, and listening. Understanding these diverse aspects allows educators to support students in developing language skills and fostering a love for literature and communication.

Understanding the Diverse Aspects of Language Arts

Language arts education covers key areas: reading, writing, speaking, and listening. Each requires distinct skills and knowledge. Reading involves decoding and comprehension, while writing focuses on mechanics and expression. Speaking and listening skills are crucial for effective communication (Moats, 2020; Zwiers, 2014). PCK helps integrate these components into a cohesive instructional approach.

Strategies for Teaching Literature, Grammar, and Communication Skills

Effective PCK includes strategies for engaging students in literature, grammar, and communication. Literature instruction benefits from close reading and discussion, helping students connect texts to their own experiences (Appleman, 2015). Grammar should be taught in context, integrating it into writing and speaking activities to show practical application (Weaver, 2018). Communication skills are best developed through interactive activities like group discussions and debates.

Developing PCK for Differentiated Instruction

Differentiated instruction is essential in language arts, addressing diverse proficiency levels among students. Teachers should provide varied reading materials, tailor writing assignments, and offer multiple opportunities for speaking and listening practice (Tomlinson, 2017). Formative assessments, such as quizzes and writing samples, are crucial for monitoring progress and adjusting instruction to meet individual needs (Burns, 2020).

Examples of Effective PCK in Language Arts Classrooms

Effective PCK is demonstrated through practices like literature circles, which foster collaborative learning and critical thinking. Process writing approaches, guiding students through drafting, revising, and editing, also highlight effective PCK (Graham, 2019).

Approaches for Fostering Creativity and Engagement

Fostering creativity and engagement is key to language arts education. Activities that promote personal expression, such as creative writing and multimedia projects, encourage students to see language as a powerful tool. Integrating technology, like digital storytelling tools, further enhances engagement (Turner & Hicks, 2017).

TRENDS IN PCK DEVELOPMENT

Pedagogical Content Knowledge (PCK) has evolved significantly, adapting to new educational paradigms and technological advancements. Originally conceptualized by Shulman (1986), PCK remains central to effective teaching, bridging the gap between subject matter expertise and teaching proficiency.

Emerging Trends in PCK Research and Practice

Recent developments in PCK emphasize integrating it with Technological Pedagogical Content Knowledge (TPACK), which combines content knowledge, pedagogy, and technology use (Mishra & Koehler, 2006). Researchers are exploring context-specific PCK, tailored to diverse student populations and classroom environments, highlighting the need for teaching practices that reflect cultural, socioeconomic, and contextual factors (Carlson & Daehler, 2019). This trend supports a more personalized approach to teaching.

Impact of Technology and Digital Tools on PCK

The rise of digital tools has led to the expansion of PCK into TPACK, integrating technology with teaching strategies (Koehler & Mishra, 2009). Technology-enhanced teaching, such as virtual labs in science and digital storytelling in language arts, has become integral to modern education (Harris, Mishra, & Koehler, 2009). Effective use of technology requires educators to blend content, pedagogy, and digital tools to enhance learning.

Professional Development Programs for Enhancing PCK

Professional development is crucial for advancing PCK among educators. Effective programs emphasize continuous learning through workshops, collaborative communities, and mentoring (Desimone & Garet, 2015). Sustained professional development and personalized learning experiences are more effective than one-time workshops, allowing teachers to integrate new knowledge into practice (Borko, Jacobs, & Koellner, 2010).

Role of Collaboration and Peer Learning in PCK Growth

Collaboration and peer learning are essential for PCK development. Collaborative practices, such as co-teaching and peer observations, enable teachers to share knowledge, reflect on their practices, and enhance their teaching strategies (Vangrieken, Meredith, Packer, & Kyndt, 2017). These methods foster a community of practice and improve teaching outcomes through shared experiences and collective problem-solving.

CHALLENGES IN DEVELOPING AND APPLYING PCK

Pedagogical Content Knowledge (PCK) integrates deep subject expertise with effective teaching strategies, but its development and application face notable challenges. These challenges often stem from systemic issues, teacher preparedness, and the dynamic nature of classroom environments.

Common Barriers to Effective PCK Implementation

A major challenge in applying PCK is bridging the gap between theoretical knowledge and practical classroom application. Teachers may understand content and pedagogy theoretically but struggle to implement them effectively due to the abstract nature of PCK and varying classroom contexts (Ball, 2018). Limited time and resources for professional development further exacerbate this issue, as available opportunities may not address specific needs or allow for reflective practice (Gess-Newsome, 2015).

Addressing Subject-Specific Challenges

Different subjects present unique challenges in PCK application. For example, mathematics teachers must use multiple representations and real-world connections to convey abstract concepts effectively (Ball, Thames, & Phelps, 2008). Science educators face the challenge of balancing structured inquiry with independent exploration (Kind, 2019). Language arts teachers must address diverse aspects of reading, writing, speaking, and listening while differentiating instruction (Grossman et al., 2018).

Role of Teacher Preparation Programs and Ongoing Professional Development

Teacher preparation programs and ongoing professional development are crucial for developing PCK but often fall short in content-specific training. Traditional programs may emphasize general strategies over detailed content instruction, leaving new teachers inadequately prepared (Darling-Hammond, 2017). Professional development needs to be continuous, context-specific, and collaborative to be effective, providing opportunities for reflection, peer learning, and hands-on experience (Desimone & Garet, 2015).**Strategies for Overcoming Challenges and Sustaining PCK Growth**

To address PCK challenges, schools should allocate time and resources for professional learning communities, integrate technology into development programs, and establish mentorship opportunities. These strategies support collaboration, reflective practice, and the continuous enhancement of PCK (Koehler & Mishra, 2016). By focusing on context, collaboration, and sustained professional growth, educators can overcome challenges and improve teaching effectiveness.

PRACTICAL APPROACHES FOR ENHANCING PCK

Pedagogical Content Knowledge (PCK) is crucial for effective teaching, blending subject expertise with pedagogical strategies. Enhancing PCK involves reflective practices, formative assessments, collaborative planning, and adapting teaching methods to diverse learning styles.

Reflective Practices and Action Research

Reflective practice helps educators critically analyze and improve their teaching methods, while action research involves systematic investigation to address teaching challenges and enhance pedagogy. These approaches support ongoing development of PCK by enabling teachers to make evidence-based adjustments and stay responsive to student needs (Khan et al., 2021; Clarke & Hollingsworth, 2020).

Integrating Formative Assessments and Feedback

Formative assessments provide ongoing feedback during instruction, allowing teachers to adjust their strategies in real time. This process helps refine PCK by highlighting effective methods and areas needing improvement (Wiliam, 2021). The continuous feedback loop facilitates better alignment of teaching practices with student learning needs (Dunn & Mulvenon, 2020).

Collaborative Lesson Planning and Peer Observation

Collaborative lesson planning and peer observation enhance PCK by allowing teachers to share expertise and learn from each other's practices. This collaborative approach fosters innovation and improvement in teaching strategies (Gore et al., 2020; Kraft & Papay, 2021). Observing peers can inspire new pedagogical methods and provide valuable feedback.

Adapting Teaching Methods to Diverse Student Needs

Adapting teaching methods to accommodate diverse learning styles is vital for effective PCK. Differentiated instruction, which tailors strategies to students' abilities and preferences, helps ensure that all students can succeed (Tomlinson, 2021). Understanding and applying varied instructional approaches based on student needs enhances overall teaching effectiveness (Hattie, 2020).

SUMMARY OF KEY POINTS AND INSIGHTS

Pedagogical Content Knowledge (PCK) is an integral concept in the field of education, forming a crucial bridge between content knowledge and effective teaching practices. It combines a teacher's deep understanding of their subject matter with the ability to convey this knowledge in ways that are comprehensible and engaging for students. This unique blend is what differentiates PCK from general teaching strategies, making it a valuable asset in the classroom. The chapter began by establishing the foundational aspects of PCK, emphasizing that it is not just about having expertise in a particular subject but also about how to present this expertise in a pedagogically sound manner. The ability to adapt and apply knowledge in various teaching contexts is a core component of PCK. For example, in mathematics, effective PCK involves using multiple representations of concepts and problem-solving strategies that help students grasp abstract ideas. In science, the emphasis is on fostering inquiry-based learning through structured experiments that encourage students to explore and understand fundamental concepts. Social sciences require a pedagogical approach that integrates historical and contemporary events to foster critical thinking and contextual understanding. In language arts, the focus is on developing reading, writing, speaking, and listening skills through differentiated instruction that addresses diverse student needs.

Addressing these subject-specific challenges requires teachers to be adaptable and reflective. For instance, mathematics teachers need to find innovative ways to help students understand complex mathematical concepts, often using visual aids and real-world applications. Science educators must balance between guiding structured experiments and encouraging independent exploration. Social science teachers need to create lessons that connect past events to current issues, promoting a deeper understanding of the subject. Language arts instructors must tailor their teaching to support various literacy skills, often adjusting their methods based on individual student needs.

Future of PCK in Education: Trends and Predictions

As education continues to evolve, so does the understanding and application of PCK. Several emerging trends are shaping the future of PCK and influencing how educators develop and apply this knowledge in their teaching practices.

Integration of Technology: One of the most significant trends is the increasing integration of technology in the classroom, which has given rise to the concept of Technological Pedagogical Content Knowledge (TPACK). TPACK extends the traditional PCK framework by incorporating digital tools and resources into teaching practices. This integration allows educators to enhance their instructional strategies and engage students in new and dynamic ways. For example, digital simulations and virtual laboratories in science education provide students with interactive and immersive learning experiences that may not be feasible in a traditional classroom setting. In language arts, digital storytelling and online discussion platforms foster greater student engagement and collaboration. The TPACK framework emphasizes the need for educators to not only understand their subject and pedagogy but also to be proficient in using technology to support and enhance student learning (Mishra & Koehler, 2006).

Professional Development: Another important trend is the increasing emphasis on professional development programs specifically designed to enhance PCK. Effective professional development is crucial for helping teachers deepen their understanding of both content and pedagogy. Recent research highlights the importance of collaborative learning environments, where educators work together to develop and refine their PCK through peer observations, lesson studies, and shared reflections. Such programs foster a supportive learning community among educators and lead to the continuous improvement of teaching practices. For example, professional development initiatives that include collaborative lesson planning and peer feedback have been shown to positively impact teachers' PCK and their ability to implement effective instructional strategies (Khan et al., 2021).

Contextual Adaptation: The growing recognition of the importance of context in shaping PCK is another key trend. As educational environments become increasingly diverse, teachers must adapt their PCK to meet the unique needs of their students. This includes considering factors such as cultural background, language proficiency, and learning abilities. Teachers need to be equipped with the skills to modify their teaching approaches based on the specific characteristics of their classroom environment. This contextual understanding ensures that PCK remains relevant and effective in addressing the diverse needs of students. For instance, teachers working in multilingual classrooms may need to adapt their instructional methods to support language development and address the challenges faced by students with varying levels of language proficiency (Mishra et al., 2020).

Practical Approaches for Enhancing PCK

To effectively enhance PCK, educators can adopt several practical approaches that support continuous development and improvement.

Reflective Practices and Action Research: Reflective practice is a foundational approach to developing PCK. It involves critically analyzing one's own teaching methods and their effectiveness in conveying subject matter. By engaging in reflective practices, educators can identify areas for improvement and refine their teaching strategies over time. Action research is a related approach that involves systematically investigating teaching practices to address specific problems and enhance instructional methods. This iterative process—comprising planning, acting, observing, and reflecting—enables teachers to make evidence-based adjustments to their pedagogy. Reflective practices and action research encourage teachers to engage deeply with their content knowledge and pedagogical approaches, fostering a more nuanced understanding of how to support student learning effectively (Zeichner, 2003).

Integrating Formative Assessments and Feedback: Formative assessments are essential for refining PCK. Unlike summative assessments, which evaluate student learning at the end of an instructional period, formative assessments provide ongoing feedback during the learning process. This immediate feedback loop allows teachers to adjust their instructional strategies in real time, addressing any misconceptions or difficulties that students may encounter. Integrating formative assessments into teaching helps educators understand how students are engaging with the material and which aspects of their teaching are most effective. By using formative assessments to gauge the effectiveness of different pedagogical techniques, teachers can make informed decisions about which strategies to continue using and which to modify or abandon (Black & Wiliam, 2009).

Collaborative Lesson Planning and Peer Observation: Collaborative lesson planning and peer observation are effective strategies for enhancing PCK. When teachers collaborate on lesson planning, they share their expertise and insights, leading to more innovative and effective teaching strategies. This collaborative process allows teachers to learn from each other's strengths and expand their own

PCK. Peer observation, where teachers observe each other's classes and provide constructive feedback, fosters a culture of continuous improvement. Observing colleagues can inspire new approaches to pedagogy and help teachers refine their PCK by incorporating successful strategies used by others (Gore, Lloyd, & Smith, 2014; Hobson & Malderez, 2013).

Adapting Teaching Methods to Diverse Student Needs: One of the critical aspects of PCK is the ability to adapt teaching methods to accommodate diverse student needs and learning styles. Differentiated instruction involves tailoring teaching strategies to meet varying abilities, interests, and learning preferences. This approach requires teachers to understand different ways students learn and design lessons that are inclusive and effective. For example, teachers may use visual, auditory, and kinesthetic methods to present material, or offer varying levels of complexity and support to address individual needs. Adapting teaching methods to diverse student needs is essential for ensuring that all students have the opportunity to succeed and for enhancing PCK in practice (Tomlinson, 2014).

Future Research Directions

Impact of Digital Technologies on CSR Effectiveness: Investigate how emerging digital technologies (e.g., blockchain, AI) enhance the transparency and effectiveness of CSR initiatives. Assess their role in improving reporting accuracy, stakeholder engagement, and tracking of sustainable practices.

Integration of CSR in Financial Performance Metrics: Explore how CSR initiatives influence financial performance and develop new metrics for incorporating CSR outcomes into financial evaluations. Examine the long-term financial impacts of CSR investments and their alignment with traditional financial indicators.

Consumer Behavior and CSR: Study how consumer perceptions and behaviors are affected by CSR activities. Analyze the effectiveness of various marketing strategies in communicating CSR efforts and their impact on brand loyalty, consumer trust, and purchasing decisions.

Cross-Sector Collaboration for Sustainable Development: Evaluate the effectiveness of partnerships between businesses, governments, and NGOs in advancing sustainable development goals. Identify best practices, challenges, and outcomes of such collaborations across different sectors.

Leadership Styles and CSR Implementation: Assess how different leadership styles (e.g., transformational, servant) influence the implementation and success of CSR strategies. Examine the impact of leadership approaches on employee engagement, organizational culture, and stakeholder perceptions.

CSR and Financial Risk Management: Explore the relationship between CSR practices and financial risk management. Investigate how CSR initiatives affect risk assessment and mitigation strategies, and how companies balance risk and reward in their CSR investments.

Ethical Implications of CSR Marketing Strategies: Examine the ethical considerations of CSR marketing strategies, focusing on issues such as "greenwashing" and its impact on consumer trust and regulatory compliance.

Regional and Cultural Differences in CSR Practices: Study how CSR practices vary across regions and cultures. Explore how local norms, values, and regulations influence CSR strategies and the effectiveness of global vs. localized approaches.

Measurement and Reporting Standards for CSR: Investigate the development of standardized metrics and reporting frameworks for CSR. Create robust, comprehensive, and comparable standards for assessing and communicating CSR performance.

Long-Term Impact of CSR on Organizational Resilience: Examine how sustained CSR efforts contribute to organizational resilience and long-term success. Assess the relationship between CSR practices and a company's ability to navigate crises and maintain a positive reputation over time.

The Role of CSR in Addressing Global Challenges: Analyze how CSR initiatives contribute to solving global challenges like climate change, inequality, and health crises. Evaluate the effectiveness of CSR strategies in making a tangible impact and identify areas for improvement.

The Influence of Employee Perceptions on CSR Implementation: Investigate how employees' views on CSR initiatives affect their engagement, performance, and advocacy. Explore how involving employees in CSR efforts impacts organizational culture and overall program effectiveness.

These research directions aim to advance understanding of the intersection between CSR, marketing, and finance, providing valuable insights for improving sustainable development practices and strategies.

CONCLUSION

Pedagogical Content Knowledge (PCK) remains a foundational concept in education, integrating content expertise with tailored teaching strategies to enhance both teaching effectiveness and student outcomes. The chapter explored the various dimensions of PCK, its development across different subject areas, and practical approaches for enhancing it. As the educational landscape evolves, the understanding and application of PCK will continue to be shaped by emerging trends such as the integration of technology, professional development, and contextual adaptation.

These advancements will support educators in creating effective, engaging, and inclusive learning environments that foster both academic and personal growth. The ongoing development of PCK is crucial for improving teaching practices and ensuring that educators are equipped to meet the diverse needs of their students. Future research and innovation in PCK will likely provide new insights and tools, further enhancing the ability of teachers to deliver high-quality instruction and support student learning.

REFERENCES

Ainsworth, S. (2006). DeFT: A conceptual framework for learning with multiple representations. *Learning and Instruction*, 16(3), 183–198. DOI: 10.1016/j.learninstruc.2006.03.001

Appleman, D. (2015). *Critical literacy in the classroom: The art of argument.* Guilford Press.

Ball, D. L. (2018). The complexity of teaching mathematics: Navigating the terrain of pedagogical content knowledge. *Journal of Mathematics Teacher Education*, 21(1), 29–48. DOI: 10.1007/s10857-017-9398-3

Ball, D. L., Thames, M. H., & Phelps, G. (2008). Content knowledge for teaching: What makes it special? *Journal of Teacher Education*, 59(5), 389–407. DOI: 10.1177/0022487108324554

Banks, J. A., & Banks, C. A. M. (2019). *Teaching strategies for the social studies: Decision-making and citizenship education.* Longman.

Barton, K. C., & Levstik, L. S. (2015). *Teaching history for the common good.* Routledge.

Bell, R. L., Smetana, L., & Binns, I. (2005). Simplifying inquiry instruction. *Science Teacher (Normal, Ill.)*, 72(7), 30–33.

Black, P., & Wiliam, D. (2009). Developing the theory of formative assessment. *Educational Assessment, Evaluation and Accountability*, 21(1), 5–31. DOI: 10.1007/s11092-008-9068-5

Boaler, J. (2016). *Mathematical mindsets: Unleashing students' potential through creative math, inspiring messages, and innovative teaching.* Jossey-Bass.

Borko, H., Jacobs, J., & Koellner, K. (2010). Sustaining professional development in the context of teaching reform. *Teachers College Record*, 112(2), 519–548.

Brass, J., & Webb, A. (2015). *Reclaiming English language arts methods courses: Critical issues and challenges for teacher educators in top-down times.* Routledge.

Burns, M. (2020). *Formative assessment in the classroom: An introduction.* Routledge.

Bybee, R. W. (2014). The BSCS 5E instructional model: Creating teachable moments. *Science and Children*, 51(8), 10–13. DOI: 10.2505/4/sc14_051_08_10

Capps, D. K., Crawford, B. A., & Constas, M. A. (2012). A review of empirical literature on inquiry professional development: Alignment with best practices and a critique of the findings. *Journal of Science Teacher Education*, 23(3), 291–318. DOI: 10.1007/s10972-012-9275-2

Carlson, D., & Daehler, K. (2019). Context-specific PCK: Adapting teaching practices to diverse educational settings. *Journal of Science Teacher Education*, 30(4), 517–532. DOI: 10.1080/1046560X.2019.1624267

Carter, A. (2021). *Culturally responsive teaching in the social studies classroom: Empowering students through critical inquiry*. Teachers College Press.

Clarke, D., & Hollingsworth, H. (2020). Building teacher professional development in the age of remote learning. *Teaching and Teacher Education*, 95, 103160. DOI: 10.1016/j.tate.2020.103160

Darling-Hammond, L. (2017). Teacher education and the opportunity gap. *Journal of Teacher Education*, 68(3), 231–245. DOI: 10.1177/0022487117692564

Darling-Hammond, L. (2020). Learning to teach: The role of practice-based teacher education. *Harvard Educational Review*.

Depaepe, F., Verschaffel, L., & Kelchtermans, G. (2013). Pedagogical content knowledge: A systematic review of the way in which the concept has pervaded mathematics educational research. *Teaching and Teacher Education*, 34, 12–25. DOI: 10.1016/j.tate.2013.03.001

Desimone, L. M. (2009). Improving impact studies of teachers' professional development: Toward better conceptualizations and measures. *Educational Researcher*, 38(3), 181–199. DOI: 10.3102/0013189X08331140

Desimone, L. M., & Garet, M. S. (2015). Best practices in professional development: Findings from recent research. *American Educational Research Journal*, 52(3), 375–402. DOI: 10.3102/0002831215577481

Di Martino, P., & Zan, R. (2010). 'Me and maths': Towards a definition of attitude grounded on students' narratives. *Journal of Mathematics Teacher Education*, 13(1), 27–48. DOI: 10.1007/s10857-009-9134-z

Dunn, K. E., & Mulvenon, S. W. (2020). Formative assessment and the role of feedback in educational practice. *Journal of Educational Measurement*, 57(3), 483–501. DOI: 10.1111/jedm.12270

Evans, L. (2019). Professional development and reflective teaching: Exploring the intersection of pedagogy and content. *Educational Research Review*, 28, 100–110. DOI: 10.1016/j.edurev.2019.01.002

Gess-Newsome, J. (2015). A model of teacher knowledge and its implications for science education research and practice. *Science Education*, 99(1), 50–75. DOI: 10.1002/sce.21125

Gess-Newsome, J., & Carlson, J. (2020). The PCK summit and its aftermath: The growth and impact of the PCK research community. *Journal of Science Teacher Education*, 31(8), 903–911. DOI: 10.1080/1046560X.2020.1832555

Gore, J., Lloyd, A., & Smith, M. (2014). Professional learning and development in schools. *Review of Educational Research*, 84(1), 1–40. DOI: 10.3102/0034654313496870

Gore, J., Lloyd, A., & Smith, M. (2020). Collaborative practices and professional learning communities: Enhancing teacher practice. *Professional Development in Education*, 46(1), 50–68. DOI: 10.1080/19415257.2019.1601326

Graham, S. (2019). *The writing workshop: A practical guide*. Heinemann.

Grossman, P., Compton, C., Igra, D., Ronfeldt, M., Shahan, E., & Williamson, P. (2018). Teaching practice: A cross-disciplinary perspective. *Teachers College Record*, 120(6), 1–29. DOI: 10.1177/016146811812000601

Harris, J., Mishra, P., & Koehler, M. J. (2009). Teachers' technological pedagogical content knowledge and learning activity types: Curriculum-based technology integration reframed. *Journal of Research on Technology in Education*, 41(4), 393–416. DOI: 10.1080/15391523.2009.10782536

Hattie, J. (2020). *Visible learning: Feedback*. Routledge.

Hess, D. E. (2009). *Controversy in the classroom: The democratic power of discussion*. Routledge. DOI: 10.4324/9780203878880

Hill, H. C., Ball, D. L., & Schilling, S. G. (2008). Unpacking pedagogical content knowledge: Conceptualizing and measuring teachers' topic-specific knowledge of students. *Journal for Research in Mathematics Education*, 39(4), 372–400. DOI: 10.5951/jresematheduc.39.4.0372

Hobson, A. J., & Malderez, A. (2013). Mentoring and coaching for new teachers. *Teacher Education Quarterly*, 40(4), 1–20.

Hofstein, A., & Lunetta, V. N. (2004). The laboratory in science education: Foundations for the twenty-first century. *Science Education*, 88(1), 28–54. DOI: 10.1002/sce.10106

Journell, W. (2016). Teaching politics in secondary education: Engaging with controversial issues in the classroom. *Social Studies*, 107(1), 24–30. DOI: 10.1080/00377996.2015.1132366

Khan, A., Li, M., & Hu, X. (2021). Action research in education: A review of current practices and future directions. *The Journal of Educational Research*, 114(2), 230–246. DOI: 10.1080/00220671.2020.1833581

Kilpatrick, J., Swafford, J., & Findell, B. (Eds.). (2001). *Adding it up: Helping children learn mathematics*. National Academy Press.

Kind, V. (2015). Preservice science teachers' PCK development during an extended practicum. *Research in Science Education*, 45(5), 851–873. DOI: 10.1007/s11165-014-9444-5

Kind, V. (2019). Science education and inquiry-based learning: Striving for balance. *International Journal of Science Education*, 41(6), 735–752. DOI: 10.1080/09500693.2019.1573466

Kind, V. (2021). The role of pedagogical content knowledge in science education: New perspectives and developments. *Research in Science Education*, 51, 569–586. DOI: 10.1007/s11165-019-09848-3

Koehler, M. J., & Mishra, P. (2009). Technological pedagogical content knowledge: A framework for teacher knowledge. *Teachers College Record*, 111(6), 1017–1054. DOI: 10.1177/016146810911100611

Koehler, M. J., & Mishra, P. (2009). What is technological pedagogical content knowledge (TPACK)? *Contemporary Issues in Technology & Teacher Education*, 9(1), 60–70.

Koehler, M. J., & Mishra, P. (2016). Technological pedagogical content knowledge: A framework for teacher knowledge. *Teachers College Record*, 118(2), 1–10. DOI: 10.1177/016146811811800201

Kraft, M. A., & Papay, J. P. (2021). Developing teacher expertise through collaborative practice. *Education Policy Analysis Archives*, 29(46), 1–24. DOI: 10.14507/epaa.29.6815

Magnusson, S., Krajcik, J., & Borko, H. (1999). Nature, sources, and development of pedagogical content knowledge for science teaching. In Gess-Newsome, J., & Lederman, N. G. (Eds.), *Examining pedagogical content knowledge* (pp. 95–132). Springer.

Minner, D. D., Levy, A. J., & Century, J. (2010). Inquiry-based science instruction—What is it and does it matter? *Journal of Research in Science Teaching*, 47(4), 474–496. DOI: 10.1002/tea.20347

Mishra, P., & Koehler, M. J. (2006). Technological pedagogical content knowledge: A framework for teacher knowledge. *Teachers College Record*, 108(6), 1017–1054. DOI: 10.1111/j.1467-9620.2006.00684.x

Mishra, P., Koehler, M. J., & Henriksen, D. (2020). The role of technological pedagogical content knowledge in the 21st century classroom. *Educational Technology*, 60(1), 3–12. DOI: 10.1007/s11423-020-09701-x

Moats, L. C. (2020). *Speech to print: Language essentials for teachers*. Brookes Publishing.

National Council for the Social Studies. (2017). College, Career, and Civic Life (C3) Framework for Social Studies State Standards. National Council for the Social Studies. https://www.socialstudies.org/c3

Park, S., & Oliver, J. S. (2008). Revisiting the conceptualization of pedagogical content knowledge. *Journal of Science Teacher Education*, 19(3), 257–277. DOI: 10.1007/s10972-008-9103-7

Pierce, R., & Stacey, K. (2010). Mapping the landscape of teachers' professional development and technology integration. *Educational Studies in Mathematics*, 73(2), 245–262. DOI: 10.1007/s10649-010-9255-4

Rutten, N., van Joolingen, W. R., & van der Veen, J. T. (2012). The learning effects of computer simulations in science education. *Computers & Education*, 58(1), 136–153. DOI: 10.1016/j.compedu.2011.07.017

Schneider, R. M., & Plasman, K. (2021). Science teacher learning progressions for pedagogical content knowledge. *Journal of Research in Science Teaching*, 58(1), 5–35. DOI: 10.1002/tea.21647

Schoenfeld, A. H. (2013). Reflections on problem solving theory and practice. *The Montana Math Enthusiast*, 10(1), 9–34. DOI: 10.54870/1551-3440.1258

Schön, D. A. (2017). *The reflective practitioner: How professionals think in action*. Routledge. DOI: 10.4324/9781315237473

Shaver, J. P. (2020). *Handbook of research on social studies teaching and learning*. Macmillan.

Shulman, L. S. (1987). Knowledge and teaching: Foundations of the new reform. *Harvard Educational Review*, 57(1), 1–22. DOI: 10.17763/haer.57.1.j463w79r56455411

Taber, K. S. (2013). Revisiting the chemistry triplet: Drawing upon the nature of chemical knowledge and the psychology of learning to inform chemistry education. *Chemistry Education Research and Practice*, 14(2), 156–168. DOI: 10.1039/C3RP00012E

Tomlinson, C. A. (2014). *The differentiated classroom: Responding to the needs of all learners*. ASCD.

Tomlinson, C. A. (2017). *How to differentiate instruction in academically diverse classrooms*. ASCD.

Turner, M., & Hicks, T. (2017). *The new literacy: Technology and learning in the classroom*. Teachers College Press.

Van Driel, J. H., & Berry, A. (2012). Teacher professional development focusing on PCK: The role of teachers' beliefs and knowledge. *Educational Researcher*, 41(1), 26–28. DOI: 10.3102/0013189X11431010

Van Driel, J. H., Berry, A., & Meirink, J. (2014). Research on teachers' professional development and its impact on educational practice. *European Journal of Education*, 49(2), 218–232. DOI: 10.1111/ejed.12064

Vangrieken, K., Meredith, C., Packer, T., & Kyndt, E. (2017). Teacher collaboration and professional development: A systematic review. *Educational Research Review*, 21, 15–32. DOI: 10.1016/j.edurev.2017.05.002

VanSledright, B. (2013). *The challenge of rethinking history education: On practices, theories, and policy*. Routledge.

Weaver, C. (2018). *Grammar to enrich and enhance writing*. Heinemann.

Wiliam, D. (2021). *Embedded formative assessment: Insights for learning*. Hodder Education.

Williams, A. (2020). *Engaging the disengaged: Creating responsive classrooms for all students*. Routledge.

Windschitl, M., Thompson, J., & Braaten, M. (2008). Beyond the scientific method: Model-based inquiry as a new paradigm of preference for school science investigations. *Science Education*, 92(5), 941–967. DOI: 10.1002/sce.20259

Wineburg, S. (2018). *Why learn history (when it's already on your phone)*. University of Chicago Press. DOI: 10.7208/chicago/9780226357355.001.0001

Yager, R. E. (2015). Real-world applications of science. *Science Education International*, 26(2), 136–145. DOI: 10.33828/sei.v26.i2.6

Zeichner, K. M. (2003). The role of action research in teacher education. *Journal of Teacher Education*, 54(1), 24–34. DOI: 10.1177/0022487102238658

Zwiers, J. (2014). *Academic conversations: Classroom talk that fosters critical thinking and content understanding*. Stenhouse Publishers.

KEY TERMS AND DEFINITIONS

Corporate Social Responsibility (CSR): A business model that integrates social and environmental concerns into a company's operations and interactions with stakeholders. CSR involves initiatives and practices that go beyond profit maximization to include contributions to societal well-being, environmental sustainability, and ethical conduct.

Sustainable Development: Development that meets the needs of the present without compromising the ability of future generations to meet their own needs. It encompasses three main pillars: economic growth, environmental protection, and social inclusion, aiming to balance these aspects to ensure long-term viability and equity.

Marketing Strategies: Plans and actions designed to promote and sell products or services effectively. In the context of CSR, marketing strategies often emphasize a company's commitment to ethical practices, sustainability, and community involvement, aiming to enhance brand reputation and customer loyalty.

Financial Strategies: Approaches and decisions related to the management of a company's financial resources. Financial strategies in CSR contexts may include investments in sustainable projects, the allocation of resources towards socially responsible initiatives, and the integration of sustainability metrics into financial reporting.

Leadership in CSR: The role of leaders in guiding and promoting CSR initiatives within an organization. Effective leadership in CSR involves setting a vision for sustainability, creating a culture of responsibility, and aligning business practices with ethical and environmental standards.

Cross-Functional Collaboration: The process of different departments or teams within an organization working together to achieve common goals. In CSR, this often involves collaboration between marketing, finance, and other departments to ensure that sustainability initiatives are integrated into all aspects of business operations.

Ethical Implications: Considerations related to the moral aspects of business practices. Ethical implications in CSR involve evaluating the impact of business activities on stakeholders, including issues such as fairness, transparency, and the potential for exploitation or harm.

Digital Transformation: The integration of digital technologies into all areas of business operations, fundamentally changing how companies operate and deliver value to customers. In CSR, digital transformation can enhance transparency, improve reporting, and engage stakeholders more effectively through online platforms.

Transparency: The degree to which an organization openly shares information about its practices, decisions, and performance. In CSR, transparency is crucial for building trust with stakeholders and demonstrating accountability in relation to social and environmental impacts.

Stakeholder Engagement: The process of involving individuals or groups who have an interest in or are affected by a company's activities. Effective stakeholder engagement in CSR involves listening to concerns, addressing issues, and collaborating with stakeholders to enhance the impact and credibility of CSR efforts.

CSR Reporting: The practice of disclosing information about a company's CSR activities and performance. CSR reporting typically includes details on social, environmental, and economic impacts, and is often guided by standards such as the Global Reporting Initiative (GRI).

Sustainable Finance: Financial practices and investments that support sustainable development goals. Sustainable finance involves allocating capital to projects and companies that have positive social and environmental outcomes, and may include green bonds, socially responsible investing (SRI), and impact investing.

Brand Reputation: The public perception of a company's brand based on its actions, values, and communication. A strong brand reputation in CSR contexts is built on consistent ethical behavior, transparency, and positive contributions to society and the environment.

Impact Assessment: The evaluation of the effects and outcomes of CSR initiatives on stakeholders and the environment. Impact assessment involves measuring both the positive and negative effects of CSR activities to understand their effectiveness and inform future strategies.

Leadership Approaches: Different methods and styles of guiding and managing an organization. In the context of CSR, leadership approaches may include transformational leadership, which inspires and motivates employees towards a shared vision of sustainability, and participative leadership, which involves stakeholders in decision-making processes.

Chapter 2
Examining the Diverse Sources Influencing the Development of Pedagogical Content Knowledge (PCK) Among Educators in Various Educational Settings

Jamila Khurshid
 https://orcid.org/0000-0002-7812-3372
University of Poonch, Rawalakot, Pakistan

Nabila Khurshid
 https://orcid.org/0000-0002-8828-548X
Comsats University, Islamabad, Pakistan

Nyela Ashraf
University of Poonch, Rawalakot, Pakistan

Arslan Arshad
 https://orcid.org/0009-0001-8757-0799
Alhamd University, Islamabad, Pakistan

ABSTRACT

This comprehensive study delves into the intricate web of diverse sources that influence

DOI: 10.4018/979-8-3693-0655-0.ch002

the development of Pedagogical Content Knowledge (PCK) among educators in a multitude of educational settings. By exploring the impact of factors such as teacher education programs, classroom experiences, professional development workshops, specialized content knowledge, mentorship programs, and technology integration, this research aims to provide a holistic understanding of how educators acquire, refine, and apply their PCK. Through an in-depth analysis of these multifaceted sources, this study seeks to shed light on the complex interplay between different influences on PCK development and their implications for enhancing teaching practices and fostering effective student learning outcomes.

INTRODUCTION

The first section of this paper presents the review and the definition of PCK as the theoretical framework that is used to examine the teaching and learning processes as they are the core aspects of the study (Jain et al., 2024). It introduces the area of knowledge that the study focuses on to establish sources of PCK pro development in educators within different frames of reference(Gomez, 2020). Less significance is given to the knowledge of such sources for the aim of enhancing the teaching practices that enhance the achievement of students(Shing et al., 2018). Teacher education programs, classroom experiences, undertaking various workshops, developing specialized content knowledge, getting mentorship programs, resorting to new technologies, and so on are some of the strategies to be addressed in the current investigation, and these are also introduced in the beginning part of the study(Loughran & Berry, 2005). The final intention is to provide a general idea regarding how teachers construct and elaborate their PCK from a variety of sources of information(Loughran & Berry, 2005). The first section of the manuscript features a discussion on Pedagogical Content Knowledge (PCK) as well as an exposition of the relationship between the four researched teachers and their participants' teaching practice(Gomez, 2020). This paper introduces the study context by defining the area of study, which concerns the various sources whereby educators in various learning settings develop the PCK. The following sources highlight how they can be understood as a means of enhancing teaching practices so as to deliver better student learning(R. Evens et al., 2016). The key somewhat related factors include teachers' education programs, their classroom experience, professional development workshops or seminars, specialized content knowledge, mentorship, and knowledge in the application of technology in education, as highlighted in the introduction section of this study (M. Evens et al., 2016). The targeted understanding is the end product of the occasions through which educators acquire and transform their PCK(Bunch, 2013).

Scholastic Content Knowledge (SCK) is an essential part of teaching practice since it is a mediator between the domain content knowledge and enacted teaching knowledge. With regard to this, (McGaw, 2024) defined PCK as the complex contextual knowledge that educators have when it comes to implementing pedagogy in order to effectively present content in a manner that is easy to understand for their students. This not only includes the content that is taught but also includes the ways and methods most appropriate to help transfer that content to learners. In the current world of education, thus it is incredibly important for teachers to understand various aspects of their PCK and where it originates from to enable them to thrive in ever-changing education environments. This study seeks to identify the various sources that contribute to the development of PCK amongst educators, with the view of providing a comprehensive understanding of the complex interaction of various factors that define practices and improve the learning achievements of learners.

Background of the Study

Over the years, the LFE has embraced the importance of Pedagogical Content Knowledge (PCK) in the creation of good teaching practices. PCK entails the procedural and propositional knowledge that teachers have in order to integrate and coordinate subject matter content with learning/teaching methodologies to enhance the learning of students(Jain et al., 2024). The pioneering work of (McGaw, 2024) has played a crucial role in our attempt to understand and elaborate on some of the key features of PCK and its centrality within the teaching and learning process. It is on this background that one is able to appreciate the need for educators to not only possess a wide and deep understanding of what he or she intends to teach but also know how to best present the content in a way that is most fitting for the learners(Vinodhen, 2020). With the emergence of educational diversification and the variations in students' characteristics and educational environments, the identification of the sources through which the construction of PCK takes place becomes important as well(Bo, 2024). For that reason, the reader who delves into the background and sources of PCK is more competent in practices that promote the betterment of learning environments and educational results for learners across contexts.

Significance of the Study

The importance of studying the various sources that shape PCK in educators' practice is in its potential to develop and improve the teaching practices and, hence, the learning achievements of students (Max et al., 2023). Knowledge about these sources can help to explain how educators develop PCK and hone the practices that enable their pupils to be more engaged and have a greater level of learning (Can & Boz, 2022)(Reza Adel & Azari Noughabi, 2023). Through the identification of the features that characterize PCK's development, it is easier to modify methods of teaching to suit the needs of learners in each context (Kholid et al., 2023). It is, therefore, the intention of this research to enhance the knowledge database regarding the multiple sources of PCK and their impact on teaching practices and student outcomes.

SOURCES

1- Teacher Education Programs

Teacher education programs have the critical task of developing PCK among educators (Reza et al., 2023). Preservice(Ngubane, 2024) teacher education programs prepare teachers with the essential skills in teaching and subject matter that are required for the conversion of content to teaching-learning experiences for students. Teachers acquire a preliminary understanding of the development of the PCK and the modification of practices by enrolling in teacher education programs (Kyi et al., 2023). High-quality teacher training programs are paramount in preparing teachers for the purpose of providing depth of knowledge to help them be effective teachers and respond to the improved teaching and learning outcomes amongst students (Kyi et al., 2023).

2- Classroom Experiences

Teachers spend most of their formative years in the classroom practices that define their professional Pedagogical Content Knowledge (PCK) (Thacker et al., 2023). Performing the hands-on session with the students affords the teachers practical ground on which to implement knowledge and teaching competencies in subject matter content (Kelly et al., 2023). In this way, these experience levels provide important information about the learning behaviors of the students, effective and possible strategies of instruction, and the uniqueness and constantly changing nature of the context of the classroom environment, which are helpful in constructing and fine-tuning educators' PCK. When educators provide meaningful feedback on the classroom experiences they undergo, the teaching practices and the students' engagement and learning achievements will be improved.

3-Professional Development Workshops

This is because workshops, as part of professional learning, bestow on teachers the opportunity to refine their Pedagogical Content Knowledge (Poulou et al., 2023). These workshops present the teachers with specific possibilities to reflect on practice, work with colleagues, and learn new approaches to teaching and new content knowledge (Bhatt et al., 2024). From workshops, educators receive current information on educational trends, new outlooks on practices, and the ability to update their pedagogy skills (Stenberg et al., 2024). Such workshops can provide a boost to the growth of educators' professional learning and development as well as promote the spirit of professionally continued education in the sphere of teaching.

4-Specialized Content Knowledge (SCK)

Thus, it can be noted that in the process of knowledge specialization, the educators' SCK actually determines how the matter of educating within specific subject matter areas is carried out, especially in conception (Özel et al., 2022). Such knowledge extends beyond the professional and structural content knowledge and covers profound knowledge of the content matter so that teachers can effectively explain it to students (Corven et al., 2022). Consequently, when teachers are able to build and hone his/ her SCK, she/he is equipped to modify the instructional practices and adapt corresponding teaching techniques that will favorably impact the students learning (Cho et al., 2023).

5- Mentorship Programs

Mentorship programs are also very helpful in the development of educators, and this can be seen from the following (Whitlock, 2024). Thus, through the establishment of professional connections with experienced mentors, educators can get useful tips, advice, and support that will help them to improve their Pedagogical Content Knowledge (PCK) (Rahal et al., 2023). These programs offer a systematic way through which knowledge and skills are acquired, disseminated, and enhanced to the advantage of both the educators and the learners (Odonkor et al., 2024).

6-Technology Integration in Education

The use of technology in the teaching and learning process has been considered to have many advantages in enhancing teaching and learning processes and students' engagement (Cahill et al., 2023). Therefore, the use of technology in teaching helps teachers to come up with lessons that are interesting and fun and at the same time help learners who have difficulties in learning (Lim et al., 2024). This is because, through technology integration, students' achievement can be increased and the students can be equipped to face the challenges of the 21st century (Ali et al., 2023). It then becomes important for educators to look for and embrace strategies that can be used to incorporate technology into the teaching and learning processes in today's teaching institutions.

CONCLUSION

Thus, it is possible to state that the integration of technology into education has numerous potentialities that can enhance the quality of teaching and learning, stimulate students' motivation, and prepare students for further life in the digital society. Technology integration in teaching and learning helps the teachers to develop a lively and stimulating classroom environment that addresses the needs of all students. Previous studies on Technology Integration show that it has a positive correlation with students' achievement and stress the need for teachers to be provided with regular training to use the technology in their classroom effectively. The use of technology in teaching and learning can, therefore, result in a shift in the teaching and learning process that will enable students to excel in society.

Discussion

In the context of Pedagogical Content Knowledge (PCK) development, the debate concerns the sources that can enhance teachers' capacity to link subject matter content and teaching methods. Teacher education programs are vital in preparing teachers to acquire the necessary knowledge and understanding of the PCK that is required in teaching (Reza et al., 2023). Classroom practice is crucial for teachers to develop and enhance their PCK in actual learning contexts and adjust the teaching strategies according to students' requirements (Thacker et al., 2023). Specialized Content Knowledge (SCK) increases the depth of knowledge of the educators in specific areas of teaching and learning disciplines. It assists them in breaking down the concepts and renders them in a way that is easier for the learners to understand (Ozel et al., 2022). Mentorship programs help in developing the PCK of the educators and the participants are able to learn from their peers (Whitlock, 2024). Technology integration as a source of influence helps educators to create an effective and creative learning environment, which meets the needs and capacities of all learners (Cahill et al., 2023). Therefore, these different sources should be considered by educators in order to enhance their teaching methods, enhance students' interest and consequently enhance students' achievement.

Future Research

Future research on examining the diverse sources influencing the development of Pedagogical Content Knowledge (PCK) among educators should focus on several key areas: the effect of integrating technology that evaluates the extent of technology integration in enhancing the professional content and pedagogical knowledge, the utility of professional development programs in providing understanding of new technologies to teachers, cross setting comparison, the utility of student feedback to influence teacher's teaching strategies and the nature of knowledge building collaborative learning among teachers. To this end, this multifaceted research approach intends to provide improvements in describing and facilitating the ways in which various sources build PCK with regard to technology integration so that teachers might be armed to construct meaningful and relevant learning environments in society that is progressively becoming technological.

Definition

Pedagogical Content Knowledge (PCK) is a component of teaching that deals with both teaching and content. It includes knowledge of how to approach the task of teaching specific content in the best way possible and using the existing knowledge, misconceptions, and learning activities of students. PCK comprises knowledge of the proper content, procedures in behavioral assessment, and strategies that can be used by the teacher in order to teach students to represent content in ways which can be easily understood by the students. In other words, it is the knowledge that teachers require in order in order to facilitate learning and 'teach'in content to learners.

Specialized Content Knowledge (SCK) is knowledge concerning specific discipline where teacher has to teach, which is relevant to the effective teaching learning process. It concerns specific knowledge extending beyond the general understanding of a subject in a given discipline or field, which is often the type of knowledge, which will encompass to a certain extent specialized knowledge of one's area of professional specialization. Through SCK educators can determine misconceptions held by the learners, plan on how to help the students transform these beliefs and enhance their knowledge and understanding of content under learning.

REFERENCES

Bhatt, M. J., Durani, H., Tanna, P., & Lathigara, A. (2024). Enhancing Real-World Applications Learning In Industrial Engineering: Integrating Out-of-Classroom Experiences for Optimal Skill Development. *Journal of Engineering Education Transformations, 37*(Special Issue 2).

Bo, N. S. W. (2024). *OECD digital education outlook 2023: Towards an effective education ecosystem*. Hungarian Educational Research Journal.

Bunch, G. C. (2013). Pedagogical language knowledge: Preparing mainstream teachers for English learners in the new standards era. *Review of Research in Education, 37*(1), 298–341. DOI: 10.3102/0091732X12461772

Can, H. B., & Boz, Y. (2022). Development of pre-service teachers' pedagogical content knowledge and the factors affecting that development: A longitudinal study. *Chemistry Education Research and Practice, 23*(4), 980–997. DOI: 10.1039/D2RP00106C

Cho, K., Ward, P., Chey, W. S., Tsuda, E., Atkinson, O. J., & Oh, D. (2023). An Assessment of Preservice Teachers' Volleyball Content Knowledge in Physical Education Teacher Education. *International Journal of Kinesiology in Higher Education, 7*(4), 335–345. DOI: 10.1080/24711616.2022.2163726

Corven, J., DiNapoli, J., Willoughby, L., & Hiebert, J. (2022). Long-Term relationships between Mathematics instructional time during teacher preparation and specialized content knowledge. *Journal for Research in Mathematics Education, 53*(4), 277–306. DOI: 10.5951/jresematheduc-2020-0036

Evens, M., Elen, J., & Depaepe, F. (2016). Pedagogical content knowledge in the context of foreign and second language teaching: A review of the research literature. *Porta Linguarum, 26*, 187–200. DOI: 10.30827/Digibug.53944

Evens, R., Hoefler, M., Biber, K., & Lueken, U. (2016). The Iowa Gambling Task in Parkinson's disease: A meta-analysis on effects of disease and medication. *Neuropsychologia, 91*, 163–172. DOI: 10.1016/j.neuropsychologia.2016.07.032 PMID: 27475264

Gomez, J. C. (2020). Development of EFL teachers pedagogical content knowledge through action research in a master's program. *Problems of Education in the 21st Century, 78*(4), 533–552.

Jain, J., Ling, L. Y., & Jin, M. S. (2024). A Systematic Review of Pedagogical Content Knowledge for Teaching Nature of Science. *Asian Journal of University Education*, 20(1), 138–151. DOI: 10.24191/ajue.v20i1.25738

Kelly, K. J., Kast, D. J., Schiksnis, C. A., & Thrash, J. C. (2023). Hands-on Hypoxia: Engaging High School Educators in the science behind Marine Microbial Dynamics in Hypoxic Coastal Areas Through Field and Classroom Experiences. *Current. Journal of Marketing Education*, 38(1).

Kholid, M. N., Hendriyanto, A., Sahara, S., Muhaimin, L. H., Juandi, D., Sujadi, I., Kuncoro, K. S., & Adnan, M. (2023). A systematic literature review of Technological, Pedagogical and Content Knowledge (TPACK) in mathematics education: Future challenges for educational practice and research. *Cogent Education*, 10(2), 2269047. DOI: 10.1080/2331186X.2023.2269047

Kyi, W. W., Errabo, D. D., & Isozaki, T. (2023). A Comparison of Pre-Service Science Teacher Education in Myanmar, the Philippines and Japan. *Education Sciences*, 13(7), 706. DOI: 10.3390/educsci13070706

Loughran, J., & Berry, A. (2005). Modelling by teacher educators. *Teaching and Teacher Education*, 21(2), 193–203. DOI: 10.1016/j.tate.2004.12.005

Max, A.-L., Weitzel, H., & Lukas, S. (2023). Factors influencing the development of pre-service science teachers' technological pedagogical content knowledge in a pedagogical makerspace. *Frontiers in Education*, 8, 1166018. DOI: 10.3389/feduc.2023.1166018

McGaw, M. A. D. (2024). Professional Content Knowledge: Increasing Instructional Quality. In *Cases on Economics Education and Tools for Educators* (pp. 121–135). IGI Global.

Ngubane, T. (2024). Influence of Teacher Training Programs on Quality of Education in South Africa. *African Journal of Education and Practice*, 9(2), 46–55. DOI: 10.47604/ajep.2524

Odonkor, T. N., Eziamaka, N. V., & Akinsulire, A. A. (2024). *Strategic mentorship programs in fintech software engineering for developing industry leaders*.

Özel, Z., Yılmaz, A., Işıksal-Bostan, M., & Özkan, B. (2022). Investigation of the Specialized Content Knowledge of the Pre-service Primary School Teachers about Multiplication. *International Journal for Mathematics Teaching and Learning*, 23(2), 115–143. DOI: 10.4256/ijmtl.v23i2.464

Poulou, M. S., Reddy, L. A., & Dudek, C. M. (2023). Teachers and school administrators' experiences with professional development feedback: The classroom strategies assessment system implementation. *Frontiers in Psychology*, 14, 1074278. DOI: 10.3389/fpsyg.2023.1074278 PMID: 36910749

Rahal, M., Alsharif, N. Z., Younes, S., Sakr, F., Mourad, N., Halat, D. H., Akel, M., & Jomha, I. (2023). The assessment of mentorship programs on pharmacy students' leadership roles and performance in experiential education. *Pharmacy Practice*, 21(3), 21. DOI: 10.18549/PharmPract.2023.3.2853

Reza Adel, S. M., & Azari Noughabi, M. (2023). Developing Pedagogical Content Knowledge (PCK) through an enriched teacher education program: Cases of four Iranian pre-service EFL teachers. *Pedagogies*, 18(3), 352–373. DOI: 10.1080/1554480X.2022.2061976

Shing, C. L., Saat, R. M., & Loke, S. H. (2018). The knowledge of teaching â€"pedagogical content knowledge (PCK). *MOJES: Malaysian Online Journal of Educational Sciences*, 3(3), 40–55.

Stenberg, E., Milosavljevic, A., Götrick, B., & Lundegren, N. (2024). Continuing professional development in general dentistry—Experiences of an online flipped classroom. *European Journal of Dental Education*, 28(3), 825–832. DOI: 10.1111/eje.13013 PMID: 38654701

Thacker, B., Hart, S., Wipfli, K., & Wang, J. (2023). The development of free-response questions to assess learning assistants PCK in the context of questioning. *ArXiv Preprint ArXiv:2304.14285*.

Vinodhen, V. (2020). The development of science education during the ability-driven phase in Singapore, 1997–2011. *Asia-Pacific Science Education*, 6(1), 207–227. DOI: 10.1163/23641177-BJA00007

Whitlock, B. (2024). Mentorship programs in schools: Bridging the character education gap. *Journal of Moral Education*, 53(1), 89–118. DOI: 10.1080/03057240.2023.2280757

Chapter 3
Leveraging Learning Progressions to Enhance Pedagogical Content Knowledge in Science Education

Sam Ramaila
https://orcid.org/0000-0002-7351-477X
University of Johannesburg, South Africa

ABSTRACT

This chapter explores how learning progressions can enhance Pedagogical Content Knowledge (PCK) in science education. By providing a structured sequence of concepts and skills, learning progressions help educators align teaching strategies with students' cognitive development. This alignment offers deeper insights into student understanding and engagement with scientific concepts, improving PCK. The chapter examines the theoretical foundations of learning progressions and PCK, discusses strategies for integrating progressions into classroom practice, and uses case studies to show how they aid in addressing misconceptions, scaffolding learning, and promoting conceptual understanding. It emphasizes the importance of learning progressions in refining PCK and improving science education, ultimately preparing students for advanced inquiry and problem-solving.

DOI: 10.4018/979-8-3693-0655-0.ch003

1. INTRODUCTION

In the realm of science education, the effective integration of Pedagogical Content Knowledge (PCK) is essential for fostering deep understanding and mastery of complex scientific concepts (Star, 2023). As educators strive to improve teaching practices and enhance student outcomes, the adoption of learning progressions offers a valuable framework for guiding instructional design and practice (Sancar, Atal & Deryakulu, 2021). Learning progressions, which delineate the developmental pathways through which students build and refine their understanding of scientific concepts, provide a roadmap for educators to scaffold instruction and address diverse learning needs (Duschl, 2019). This chapter explores how leveraging learning progressions can significantly enhance PCK within the context of science education. It delves into the intersection of these two crucial elements—learning progressions and PCK—highlighting how their integration can lead to more effective and responsive teaching practices. By examining the theoretical foundations of learning progressions and their practical applications, this chapter aims to illustrate how educators can use these frameworks to deepen their understanding of both content and pedagogy.

I will begin by defining learning progressions and their role in science education, outlining how they provide a structured approach to understanding student learning trajectories and identifying key milestones in concept development. Next, I will explore the concept of PCK, emphasizing its importance in bridging content knowledge with instructional strategies to facilitate student comprehension. The chapter will then demonstrate how learning progressions can be leveraged to enhance PCK by providing targeted strategies for aligning instructional practices with students' developmental needs. Through a series of case studies and practical examples, this chapter will illustrate how educators can apply learning progressions to refine their teaching practices, design effective instructional interventions, and support students' conceptual growth in science. Additionally, I will address the challenges and opportunities associated with implementing learning progressions, offering insights into best practices and strategies for overcoming common obstacles.

By the end of this chapter, readers will have a comprehensive understanding of how learning progressions can be utilized to enhance PCK in science education, equipping them with the tools and knowledge needed to improve instructional effectiveness and support student learning. As educators continue to seek innovative approaches to teaching and learning, the integration of learning progressions and PCK represents a promising avenue for advancing science education and achieving educational excellence.

2. THEORETICAL FOUNDATIONS

2.1 Definition and Conceptualization of Learning Progressions

Learning progressions are foundational frameworks in education that chart the typical pathways students follow as they deepen their understanding of a subject (Duschl, 2019). Unlike traditional curricula that may present content in a linear or compartmentalized fashion, learning progressions capture the dynamic and often non-linear nature of learning (Duschl, Maeng & Sezen, 2011). They are descriptive continuums that outline how students' thinking evolves over time, from initial, often simplistic notions to more sophisticated, integrated understandings. The concept of learning progressions is anchored in the recognition that learning is a cumulative process (Sikorski, 2019). It builds on prior knowledge and experiences, with students progressively refining and expanding their conceptual frameworks. This process involves moving from novice-like understandings to expert-like comprehension, where learners can apply knowledge flexibly and creatively in various contexts. Learning progressions, therefore, provide a map of these developmental milestones, highlighting key conceptual shifts and critical junctures in a student's learning journey (Duschl, Maeng & Sezen, 2011).

At the core of learning progressions is the idea of incremental development (Fonger et al., 2017). They emphasize that understanding does not emerge fully formed but grows through a series of stages. Each stage represents a qualitatively different level of understanding, characterized by increasingly complex and abstract thinking. For instance, in science education, a progression might begin with students recognizing observable phenomena, advance to identifying patterns and relationships, and culminate in explaining underlying scientific principles. This staged approach helps educators recognize that students may require time and multiple experiences to achieve a robust understanding. Importantly, learning progressions acknowledge multiple pathways to learning. While they describe typical sequences of conceptual development, they also accommodate individual variations. Students come to the classroom with diverse backgrounds, experiences, and prior knowledge, all of which influence their learning trajectories. Thus, learning progressions are not rigid scripts but flexible guides that can be adapted to meet the unique needs of each learner ((Duschl, Maeng & Sezen, 2011). This flexibility is crucial for differentiating instruction and providing targeted support.

A central feature of learning progressions is their focus on big ideas—the core concepts and practices that are essential for understanding a subject. In science, these big ideas might include concepts like energy, matter, ecosystems, or the nature of scientific inquiry. Learning progressions help educators prioritize these foundational concepts and explore how they connect across different topics and grade levels (Upahi & Ramnarain, 2022). By focusing on big ideas, teachers can ensure that students build a coherent and connected understanding of the subject matter, rather than a fragmented collection of facts. Learning progressions also play a critical role in informative assessment (Hassel, Launius & Rensing, 2021). They provide a framework for assessing where students are in their learning and identifying the next steps in their development. Formative assessments, designed in alignment with learning progressions, allow teachers to gather evidence of students' thinking, understand their current level of understanding, and plan instruction accordingly (Harris, Adie & Wyatt-Smith, 2022). This approach shifts the focus from merely evaluating student performance to supporting ongoing learning and growth.

The conceptualization of learning progressions involves understanding them as both research-based constructs and practical tools. They are grounded in empirical studies that explore how students' thinking evolves in various domains. Researchers analyse patterns in student responses, misconceptions, and reasoning processes to develop models of typical learning pathways ((Upahi & Ramnarain, 2022). These models are then validated and refined through further research and classroom applications. In practice, learning progressions guide curriculum design, instructional planning, and professional development (Yao, Liu & Guo, 2023). They help educators scaffold instruction, providing appropriate challenges at each stage of learning. For example, in teaching complex scientific ideas, teachers might first engage students with concrete experiences and observations before moving on to more abstract explanations and theoretical models. Learning progressions also support teachers in diagnosing and addressing misconceptions, guiding students towards more scientifically accurate understandings (Shepard, 2018).

Ultimately, learning progressions are powerful tools for enhancing educational practice. They offer a structured yet flexible approach to understanding and supporting student learning, grounded in the reality that learning is a gradual, complex process. By making the pathways of learning visible, they empower educators to make informed instructional decisions, fostering deeper and more meaningful learning experiences for all students.

2.2 Understanding Pedagogical Content Knowledge (PCK)

Pedagogical Content Knowledge (PCK) (Shulman, 1986) represents a critical facet of effective teaching, embodying the intersection of subject matter expertise and pedagogical acumen. Coined by Lee Shulman in 1986, PCK transcends simple mastery of content and pedagogy; it is the unique amalgamation of both that enables teachers to deliver content in ways that are not only comprehensible but also engaging and meaningful to students. At the heart of PCK lies the teacher's deep understanding of the content they teach (Fraser, 2016). This knowledge extends beyond rote facts and figures to encompass the underlying concepts, theories, and frameworks that define a discipline. In science education, for instance, it involves grasping not just scientific facts but also the processes of scientific inquiry and the nature of scientific knowledge. This foundational content knowledge is the bedrock upon which all other elements of PCK are built.

However, content knowledge alone is insufficient for effective teaching (Chew & Cerbin, 2020). Teachers must also possess a robust repertoire of pedagogical strategies. These strategies include various instructional methods, such as inquiry-based learning, hands-on experiments, and collaborative projects, all tailored to facilitate student understanding. A teacher's pedagogical skills enable them to present content in diverse ways, accommodating different learning styles and making complex concepts accessible (Kleickmann et al., 2013). For example, using analogies and visual aids can help demystify abstract scientific phenomena, making them more relatable to students' everyday experiences. Integral to PCK is an understanding of students and their learning processes. This includes awareness of the typical preconceptions and misconceptions students may hold about specific topics, as well as an appreciation of their developmental stages and cultural backgrounds (Velliaris & Pierce, 2016). For instance, students may enter a physics classroom with preconceived notions about motion and force that differ from scientific explanations. A teacher with strong PCK anticipates these misconceptions and uses targeted instructional strategies to guide students toward accurate scientific understanding.

Curriculum knowledge is another crucial component of PCK (Park & Oliver, 2008). It involves knowing the structure and goals of the curriculum, including the standards and benchmarks students are expected to achieve. This knowledge allows teachers to align their instruction with curriculum objectives and ensure that students are adequately prepared for assessments. Moreover, understanding the broader curriculum context enables teachers to make interdisciplinary connections, enriching the learning experience (Mora-Flores & Kaplan, 2022). The context in which teaching occurs also plays a pivotal role in shaping PCK. This includes the classroom environment, school culture, and community expectations, as well as the availability of resources and support systems. Teachers must navigate these contextual factors, adapting their teaching methods to the specific needs and constraints of their educational setting. For example, a teacher in a resource-limited school may rely more on improvised teaching aids or digital resources to facilitate learning.

Developing and enhancing PCK is a dynamic and ongoing process. Teachers refine their PCK through reflective practice, analysing their teaching experiences, and seeking ways to improve (Kuswandono, 2012). Professional development opportunities, such as workshops, seminars, and collaborative discussions, provide valuable platforms for teachers to deepen their knowledge and exchange best practices. Engaging with the latest research in education and subject-specific fields further enriches teachers' PCK, equipping them with evidence-based strategies and innovative approaches (van Dijk & Kattmann, 2007). In the realm of science education, PCK is particularly vital due to the subject's inherent complexity and the abstract nature of many scientific concepts (Almonacid-Fierro et al., 2023). Teachers must bridge the gap between students' everyday experiences and the sophisticated explanations offered by science. For instance, explaining the concept of chemical bonding requires not only a solid understanding of chemistry but also the ability to relate it to familiar experiences, such as the attraction between magnets. A teacher's PCK enables them to create a learning environment that encourages inquiry, fosters critical thinking, and supports students in constructing a deep and coherent understanding of scientific principles (Shinana, Ngcoza & Mavhunga, 2021).

Ultimately, PCK is more than just a set of discrete knowledge areas; it is an integrative framework that informs every aspect of teaching. It allows teachers to make informed decisions about how to present content, respond to student needs, and adapt to the teaching context. By continually developing their PCK, teachers enhance their ability to foster meaningful and transformative learning experiences, preparing students not only to excel academically but also to apply their knowledge in real-world contexts.

2.3 Pedagogical Content Knowledge (PCK) for Specific Sub-Disciplines and Populations

Pedagogical Content Knowledge (PCK) is a critical framework for understanding how teachers blend subject matter expertise with effective teaching strategies to facilitate learning (Sarkar et al, 2024). However, to fully appreciate the depth and applicability of PCK, it is essential to delve into its nuances by focusing on specific sub-disciplines and populations. Expanding the discussion in this way provides a more comprehensive understanding of how PCK operates within various educational contexts and enhances its relevance for diverse teaching scenarios.

In the context of science education, PCK involves understanding how to teach complex scientific concepts and processes effectively (Depaepe, Verschaffel & Kelchtermans, 2013). For example, in physics, teachers need to convey abstract concepts like forces and motion in ways that make them tangible for students. This involves selecting appropriate instructional strategies, such as using visual aids or simulations, and addressing common misconceptions. PCK in science education also includes knowing how to sequence content to build foundational knowledge progressively, from simple to more complex concepts (Almonacid-Fierro et al., 2023).

PCK in mathematics education focuses on how to teach mathematical concepts and problem-solving skills (Depaepe, Verschaffel & Kelchtermans, 2013). Teachers must be adept at presenting abstract mathematical ideas in concrete ways, using visual representations and real-world applications. For instance, teaching geometry might involve hands-on activities with physical shapes to help students grasp spatial relationships. Effective mathematics instruction also requires understanding common student errors and misconceptions and knowing how to address them through targeted interventions (Benecke & Kaiser, 2023).

In language arts, PCK involves understanding how to teach reading and writing skills effectively (Star, 2023). Teachers need to know how to scaffold instruction for different stages of literacy development, from phonemic awareness in early grades to advanced literary analysis in higher grades. This includes selecting appropriate texts, designing engaging writing assignments, and using formative assessments to guide instruction. PCK in language arts also involves recognizing the diverse linguistic backgrounds of students and adapting instruction to support their unique needs (Hossain, 2024).

PCK in social studies involves teaching historical, geographical, and cultural concepts in ways that foster critical thinking and historical inquiry (Deng, 2018). Teachers need to select appropriate sources, such as primary documents or maps, and design activities that help students analyse and interpret historical events or social phenomena. Effective social studies instruction also requires understanding how to make connections between past and present issues and addressing diverse perspectives and interpretations (Popa, 2022).

PCK must also account for the diverse needs of learners, including those with different cultural, linguistic, and ability backgrounds. For example, teachers working with English Language Learners (ELLs) need to adapt their instruction to include language support strategies, such as visual aids and collaborative learning opportunities. PCK for diverse learners involves recognizing and addressing cultural differences in learning styles and experiences, ensuring that all students have equitable access to the curriculum (Caingcoy, 2023).

For students with special needs, PCK involves modifying instructional practices to accommodate various learning challenges (Depaepe, Verschaffel & Kelchtermans, 2013). This may include implementing differentiated instruction, using assistive technology, and creating individualized education plans (IEPs). Teachers need to understand how to adapt content and teaching methods to support students with disabilities, ensuring that they can participate fully in the learning process and achieve their potential (Adewumi, Mosito & Agosto, 2019).

PCK for gifted and talented students requires understanding how to provide enrichment and advanced learning opportunities that challenge and engage these students (Reis, Renzulli & Renzulli, 2021). Teachers need to design instruction that goes beyond the standard curriculum, offering opportunities for independent research, complex problem-solving, and higher-order thinking (Panke, 2019). PCK in this context also involves creating a learning environment that nurtures creativity and intellectual curiosity.

In early childhood education, PCK involves knowing how to teach foundational skills in a developmentally appropriate manner (Gasteiger et al., 2020). Teachers need to understand how young children learn through play and exploration and design activities that support language development, numeracy, and social skills. Effective PCK for early childhood educators also includes knowing how to create a supportive and engaging classroom environment that fosters curiosity and a love of learning (Liu, Hedges & Cooper, 2023.

Expanding the discussion of Pedagogical Content Knowledge (PCK) to include specific sub-disciplines and populations offers a richer and more nuanced understanding of how teachers integrate content knowledge with effective teaching strategies. By exploring PCK in various educational contexts and for diverse learner groups, educators can enhance their instructional practices, address unique challenges, and better support student learning. This comprehensive approach ensures that PCK remains a dynamic and relevant framework for improving educational outcomes across different subjects and student populations.

2.4 The relationship Between Learning Progressions and PCK

The relationship between learning progressions and Pedagogical Content Knowledge (PCK) is a synergistic one, with each concept enhancing and informing the other (Suh & Park, 2017). Both are crucial for effective teaching and learning, especially in complex fields like science education, where understanding both the content and the nuances of how students learn is vital. Learning progressions offer a detailed map of how students typically develop understanding in a particular subject area over time (Fortus & Krajcik, 2012). They describe the stages through which students' thinking evolves, from basic, often naive conceptions to more sophisticated, nuanced understandings. These stages are informed by extensive research into how students learn and how their misconceptions and ideas can change through instruction and experience. Pedagogical Content Knowledge, on the other hand, is the knowledge teachers use to effectively teach their subject matter. PCK involves knowing not only the content but also the most effective ways to convey it to students (Depaepe, Verschaffel & Kelchtermans, 2013). This includes understanding the common misconceptions students may have, the typical challenges they might face, and the best strategies to address these issues.

Learning progressions provide a framework that enhances a teacher's PCK by offering a clear understanding of where students are likely to be in their learning journey and what they are ready to learn next (Schneider & Plasman, 2011). This understanding helps teachers tailor their instructional strategies to meet students' needs at each developmental stage. For instance, if a learning progression indicates that students often struggle with the concept of energy transfer, a teacher can anticipate this and prepare specific interventions or analogies to clarify the concept. Both learning progressions and PCK emphasize the importance of addressing students' misconceptions. Learning progressions highlight common misconceptions that arise at different stages of learning, while PCK equips teachers with the pedagogical tools to address these misconceptions effectively (Yang et al., 2023). Together, they guide teachers in diagnosing student misunderstandings and selecting appropriate teaching methods to correct them. For example, understanding that students may initially believe that heavier objects fall faster than lighter ones can inform a teacher's approach to teaching gravity and motion.

Learning progressions support the differentiation of instruction, a key component of PCK. By identifying where each student is along the progression, teachers can differentiate their teaching, offering more support to those who need it and more challenging tasks to those ready to advance (Godor, 2021). This scaffolding is a critical aspect of effective pedagogy, ensuring that all students are appropriately challenged and supported in their learning. Learning progressions also inform formative assessment practices, which are integral to PCK. By understanding the typical learning pathways outlined in progressions, teachers can design assessments that diagnose students' current levels of understanding and provide targeted feedback (Duschl, Maeng & Sezen, 2011). This feedback can then inform subsequent instruction, helping students progress to the next stage of their learning. The integration of learning progressions into curriculum design ensures that instructional content is sequenced in a way that aligns with students' cognitive development (Fonger et al., 2017). This alignment is a core aspect of PCK, as it requires a deep understanding of how to present content logically and coherently. For example, a curriculum designed with learning progressions in mind might introduce fundamental scientific principles before moving on to more complex topics, ensuring a solid foundational understanding. Engaging with learning progressions can be a valuable part of professional development for teachers, helping them refine their PCK. By exploring the research behind learning progressions and their application in the classroom, teachers can deepen their understanding of both content and pedagogy (Harris, Adie & Wyatt-Smith, 2022). This professional growth, in turn, enhances their ability to teach more effectively and support student learning.

The relationship between learning progressions and PCK is dynamic. As research in educational psychology and content-specific pedagogy evolves, so do learning progressions. Similarly, teachers continually refine their PCK through experience, reflection, and ongoing professional learning. The interplay between these elements allows for a responsive and adaptive approach to teaching, where both the content and methods are continually aligned with the best understanding of student learning (Schipper, Goei & de Vries, 2023). In summary, the integration of learning progressions into PCK represents a powerful approach to teaching that is both informed by research and responsive to students' needs. This relationship ensures that teachers are not only knowledgeable about their subject matter but also skilled in the art of teaching it, capable of guiding students through a thoughtful and systematic progression of understanding.

2.5 The Role of Technology in Supporting Learning Progressions and Pedagogical Content Knowledge (PCK)

In the evolving landscape of education, technology has emerged as a transformative force, profoundly shaping the way educators approach teaching and learning. Central to this transformation is its role in supporting learning progressions and enhancing Pedagogical Content Knowledge (PCK) (Star, 2023). As educators seek to navigate the complexities of modern classrooms, technology provides innovative tools and strategies that enrich instructional practices and foster deeper student understanding. At the heart of technology's impact on learning progressions is its ability to facilitate personalized learning. Adaptive learning systems, powered by sophisticated algorithms, analyse students' interactions and performance to tailor educational experiences (Zheng et at., 2022). These systems offer customized resources and feedback that align with each student's current understanding and needs. This personalization ensures that students' progress through learning stages at their own pace, receiving targeted support that addresses their unique challenges and strengths. As a result, educators can more effectively guide students through a continuum of learning, from foundational concepts to advanced applications.

Technology also plays a crucial role in deepening educators' Pedagogical Content Knowledge (PCK)—the intersection of what teachers know about content and how to teach it (Koehler, Mishra & Cain, 2013). Interactive tools such as simulations and virtual labs provide dynamic representations of complex concepts (Haleem et al., 2022). For instance, PhET simulations allow educators to visualize and manipulate scientific phenomena that might be difficult to demonstrate in a traditional classroom. This hands-on experience enhances teachers' understanding of the content and enables them to convey complex ideas in more accessible and engaging ways. Moreover, interactive whiteboards and digital resources allow for real-time adjustments during lessons. Teachers can modify explanations, display multiple representations of content, and interactively address students' questions and misconceptions. This flexibility not only enhances the clarity of instruction but also equips educators with a richer toolkit for explaining challenging concepts, thereby refining their PCK.

Learning analytics, powered by technology, offer valuable insights into student progress and achievement (Lee, Cheung & Kwok, 2020). Learning management systems with analytics capabilities enable educators to monitor individual and group performance, identify trends, and make data-driven decisions (Aguilar, 2018). By analysing patterns in student data, teachers can adjust their instructional approaches, provide targeted support, and ensure that students remain on track to meet learning objectives. This analytical approach enhances the effectiveness of instruction and supports students' progression through learning stages. Augmented Reality (AR) and Virtual Reality (VR) technologies offer immersive learning experiences that bring abstract concepts to life (Al-Ansi et al., 2023). These technologies allow students to explore virtual environments, interact with three-dimensional models, and engage in experiential learning activities. For educators, AR and VR provide new avenues for presenting content and fostering student engagement (Sümer & Vaněček, 2024). By incorporating these technologies into their teaching, educators can enhance their PCK and offer students innovative ways to understand and apply knowledge.

Technology's role in supporting learning progressions and enhancing Pedagogical Content Knowledge is multifaceted and profound. From personalizing learning experiences to deepening educators' understanding of content and teaching methods, technology provides tools and strategies that enrich the educational experience. By leveraging these technological advancements, educators can more effectively support student progress, refine their instructional practices, and navigate the complexities of modern teaching with greater confidence and skill.

3. RELEVANT EDUCATIONAL THEORIES AND RESEARCH

The interplay between learning progressions and Pedagogical Content Knowledge (PCK) is deeply rooted in various educational theories and research findings that have shaped our understanding of teaching and learning (Suh & Park, 2017). These theories provide a conceptual foundation for why and how students learn, informing the development of both learning progressions and PCK. At the core of learning progressions and PCK is the constructivist view of learning, which posits that learners actively construct their own understanding based on their experiences and interactions with the world. This theory, influenced by scholars like Jean Piaget and Lev Vygotsky, suggests that knowledge is not passively received but actively built by the learner. Piaget's theory emphasizes the stages of cognitive development, where learners progress through a series of stages characterized by increasingly sophisticated thinking. This idea is reflected in learning progressions, which map out the stages students typically go through as they deepen their understanding of a subject. For instance, in science education, students might progress from concrete operational thinking, where they rely on tangible experiences, to formal operational thinking, where they can understand abstract concepts and hypotheses.

Vygotsky introduced the concept of the Zone of Proximal Development (ZPD), which refers to the range of tasks that a learner can perform with guidance but cannot yet perform independently (Vygotsky, 1978). This concept is central to PCK, as it underscores the importance of scaffolding—providing support structures that help students progress to higher levels of understanding. Teachers use their knowledge of the ZPD to tailor instruction and support students' learning progression, gradually removing scaffolds as students become more competent (Shabani, Khatib & Ebadi, 2010). Theories of conceptual change explore how learners modify their existing beliefs and understandings considering new information. These theories are particularly relevant in science education, where students often enter the classroom with misconceptions that must be addressed for accurate understanding to develop. Posner et at. (1982) proposed that conceptual change occurs when students encounter new information that is inconsistent with their existing beliefs, leading to cognitive conflict. For conceptual change to happen, students must experience dissatisfaction with their current understanding, find the new concept intelligible and plausible, and see it as useful. This theory informs PCK by highlighting the importance of addressing misconceptions directly and helping students reconstruct their understanding considering scientific explanations.

Bloom's Taxonomy provides a hierarchical classification of cognitive skills, ranging from basic recall of facts (knowledge) to higher-order thinking skills such as analysis, synthesis, and evaluation (Bloom, 1956). This taxonomy is instrumental in designing learning progressions, as it outlines the types of cognitive processes students engage in at different levels of understanding. In the context of PCK, Bloom's Taxonomy helps teachers plan lessons and assessments that target various cognitive levels. For instance, in a science class, teachers might first focus on ensuring students understand key concepts (comprehension) before asking them to apply these concepts to solve real-world problems (application) or analyse data (analysis).

4. RESEARCH ON FORMATIVE ASSESSMENT

Formative assessment research has shown that continuous, real-time assessment of student understanding can significantly enhance learning outcomes (Schildkamp et al., 2020). Formative assessments are closely linked to learning progressions, as they provide evidence of where students are along the progression and what they need to move forward. A research conducted by Wiliam and Black (2018) emphasizes that formative assessment is not just about assessing students' knowledge but also about informing instruction. Effective formative assessment involves feedback that is specific, timely, and actionable, helping students understand their current level of understanding and the steps they need to take to improve (Adarkwah, 2021). This practice is a crucial component of PCK, as it requires teachers to interpret assessment data and adjust their teaching strategies accordingly.

The concept of situated learning, proposed by Lave and Wenger (1991), suggests that learning occurs within a context and is deeply tied to social interactions and the environment. This theory supports the idea that learning is a participatory process, where learners engage with more knowledgeable others within a community of practice. In terms of PCK, situated learning emphasizes the importance of creating authentic learning experiences that are relevant to students' lives (Stansberry, 2017) Teachers with strong PCK design learning activities that immerse students in real-world contexts, facilitating deeper understanding and application of knowledge. For example, in a science class, a teacher might create a project-based learning experience where students investigate local environmental issues, applying their scientific knowledge in a meaningful context. Research on teacher expertise underscores that expert teachers possess a deep and flexible understanding of their subject matter and are adept at using various instructional strategies (van Dijk et al., 2020). This expertise is not innate but develops over time through reflection, experience, and continuous professional development.

Professional development programs that focus on both content knowledge and pedagogical strategies are crucial for enhancing PCK. Research by Desimone (2009) and others has shown that effective professional development is sustained, collaborative, and closely tied to teachers' instructional practices. Such programs often include opportunities for teachers to explore learning progressions, discuss common student misconceptions, and share best practices for addressing these challenges (Harris, Adie & Wyatt-Smith, 2022). The relationship between learning progressions and PCK is deeply informed by these educational theories and research findings. Together, they provide a comprehensive framework for understanding how students learn and how teachers can best support this learning. By integrating these theoretical perspectives and research insights, educators can develop rich PCK that enables them to design effective instruction, address student misconceptions, and foster meaningful learning experiences. Designing and constructing learning progressions in science education involves a systematic approach to outlining the typical pathways through which students develop scientific understanding (Yao, Liu & Guo, 2023). These progressions serve as valuable tools for educators, offering a roadmap for instruction that aligns with students' cognitive development and conceptual growth.

5. UNDERSTANDING THE PURPOSE OF LEARNING PROGRESSIONS

The primary purpose of learning progressions is to provide a coherent framework for guiding student learning over time. They describe how students' understanding of scientific concepts evolves from simple, often naive notions to more sophisticated, scientific understandings. Learning progressions help educators identify the key conceptual milestones that students typically achieve and the common challenges they face along the way (Harris, Adie & Wyatt-Smith, 2022).

Step 1: Defining the Target Learning Goals

The first step in designing a learning progression is to clearly define the target learning goals. These goals are derived from educational standards, curriculum frameworks, and the essential concepts of the scientific discipline being taught. In science education, these goals might include fundamental concepts such as energy, matter, ecosystems, or scientific inquiry processes. Defining these learning goals involves specifying what students should know and be able to do at various stages of their education. For instance, in teaching the concept of chemical reactions, the target learning goals might range from understanding basic reactants and products in elementary grades to exploring complex reaction mechanisms and stoichiometry in advanced levels.

Step 2: Mapping the Developmental Stages

Once the target learning goals are established, the next step is to map out the developmental stages through which students typically progress. This involves identifying the intermediate concepts and skills that students need to acquire to achieve the target learning goals. To construct these stages, educators and researchers draw on empirical studies of student thinking and learning in science. This research often involves analysing how students' conceptual understanding evolves, identifying common misconceptions, and understanding the cognitive processes underlying scientific reasoning (Mills, 2016). For example, in learning about ecosystems, the developmental stages might include:

Initial Stage: Recognizing individual organisms and their basic needs.
Intermediate Stage: Understanding interactions between organisms and their environment.
Advanced Stage: Exploring complex relationships within ecosystems, including energy flow and nutrient cycles.

Step 3:   Integrating Research Findings and Theoretical Perspectives

Designing learning progressions requires integrating research findings on how students learn science and applying relevant educational theories. Research on cognitive development, conceptual change, and pedagogical strategies informs the design of learning progressions by providing insights into how students' understanding of scientific concepts evolves and how best to support this development. For example, theories such as Piaget's stages of cognitive development and Vygotsky's Zone of Proximal Development help guide the design of learning progressions by outlining the cognitive capabilities of students at different ages and stages of development. Incorporating these theories ensures that the learning progressions are developmentally appropriate and align with students' cognitive abilities.

Step 4: Designing Instructional Activities and Assessments

With a clear learning progression in place, educators can design instructional activities and assessments that align with each stage of the progression. Instructional activities should be tailored to the specific concepts and skills students are expected to learn at each stage, using strategies that build on their prior knowledge and address their current needs. For instance, if the learning progression includes a stage where students need to understand the role of producers in an ecosystem, instructional activities might involve hands-on experiments with plants, interactive simulations, or field trips. Assessments should be designed to evaluate students' understanding at each stage, providing insights into their progress and areas where they may need additional support.

Step 5: Iterating and Refining the Progression

Designing learning progressions is not a one-time process but an iterative one. Educators need to continuously evaluate and refine the learning progressions based on classroom experiences, student feedback, and ongoing research. This process involves:

> *Collecting Data*: Gathering information on how well students are progressing through the stages and identifying any areas where they may struggle.
> *Analysing and Reflecting*: Reviewing assessment data and student feedback to determine whether the learning progression is effective in supporting student understanding.

Adjusting: Modifying the learning progression, instructional strategies, and assessments as needed to better align with students' learning needs and ensure their success.

Step 6: Providing Professional Development and Support

Effective implementation of learning progressions requires that educators are well-versed in their design and application. Providing professional development opportunities for teachers is essential for helping them understand and utilize learning progressions effectively (Sims et al., 2023). Professional development should focus on:

Understanding the Progressions: Helping teachers grasp the developmental stages and target learning goals outlined in the progressions.
Designing Instruction: Assisting teachers in designing and implementing instructional activities and assessments that align with the learning progressions.
Using Data: Training teachers to use assessment data to monitor student progress and adjust instruction accordingly.

Designing and constructing learning progressions in science education involves a comprehensive approach that integrates research, theoretical frameworks, and practical considerations (Duschl, 2019). By defining clear learning goals, mapping developmental stages, incorporating research findings, designing aligned instructional activities, and iteratively refining the progressions, educators can create effective frameworks that support students' scientific understanding and facilitate their cognitive development (Wijngaards-de Meij & Merx, 2018). This structured approach not only enhances teaching practices but also ensures that students receive coherent, developmentally appropriate instruction that fosters deep and lasting learning in science.

6. KEY CONSIDERATIONS AND CHALLENGES IN DEVELOPING LEARNING PROGRESSIONS

Developing learning progressions in science education involves careful planning and consideration of various factors to ensure that these frameworks effectively support student learning. While learning progressions offer significant benefits in guiding instructional practices and improving educational outcomes, several key considerations and challenges must be addressed to create effective and meaningful progressions (Shepard, 2018). Learning progressions should be aligned with educational standards and curricula to ensure that they meet the requirements set by educational authorities. This alignment ensures that the progression not only reflects the essential concepts and skills students need to acquire but also adheres to the broader educational goals and expectations. Close alignment helps integrate learning progressions into existing curricula and makes it easier for educators to implement them effectively (Wijngaards-de Meij & Merx, 2018).

The stages outlined in a learning progression must be developmentally appropriate, reflecting the cognitive and conceptual abilities of students at different ages and grade levels. This requires a deep understanding of students' cognitive development and how their thinking evolves over time. The progression should be neither too simplistic nor too complex for the target age group, ensuring that students can engage with the material meaningfully and build on their prior knowledge (Goldstone & Landy, 2012). Effective learning progressions are grounded in empirical research on how students learn and develop understanding in science (Fonger et al., 2017). This research includes studies on cognitive development, conceptual change, and common misconceptions. Drawing on this research helps ensure that the progression accurately reflects students' typical learning pathways and addresses common challenges and misconceptions.

Learning progressions should be clearly articulated and precisely defined. Each stage of the progression needs to be described in detail, outlining the specific concepts, skills, and understandings students are expected to achieve. Clear descriptions help teachers understand the goals for each stage and design appropriate instructional activities and assessments. While learning progressions provide a structured framework, they should also be flexible and adaptable to accommodate the diverse needs of students and variations in instructional contexts (Shepard, 2018). Teachers may need to adjust the progression based on students' unique learning needs, backgrounds, and experiences. This flexibility ensures that the progression remains relevant and effective in different educational settings. Incorporating formative assessment into the learning progression is crucial for monitoring students' progress and informing instruction (Harris, Adie & Wyatt-Smith, 2022). Formative assessments should be designed to evaluate students' understanding at each stage of the progression and provide feedback that helps them advance to the next stage. Effective integration of formative assessment supports ongoing adjustment of instruction and helps address students' specific learning needs (van der Steen et al., 2023).

One of the primary challenges in developing learning progressions is accurately mapping the complexity of cognitive development. Understanding how students' conceptual understanding evolves over time requires detailed knowledge of cognitive development theories and extensive research (Chand, 2024). Translating this understanding into practical, sequential stages can be challenging, especially when dealing with abstract or complex scientific concepts. Students come to the classroom with diverse backgrounds, prior knowledge, and learning needs. Developing learning progressions that cater to this diversity while maintaining coherence and consistency can be challenging (Fonger et al., 2017). Ensuring that the progression addresses various learning styles and levels of prior knowledge without becoming overly fragmented or complex requires careful consideration. Students often have pre-existing misconceptions about scientific concepts that can hinder their learning. Designing learning progressions that effectively address and correct these misconceptions while guiding students towards accurate scientific understanding is a significant challenge (Duschl, Maeng & Sezen-Barrie, 2011). It requires a deep understanding of common misconceptions and strategies for overcoming them.

Ensuring that learning progressions maintain student engagement throughout the progression can be challenging. Students may lose interest or struggle with concepts that are too abstract or disconnected from their experiences. Designing engaging and meaningful instructional activities that align with each stage of the progression is crucial for sustaining students' motivation and interest. Successfully implementing learning progressions in the classroom requires adequate support and training for teachers (Duschl, Maeng & Sezen-Barrie, 2011). Teachers need to understand the progression, its goals, and how to design instruction and assessments that align with it. Providing professional development and ongoing support is essential for effective implementation. Educational contexts and standards are continually evolving, which can impact the relevance and effectiveness of learning progressions. Keeping learning progressions up to date with current research, educational standards, and instructional practices is an ongoing challenge. Regular review and revision of progressions are necessary to ensure their continued relevance and effectiveness.

Developing learning progressions in science education involves a nuanced approach that considers developmental appropriateness, alignment with standards, and empirical research. While there are significant challenges, such as addressing cognitive complexity, diverse student needs, and misconceptions, these can be mitigated through careful planning, ongoing assessment, and support for educators. By addressing these considerations and challenges, educators can create effective learning progressions that enhance teaching practices, support student learning, and foster a deeper understanding of science.

7. EXAMPLES OF LEARNING PROGRESSIONS IN VARIOUS SCIENTIFIC DOMAINS

Learning progressions offer a structured framework for understanding how students' knowledge and skills in various scientific domains evolve over time. They provide a roadmap for educators to guide students from basic concepts to more advanced understanding. Here, I explore examples of learning progressions in several key scientific domains, illustrating how these frameworks can be applied to support student learning in different areas of science.

a. Physics: Understanding Forces and Motion

Early Elementary (Grades K-2): At the earliest stages, students begin by observing and describing basic physical phenomena. They might explore concepts such as pushing and pulling objects and recognize that these actions can change the motion of objects. Students learn to identify simple forces and their effects, such as making objects move faster or slower (Wiseman, 2011).

Late Elementary (Grades 3-5): As students progress, they develop a more detailed understanding of forces and motion. They learn about different types of forces (e.g., gravity, friction) and how they affect the movement of objects. Students explore concepts like the direction of forces and how they can be measured using simple tools. They begin to understand that forces can be represented as vectors with both magnitude and direction (Valentine eta l., 2021).

Middle School (Grades 6-8): In middle school, students delve into Newton's laws of motion and explore more complex interactions between forces and motion. They investigate how forces are balanced or unbalanced, and how this affects the motion of objects. Students also start to apply mathematical relationships to describe and predict motion, such as using formulas to calculate speed, acceleration, and force (Lee & Liu, 2009).

High School (Grades 9-12): At the high school level, students study more sophisticated concepts related to forces and motion, such as projectile motion, circular motion, and dynamics. They use advanced mathematical models to analyse and predict the behaviour of objects under various forces. Students also explore the principles of momentum and energy, applying these concepts to real-world scenarios and experimental data (Fortus, Shwartz & Rosenfeld, 2016).

b. Biology: Understanding Ecosystems

Early Elementary (Grades K-2): Young students begin by learning about living and non-living components of their environment. They might explore simple food chains and the basic needs of plants and animals. Students recognize that living organisms interact with their environment and depend on each other for survival (Adelson et al., 2009).

Late Elementary (Grades 3-5): As students advance, they explore more complex interactions within ecosystems. They study various biomes and the roles of producers, consumers, and decomposers. Students learn about habitats, adaptation, and how environmental changes can impact ecosystems. They start to understand the concept of ecological balance and how different organisms contribute to this balance (Valentine et al., 2021).

Middle School (Grades 6-8): Middle school students investigate energy flow and nutrient cycling within ecosystems. They explore the dynamics of populations, communities, and ecosystems, examining factors like biodiversity, competition, and symbiosis. Students use models to understand how changes in one part of an ecosystem can affect the whole system (Lee & Liu, 2009).

High School (Grades 9-12): At the high school level, students study ecosystems in greater depth, focusing on complex interactions and ecological processes. They analyse ecosystems at a larger scale, such as global biomes and their interactions with climate change. Students apply ecological principles to address real-world issues like conservation and environmental management (Lumpkin & Favor, 2012).

c. Chemistry: Understanding Chemical Reactions

Early Elementary (Grades K-2): In the early years, students explore the basic concepts of matter and simple changes in materials. They might observe physical changes, such as melting or dissolving, and recognize that substances can change form but remain the same substance (Roberts et al., 2022).

Late Elementary (Grades 3-5): As students progress, they learn about chemical reactions, including mixing substances and observing observable changes like colour changes, gas production, or temperature changes. Students begin to understand that chemical reactions involve the formation of new substances with different properties (Garza et al., 2014).

Middle School (Grades 6-8): In middle school, students study more detailed aspects of chemical reactions, including the concept of conservation of mass, reaction rates, and the role of energy in reactions. They explore different types of chemical reactions, such as synthesis, decomposition, and combustion, using models and experiments to understand the underlying principles ((Lee & Liu, 2009).

Examples of learning progressions in various scientific domains illustrate how students' understanding of scientific concepts evolves from basic observations to sophisticated analyses. By providing a clear framework for conceptual development, learning progressions help educators design effective instructional strategies and assessments that support students' growth. Understanding these progressions allows educators to tailor their teaching to meet students' needs at different stages of their learning journey, ultimately fostering a deeper and more comprehensive understanding of science.

8. ENHANCING PCK THROUGH LEARNING PROGRESSIONS

Learning progressions play a crucial role in informing and refining Pedagogical Content Knowledge (PCK) by providing a structured framework for understanding how students' knowledge and skills develop over time (Star, 2023). They help educators align instructional strategies, identify and address misconceptions, and implement scaffolding and differentiation to support effective teaching and learning.

8.1 How Learning Progressions Inform and Refine PCK

Learning progressions provide insights into the typical pathways through which students develop understanding in specific scientific domains (Merritt & Krajcik, 2013). By outlining the stages of conceptual development, learning progressions help educators understand the cognitive processes underlying students' learning. This understanding is fundamental to refining PCK, as it enables teachers to tailor their instruction to align with students' current levels of understanding and guide them effectively towards more advanced concepts. By detailing the progression from basic to advanced understanding, learning progressions inform instructional planning and design. Educators can use these frameworks to plan lessons and activities that build on students' existing knowledge and lead them through the necessary conceptual milestones (Darling-Hammond et al., 2023). This alignment ensures that instruction is coherent, logically sequenced, and responsive to students' developmental needs, thereby refining teachers' PCK and improving their ability to deliver effective science instruction. Learning progressions help educators design assessments that are aligned with students' developmental stages. By understanding the expected progression of knowledge and skills, teachers can create assessments that accurately measure students' understanding and identify gaps in their learning. This alignment with learning progressions helps refine assessment practices and ensures that assessments provide meaningful feedback for both students and educators.

8.1.1 Identifying and Addressing Students' Misconceptions Using Learning Progressions

Learning progressions are valuable tools for identifying students' misconceptions by providing a clear map of typical conceptual development (Shepard, 2018). Educators can compare students' current understanding with the expected stages in the progression to pinpoint areas where misconceptions may arise. For instance, if students are struggling with the concept of chemical reactions, learning progressions can help identify whether they have misconceptions about the nature of substances or the process of reactions. Once misconceptions are identified, learning progressions guide educators in designing targeted interventions. By understanding the common misconceptions associated with each stage of the progression, teachers can develop specific instructional strategies and activities to address these misconceptions. For example, if students misunderstand the concept of force and motion, educators can use hands-on experiments and visual models to clarify these concepts and correct misunderstandings. Learning progressions enable educators to provide constructive feedback that is aligned with students' developmental stages (Harris, Adie & Wyatt-Smith, 2022). Feedback can be tailored to address specific misconceptions and guide students towards the next stage of understanding. For instance, feedback on a student's explanation of a scientific phenomenon can be framed in the context of the progression, helping the student understand how their current thinking aligns with or deviates from scientific concepts.

8.1.2 Aligning Instructional Strategies with Learning Progressions to Support Student Learning

Learning progressions help educators design instructional strategies that build logically from one stage to the next (Fonger et al., 2017). By aligning instructional activities with the stages of the progression, teachers can ensure that lessons are designed to progressively develop students' understanding. For example, in teaching ecosystems, instruction can start with basic concepts like the needs of living organisms and gradually introduce more complex ideas such as energy flow and nutrient cycling. Learning progressions guide the implementation of evidence-based instructional practices that are aligned with students' developmental stages (Harris, Adie & Wyatt-Smith, 2022). Educators can use strategies such as inquiry-based learning, hands-on experiments, and collaborative projects that are appropriate for each stage of the progression. This alignment supports students' active engagement with the material and facilitates deeper understanding. As students progress through the learning stages, their needs and understanding may change. Learning progressions help educators adjust instruction based on ongoing assessment and feedback. Teachers can modify their strategies and provide additional support as needed to ensure that instruction remains aligned with students' evolving needs and promotes continued growth.

8.1.3 Scaffolding and Differentiation Strategies Based on Learning Progressions

Scaffolding involves providing support to help students achieve higher levels of understanding. Learning progressions inform scaffolding strategies by identifying the specific skills and concepts that students need to master at each stage (Duschl, 2019). Educators can design scaffolded activities that provide incremental support, such as guided practice, step-by-step instructions, and modelling, to help students build the necessary skills and knowledge. Differentiation involves tailoring instruction to meet the diverse needs of students. Learning progressions help educators differentiate instruction by providing insights into the range of developmental stages and learning needs within a classroom (Shepard, 2018). Teachers can use strategies such as grouping students by their current stage of understanding, providing tiered assignments, and offering varying levels of complexity to accommodate different learners.

Learning progressions help educators address individual learning needs by highlighting the specific areas where students may require additional support (Harris, Adie & Wyatt-Smith, 2022). Teachers can use formative assessments and progress monitoring to identify students who may be struggling and provide targeted interventions based on their position within the progression. This individualized approach ensures that all students receive the support they need to advance in their learning. Learning progressions play a vital role in informing and refining Pedagogical Content Knowledge (PCK) by providing a structured framework for understanding students' conceptual development (Sarkar et al., 2024). They help educators identify and address misconceptions, align instructional strategies with students' developmental stages, and implement effective scaffolding and differentiation strategies. By leveraging learning progressions, educators can enhance their instructional practices, support student learning more effectively, and foster a deeper understanding of scientific concepts. Integrating learning progressions into curriculum planning and lesson design, exploring case studies of successful implementation, examining their impact on student outcomes and teacher practice, and addressing the challenges and solutions associated with their use are essential aspects of leveraging learning progressions to enhance Pedagogical Content Knowledge (PCK).

8.1.4 Integrating Learning Progressions into Curriculum Planning and Lesson Design

Learning progressions provide a framework for mapping out curriculum content in a coherent and sequential manner (Fortus & Krajcik, 2012). Educators can use these progressions to ensure that the curriculum aligns with the developmental stages of student understanding. For instance, in a biology curriculum, learning progressions can guide the sequencing of topics from basic concepts like cell structure to more complex topics such as genetic inheritance. By mapping out the curriculum according to the progression, teachers can create a logical flow that builds students' knowledge incrementally. When designing lessons, educators can use learning progressions to tailor activities, materials, and assessments to the specific stage of understanding that students are expected to achieve (Yao, Liu & Guo, 2023). For example, in a chemistry class, a lesson on chemical reactions might start with simple observations and gradually introduce more complex concepts such as reaction mechanisms and stoichiometry. By aligning lesson objectives and activities with the stages of the progression, teachers can ensure that each lesson contributes to students' overall understanding in a structured and meaningful way. Learning progressions inform differentiation and scaffolding strategies by highlighting the specific needs and challenges of students at different stages of development. Teachers can use these insights to design differentiated instruction that targets varying levels of understanding within the classroom. Scaffolding strategies, such as providing step-by-step guidance or using visual aids, can be incorporated based on the progression to support students as they advance through the stages.

8.1.5 The Influence of Standardized Testing on Curriculum Design and Instructional Practice

Standardized testing has become a cornerstone of the educational system, wielding significant influence over curriculum design and instructional practices (Cunningham, 2019). While these assessments are intended to measure student achievement and ensure accountability, their impact on education extends far beyond the classroom (Shepard, 2019). Understanding this influence involves examining both the benefits and challenges associated with standardized testing, and how they shape educational practices. One of the primary ways standardized testing influences curriculum design is through the alignment with state and national standards (Wijngaards-de Meij & Merx, 2018). Schools and educators often adjust their curricula to ensure that they address the content and skills assessed by standardized tests. This alignment is aimed at improving student performance on these assessments, leading to a more focused and streamlined curriculum that emphasizes tested subjects and skills.

The pressure to perform well on standardized tests can lead to an increased emphasis on testable content, sometimes at the expense of a more comprehensive or balanced curriculum (Heissel, Levy & Adam, 2017). Subjects and topics that are heavily tested may receive more instructional time, while other important areas, such as critical thinking, creativity, or social-emotional learning, might be marginalized. This focus on testable content can shape the scope and sequence of the curriculum, often narrowing the breadth of what students are exposed to. In response to standardized testing, some educators and policymakers advocate for curricular reforms that integrate higher-order thinking skills and real-world applications (Pak et al., 2020). For example, there may be a push to incorporate project-based learning, interdisciplinary approaches, or experiential learning opportunities that align with test requirements while also fostering deeper understanding and skills development.

A common consequence of standardized testing is the phenomenon of "teaching to the test" (Benjamin & Pashler, 2015. Educators may focus their instruction on the specific content and question formats that appear on the assessments. While this can help students become familiar with the types of questions they will encounter, it can also limit the scope of learning and detract from broader educational goals. Teaching to the test may emphasize rote memorization and procedural skills over critical thinking and problem-solving. Standardized testing often leads to an increased focus on test preparation activities (Cunningham, 2019). Schools may implement practice tests, review sessions, and test-taking strategies to improve student performance. While these practices can help students familiarize themselves with the testing format and reduce anxiety, they may also detract from regular instruction and limit opportunities for exploration and creativity (Yang et al., 2023).

Standardized test results provide valuable data that can inform instructional practices. Educators can use this data to identify areas of strength and weakness, tailor instruction to meet students' needs, and monitor progress over time (Pitsia, Karakolidis & Lehane, 2021). However, an overreliance on test data can lead to a narrow view of student achievement, potentially overlooking other important aspects of learning such as social skills, emotional development, and creativity (Buçinca, Malaya & Gajos, 2021). Standardized test scores are often used as a metric for evaluating teacher performance and effectiveness (Steinberg & Garrett, 2016). This reliance on test scores can create pressure on teachers to prioritize test preparation over other aspects of instruction. It can also influence hiring practices, professional development, and compensation, shaping instructional practices in ways that align with test performance metrics.

While standardized testing undeniably influences curriculum design and instructional practices, it is important to strike a balance that ensures comprehensive education (Whitaker, Jenkins & Duer, 2022). Efforts to mitigate the negative impacts of standardized testing include: Incorporating a variety of assessment methods, such as formative assessments, portfolios, and performance-based assessments, can provide a more holistic view of student learning (Huber & Skedsmo, 2017). These assessments complement standardized tests by capturing a broader range of skills and competencies. Curriculum design should aim to balance test preparation with a focus on critical thinking, creativity, and other essential skills. Ensuring that students are exposed to a well-rounded education helps them develop a more comprehensive skill set that extends beyond test content. Providing educators with professional development opportunities focused on innovative instructional strategies and assessment practices can help them adapt to the demands of standardized testing while maintaining a rich and engaging curriculum. Emphasizing a growth mindset in education—where the focus is on continuous improvement and learning rather than solely on test scores—can help shift the emphasis from test performance to overall student development.

Standardized testing has a profound impact on curriculum design and instructional practices, shaping the educational landscape in significant ways. While these assessments aim to provide valuable insights into student achievement and ensure accountability, they also present challenges that can narrow the scope of education and influence teaching methods. By acknowledging these influences and striving to balance test preparation with comprehensive, student-centred learning, educators and policymakers can work towards an educational approach that fosters both academic success and holistic development.

9. CASE STUDIES OF SUCCESSFUL IMPLEMENTATION OF LEARNING PROGRESSIONS IN SCIENCE CLASSROOMS

a. Case Study: Elementary School Ecosystem Project

In an elementary school setting, a team of teachers implemented a learning progression for teaching ecosystems. The progression began with basic concepts such as the needs of living organisms and expanded to more complex ideas like energy flow and ecological interactions. Teachers used hands-on activities, such as creating terrariums and conducting field observations, to engage students at each stage. The implementation led to improved student understanding of ecosystem dynamics and enhanced their ability to apply concepts to real-world scenarios (Hatch & Clark, 2021).

b. Case Study: High School Physics Unit on Forces and Motion

A high school physics teacher implemented a learning progression for teaching forces and motion. The progression included stages from basic force concepts to advanced topics like projectile motion and dynamics. The teacher used interactive simulations, lab experiments, and problem-solving exercises aligned with the progression. Students showed significant improvements in their ability to apply Newton's laws and analyse motion, as evidenced by their performance in assessments and increased confidence in tackling complex physics problems (Nguyen, Thuan & Giang, 2023).

c. Case Study: Middle School Chemistry Investigation

In a middle school chemistry class, a learning progression was used to teach chemical reactions. The progression started with observing simple reactions and gradually introduced concepts like conservation of mass and reaction rates. Teachers incorporated visual models, guided experiments, and formative assessments aligned with the progression. Students demonstrated enhanced conceptual understanding and were better able to predict and explain chemical reactions, leading to higher achievement in chemistry assessments (Sevian & Talanquer, 2014).

10. THE ROLE OF TEACHER AGENCY IN THE ADOPTION AND ADAPTATION OF LEARNING PROGRESSIONS

Teacher agency plays a pivotal role in the successful adoption and adaptation of learning progressions within educational settings (Li & Ruppar, 2021). Learning progressions, which outline the sequential development of students' understanding and skills over time, offer a framework for guiding instruction and supporting student growth (Harris, Adie & Wyatt-Smith, 2022). However, the effective implementation of these progressions relies significantly on the autonomy, expertise, and adaptability of educators (Gotwals & Cisterna, 2022). Understanding the role of teacher agency in this process illuminates how teachers can drive educational innovation and enhance student learning. Teachers possess unique insights into their students' needs, learning styles, and classroom dynamics. With agency, educators can tailor learning progressions to fit their specific context, adjusting based on their observations and the diverse needs of their students (Gebre & Polman, 2020). This customization ensures that the progression of learning is relevant and effective, addressing individual and group needs in a way that standardized approaches may not fully capture.

Teacher agency allows educators to adapt and innovate within the framework of learning progressions (Cong-Lem, 2024). While learning progressions provide a structured pathway for student development, teachers can integrate creative and innovative teaching methods to enhance engagement and comprehension (Harris, Adie & Wyatt-Smith, 2022). For instance, a teacher might incorporate technology, project-based learning, or interdisciplinary approaches to make the progression more engaging and relevant to students. Teachers play a crucial role in collecting and analysing feedback from their students regarding the effectiveness of learning progressions. By actively seeking input and reflecting on student performance, teachers can make informed decisions about how to refine and improve their instructional practices. This iterative process of feedback and adaptation is essential for ensuring that learning progressions remain dynamic and responsive to student needs. Teacher agency is supported by ongoing professional development, which equips educators with the knowledge and skills necessary to effectively implement and adapt learning progressions (Cong-Lem, 2024). Professional learning opportunities, such as workshops, collaborative planning sessions, and coaching, help teachers stay informed about best practices and emerging trends, enhancing their ability to apply learning progressions in their teaching (Clark et al., 2023).

While teacher agency allows for customization and innovation, it also requires a balance with standardized expectations and guidelines (Poulton, 2020). Teachers must navigate between adhering to mandated curricula and exercising their professional judgment to adapt learning progressions. Striking this balance is crucial for ensuring that students receive consistent and equitable instruction while also benefiting from personalized and responsive teaching (Comstock et al., 2023). To maximize the impact of teacher agency, educators need support from school leaders and colleagues. Collaborative planning and shared expertise can enhance the implementation of learning progressions, providing teachers with valuable resources and ideas (Liu, Hedges & Cooper, 2023). Additionally, school leadership can foster an environment that values teacher autonomy and encourages experimentation, further empowering educators to take ownership of their instructional practices (Nadeem, 2024).

Effective adoption and adaptation of learning progressions require access to appropriate resources, including teaching materials, technology, and time for planning and reflection (Ngoasong, 2022). Schools and educational systems need to ensure that teachers have the necessary resources and support to implement and adjust learning progressions effectively. Developing a culture that values teacher agency involves recognizing and celebrating the contributions of educators in shaping and enhancing learning progressions (Nagel, Guðmundsdóttir & Afdal, 2023). Schools can create platforms for teachers to share their successes, challenges, and innovations, fostering a collaborative environment that supports continuous improvement and professional growth (Kolleck et al., 2021).

Teacher agency is integral to the successful adoption and adaptation of learning progressions, as it empowers educators to tailor instruction, innovate, and respond to the needs of their students. By balancing autonomy with standardized expectations, providing support and resources, and fostering a collaborative and supportive culture, educators can enhance the effectiveness of learning progressions and positively impact student outcomes. Recognizing and nurturing teacher agency not only strengthens instructional practices but also contributes to a more dynamic and responsive educational environment.

11. IMPACT OF LEARNING PROGRESSIONS ON STUDENT OUTCOMES AND TEACHER PRACTICE

Learning progressions have been shown to improve student outcomes by providing a clear pathway for conceptual development. Students who engage with instruction aligned with learning progressions often achieve a deeper understanding of scientific concepts (Upahi & Ramnarain, 2022). They are better able to connect new knowledge with existing understanding and apply concepts to novel situations, leading to improved performance in assessments and a more robust grasp of scientific principles. For teachers, learning progressions offer a valuable tool for refining instructional practices. They help teachers design lessons that are more coherent and aligned with students' developmental stages. Educators who use learning progressions often report greater clarity in planning and delivering instruction, as well as more effective differentiation and scaffolding (Harris, Adie & Wyatt-Smith, 2022). Additionally, learning progressions support formative assessment practices by providing a clear framework for evaluating student progress and adjusting instruction accordingly (Alonzo, 2011). Teachers who integrate learning progressions into their practice often experience increased confidence and competence in their teaching. The structured framework provided by learning progressions helps teachers feel more prepared to address students' needs and respond to emerging challenges. This increased confidence can lead to more effective and engaging instruction, benefiting both students and teachers.

12. CHALLENGES AND SOLUTIONS IN USING LEARNING PROGRESSIONS TO ENHANCE PCK

To address the complexity of developmental stages, educators can collaborate with colleagues and experts to gain a deeper understanding of the learning progressions relevant to their subject area. Professional development workshops and training sessions can provide valuable insights into interpreting and applying learning progressions effectively. Additionally, creating simplified versions of progressions for practical classroom use can help manage complexity (Shepard, 2018). Differentiation and scaffolding are key strategies for addressing diverse student needs. Learning progressions help identify the specific needs of students at different stages, allowing teachers to design targeted interventions and support (Shepard, 2018). Using formative assessments and ongoing feedback can help teachers adjust their instruction to meet the varied needs of their students and ensure that all learners make progress.

Integrating learning progressions with existing curricula requires careful planning and alignment. Teachers can start by mapping learning progressions onto their current curriculum to identify areas of overlap and gaps. Collaboration with curriculum developers and instructional designers can also help align learning progressions with curriculum goals and standards, ensuring a seamless integration. Resistance to change can be mitigated by involving teachers in the development and implementation of learning progressions. Providing opportunities for teachers to share their experiences, discuss challenges, and offer feedback can foster a collaborative approach to adoption. Additionally, highlighting the benefits of learning progressions for student learning and providing ongoing support can help build buy-in and enthusiasm among educators.

Integrating learning progressions into curriculum planning and lesson design offers a structured approach to enhancing Pedagogical Content Knowledge (PCK) (Deng, 2018). Successful implementation, as demonstrated in case studies, shows that learning progressions can significantly improve student outcomes and support effective teaching practices (Ventista & Brown, 2023). While challenges such as the complexity of developmental stages and diverse student needs exist, targeted solutions like differentiation, professional development, and collaborative planning can help overcome these obstacles (Freeman-Green, Williamson & Cornelius, 2023). By leveraging learning progressions, educators can refine their PCK, design more effective instruction, and ultimately enhance student learning in science education.

13. EMERGING TRENDS IN EDUCATION: TECHNOLOGY AND INTERDISCIPLINARY APPROACHES IN LEARNING PROGRESSIONS

In exploring the integration of learning progressions into instructional design, it is crucial to acknowledge and incorporate contemporary trends that are shaping the educational landscape. While the chapter effectively outlines the fundamental principles of learning progressions and their application in instructional design, it is essential to further examine how emerging trends, such as technology and interdisciplinary approaches, are transforming these concepts. Technology has revolutionized education, offering innovative tools and methods that enhance and support learning progressions (Wang, Chen, Yu & Wang, 2024). The integration of technology into instructional design is not merely an enhancement but a fundamental shift in how we approach teaching and learning.

Adaptive technologies are at the forefront of this transformation. These systems utilize algorithms to analyse individual student performance and adapt instructional materials to meet their specific needs. By offering personalized learning experiences, adaptive learning systems help students advance through learning progressions at their own pace (Alrawashdeh et al., 2024). This individualized approach ensures that each student receives the support necessary to master concepts and skills, leading to more effective and efficient learning pathways. The use of interactive tools, such as virtual labs and simulations, provides students with opportunities to engage with complex concepts in a dynamic and hands-on manner (Laseinde, & Dada, 2023). For instance, virtual experiments in a science class allow students to explore scientific principles in ways that might be impractical or impossible in a traditional classroom setting. These technologies not only facilitate a deeper understanding of content but also support the progression of learning by allowing students to experiment and apply knowledge in interactive environments (Haleem et al., 2022).

Learning analytics play a critical role in tracking and supporting student progress (Banihashem et al., 2022). By analysing data from various sources, such as student assessments and interactions, educators can gain insights into students' learning trajectories. This data-driven approach enables teachers to make informed decisions about instructional adjustments, identify areas where students may need additional support, and tailor learning experiences to better align with each student's progression (Ndukwe & Daniel, 2020). Online platforms that facilitate collaboration, such as Google Classroom and Microsoft Teams, enable students to work together on projects and share ideas. These tools support collaborative learning, which is essential for developing problem-solving skills and advancing through learning progressions (Xu, Wang & Wang, 2023). Collaborative platforms also allow teachers to monitor group interactions and provide feedback, further enhancing the learning experience (Moore et al., 2019).

While the chapter provides a solid foundation on integrating learning progressions into instructional design, it is crucial to address emerging trends that significantly impact this integration. Technology and interdisciplinary approaches offer powerful tools and methods that enhance learning progressions and enrich the educational experience. By embracing these trends, educators can better support student learning, ensure more effective progression through content, and prepare students for the complexities of the modern world. The evolving landscape of education demands that we continuously adapt our instructional strategies to incorporate these innovations, ultimately leading to more engaging and impactful learning experiences.

14. EMPIRICAL EVIDENCE AND RESEARCH FINDINGS

14.1 Overview of Research Studies on the Effectiveness of Learning Progressions in Science Education

Research into the effectiveness of learning progressions in science education has increasingly highlighted their value in improving both student outcomes and teacher practices. Learning progressions are designed to map out the stages of cognitive development in specific scientific domains, providing a framework for curriculum and instruction that aligns with how students typically learn. Several studies have examined the impact of these frameworks on various aspects of science education, revealing positive outcomes in terms of student achievement and instructional effectiveness (Kyriakides, Christoforou & Charalambous, 2013). Studies on learning progressions often focus on various aspects, including their impact on student understanding, instructional design, and teacher effectiveness (Harris, Adie & Wyatt-Smith, 2022). Methodologies employed in these studies include quasi-experimental designs, case studies, and longitudinal analyses. For instance, research might involve comparing student performance in classrooms where learning progressions are implemented with performance in classrooms using traditional instructional methods. Other studies use qualitative methods, such as interviews and classroom observations, to gain insights into how learning progressions influence teaching practices and student engagement.

Research has generally found that learning progressions lead to significant improvements in student learning outcomes. For example, studies have shown that students in classrooms using learning progressions demonstrate better conceptual understanding of scientific concepts, improved problem-solving skills, and enhanced ability to apply knowledge in novel situations (Panizzon et al., 2021). Additionally, research indicates that learning progressions help teachers design more effective and coherent instruction, leading to better alignment between curriculum, assessment, and student learning (Jin et al., 2019). A study conducted by Alonzo and Elby (2019) found that students in classrooms where learning progressions were used showed greater improvement in their ability to explain ecological concepts and apply them to real-world scenarios). A study by Harris, Adie and Wyatt-Smith (2022) reported that students exposed to progression-based instruction performed better on assessments and exhibited a deeper understanding of chemical principles.

14.2 Analysis of Empirical Data on the Impact of Learning Progressions on PCK

Empirical data consistently show that learning progressions help teachers refine their Pedagogical Content Knowledge (PCK) by providing a clear framework for understanding students' developmental stages (Depaepe, Verschaffel & Kelchtermans, 2013). Studies indicate that teachers who use learning progressions are better able to design instruction that aligns with students' current levels of understanding and progressively builds their knowledge (Yao, Liu & Guo, 2023). This alignment supports more effective lesson planning, implementation, and assessment, leading to improved instructional quality. Data analysis reveals that learning progressions enhance teachers' ability to differentiate instruction and provide targeted scaffolding (Langelaan et al., 2024). Research shows that teachers who use learning progressions are more adept at identifying students' individual needs and designing appropriate interventions (Harris, Adie & Wyatt-Smith, 2022). For example, learning progressions help teachers create scaffolded activities that support students at various stages of understanding, leading to more personalized and effective instruction. Empirical studies highlight that learning progressions are valuable tools in professional development programs (Kranjc Horvat et al., 2021). Teachers who engage with learning progressions through training and workshops report increased confidence and competence in their teaching practice. Research shows that professional development focused on learning progressions helps teachers develop a deeper understanding of instructional design, assessment, and differentiation, thereby enhancing their overall PCK (Sims et al., 2023).

14.3 Synthesis of Findings and Implications for Practice

The synthesis of research findings indicates that learning progressions significantly contribute to instructional coherence. By providing a structured framework for curriculum and lesson design, learning progressions help ensure that instruction is logically sequenced and aligned with students' developmental stages. This coherence supports more effective teaching and learning, as students receive instruction that builds progressively on their existing knowledge and skills. Learning progressions enhance teacher effectiveness by equipping educators with tools and strategies to better understand and address students' learning needs (Harris, Adie & Wyatt-Smith, 2022). The evidence suggests that teachers who use learning progressions are better at designing differentiated instruction, identifying and addressing misconceptions, and providing targeted feedback. As a result, teachers can support student learning more effectively and achieve better educational outcomes.

The positive impact of learning progressions on both student outcomes and teacher practice suggests several implications for future research and practice. Continued research is needed to explore the long-term effects of learning progressions, their applicability across different scientific domains, and their impact on diverse student populations. Additionally, professional development programs should incorporate training on learning progressions to support teachers in implementing these frameworks effectively. Further studies can also investigate the integration of learning progressions with other instructional strategies and technologies to enhance science education. While learning progressions offer numerous benefits, challenges such as the complexity of developmental stages and the need for alignment with existing curricula must be addressed. Solutions include providing ongoing professional development, simplifying the use of learning progressions for practical classroom application, and fostering collaboration among educators to share best practices and experiences.

The research on learning progressions highlights their effectiveness in improving science education by enhancing both student outcomes and teacher practice. Empirical data support the positive impact of learning progressions on instructional design, differentiation, and professional development. The synthesis of findings underscores the value of learning progressions in creating coherent and effective science instruction and suggests important implications for future research and practice. By addressing challenges and leveraging the benefits of learning progressions, educators can continue to advance science education and support student success.

15. CONCLUSION

The integration of learning progressions into science education represents a significant advancement in enhancing Pedagogical Content Knowledge (PCK) among educators. By providing a structured framework for understanding how students develop and deepen their scientific knowledge over time, learning progressions offer a powerful tool for designing effective instructional strategies, assessments, and curricular materials. This chapter has explored the multifaceted role of learning progressions in enriching PCK, highlighting several key points. Learning progressions illuminate the developmental paths that students follow as they acquire and refine their scientific understanding. This clarity allows educators to tailor their instruction to align with students' current levels of comprehension and to anticipate and address potential misconceptions. By grounding instruction in a detailed understanding of these trajectories, teachers can foster more effective and targeted learning experiences. Integrating learning progressions into instructional design helps educators create coherent and logically sequenced lessons that build upon students' prior knowledge and scaffold their learning. Research indicates that this approach leads to improved student outcomes, as instruction becomes more aligned with students' cognitive development and learning needs. Furthermore, learning progressions support the development of differentiated instruction and scaffolding strategies, enabling teachers to better meet the diverse needs of their students.

Professional development programs focused on learning progressions and PCK equip educators with the knowledge and skills needed to effectively implement these frameworks in their teaching. By participating in targeted training, collaborative learning communities, and coaching programs, teachers can enhance their understanding of PCK and learning progressions, leading to more effective classroom practices and improved student learning. While the use of learning progressions offers numerous benefits, it also presents challenges, such as the need for ongoing support and the integration of progressions with existing curricula. Addressing these challenges requires a commitment to continuous professional development, collaboration among educators, and the development of resources and tools that facilitate the practical application of learning progressions. The continued exploration and refinement of learning progressions hold promise for further enhancing science education. Future research should focus on evaluating the long-term impact of learning progressions on student outcomes and teacher practice, exploring their application across various scientific domains, and addressing the evolving needs of diverse student populations. Additionally, integrating learning progressions with emerging educational technologies and instructional strategies could further enrich the teaching and learning experience.

In conclusion, leveraging learning progressions to enhance PCK in science education offers a transformative approach to teaching and learning. By providing a framework for understanding student development and aligning instruction with their cognitive needs, learning progressions help educators create more effective and responsive educational environments. As educators continue to embrace and integrate these frameworks, the potential for improved student achievement and instructional quality in science education will grow, leading to more equitable and meaningful learning experiences for all students.

REFERENCES

Adarkwah, M. (2021). The power of assessment feedback in teaching and learning: A narrative review and synthesis of the literature. *SN Social Sciences*, 1(3), 75. DOI: 10.1007/s43545-021-00086-w

Adelson, L., Culp, R., & Bunn, S.. (2009). Teaching evolution concepts to early elementary school students. *Evolution (New York)*, 2(4), 458–473. DOI: 10.1007/s12052-009-0148-x

Adewumi, T. M., Mosito, C., & Agosto, V. (2019). Experiences of teachers in implementing inclusion of learners with special education needs in selected Fort Beaufort District primary schools, South Africa. *Cogent Education*, 6(1), 1703446. Advance online publication. DOI: 10.1080/2331186X.2019.1703446

Aguilar, S. J. (2018). Learning analytics: At the nexus of big data, digital innovation, and social justice in education. *TechTrends*, 62(1), 37–45. DOI: 10.1007/s11528-017-0226-9

Al-Ansi, A. M., Jaboob, M., Garad, A., & Al-Ansi, A. (2023). Analyzing augmented reality (AR) and virtual reality (VR) recent development in education. *Social Sciences & Humanities Open*, 8(1), 100532. DOI: 10.1016/j.ssaho.2023.100532

Almonacid-Fierro, A., Sepúlveda-Vallejos, S., Valdebenito, K., & Aguilar-Valdés, M. (2023). Analysis of pedagogical content knowledge in science teacher education: A systematic review 2011-2021. *International Journal of Educational Methodology*, 9(3), 525–534. DOI: 10.12973/ijem.9.3.525

Almonacid-Fierro, A., Sepúlveda-Vallejos, S., Valdebenito, K., Montoya-Grisales, N., & Aguilar-Valdés, M. (2023). Analysis of pedagogical content knowledge in science teacher education: A systematic review 2011-2021. *International Journal of Educational Methodology*, 9(3), 525–534. DOI: 10.12973/ijem.9.3.525

Alonzo, A. C. (2011). Learning progressions that support formative assessment practices. *Measurement: Interdisciplinary Research and Perspectives*, 9(2–3), 124–129. DOI: 10.1080/15366367.2011.599629

Alonzo, A. C., & Elby, A. (2019). Beyond empirical adequacy: Learning progressions as models and their value for teachers. *Cognition and Instruction*, 37(1), 1–37. DOI: 10.1080/07370008.2018.1539735

Alrawashdeh, G. S., Fyffe, S., Azevedo, R. F. L., & Castillo, N. M. (2024). Exploring the impact of personalized and adaptive learning technologies on reading literacy: A global meta-analysis. *Educational Research Review*, 42, 100587. Advance online publication. DOI: 10.1016/j.edurev.2023.100587

Banihashem, S. K., Noroozi, O., van Ginkel, S., Macfadyen, L. P., & Biemans, H. J. A. (2022). A systematic review of the role of learning analytics in enhancing feedback practices in higher education. *Educational Research Review*, 37, 100489. Advance online publication. DOI: 10.1016/j.edurev.2022.100489

Benecke, K., & Kaiser, G. (2023). Teachers' approaches to handling student errors in mathematics classes. *Asian Journal for Mathematics Education*, 2(2), 161–182. DOI: 10.1177/27527263231184642

Benjamin, A. S., & Pashler, H. (2015). The value of standardized testing: A perspective from cognitive psychology. *Policy Insights from the Behavioral and Brain Sciences*, 2(1), 13–23. DOI: 10.1177/2372732215601116

Black, P., & Wiliam, D. (2018). Classroom assessment and pedagogy. *Assessment in Education: Principles, Policy & Practice*, 25(6), 1–25. DOI: 10.1080/0969594X.2018.1441807

Bloom, B. S. (1956). Taxonomy of educational objectives: the classification of educational goals; Handbook I: Cognitive domain. In Engelhart, M. D., Furst, E. J., Hill, W. H., & Krathwohl, D. R. (Eds.), *Taxonomy of educational objectives: the classification of educational goals; Handbook I: Cognitive domain*. David McKay.

Buçinca, Z., Malaya, M. B., & Gajos, K. Z. (2021). To trust or to think: Cognitive forcing functions can reduce overreliance on AI in AI-assisted decision-making. Proceedings of the ACM on Human-Computer Interaction, 5(CSCW1), 1–21. https://doi.org/DOI: 10.1145/3449287

Caingcoy, M. E. (2023). Culturally responsive pedagogy: A systematic overview. *Diversitas Journal*, 8(4), 3203–3212. DOI: 10.48017/dj.v8i4.2780

Chand, S. P. (2024). Constructivism in education: Exploring the contributions of Piaget, Vygotsky, and Bruner. [IJSR]. *International Journal of Science and Research (Raipur, India)*, 12(7), 274–278. DOI: 10.21275/SR23630021800

Chew, S., & Cerbin, W. (2020). The cognitive challenges of effective teaching. *The Journal of Economic Education*, 52(1), 1–24. DOI: 10.1080/00220485.2020.1845266

Clark, A. M., Zhan, M., Dellinger, J. T., & Semingson, P. L. (2023). Innovating teaching practice through professional learning communities: Determining knowledge sharing and program value. *SAGE Open*, 13(4), 21582440231200983. Advance online publication. DOI: 10.1177/21582440231200983

Comstock, M., Litke, E., Hill, K. L., & Desimone, L. M. (2023). A culturally responsive disposition: How professional learning and teachers' beliefs

Cong-Lem, N. (2024). Teacher agency for change and development in higher education: A scoping literature review. *International Journal of Educational Reform*, 0(0), 10567879231224744. Advance online publication. DOI: 10.1177/10567879231224744

Cunningham, J. (2019). Missing the mark: Standardized testing as epistemological erasure in U.S. schooling. *Power and Education*, 11(1), 111–120. DOI: 10.1177/1757743818812093

Darling-Hammond, L., Schachner, A. C. W., Wojcikiewicz, S. K., & Flook, L. (2023). Educating teachers to enact the science of learning and development. *Applied Developmental Science*, 28(1), 1–21. DOI: 10.1080/10888691.2022.2130506 PMID: 36704361

Deng, Z. (2018). Pedagogical content knowledge reconceived: Bringing curriculum thinking into the conversation on teachers' content knowledge. *Teaching and Teacher Education*, 72, 155–164. DOI: 10.1016/j.tate.2017.11.021

Depaepe, F., Verschaffel, L., & Kelchtermans, G. (2013). Pedagogical content knowledge: A systematic review of the way in which the concept has pervaded mathematics educational research. *Teaching and Teacher Education*, 34, 12–25. DOI: 10.1016/j.tate.2013.03.001

Desimone, L. M. (2009). Improving impact studies of teachers' professional development: Toward better conceptualizations and measures. *Educational Researcher*, 38(3), 181–200. DOI: 10.3102/0013189X08331140

Duschl, R. (2019). Learning progressions: Framing and designing coherent sequences for STEM education. *Disciplinary and Interdisciplinary Science Education Research*, 1(1), 4. DOI: 10.1186/s43031-019-0005-x

Duschl, R., Maeng, S., & Sezen-Barrie, A. (2011). Learning progressions and teaching sequences: A review and analysis. *Studies in Science Education*, 47(2), 123–182. DOI: 10.1080/03057267.2011.604476

Fonger, N. L., Stephens, A., Blanton, M., Isler, I., Knuth, E., & Gardiner, A. M. (2017). Developing a learning progression for curriculum, instruction, and student learning: An example from mathematics education. *Cognition and Instruction*, 36(1), 30–55. DOI: 10.1080/07370008.2017.1392965

Fortus, D., & Krajcik, J. (2012). Curriculum coherence and learning progressions. In Fraser, B., Tobin, K., & McRobbie, C. (Eds.), *Second international handbook of science education* (pp. 783–798). Springer., DOI: 10.1007/978-1-4020-9041-7_52

Fortus, D., & Krajcik, J. (2012). Curriculum coherence and learning progressions. In Fraser, B., Tobin, K., & McRobbie, C. (Eds.), *Second international handbook of science education* (pp. 783–798). Springer., DOI: 10.1007/978-1-4020-9041-7_52

Fortus, D., Shwartz, Y., & Rosenfeld, S. (2016). High school students' meta-modelling knowledge. *Research in Science Education*, 46(4), 787–810. DOI: 10.1007/s11165-015-9480-z

Fraser, S. P. (2016). Pedagogical content knowledge (PCK): Exploring its usefulness for science lecturers in higher education. *Research in Science Education*, 46(1), 141–161. DOI: 10.1007/s11165-014-9459-1

Freeman-Green, S., Williamson, P., & Cornelius, K. E. (2023). Promoting inclusive practices in education: Bridging gaps and fostering independence. *Teaching Exceptional Children*, 56(2), 68–69. DOI: 10.1177/00400599231223785

Garza, R., Alejandro, E. A., Blythe, T., & Fite, K. (2014). Caring for students: What teachers have to say. *ISRN Education*, 2014(4), 1–7. DOI: 10.1155/2014/425856

Gasteiger, H., Bruns, J., Benz, C., Brunner, E., & Sprenger, P. (2020). Mathematical pedagogical content knowledge of early childhood teachers: A standardized situation-related measurement approach. *ZDM Mathematics Education*, 52(2), 193–205. DOI: 10.1007/s11858-019-01103-2

Gebre, E. H., & Polman, J. L. (2020). From "context" to "active contextualization": Fostering learner agency in contextualizing learning through science news reporting. *Learning, Culture and Social Interaction*, 24, 100374. Advance online publication. DOI: 10.1016/j.lcsi.2019.100374

Godor, B. P. (2021). The many faces of teacher differentiation: Using Q methodology to explore teachers' preferences for differentiated instruction. *Teacher Educator*, 56(1), 43–60. DOI: 10.1080/08878730.2020.1785068

Goldstone, R. L., & Landy, D. H. (2012). The Goldilocks effect: Human infants allocate attention to visual sequences that are neither too simple nor too complex. *PLoS One*, 7(5), e36399. DOI: 10.1371/journal.pone.0036399 PMID: 22649492

Gotwals, A. W., & Cisterna, D. (2022). Formative assessment practice progressions for teacher preparation: A framework and illustrative case. *Teaching and Teacher Education*, 110, 103601. Advance online publication. DOI: 10.1016/j.tate.2021.103601

Haleem, A., Javaid, M., Qadri, M. A., & Suman, R. (2022). Understanding the role of digital technologies in education: A review. *Sustainable Operations and Computers*, 3, 275–285. DOI: 10.1016/j.susoc.2022.05.004

Harris, L. R., Adie, L., & Wyatt-Smith, C. (2022). Learning progression–based assessments: A systematic review of student and teacher uses. *Review of Educational Research*, 92(6), 996–1040. DOI: 10.3102/00346543221081552

Harris, L. R., Adie, L., & Wyatt-Smith, C. (2022). Learning progression–based assessments: A systematic review of student and teacher uses. *Review of Educational Research*, 92(6), 996–1040. DOI: 10.3102/00346543221081552

Hassel, H., Launius, C., & Rensing, S. (2021). Student learning and principles for assessment. In *A guide to teaching introductory women's and gender studies* (pp. 83–106). Palgrave Macmillan., DOI: 10.1007/978-3-030-71785-8_4

Hatch, L., & Clark, S. K. (2021). A study of the instructional decisions and lesson planning strategies of highly effective rural elementary school teachers. *Teaching and Teacher Education*, 108, 103505. DOI: 10.1016/j.tate.2021.103505

Heissel, J. A., Levy, D. J., & Adam, E. K. (2017). Stress, sleep, and performance on standardized tests: Understudied pathways to the achievement gap. *AERA Open*, 3(3), 2332858417713488. Advance online publication. DOI: 10.1177/2332858417713488

Hossain, K. I. (2024). Reviewing the role of culture in English language learning: Challenges and opportunities for educators. *Social Sciences & Humanities Open*, 9, 100781. DOI: 10.1016/j.ssaho.2023.100781

Huber, S. G., & Skedsmo, G. (2017). Standardization and assessment practices. *Educational Assessment, Evaluation and Accountability*, 29(1), 1–3. DOI: 10.1007/s11092-017-9257-1

Jin, H., Mikeska, J., Hokayem, H., & Mavronikolas, E. (2019). Toward coherence in curriculum, instruction, and assessment: A review of learning progression literature. *Science Education*, 103(5), 1206–1234. Advance online publication. DOI: 10.1002/sce.21525

Kleickmann, T., Richter, D., Kunter, M., Elsner, J., Besser, M., Krauss, S., & Baumert, J. (2013). Teachers' content knowledge and pedagogical content knowledge: The role of structural differences in teacher education. *Journal of Teacher Education*, 64(1), 90–106. DOI: 10.1177/0022487112460398

Koehler, M. J., Mishra, P., & Cain, W. (2013). What is Technological Pedagogical Content Knowledge (TPACK)? *Journal of Education*, 193(3), 13–19. DOI: 10.1177/002205741319300303

Kolleck, N., Schuster, J., Hartmann, U., & Gräsel, C. (2021). Teachers' professional collaboration and trust relationships: An inferential social network analysis of teacher teams. *Research in Education*, 111(1), 89–107. DOI: 10.1177/00345237211031585

Kranjc Horvat, A., Wiener, J., Schmeling, S., & Borowski, A. (2021). Learning goals of professional development programs at science research institutions: A Delphi study with different stakeholder groups. *Journal of Science Teacher Education*, 33(1), 32–54. DOI: 10.1080/1046560X.2021.1905330

Kuswandono, P. (2012). Reflective practices for teacher education. LLT Journal: A Journal on Language and Language Teaching, 15(01), 149–162. https://doi.org/ DOI: 10.24071/llt.2012.150102

Kyriakides, L., Christoforou, C., & Charalambous, C. Y. (2013). What matters for student learning outcomes: A meta-analysis of studies exploring factors of effective teaching. *Teaching and Teacher Education*, 36, 143–152. DOI: 10.1016/j.tate.2013.07.010

Langelaan, B. N., Gaikhorst, L., Smets, W., & Oostdam, R. J. (2024). Differentiating instruction: Understanding the key elements for successful teacher preparation and development. *Teaching and Teacher Education*, 140, 104464. DOI: 10.1016/j.tate.2023.104464

Laseinde, P. T., & Dada, D. (2023). Enhancing teaching and learning in STEM labs: The development of an Android-based virtual reality platform. *Materials Today: Proceedings*. Advance online publication. DOI: 10.1016/j.matpr.2023.09.020

Lave, J., & Wenger, E. (1991). *Situated learning: Legitimate peripheral participation.* Cambridge University Press. DOI: 10.1017/CBO9780511815355

Lee, E. S., & Liu, U. L. (2009). Assessing learning progression of energy concepts across middle school grades: The knowledge integration perspective. *Science Education*, •••, 665–688.

Lee, L. K., Cheung, S. K. S., & Kwok, L. F. (2020). Learning analytics: Current trends and innovative practices. *Journal of Computers in Education*, 7(1), 1–6. DOI: 10.1007/s40692-020-00155-8

Li, L., & Ruppar, A. (2021). Conceptualizing teacher agency for inclusive education: A systematic and international review. *Teacher Education and Special Education*, 44(1), 42–59. DOI: 10.1177/0888406420926976

Liu, M., Hedges, H., & Cooper, M. (2023). Effective collaborative learning for early childhood teachers: Structural, motivational and sustainable features. *Professional Development in Education*, 50(2), 420–438. DOI: 10.1080/19415257.2023.2235578

Lumpkin, A., & Favor, J. (2012). Comparing the academic performance of high school athletes and non-athletes in Kansas in 2008-2009. *Journal of Sport Administration & Supervision*, 4(1), 41–62.

Merritt, J., & Krajcik, J. (2013). Learning progression developed to support students in building a particle model of matter. In Tsaparlis, G., & Sevian, H. (Eds.), *Concepts of matter in science education* (pp. 11–45). Springer., DOI: 10.1007/978-94-007-5914-5_2

Mills, S. (2016). Conceptual understanding: A concept analysis. *The Qualitative Report*, 21(3), 546–557. DOI: 10.46743/2160-3715/2016.2308

Moore, B., Boardman, A. G., Smith, C., & Ferrell, A. (2019). Enhancing collaborative group processes to promote academic literacy and content learning for diverse learners through video reflection. *SAGE Open*, 9(3), 2158244019861480. Advance online publication. DOI: 10.1177/2158244019861480

Mora-Flores, E., & Kaplan, S. N. (2022). Interdisciplinary learning: Connecting language and literacy across the curriculum. *Gifted Child Today*, 45(2), 110–112. DOI: 10.1177/10762175211070845

Nadeem, M. (2024). Distributed leadership in educational contexts: A catalyst for school improvement. *Social Sciences & Humanities Open*, 9, 100835. Advance online publication. DOI: 10.1016/j.ssaho.2024.100835

Nagel, I., Guðmundsdóttir, G. B., & Afdal, H. W. (2023). Teacher educators' professional agency in facilitating professional digital competence. *Teaching and Teacher Education*, 132, 104238. Advance online publication. DOI: 10.1016/j.tate.2023.104238

Ndukwe, I. G., & Daniel, B. K. (2020). Teaching analytics, value, and tools for teacher data literacy: A systematic and tripartite approach. *International Journal of Educational Technology in Higher Education*, 17(1), 22. DOI: 10.1186/s41239-020-00201-6

Ngoasong, M. Z. (2022). Curriculum adaptation for blended learning in resource-scarce contexts. *Journal of Management Education*, 46(4), 622–655. DOI: 10.1177/10525629211047168

Nguyen, L. C., Thuan, H. T., & Giang, T. T. H. (2023). Application of G. Polya's problem-solving process in teaching high-school physics. *Journal of Law and Society*, 4(1), 26–33. DOI: 10.37899/journal-la-sociale.v4i1.761

Nilsson, P., & Karlsson, G. (2018). Capturing student teachers' pedagogical content knowledge (PCK) using CoRes and digital technology. *International Journal of Science Education*, 41(4), 419–447. DOI: 10.1080/09500693.2018.1551642

Pak, K., Polikoff, M. S., Desimone, L. M., & Saldívar García, E. (2020). The adaptive challenges of curriculum implementation: Insights for educational leaders driving standards-based reform. *AERA Open*, 6(2), 2332858420932828. Advance online publication. DOI: 10.1177/2332858420932828

Panizzon, D., Pegg, J., Arthur, D., & McCloughan, G. (2021). Designing a developmental progression to assess students' conceptual understandings by focusing on the language demands in science. *Australian Journal of Education*, 65(3), 265–279. DOI: 10.1177/00049441211036518

Panke, S. (2019). Design thinking in education: Perspectives, opportunities, and challenges. *Open Education Studies*, 1(1), 281–306. DOI: 10.1515/edu-2019-0022

Park, S., & Oliver, J. S. (2008). Revisiting the conceptualisation of pedagogical content knowledge (PCK): PCK as a conceptual tool to understand teachers as professionals. *Research in Science Education*, 38(3), 261–284. DOI: 10.1007/s11165-007-9049-6

Piaget, J. (1964). Cognitive development in children: Development and learning. *Journal of Research in Science Teaching*, 2(3), 176–186. DOI: 10.1002/tea.3660020306

Pitsia, V., Karakolidis, A., & Lehane, P. (2021). Investigating the use of assessment data by primary school teachers: Insights from a large-scale survey in Ireland. *Educational Assessment*, 26(3), 145–162. DOI: 10.1080/10627197.2021.1917358

Popa, N. (2022). Operationalizing historical consciousness: A review and synthesis of the literature on meaning making in historical learning. *Review of Educational Research*, 92(2), 171–208. DOI: 10.3102/00346543211052333

Posner, G. J., Strike, K. A., Hewson, P. W., & Gertzog, W. A. (1982). Accommodation of scientific conception: Toward a theory of conceptual change. *Science Education*, 66(2), 211–227. DOI: 10.1002/sce.3730660207

Poulton, P. (2020). Teacher agency in curriculum reform: The role of assessment in enabling and constraining primary teachers' agency. *Curriculum Perspectives*, 40(1), 35–48. DOI: 10.1007/s41297-020-00100-w

Reis, S. M., Renzulli, S. J., & Renzulli, J. S. (2021). Enrichment and gifted education pedagogy to develop talents, gifts, and creative productivity. *Education Sciences*, 11(10), 615. DOI: 10.3390/educsci11100615

Roberts, G. J., Hall, C., Cho, E., Coté, B., Lee, J., Qi, B., & Van Ooyik, J. (2022). The state of current reading intervention research for English learners in grades K–2: A best-evidence synthesis. *Educational Psychology Review*, 34(2), 335–361. DOI: 10.1007/s10648-021-09629-2

Sancar, R., Atal, D., & Deryakulu, D. (2021). A new framework for teachers' professional development. *Teaching and Teacher Education*, 101, 103305. DOI: 10.1016/j.tate.2021.103305

Sarkar, M., Gutierrez-Bucheli, L., Yip, S. Y., Lazarus, M., Wright, C., White, P. J., Ilic, D., Hiscox, T. J., & Berry, A. (2024). Pedagogical content knowledge (PCK) in higher education: A systematic scoping review. *Teaching and Teacher Education*, 144, 104608. DOI: 10.1016/j.tate.2024.104608

Schildkamp, K., van der Kleij, F. M., Heitink, M. C., Kippers, W. B., & Veldkamp, B. P. (2020). Formative assessment: A systematic review of critical teacher prerequisites for classroom practice. *International Journal of Educational Research*, 103, 101602. DOI: 10.1016/j.ijer.2020.101602

Schipper, T. M., Goei, S. L., & de Vries, S. (2023). Dealing with the complexity of adaptive teaching through collaborative teacher professional development. In Maulana, R., Helms-Lorenz, M., & Klassen, R. M. (Eds.), *Effective teaching around the world* (pp. 707–722). Springer., DOI: 10.1007/978-3-031-31678-4_32

Schneider, R. M., & Plasman, K. (2011). Science teacher learning progressions: A review of science teachers' pedagogical content knowledge development. *Review of Educational Research*, 81(4), 530–565. DOI: 10.3102/0034654311423382

Sevian, H., & Talanquer, V. (2014). Rethinking chemistry: A learning progression on chemical thinking. *Chemistry Education Research and Practice*, 15(1), 10–23. DOI: 10.1039/C3RP00111C

Shabani, K., Khatib, M., & Ebadi, S. (2010). Vygotsky's Zone of Proximal Development: Instructional implications and teachers' professional development. *English Language Teaching*, 3(4), 237–248. DOI: 10.5539/elt.v3n4p237

Shepard, L. A. (2018). Learning progressions as tools for assessment and learning. *Applied Measurement in Education*, 31(2), 165–174. DOI: 10.1080/08957347.2017.1408628

Shepard, L. A. (2019). Classroom assessment to support teaching and learning. *The Annals of the American Academy of Political and Social Science*, 683(1), 183–200. DOI: 10.1177/0002716219843818

Shinana, E., Ngcoza, K. M., & Mavhunga, E. (2021). Development of teachers' PCK for a scientific inquiry-based teaching approach in Namibia's rural schools. African Journal of Research in Mathematics. *Science and Technology Education*, 25(1), 1–11. DOI: 10.1080/18117295.2021.1913375

Sikorski, T. R. (2019). Context-dependent "upper anchors" for learning progressions. *Science & Education*, 28(6), 957–981. DOI: 10.1007/s11191-019-00074-w

Sims, S., Fletcher-Wood, H., O'Mara-Eves, A., Cottingham, S., Stansfield, C., Goodrich, J., Van Herwegen, J., & Anders, J. (2023). Effective teacher professional development: New theory and a meta-analytic test. *Review of Educational Research*, 0(0), 00346543231217480. Advance online publication. DOI: 10.3102/00346543231217480

Stansberry, S. L. (2017). Authentic teaching with technology through situated learning. *Journal of Formative Design in Learning*, 1(1), 16–30. DOI: 10.1007/s41686-017-0004-2

Star, J. R. (2023). Revisiting the origin of, and reflections on the future of, pedagogical content knowledge. *Asian Journal for Mathematics Education*, 2(2), 147–160. DOI: 10.1177/27527263231175885

Steinberg, M. P., & Garrett, R. (2016). Classroom composition and measured teacher performance: What do teacher observation scores really measure? *Educational Evaluation and Policy Analysis*, 38(2), 293–317. DOI: 10.3102/0162373715616249

Suh, J. K., & Park, S. (2017). Exploring the relationship between pedagogical content knowledge (PCK) and sustainability of an innovative science teaching approach. *Teaching and Teacher Education*, 64, 246–259. DOI: 10.1016/j.tate.2017.01.021

Suh, J. K., & Park, S. (2017). Exploring the relationship between pedagogical content knowledge (PCK) and sustainability of an innovative science teaching approach. *Teaching and Teacher Education*, 64, 246–259. DOI: 10.1016/j.tate.2017.01.021

Sümer, M., & Vaněček, D. (2024). A systematic review of virtual and augmented realities in higher education: Trends and issues. *Innovations in Education and Teaching International*, •••, 1–12. DOI: 10.1080/14703297.2024.2382854

Upahi, J. E., & Ramnarain, U. (2022). Evidence of foundational knowledge and conjectural pathways in science learning progressions. *Science & Education*, 31(1), 55–92. DOI: 10.1007/s11191-021-00226-x

Valentine, K. A., Truckenmiller, A. J., Troia, G. A., & Aldridge, S. (2021). What is the nature of change in late elementary writing and are curriculum-based measures sensitive to that change? *Assessing Writing*, 50, 100567. DOI: 10.1016/j.asw.2021.100567

van der Steen, J., van Schilt-Mol, T., van der Vleuten, C., & Joosten-ten Brinke, D. (2023). Designing formative assessment that improves teaching and learning: What can be learned from the design stories of experienced teachers? *Journal of Formative Design in Learning*, 7(2), 182–194. DOI: 10.1007/s41686-023-00080-w

van Dijk, E. E., van Tartwijk, J., van der Schaaf, M. F., & Kluijtmans, M. (2020). What makes an expert university teacher? A systematic review and synthesis of frameworks for teacher expertise in higher education. *Educational Research Review*, 31, 100365. DOI: 10.1016/j.edurev.2020.100365

van Dijk, E. M., & Kattmann, U. (2007). A research model for the study of science teachers' PCK and improving teacher education. *Teaching and Teacher Education*, 23(6), 885–897. DOI: 10.1016/j.tate.2006.05.002

Velliaris, D. M., & Pierce, J. M. (2016). Cultural diversity: Misconceptions, misinterpretations, and misunderstandings in the classroom. In Jones, K., & Mixon, J. R. (Eds.), *Intercultural responsiveness in the second language learning classroom* (pp. 85–105). IGI Global., DOI: 10.4018/978-1-5225-2069-6.ch006

Ventista, O. M., & Brown, C. (2023). Teachers' professional learning and its impact on students' learning outcomes: Findings from a systematic review. *Social Sciences & Humanities Open*, 8(1), 100565. DOI: 10.1016/j.ssaho.2023.100565

Vygotsky, L. S. (1978). Interaction between learning and development. In Cole, M., John-Steiner, V., Scribner, S., & Souberman, E. (Eds.), *Mind in Society: The Development of Higher Psychological Processes* (pp. 79–91). Harvard University Press.

Wang, C., Chen, X., Yu, T., & Wang, Y. (2024). Education reform and change driven by digital technology: A bibliometric study from a global perspective. *Humanities & Social Sciences Communications*, 11(1), 256. Advance online publication. DOI: 10.1057/s41599-024-02717-y

Whitaker, A. A., Jenkins, J. M., & Duer, J. K. (2022). Standards, curriculum, and assessment in early childhood education: Examining alignment across multiple state systems. *Early Childhood Research Quarterly*, 58, 59–74. DOI: 10.1016/j.ecresq.2021.07.008

Wijngaards-de Meij, L., & Merx, S. (2018). Improving curriculum alignment and achieving learning goals by making the curriculum visible. *The International Journal for Academic Development*, 23(3), 219–231. DOI: 10.1080/1360144X.2018.1462187

Wiseman, A. (2011). Interactive read alouds: Teachers and students constructing knowledge and literacy together. *Early Childhood Education Journal*, 38(6), 431–438. DOI: 10.1007/s10643-010-0426-9

Xu, E., Wang, W., & Wang, Q. (2023). The effectiveness of collaborative problem solving in promoting students' critical thinking: A meta-analysis based on empirical literature. *Humanities & Social Sciences Communications*, 10(1), 16. DOI: 10.1057/s41599-023-01508-1

Yang, C., Li, J., Zhao, W., Luo, L., & Shanks, D. R. (2023). Do practice tests (quizzes) reduce or provoke test anxiety? A meta-analytic review. *Educational Psychology Review*, 35(3), 87. DOI: 10.1007/s10648-023-09801-w

Yang, Y., Liu, Y. X., Song, X. H., Yao, J.-X., & Guo, Y.-Y. (2023). A tale of two progressions: Students' learning progression of the particle nature of matter and teachers' perception on the progression. *Disciplinary and Interdisciplinary Science Education Research*, 5(1), 18. DOI: 10.1186/s43031-023-00085-2

Yao, J. X., Liu, Y. X., & Guo, Y. Y. (2023). Learning progression-based design: Advancing the synergetic development of energy understanding and scientific explanation. *Instructional Science*, 51(3), 397–421. DOI: 10.1007/s11251-023-09620-0

Zheng, L., Long, M., Zhong, L., & Gyasi, J. F. (2022). The effectiveness of technology-facilitated personalized learning on learning achievements and learning perceptions: A meta-analysis. *Education and Information Technologies*, 27(11), 11807–11830. DOI: 10.1007/s10639-022-11092-7

Chapter 4
Phronesis as a Pathway for the Nature and Development of Pedagogical Content Knowledge (PCK):
Seeing Through Indigenous Gnoseology

Jahid Siraz Chowdhury
https://orcid.org/0000-0002-1016-0441
Universiti Malaya, Malaysia

Zulkarnain A. Hatta
https://orcid.org/0000-0002-7339-3939
Lincoln University Collge, Malaysia

Sneha Singh
https://orcid.org/0000-0002-4221-7203
University of Auckland, New Zealand

ABSTRACT

This chapter examines the relationship between Indigenous Science and the new Western Baconian History of Philosophy of Science. It focuses on the Durkheimian Sociology of Knowledge and the connection between knowledge production and democracy. It rejects the notion that knowledge is merely labor and reflects Aristotle's stance that knowledge benefits societies. In critiquing the qualitative-quantitative

DOI: 10.4018/979-8-3693-0655-0.ch004

dichotomy in the social sciences, this article reveals its deceptive nature, departing from empirical data analysis. This chapter explores the function of social science as a transition between the pre-colonial and post-colonial eras. Reconstructing a colonial history that marginalized non-Western thinkers and proposes a synthesis of Aristotelian Gnoseology, Indigenous Holism, Al-Farabian volunteerism, Patanjali's mind-body-spiritual odyssey, and Buddha's enlightenment, this chapter synthesis gives rise to Indigenous Gnosticism, which guides social scientists to contribute to human welfare and intellectual happiness while grounding their assertions in philosophical rigor.

BACKGROUND: HOW WE THINK ABOUT HUMAN SUFFERINGS

Philosophers, known as "lovers of wisdom" (Horrigan, 2007, p. vii, n. 2; Dilley, 2010), are dedicated to seeking knowledge that transcends personal gain, aiming instead for understanding that benefits society. Derived from the Greek 'philos' (love) and 'sophia' (wisdom), this pursuit reflects a devotion to exploring existence, morality, and knowledge (Russell, 1945). Philosophy's role in understanding truth and reality (Gadamer, 1975; Habermas, 1984) contrasts sharply with the ongoing qualitative-quantitative division in social sciences, a dichotomy critiqued for distorting complex human experiences (Crotty, 1998). This binary, particularly in postcolonial contexts, prompts reflection on the real purpose of knowledge (Said, 1978; Smith, 1999).

Knowledge serves beyond abstract discourse, functioning as a pathway toward societal well-being, particularly within anthropology and social sciences (Wilkinson & Kleinman, 2016). This awareness underscores the importance of examining human suffering and other universal experiences, suggesting that knowledge production must address core ethical issues in social sciences (Foucault, 1972). History and philosophy of science reveal the need to re-evaluate contributions, especially where Indigenous perspectives have been historically sidelined. Examining the limitations and biases within documented knowledge, as observed by historians of science (Kuhn, 1962), urges social scientists to foster well-being through culturally sensitive research.

This chapter advocates a move from epistemology alone to gnoseology, promoting an expanded concept of knowledge that integrates experiential, ethical, and cultural dimensions beyond conventional empirical methods. Unlike traditional epistemology, which emphasizes the methodology of knowing (Audi, 2010), gnoseology considers the purpose and essence of knowledge in human life, recognizing that knowledge extends beyond information to encompass wisdom and ethical application (Gadamer, 1975; Scheler, 2009). Philosophers like Aristotle (2004) suggested that knowledge serves to realize human flourishing (eudaimonia), underscoring the importance of knowledge as beneficial to society and morally rooted.

Gnoseology resonates with ancient philosophical traditions, where knowledge was considered both transformative and relational (Heidegger, 1962). This relational knowledge connects to existential questions and the search for meaning within community life, contrasting the Western, often individualistic, epistemic models. Gadamer's (1975) Truth and Method similarly argues that understanding requires dialogical engagement, situating knowledge within social and historical contexts rather than detached analysis.

In this sense, gnoseology aligns with contemporary critiques of objective knowledge, where the knower is often separated from the known. Scheler's (2009) Phenomenology of Knowledge elaborates on this by suggesting that knowledge must reflect the ontological depth of human experience, encompassing subjective, intersubjective, and ethical dimensions. This philosophical foundation for gnoseology thus broadens the concept of knowledge, encouraging researchers to pursue not only scientific truth but also wisdom grounded in human welfare and moral responsibility (MacIntyre, 1984), emphasizing philosophical rigor and scientific inquiry for broader societal good (Habermas, 1984). This framework considers the welfare of people as integral to the pursuit of knowledge, aligning with critical postmodernist views that call for dismantling oppressive structures embedded in traditional scholarship (Bhabha, 1994; Spivak, 1988). Addressing essential questions—such as anthropology's mission and the ethical basis of knowledge production—compels scholars to critique claims of objectivity, noting how figures like Malinowski were entwined with colonial hierarchies (Clifford & Marcus, 1986).

Indigenous gnoseology meaningfully contributes to Pedagogical Content Knowledge (PCK) by incorporating holistic, culturally ingrained perspectives into education (Battiste & Henderson, 2000). Indigenous methods, oral traditions, and holistic epistemologies enhance educators' cultural sensitivity, aligning PCK with diverse student needs and fostering inclusive pedagogy (Smith, 1999; Dei, 2000; Chowdhury, 2023a). This culturally responsive PCK honors Indigenous values and empowers students to engage meaningfully with curriculum content, nurturing a pedagogical environment that resonates with their cultural identities and academic success

As Nancy Scheper-Hughes emphasizes, "Anthropology requires strength, courage, and perseverance" (Scheper-Hughes, 1995). Farid Alatas builds on this notion by suggesting that silence can serve as a powerful method in uncovering truth, highlighting the resilience needed in scholarship (Alatas, 2018). Such perspectives aim to renew the role of knowledge in fostering a bold, enduring approach rooted in the etymology of gnoseology, derived from the Greek gnosis (knowledge) and Latin -logia (study) (Merriam-Webster, 2022). Early academia often resisted internal critique, but contemporary scholarship increasingly merges scientific rigor with personal insight, as ethical scholarship demands transparency and depth (MacIntyre, 1984). This embrace of self-reflective knowledge aligns with Indigenous Gnoseology, which challenges distinctions between personal narrative and ethnography, shifting ontological boundaries within scientific analysis (Hanson, 1984; Gadamer, 1975).

Gnoseology, unlike epistemology, which Descartes framed around validity, operates as a practical philosophy that connects with Aristotelian Nicomachean Ethics to pursue knowledge as a virtue through episteme (scientific knowledge) and techne (practical skill) (Aristotle, 2004). This synthesis of Eastern and Western philosophies emphasizes knowledge as a means to ethical and societal good, merging Indigenous wisdom and philosophical inquiry. Drawing on Aristotle's phronesis (practical wisdom), Farabi's concept of intellectual happiness, Patanjali's enlightenment, and Buddhist ethical values, gnoseology contributes a unique perspective that values diverse knowledge systems and practices (Dei, 2000; Battiste & Henderson, 2000). This broadened approach echoes Thomas' notion of universal connections, reflecting cross-cultural insights within an Indigenous framework that respects the knowledge structures of all societies (Hanson, 1984).

Indigenous Gnoseology, as proposed here, aims to blend Aristotelian gnoseology with Indigenous holism, Al-Farabian ethical grounding, Patanjali's mind-body-spiritual integration, and Buddha's enlightenment to create a knowledge system for social scientists that contributes to human welfare and intellectual fulfillment (Gadamer, 1975). This approach shifts the historical narrative, advocating for a revised understanding of knowledge that combines scientific logic with ethical imperatives. Such a gnoseological framework aims to remind scholars of their roles as "lovers of wisdom" (Russell, 1945), motivating them to act as agents of positive change and inclusive knowledge production

In proposing Indigenous Gnoseology, we introduce a conceptual framework that allows social scientists to contribute meaningfully to human welfare and intellectual fulfillment through knowledge rooted in ethical and cultural understanding. This approach, positioned within the broader context of Pedagogical Content Knowledge (PCK), aligns with the educational goal of equipping educators and learners with the wisdom and tools necessary to grasp knowledge's social and practical significance (Shulman, 1987). PCK traditionally refers to educators' capacity to transform subject matter into teachable content by understanding how students learn and which teaching methods best convey complex ideas (Grossman, 1990). By integrating Indigenous Gnoseology into PCK, we aim to develop a pedagogy that prioritizes ethical reasoning and respects diverse epistemologies, creating a more holistic approach to teaching and learning (Dei, 2000; Battiste & Henderson, 2000).

Indigenous Gnoseology, as an epistemic approach, combines Aristotelian practical wisdom (phronesis), Al-Farabian intellectual joy, Patanjali's spiritual insights, and Buddhist morality, thus embodying a knowledge system that honors the ethical and relational dimensions of learning (Aristotle, 2004; Farabi, trans. 2001). This blend of philosophical and cultural insights highlights that knowledge must extend beyond theoretical concepts, fostering intellectual joy and contributing to personal and communal well-being (MacIntyre, 1984). In the context of PCK, this means that educators are not merely transmitters of information but facilitators who cultivate intellectual growth by connecting knowledge with cultural relevance and ethical purpose (Gadamer, 1975; Dei, 2000). Consequently, Indigenous Gnoseology enriches the teaching process by challenging educators to consider not only what is taught but also why and how knowledge should be conveyed to foster a sense of interconnectedness among learners (Smith, 1999).

Historically, dominant epistemologies have often excluded non-Western perspectives, leading to a narrow understanding of knowledge that disregards ethical and communal dimensions (Battiste & Henderson, 2000). Indigenous Gnoseology advocates rewriting this history by validating diverse epistemic traditions and aligning them with scientific rigor, thereby challenging the limitations of purely empirical approaches. This reorientation is essential for pedagogical frameworks like PCK, which must evolve to reflect a broader, more inclusive understanding of knowledge and teaching methods (Shulman, 1987). Incorporating Indigenous Gnoseology into PCK reinforces the educator's role as a guide who nurtures students' intellectual happiness and moral development, bridging the gap between knowledge as an abstract concept and its practical, ethical applications (Gadamer, 1975).

Additionally, Indigenous Gnoseology encourages educators to pursue what Aristotle (2004) terms "virtue knowledge"—knowledge that is not only accurate but also oriented toward the betterment of society. This perspective aligns with PCK's objective to deepen content knowledge by integrating cultural and ethical awareness, thus enabling students to connect with their cultural identities and fostering inclusivity in the learning environment (Dei, 2000; Grossman, 1990). By incorporating Indigenous Gnoseology, educators can redefine PCK to create educational spaces where students from diverse backgrounds feel represented and understood, cultivating a sense of belonging and purpose within their educational journey (Wilson, 2008).

So, here, we propose Indigenous Gnoseology as an invaluable guide for PCK, where the purpose of teaching transcends content delivery to foster holistic intellectual development. This framework invites educators to embrace their role as "lovers of knowledge" who contribute to societal welfare, intellectual joy, and moral growth (Russell, 1945). In doing so, PCK becomes not just a model of pedagogical practice but a pathway to inclusive, culturally responsive education that reaffirms the shared human pursuit of wisdom and understanding (Gadamer, 1975; Smith, 1999)..

VISUALIZING GNOSEOLOGY

During my (first author) PhD journey, I confronted the limitations of understanding ontology and epistemology, particularly amid the challenges posed by the COVID-19 pandemic. The silence from anthropological and sociological associations during this crisis, as I observed, seemed to stem from an entrenched adherence to Durkheimian sociology, which views "social facts as things"—objective, measurable phenomena often detached from lived human experience (Durkheim, 1982). This method, rigorously framed in *The Rules of Sociological Method*, can unintentionally hinder the relational and contextual dimensions of knowledge, especially during societal upheavals when social science must connect more deeply with the human aspects it aims to study (Durkheim, 1982).

In seeking a more inclusive framework, I discovered that Rene Descartes, by advancing epistemology as the primary mode of understanding, transformed gnoseology's broader scope into a narrower focus on method and certainty (Descartes, 1985). This Cartesian shift emphasizes objective knowledge at the expense of relational, action-oriented understanding, a transformation that some, including Olav Eikeland, argue has contributed to a disembodied and often ethically distant approach within social sciences. Eikeland's (2006a) critique of "condescending ethics" in research warns that reducing knowledge to abstract reasoning severs it from the moral and social obligations integral to applied sciences. In his view, knowledge must be action-oriented, rooted in real-life contexts, and ethically aware—principles often neglected in traditional epistemology.

Eikeland's (2006b) discussion of *phronesis*, Aristotle's concept of practical wisdom, provides a valuable lens for rethinking knowledge as not merely something to be accumulated but as something to be practiced ethically within community contexts. For Eikeland, *phronesis* embodies a gnoseological approach by encouraging researchers to engage with knowledge as a dynamic process that requires critical reflection and ethical commitment (Eikeland, 2006b). This aligns with the Indigenous concept of knowledge as inherently communal and moral, underscoring that research should not only produce insights but also contribute positively to the communities involved (Battiste & Henderson, 2000).

Gnoseology, in this framework, reconnects social scientists to a holistic understanding of knowledge that includes ethical and cultural responsibility. The pandemic, particularly, highlighted the limitations of a purely epistemological approach and underscored the importance of a gnoseological perspective, which recognizes knowledge as lived and relational rather than abstract. Eikeland's work supports this shift by challenging social scientists to embrace the moral implications of their research, positioning knowledge as a means to foster community well-being and resilience rather than merely producing "social facts" (Eikeland, 2006a).

This journey toward gnoseology ultimately encourages us to move beyond the Cartesian dichotomy and reframe knowledge as an active, culturally resonant process. In times of crisis, such as the COVID-19 pandemic, the shift from epistemology to gnoseology becomes crucial, inviting researchers to engage in knowledge practices that are not only insightful but also compassionate and transformative (Wilson, 2008; MacIntyre, 1984). By embracing gnoseology, we are reminded of the purpose of social science: not just to observe but to contribute meaningfully to human understanding and well-being.

This realization pushed me to expand my understanding, drawing insights from diverse philosophical traditions, including Buddhism, the teachings of Sufi Master Al-Ghazali, and the writings of Patanjali. These influences shape research by grounding it in concepts of reality (ontology) and approaches to knowledge acquisition (epistemology). In this sense, gnoseology acts as an overarching framework within which epistemology operates, similar to how John Locke's empiricism and René Descartes' rationalism contribute distinct perspectives to knowledge theory (Horrigan, 2007; Alonso-Amo et al., 1992). Descartes, in particular, initiated a shift from gnoseology to epistemology, which Locke and others expanded upon (Hatfield, 2014). Locke, emphasizing the importance of distinct identity and empirical investigation, argued that an entity's identity, like that of a living organism, is tied to its continuity, whereas individual identity relies on sustained self-consciousness over time (Locke, 1847).

This debate has since led to the development of frameworks like descriptive positivism, interpretative phenomenology, and critical postcolonial analysis. However, these models often neglect normative aspects of knowledge. Interestingly, Kant, regarded by some as the father of anthropology, diverges here by addressing the normative dimensions of knowledge and ethics, bridging the gap between descriptive and ethical thought (Urban, 2013). Today, four primary paradigms—positivism, phenomenology, postcolonial critique, and Indigenous gnoseology—inform the ethics, axiology, and methodologies of research and knowledge practices (Kuhn, 2012).

While Indigenous gnoseology acknowledges a holistic view of knowledge, it sometimes overlooks foundational aspects that contribute to a more complete research approach, emphasizing instead practical and community-oriented applications (Mignolo, 2012; Sanguineti, 1988). This aligns with Indigenous methods of knowledge and practice, which depart significantly from traditional Western research methodologies, fostering an inclusive and context-sensitive approach to understanding human experience.

Table 1. Visualizing gnoseology

	Conceptualizing Gnoseology		
1	The philosophic theory of knowledge: inquiry into the basis, nature, validity, and limits of knowledge		*Merriam-Webster* (2022)
2	Gnoseology is Epistemology "This new approach to studying knowledge, linked with the incredible development of scientific epistemology since the end of the last century,		Alonso-Amo et al., 1992, p.141
3	Pramāna Epistemology	Pratyaksa (perception	Perrett, 1998. De Wet, 2021.
		Anumāna (inference, reasoning	
		Upamāna (comparison and analogy),	
		Arthāpatti (postulation, derivarion from circumstances),	
		Anupalabdi (non-perception, negative/cognitive proof),	
		Śabda (word, testimony of past or present from reliable experts),	
		and sm ti (tradition or scripture	
4	Buddhist Ethics	Cause and Karma 8 Fold Morality is source of knwoeldge	MacKenzie, 2022
5	Human Possibility	Gnoseological optimism upholds the thesis that humanity in a finite period of time	Sanguineti, 1988
6	By Christian Faith Thomas Aquinas,	Philosophy of Knowledge	Ferrier, 1856.
7	By Christian Faith	Gnoseology is as the philosophy of knowledge	Gallagher, 2021 [1964]
7	Rational Philosophy	Idealism	Descartes, Kant
8	Empiricist Philosophy	Material World	Locke, Hume, Berekly,

Source: Chowdhury et al. (2023a)

Table 1 illustrates critical perspectives on Indigenous Gnoseology (IG), highlighting its role in reshaping our understanding of knowledge by integrating advances in scientific epistemology. IG emphasizes a shift from dependence on raw power to a reliance on intellectual capability, promoting a future where knowledge and reasoning take precedence (Alonso-Amo et al., 1992, p.141). One foundational approach within IG suggests that knowledge originates from sensory experience; information without sensory traceability is thus not regarded as genuine knowledge (Chowdhury & Roy, 2023). This view introduces complexities between possibility and certainty, with some scholars asserting that empirical knowledge is absolute, while fallibilists argue that the vast scope of sensory data makes complete verification unattainable. Such perspectives can contextualize Al-Biruni's anthropological contributions, offering a lens through which to understand non-Western epistemological traditions that are often overlooked.

In examining the roots of scientific thought, IG also reclaims overlooked contributions from Eastern and Arabic scholars. Methodology, a critical aspect of the History and Philosophy of Science (HPS), encompasses insights that extend well before the New Science Era, reflecting deep-rooted intellectual traditions (Clammer & Giri, 2013). For example, Darwin's evolutionary theory is commonly associated with the study of biology; however, early evolutionary ideas appeared nearly 900 years earlier. Al-Jahiz, an early rationalist philosopher, proposed theories on environmental influences on species survival, anticipating concepts such as natural selection and adaptation (Al-Jahiz, 789). Thus, IG not only provides a bridge to scientific epistemology but also challenges established views on the origins of evolutionary thought, advocating for a broader understanding of knowledge traditions (Alonso-Amo et al., 1992; Al-Jahiz, 789; Chowdhury et al., 2023b).

WHY INDIGENOUS GNOSEOLOGY IS VITAL: FILLING GAPS IN DECOLONIAL AND ANTICOLONIAL SCHOLARSHIP

Indigenous Gnoseology—the study of knowledge from Indigenous perspectives—offers an essential framework for addressing gaps in decolonial and anticolonial scholarship. Although decolonial and anticolonial movements aim to challenge colonial power structures and advocate for Indigenous rights, they often lack a focus on Indigenous ways of knowing, being, and relating to the world. By emphasizing culturally rooted epistemologies, spirituality, and ethical responsibility, Indigenous Gnoseology brings unique insights into the limitations of current approaches, expanding the scope of decolonial and anticolonial studies (Battiste & Henderson, 2000; Wilson, 2008; Tuck & Yang, 2012).

Decolonial and anticolonial frameworks have significantly contributed to critiquing Eurocentric knowledge systems and promoting marginalized perspectives (Mignolo, 2011; Grosfoguel, 2013). However, these frameworks frequently rely on analytical models that, despite their critical stance, do not fully incorporate Indigenous epistemologies. Linda Tuhiwai Smith (2012) suggests that even decolonial scholarship can remain anchored in Western academic traditions that emphasize empirical, positivist research methodologies. This approach may inadvertently marginalize Indigenous knowledge systems, which prioritize interconnectedness, relationality, and spirituality as fundamental aspects of understanding (Kovach, 2009; Simpson, 2014).

Decolonial and anticolonial scholarship often lacks the essential components of Indigenous epistemologies, which provide a foundation for more inclusive approaches to knowledge production. Indigenous knowledge systems are not merely extensions of Western knowledge; rather, they constitute complete epistemologies that offer distinct contributions to fields such as environmental science, ethics, and community health (Battiste, 2011; Nakata, 2007). The absence of Indigenous Gnoseology in decolonial and anticolonial scholarship leaves a significant gap, as it fails to engage fully with Indigenous perspectives that see knowledge as deeply interconnected with ethical, communal, and ecological responsibilities.

A central tenet of Indigenous Gnoseology is its focus on relational and ethical dimensions of knowledge, often missing from Western-derived frameworks. While traditional epistemology is frequently centered around individual cognition and empirical evidence, Indigenous Gnoseology incorporates ethical and communal considerations, viewing knowledge as a shared, community-oriented resource (Wilson, 2008; Chilisa, 2012). Shawn Wilson (2008) describes this as "relational accountability," where researchers are ethically responsible to the community and must ensure their work is mutually beneficial. This framework contrasts with individualistic, data-driven research models and aligns with Indigenous values of reciprocity and respect.

This relational approach is crucial in addressing current global issues, particularly ecological and social crises. Indigenous Gnoseology emphasizes sustainability and interdependence, principles deeply rooted in Indigenous cultural practices (Kimmerer, 2013). By integrating these values, Indigenous Gnoseology provides a knowledge system that aligns with ethical responsibilities toward people and the planet. In contrast, decolonial and anticolonial frameworks may focus more on structural critiques than on positive, community-based outcomes. As Vine Deloria Jr. (2001) notes, Indigenous knowledge systems inherently promote stewardship of the Earth and are vital for sustainable futures.

Indigenous Gnoseology offers an essential expansion of decolonial frameworks by broadening the understanding of knowledge and challenging the dominance of Eurocentric paradigms. Walter Mignolo (2011) argues that decolonial thought must move beyond Western constructs to fully achieve its transformative potential. Indigenous Gnoseology contributes to this goal by offering a perspective that operates independently of Western epistemic traditions, instead valuing Indigenous knowledge systems as legitimate sources of understanding and empowerment (Simpson, 2014).

In addition to challenging Western epistemology, Indigenous Gnoseology enriches decolonial and anticolonial scholarship by incorporating spiritual and ethical elements often neglected in conventional frameworks. Robin Wall Kimmerer (2013) describes Indigenous knowledge as inherently spiritual, where the relationship with the natural world is integral to personal and communal identity. This holistic approach goes beyond individual empowerment, fostering resilience within the community and promoting a way of knowing that emphasizes reciprocity and respect for the natural world.

The inclusion of Indigenous Gnoseology within decolonial frameworks also addresses the need for "ontological pluralism" in scholarship, or the acknowledgment of multiple, valid ways of being and knowing (Todd, 2016). Such pluralism is essential for recognizing the diversity of Indigenous experiences and perspectives, which are often marginalized in the pursuit of universality within Western knowledge systems. Leanne Betasamosake Simpson (2014) argues that by adopting Indigenous approaches to knowledge, scholars can create space for voices that have historically been silenced or undervalued, thus contributing to a more equitable knowledge landscape.

To understand the gaps in decolonial scholarship, we must reflect on the historical trajectory of decolonial thinkers, from early figures like José Rizal (1885) and Antenor Firmin (1890) to more recent scholars. Table 2 summarizes three generations of decolonial thinkers, emphasizing their contributions and uncovering an overlooked dimension: the practical, or phronetic, application of knowledge in Indigenous contexts.

In the first wave of decolonization (1885-1980), influential figures like Rizal, Firmin, and Fanon challenged colonial ideologies, while Vine Deloria clarified Indigenous metaphysical frameworks (Deloria, 1999). The following period (1980-2000) saw scholars like Garcia and Wang examining colonialism through ethnography, and Wolfe investigating settler colonialism's systemic nature (Wolfe, 1999). Moving into the third generation (post-2000), works by de la Rosa and Dieste critique colonial power within historical anthropology, while Roque explores anthropology's role in trading human remains in colonial Portugal (Dieste, 2017; Roque, 2017). In addition, more recent publications like Indigenous Anthropology Around the World emphasize culturally sensitive approaches and the integration of Indigenous methodologies, highlighting the decolonial movement's progress and limitations (Smith, 2021; Nakata, 2007).

Linda Tuhiwai Smith argues that "Localized Critical Theory" encounters linguistic and cultural barriers within Indigenous contexts, often reducing complex Indigenous perspectives to simplistic tropes (Smith, 2012). Ferrier (1856) echoes this by arguing that institutional knowledge often repeats existing ideas without generating new insights. Edward Said (1993) further contends that such intellectual repetition prevents meaningful innovation. Spivak (2004) calls for addressing this gap, asserting that genuine intellectual engagement requires moving beyond Western paradigms.

Table 2 thus serves a dual purpose: it highlights the growth of decolonial thought while exposing the need for Indigenous Gnoseology (IG) to enrich methodologies and broaden perspectives. Although prominent decolonial figures like Firmin, Smith, and Nakata advocate for Indigenous knowledge, the use of the Indigenous Research Paradigm (IRP) remains limited, particularly in Southeast Asia and institutions like the University of Malaya (Nakata, 2007, 2017; Alatas, 2018). This gap underscores the need for methodologies that prioritize relational accountability—a concept central to IG—over Western individualism (Wilson, 2008).

Indigenous Gnoseology's emphasis on relational knowledge contrasts sharply with dominant paradigms, which treat knowledge as a possession of the individual researcher. IG posits that knowledge is inherently relational, encompassing interactions not only among humans but also with animals, plants, the cosmos, and Earth itself (Wilson, 2008). This view of knowledge as interconnected and collective implies a higher ethical responsibility, where researchers must honor all relationships affected by their work. IG, therefore, extends beyond traditional epistemology to encompass a more inclusive and accountable knowledge system.

Historically, philosophy and science have often dismissed these Indigenous views. From Bacon's mechanistic approach to Kant's cosmopolitan but racially divisive ideologies, Western frameworks have frequently positioned knowledge as objective and value-neutral, erasing relational and ethical dimensions (Bacon, 2008; Sandford, 2018). For instance, Daly (2019) critiques Bacon's New Organon, noting its departure from Aristotelian ethics, which valued wisdom for the welfare of the community or polis (Aristotle, trans. 2009). Bacon's disregard for practical wisdom epitomizes the Eurocentric bias that has long excluded Indigenous knowledge from academic discourse.

Similarly, Kant's Toward Perpetual Peace (1795) and Groundwork for the Metaphysics of Morals (1797) criticize colonialism, yet his earlier work, Idea for a Universal History (1784), upheld a racially stratified worldview, thus reflecting an inherent contradiction in his ethics (Kant, 2013; Kleingeld, 2014). Kant's contemporary, Johann Blumenbach, classified humans by race, solidifying Eurocentric hierarchies in Western thought (Blumenbach, 1775; Mensch, 2018).

Hegel, revered by scholars like Pippin and Zizek, is similarly problematic when read through an anticolonial lens. His notion of the "Spirit" prioritizes European civilization while ignoring Indigenous contributions to human history (Hegel, 2001). As Foucault (1972) critiques in his concept of the "archaeology of knowledge," such Eurocentric paradigms define what is considered legitimate knowledge, systematically erasing non-Western epistemologies.

This archaeological analysis reveals the structural biases embedded in Western knowledge systems. Indigenous Gnoseology challenges this by restoring the relational, ethical, and collective dimensions of knowledge that have been marginalized. Integrating IG within academic frameworks can empower Indigenous voices, promote genuine knowledge pluralism, and encourage responsible scholarship that respects all forms of life and knowledge.Incorporating Indigenous Gnoseology into decolonial and anticolonial scholarship is essential for fostering inclusive, ethical, and holistic approaches to knowledge. By integrating Indigenous ways of knowing, scholars can advance beyond critique alone, promoting knowledge practices that respect relationality, environmental stewardship, and community accountability. Indigenous Gnoseology provides an invaluable framework for addressing the limitations of decolonial and anticolonial frameworks, challenging Eurocentric paradigms, and enhancing academic discourse with Indigenous insights long marginalized by conventional academia. This paradigm shift not only empowers Indigenous voices but also offers all scholars a model for engaging with knowledge in ways that are ethically sound, socially responsible, and environmentally sustainable.

In essence, the archaeology of Western knowledge entails examining how various types of information, such as scientific, philosophical, and social knowledge, arose, evolved, and interacted across time. This approach looks beyond the content of knowledge to examine the deeper structures, discursive formations, and power dynamics that determine how knowledge is generated and interpreted. The archaeology of Foucault investigates how information is classified, categorized, and linked through diverse systems of thought and institutions. It highlights the importance of language, concepts, and institutions in shaping and controlling knowledge. By exposing these underlying frameworks, Foucault hoped to challenge standard historical narratives and demonstrate how knowledge is a complex web of interconnected ideas impacted by social, cultural, and political influences. In essence, Western knowledge archaeology is a methodological approach that tries to unearth the historical, linguistic, and institutional underpinnings of knowledge systems in Western societies, with the goal of understanding how knowledge is produced, structured, and utilized in various situations. The relationships between Foucault and Said are relevant in the context of Indigenous Gnoseology and the goal of humanistic knowledge generation through philosophical means. The emphasis on power relations and the formation of knowledge by Foucault aligns with the need to critically evaluate how Indigenous knowledge has been neglected and controlled by dominant structures. Said's critique of Orientalism gives light on how colonial discourses warped Indigenous viewpoints. In seeking humanistic knowledge production in Indigenous Gnoseology, their disagreements highlight the necessity of decolonizing knowledge, respecting multiple worldviews, and strengthening Indigenous perspectives. Engaging with Indigenous viewpoints philosophically can help to resist oppressive hierarchies and promote a more inclusive and respectful exchange of ideas. I am giving a little example of Figure 1. As I understand it, look at Table 2, the bolded names but not in the mainstream text. Even in this shadow, there was a big question that is the basis of today's nation-state. Agina, German Wizard, Hegel.

For Hegel, history was the stage upon which an abstract cosmic mind called the "World Spirit" evolved—from a state of unconsciousness to one self-conscious freedom grounded in ethical responsibility—by morphing into a succession of "folk" or "national spirits" (Volksgeists) spurred by the acts of "world historical individuals"

HOW IG IS A SOURCE OF KNOWLEDGE

Figure 1. Equation of gnoseology and epistemology

$E \triangleq G$ (by Definition: theory of Knowledge),

so, one can say, $E \sim G$

But, in practice, $E = \{TK \text{ and } WP, C, CC\}$

Whereas, $G (E, T, P, TK, RP)$

So, $G \subseteq E$ is not a correct methodological position

But, $E \subseteq G$, (Epistemology is a part of Gnoselogy [Aristotlian Logic, Alfarabian Philosophy, and Saadian theory of Knowledge]

Notes: WP=Western Philosophy, E= Epistemology, RP=Reciprocity, TK= Tacit Knowledge (Karl Polany), T= Techne, C= Colonialism, CC=Christian Commonwealth, P= Phronesis (Wise use of knowledge, Aristotle in Eikerland, 2007, p. 348), G= Gnoseology

Source: Chowdhury et al., (2022, p. 49)

This figure illustrates the relationship between epistemology (E) and gnoseology (G), framing epistemology as a subset of gnoseology. It begins by defining both E and G as theories of knowledge, suggesting that while they may overlap in purpose, their scope and focus differ. Epistemology, in this context, is limited to Western Philosophy (WP) and practical knowledge like Karl Polanyi's tacit knowledge (TK), techne (T), colonialism (C), and the Christian Commonwealth (CC). In contrast, gnoseology encompasses a broader range of elements, including Aristotle's *phronesis* (wise application of knowledge), reciprocity (RP), and alternative philosophies like Alfarabian and Saadian theories. The figure argues that while epistemology (E) is a component of gnoseology (G), treating gnoseology as a subset of epistemology would be an incorrect methodological stance, given the broader and more inclusive nature of gnoseology.

Revitalizing Oral Tradition: A Core of Indigenous Epistemology

Oral tradition forms a central element of Indigenous epistemology, offering rich insights that have traditionally been underrepresented in Western frameworks. The Indigenous Research Paradigm (IRP) actively restores and honors these oral practices, seamlessly incorporating them into Indigenous Gnoseology (IG). Scholars such as Linda Tuhiwai Smith, Shawn Wilson, Manulani Aluli Meyer, Martin Nakata, Karen Martin, and Jeff Corntassel have illuminated the critical role of oral tradition, not merely as a means of storytelling but as a vehicle for preserving Indigenous culture and communal knowledge (Smith, 2012; Wilson, 2008).

Smith argues that oral narratives communicate historical wisdom and cultural essence, acting as a living archive passed through generations. Wilson views oral tradition as a bridge that connects past, present, and future, sustaining a continuous dialogue across time. Aluli Meyer, Nakata, Martin, and Corntassel further stress that oral narratives convey complete worldviews, including ecological insights, spiritual connections, and collective values (Corntassel et al., 2018). Nakata's concept of "cultural interface" presents oral tradition as a challenge to Western assumptions, integrating Indigenous perspectives into academic discourse (Nakata, 2007). Through Indigenous Gnoseology, oral tradition reestablishes the relationship between people and nature, offering an ecological consciousness and a profound respect for the interconnectedness of life.

Holistic Wisdom: A Foundation of Indigenous Epistemology

Indigenous epistemology embodies a holistic perspective, embracing an interdependent view of all life forms and the environment. This contrasts with the compartmentalized nature of mainstream discourse. As Smith and Wilson emphasize, Indigenous knowledge systems view human well-being and ecological health as interconnected, resonating with a broader understanding of existence that has been cultivated over generations (Smith, 2012; Wilson, 2008). Aluli Meyer, Nakata, Martin, and Corntassel extend this holistic viewpoint by advocating for the inseparability of human health and Earth's ecosystems, arguing that this awareness can help bridge the artificial divide between humanity and nature (Corntassel et al., 2018; Nakata, 2007).

Nakata's concept of "cultural interface" further highlights this integrated knowledge approach, inviting us to move beyond isolated understanding and appreciate knowledge as a woven tapestry. This holistic framework aligns with the Indigenous belief that harmony with nature enriches the human experience, offering an alternative to the pervasive disconnection in contemporary society. In embracing this holistic wisdom, Indigenous Gnoseology guides us toward a more harmonious coexistence with the Earth, recognizing that human actions ripple through the fabric of life.

Spirituality and Animism: Anchoring Indigenous Epistemology

Indigenous epistemology is deeply intertwined with spirituality and animism, seeing the natural world as imbued with spiritual forces. This worldview fosters a deep connection with the environment, framing human existence as part of a greater cosmic web (Van Meijl, 2019; Chao, 2020). Animism, which views all life forms and elements as spiritually significant, contributes to a cosmology where humans coexist with the larger universe rather than dominating it (Studley & Horsley, 2018; Demeulenaere et al., 2021). This perspective influences how Indigenous communities interact with their environment, engaging with the land, water, and wildlife through a lens of respect and interdependence.

Indigenous knowledge is cultivated through centuries of observation and an intimate relationship with the environment. Unlike Western knowledge, which often separates information from lived experience, Indigenous knowledge is transmitted through oral tradition, songs, and ceremonies that celebrate and maintain cultural identity (King, 2016; Smith, 2023). This communal learning process contrasts sharply with the individualistic approach common in Western societies, creating a dynamic intergenerational knowledge exchange where elders share wisdom with younger generations in informal, community-centered settings (Chao, 2020).

Additionally, Indigenous epistemology is often experienced directly, in contrast to the abstract learning typical of Western education. This immersive approach enables Indigenous people to acquire knowledge through practices that honor the land and its spirits, fostering a profound connection with the cosmos (Demeulenaere et al., 2021; Morrison, 2014). By preserving Indigenous languages, traditions, and stories, this spiritual foundation supports cultural resilience and counteracts the erosion of identity caused by colonization. Indigenous Gnoseology, with its spiritual and animistic foundation, thus acts as both a guiding philosophy and a safeguard, nurturing the enduring spirit of Indigenous communities (Yannakakis, 2023; Studley & Horsley, 2018).

In summary, Indigenous Gnoseology as a source of knowledge integrates oral tradition, holistic wisdom, and spirituality, challenging Western epistemological frameworks by emphasizing relational accountability and ecological interdependence. Through the revival of Indigenous epistemology, scholars and practitioners are encouraged to recalibrate their approach to knowledge, fostering a deeper, more inclusive understanding of the world that aligns with Indigenous values of harmony, respect, and unity with the Earth

CONCLUSION AND IMPLICATIONS

This paper emphasizes the profound philosophical and practical implications of integrating Indigenous Gnoseology and Saadia Gaon's reverence for religious scriptures as sources of knowledge. Both frameworks advocate for a radical rethinking of knowledge, treating it not as a mere accumulation of facts but as a holistic, ethical, and relational pursuit. This perspective challenges the dominant Western epistemology, which often prioritizes objectivity, individualism, and empirical validation over relational accountability, spiritual depth, and communal well-being. By embracing Indigenous Gnoseology alongside Gaon's insights, we unlock a more comprehensive understanding of knowledge, one that transcends rigid boundaries and acknowledges the ethical, ecological, and spiritual dimensions of human existence.

Implications for Social Sciences and Education

This expanded epistemology calls upon the entire field of social sciences to re-evaluate its methodologies and objectives. Social science research, which traditionally emphasizes objectivity and empirical rigor, could benefit immensely from incorporating relational accountability, where knowledge is understood as a communal and ethical responsibility. This shift would foster research practices that honor the connections between researchers, communities, and the natural world, creating a more inclusive approach that resonates with the values of diverse cultures (Wilson, 2008). In anthropology, sociology, and psychology, practitioners are invited to explore knowledge as an interdependent process, viewing human experience through the lens of ecological and spiritual interconnectedness rather than isolated behavior.

Educational Policy and Curriculum Development

The implications for education policy are equally transformative. A curriculum rooted in Indigenous Gnoseology and respect for spiritual knowledge would prioritize holistic development, teaching students to view knowledge as both a communal responsibility and a source of ethical action. This shift from an individualistic, test-driven model to a relational model would instill in learners a respect for diverse knowledge systems and a deeper sense of responsibility toward the environment and society (Smith, 2012; Battiste, 2011). Educational policies might encourage teaching practices that integrate oral traditions, place-based learning, and experiential engagement, creating educational environments where students learn not only through facts but through relationships—with people, culture, and nature.

Policy Implications for Sustainable Development and Global Governance

In the policy-making sphere, Indigenous Gnoseology and Saadia Gaon's view of scripture-based wisdom could inform frameworks for sustainable development and global governance. Embracing these perspectives would mean recognizing that ethical and spiritual considerations are crucial to environmental and social policies. Policy-makers could integrate Indigenous values of reciprocity, sustainability, and spiritual connection with the land into conservation efforts and climate action plans, creating policies that respect and protect Indigenous lands and wisdom (Cajete, 2000). This approach could foster collaboration between governments and Indigenous communities, acknowledging their knowledge systems as vital to global well-being.

Toward a New Paradigm of Knowledge

Ultimately, integrating Indigenous Gnoseology and spiritual epistemologies into mainstream thought could catalyze a paradigm shift in global knowledge practices. This approach encourages a pluralistic epistemology where diverse knowledge systems coexist, fostering intercultural respect and collaborative problem-solving. In a world facing complex challenges, such as environmental degradation and social disconnection, a holistic approach to knowledge—one that combines scientific inquiry with ethical and spiritual understanding—could provide a pathway toward global harmony. This inclusive, relational framework recognizes knowledge as a shared human heritage, guiding us toward a future where wisdom is measured not by individual achievement but by our collective ability to nurture and sustain life on Earth.

In conclusion, embracing Indigenous Gnoseology and the reverence for religious and spiritual knowledge has the potential to reshape not only the academy but also the foundational structures of society, infusing them with respect, reciprocity, and responsibility. Such a transformation would not only democratize knowledge but also cultivate a world that values wisdom as a communal pursuit dedicated to the flourishing of all beings. Indigenous Gnoseology can be effectively aligned with the concept of Pedagogical Content Knowledge (PCK) by expanding PCK's framework to incorporate Indigenous ways of knowing. While PCK focuses on teachers' ability to convey subject knowledge effectively, integrating Indigenous Gnoseology introduces a relational and holistic approach to teaching, where knowledge is not merely transmitted but experienced through community, environment, and spirituality. This enriched PCK model would emphasize not only cognitive skills but also ethical responsibility, cultural relevance, and ecological sensitivity, fostering a more inclusive and sustainable pedagogy that respects diverse epistemologies and prepares learners to engage with the world meaningfully and responsibly.

REFERENCES

Al-Bīrūnī, A. R. (2020). *The Yoga Sutras of Patañjali*. New York University Press.

Alatas, F. (2018). *Applying Ibn Khaldun: The Recovery of a Lost Tradition in Sociology*. Routledge.

Alatas, F. (2018). *Silencing as method: Leaving Malay studies out*. Department of Malay Studies, National University of Singapore.

Alatas, S. H. (1972). Captive Mind in Development Studies. *International Social Science Journal*, 24(1), 9–25.

Alonso-Amo, F., Mate, J. L., Morant, J. L., & Pazos, J. (1992). From epistemology to Gnoseology: Foundations of the knowledge industry. *AI & Society*, 6(2), 140–165. DOI: 10.1007/BF02472778

Alonso-Amo, R., et al. (1992). an attempt at understanding the nature of the world and a subsequent endeavour to understand the nature of knowledge itself. This is the step from a purely epistemological approach to a gnoseological one.

Aristotle, . (2004). *The Nicomachean Ethics* (Thomson, J. A. K., Trans.). Penguin Books. (Original work published 350 BCE)

Aristotle, . (2009). *The Nicomachean Ethics* (Ross, D., Trans.). Oxford University Press.

Audi, R. (2010). *Epistemology: A Contemporary Introduction to the Theory of Knowledge* (3rd ed.). Routledge. DOI: 10.4324/9780203846469

Bacon, F. (2008). *The New Organon* (Jardine, L., & Silverthorne, M., Trans.). Cambridge University Press. (Original work published 1620)

Battiste, M. (2011). *Reclaiming Indigenous Voice and Vision*. UBC Press.

Battiste, M., & Henderson, J. Y. (2000). *Protecting Indigenous Knowledge and Heritage: A Global Challenge*. Purich Publishing. DOI: 10.59962/9781895830439

Bhabha, H. K. (1994). *The Location of Culture*. Routledge.

Bhambra, G., Krabbe, J. S., Shilliam, R., Boatcă, M., Rutazibwa, O., Hansen, P., & Popal, M. (2020). Intermezzo I–Knowledge Orders. *Beyond the Master's Tools?: Decolonizing Knowledge Orders, Research Methods and Teaching*, 63.

Blumenbach, J. F. (1775). *On the Natural Varieties of Mankind*. T. Cadell.

Cajete, G. (1994). *Look to the mountain: An ecology of indigenous education.* Kivaki Press, Cajete, G. (2000). *Native Science: Natural Laws of Interdependence.* Clear Light Publishers.

Chao, S. (2020). A tree of many lives: Vegetal teleontologies in West Papua. *HAU,* 10(2), 514–529. DOI: 10.1086/709505

Chilisa, B. (2012). *Indigenous Research Methodologies.* SAGE Publications.

Chowdhury, J. S. (2023a). Voice and Photovoice of the Bangladeshi Migrant Workers in Malaysia: An Ethnography of the 3rd Space With Reciprocity. In *Handbook of Research on Implications of Sustainable Development in Higher Education* (pp. 314-336). IGI Global.

Chowdhury, J. S., Abd Wahab, H., Saad, M. R. M., Mathbor, G. M., & Hamidi, M. (2023a). *Ubuntu Philosophy for the New Normalcy.* Springer Nature. DOI: 10.1007/978-981-19-7818-0

Chowdhury, J. S., & Roy, P. K. (2023). A Philosophical Reflection of SDG 4 and Our Education Policy: Justified Self-Interest vs. Common Interest. In *Positive and Constructive Contributions for Sustainable Development Goals* (pp. 200–219). IGI Global.

Chowdhury, J. S., Saad, M. R. M., Abd Wahab, H., & Roy, P. K. (2023b). An Introduction to the Critique of Critical Paradigm: Jürgen Habermas and Social Justice. In *Implications of Marginalization and Critical Race Theory on Social Justice* (pp. 49–67). IGI Global. DOI: 10.4018/978-1-6684-3615-8.ch003

Chowdhury, J. S., Wahab, H. A., Saad, R. M., Reza, H., & Ahmad, M. M. (Eds.). (2022). *Reciprocity and its practice in social research.* IGI Global. DOI: 10.4018/978-1-7998-9602-9

Clammer, J., & Giri, A. K. (2013). *Philosophy and Anthropology in Dialogues and Conversations. Philosophy and Anthropology. Border Crossing and Transformations.* Anthem Press.

Clifford, J., & Marcus, G. E. (1986). *Writing Culture: The Poetics and Politics of Ethnography.* University of California Press. DOI: 10.1525/9780520946286

Corntassel, J.. (2018). *Everyday Acts of Resurgence: People, Places, Practices.* Daykeeper Press.

Crotty, M. (1998). The Foundations of Social Research: Meaning and Perspective in the Research Process. *Sage (Atlanta, Ga.).*

Daly, J. (2019). *How Europe Made the Modern World: Creating the Great Divergence*. Bloomsbury Publishing.

Datta, D. M. (1997). *The six ways of knowing: A critical study of the Advaita theory of knowledge*. Motilal Banarsidass.

de Sousa Santos, B. (2018). *The end of the cognitive empire: the coming of age of epistemologies of the south*. Duke University Press. DOI: 10.1215/9781478002000

De Wet, C. H. (2021). *The science of Public Administration: a theoretical and metatheoretical enquiry* (Doctoral dissertation, North-West University (South Africa).

Dei, G. J. S. (2000). *Indigenous Knowledge in Global Contexts: Multiple Readings of Our World*. University of Toronto Press.

Dei, G. J. S. (2000). *Indigenous Knowledge in Global Contexts: Multiple Readings of Our World*. University of Toronto Press.

Deloria, V. (1969). *Custer died for your sins: An Indian manifesto*. University of Oklahoma Press.

Deloria, V. Jr. (1999). *Spirit and Reason: The Vine Deloria Jr. Reader*. Fulcrum Publishing.

Deloria, V. Jr. (2001). *Power and Place: Indian Education in America*. Fulcrum Publishing.

Demeulenaere, E.. (2021). *Animism and Indigenous Epistemology*. Routledge.

Demeulenaere, E., Yamin-Pasternak, S., Rubinstein, D. H., Lovecraft, A. L., & Ickert-Bond, S. M. (2021). Indigenous spirituality surrounding Serianthes trees in Micronesia: Traditional practice, conservation, and resistance. *Social Compass*, 68(4), 548–561. DOI: 10.1177/00377686211032769

Descartes, R. (1985). *The Philosophical Writings of Descartes* (Vol. I). Cambridge University Press.

Dieste, J. (2017). *Praise of Historical Anthropology*. Routledge.

Dilley, R. (2010). [Title of the work if available].

Dilley, R. (2010). Reflections on knowledge practices and the problem of ignorance. *Journal of the Royal Anthropological Institute*, 16(s1), S176–S192. DOI: 10.1111/j.1467-9655.2010.01616.x

Dudley, J. R. (2016). *Spirituality matters in social work: Connecting spirituality, religion, and practice.* Routledge. https://socialwork.uncc.edu/news/2016-08-04/why-spirituality-matters-social-work

Durkheim, E. (1982). *The Rules of Sociological Method* (Halls, W. D., Trans.). Free Press. (Original work published 1895) DOI: 10.1007/978-1-349-16939-9

Efros, I. (1942). Saadia's Theory of Knowledge. *Jewish Quarterly Review (Philadelphia, Pa.)*, 33(2), 133–170. DOI: 10.2307/1451990

Eikeland, O. (2006a). Condescending ethics and action research: Extended review article. *Action Research*, 4(1), 37–47. DOI: 10.1177/1476750306060541

Eikeland, O. (2006b). Phrónêsis, Aristotle, and action research. *International Journal of Action Research*, 2(1), 5–53.

Eikeland, O. (2007). From epistemology to Gnoseology–understanding the knowledge claims of action research. *Management Research News*, 30(5), 344–358. DOI: 10.1108/01409170710746346

Emon, A. M., Levering, M., & Novak, D. (2014). *Natural Law: A Jewish, Christian, and Islamic Trialogue.* Oxford University Press. DOI: 10.1093/acprof:oso/9780198706601.001.0001

Fakhry, M. (2002). *Alfarabi, founder of Islamic Neoplatonism: His life, works and influence.* Oneworld.

Fanon, F. (1967). *White skin, black masks.* Grove Press.

Farabi, A. (2001). *The Political Regime* (Mahdi, F., Trans.). University of Chicago Press.

Ferrier, J. F. (1856). *Institutes of metaphysic: the theory of knowing and being.* W. Blackwood and sons.

Foucault, M. (1972). *The Archaeology of Knowledge.* Pantheon Books.

Gadamer, H. G. (1975). Truth and Method. *Continuum: an Interdisciplinary Journal on Continuity of Care.*

Gallagher, K. T. (2021). The philosophy of knowledge. In *The Philosophy of Knowledge.* Fordham University Press. (Original work published 1964)

Gill, A. (2006). *In search of intuitive knowledge: A comparison of eastern and western epistemology* (Doctoral dissertation, Faculty of Education-Simon Fraser University).

Giri, A. K. (2013). Kant and Anthropology. Philosophy and Anthropology: Border Crossing and Transformations, 141.

Gordon, H. S. (2002). *The history and philosophy of social Science*. Routledge. DOI: 10.4324/9780203423226

Gould, S. J. (1994). The Geometer of Race. Discover governmentality. *Annual Review of Anthropology*, 26(1), 163–183.

Grosfoguel, R. (2013). The structure of knowledge in westernized universities: Epistemic racism/sexism and the four genocides/epistemicides of the long 16th century. *Human Architecture*, 11(1), 73–90.

Grossman, P. (1990). *The Making of a Teacher: Teacher Knowledge and Teacher Education*. Teachers College Press.

Grove, J. (2015). Social sciences and humanities faculties 'to close' in Japan after ministerial intervention Universities to scale back liberal arts and social science courses. https://www.timeshighereducation.com/news/social-sciences-and-humanities-faculties-close-japan-after-ministerial-decree

Habermas, J. (1984). The Theory of Communicative Action, Vol. 1: Reason and the Rationalization of Society. Beacon Press.

Hanson, N. R. (1984). *Patterns of Discovery: An Inquiry into the Conceptual Foundations of Science*. Cambridge University Press.

Hatfield, G. (2014). *Descartes and the Meditations*. Routledge.

Hegel, G. W. F. (2001). *The Phenomenology of Spirit* (Miller, A. V., Trans.). Oxford University Press. (Original work published 1807)

Heidegger, M. (1962). *Being and Time* (Macquarrie, J., & Robinson, E., Trans.). Harper & Row.

Honi Soit. (2021, July 13, 2021). Anthropology and Sociology dissolved at UWA as nationwide job losses continue, https://honisoit.com/2021/07/anthropology-and-sociology-dissolved-at-uwa-as-nationwide-job-losses-continue/

Horrigan, P. G. (2007). *Epistemology: An introduction to the philosophy of knowledge*. IUniverse.

Horrigan, P. G. (2007). *Epistemology: An introduction to the philosophy of knowledge*. IUniverse.

Jeff, B., & Vencovská, A. (2016, December). Ancient Indian Logic and Analogy. In *Logic and Its Applications: 7th Indian Conference, ICLA 2017, Kanpur, India, January 5-7, 2017* [). Springer.]. *Proceedings*, 10119, 198.

Kant, I. (1847). The Critique of Pure Reason. (Original work published 1781).

Kant, I. (2013). *Toward Perpetual Peace and Other Writings on Politics, Peace, and History*. Yale University Press.

Kapila, S. (2007). Race matters: Orientalism and religion, India and beyond c. 1770-1880. *Modern Asian Studies*, 41(3), 471–513. DOI: 10.1017/S0026749X06002526

Kidd, I. J., Medina, J., & Pohlhaus, G. (2017). *Introduction to the Routledge handbook of epistemic injustice*. Routledge. DOI: 10.4324/9781315212043-1

Kimmerer, R. W. (2013). *Braiding Sweetgrass: Indigenous Wisdom, Scientific Knowledge, and the Teachings of Plants*. Milkweed Editions.

King, M. (2016). The Epistemology of Spiritual Happiness. *Journal for the Study of Spirituality*, 6(2), 142–154. DOI: 10.1080/20440243.2016.1235169

King, T. (2016). *The Inconvenient Indian: A Curious Account of Native People in North America*. University of Minnesota Press.

Kleingeld, P. (2014). *Kant and Cosmopolitanism: The Philosophical Ideal of World Citizenship*. Cambridge University Press.

Koller, J. M. (2018). *Asian philosophies*. Routledge. DOI: 10.4324/9781315210254

Kovach, M. (2009). *Indigenous Methodologies: Characteristics, Conversations, and Contexts*. University of Toronto Press.

Kovach, M. (2021). *Indigenous methodologies: Characteristics, conversations, and contexts*. University of Toronto press.

Kuhn, T. (2012). *The Structure of Scientific Revolutions*. University of Chicago Press. DOI: 10.7208/chicago/9780226458144.001.0001

Kuhn, T. S. (1962). *The Structure of Scientific Revolutions*. University of Chicago Press.

Locke, J. (1847). An Essay Concerning Human Understanding. (Original work published 1690).

MacIntyre, A. (1984). *After Virtue: A Study in Moral Theory*. University of Notre Dame Press.

MacKenzie, M. (2022). *Buddhist Philosophy and the Embodied Mind: A Constructive Engagement*. Rowman & Littlefield. DOI: 10.5771/9781538160138

Matilal, B. K. (2017). *Epistemology, logic, and grammar in Indian philosophical analysis*. De Gruyter Mouton.

McCrea, N., Meade, R. R., & Shaw, M. (2017). Solidarity, organising and tactics of resistance in the 21st century: Social movements and community development praxis in dialogue. *Community Development Journal: An International Forum*, 52(3), 385–404. DOI: 10.1093/cdj/bsx029

Meghji, A. (2022). Towards a theoretical synergy: Critical race theory and decolonial thought in Trumpamerica and Brexit Britain. *Current Sociology*, 70(5), 647–664. DOI: 10.1177/0011392120969764

Mensch, J. (2018). *Race and Racism in Continental Philosophy*. Indiana University Press.

Mensch, R. J. (2000). Kant and Blumenbach on the Bildungstrieb: A historical misunderstanding. *Studies in History and Philosophy of Science Part C Studies in History and Philosophy of Biological and Biomedical Sciences*, 31(1), 11–32. DOI: 10.1016/S1369-8486(99)00042-4

Merriam-Webster. (2022). Gnoseology. In Merriam-Webster.com dictionary. Retrieved from https://www.merriam-webster.com

Merriam-Webster (2022). "Gnoseology." *Merriam-Webster.com Dictionary*, Merriam-Webster, https://www.merriam-webster.com/dictionary/gnoseology. Accessed 12 Jul. 2022.

Mignolo, W. D. (2012). *The Darker Side of Western Modernity: Global Futures, Decolonial Options*. Duke University Press.

Moosavi, L. (2020). The decolonial bandwagon and the dangers of intellectual decolonisation. *International Review of Sociology*, 30(2), 332–354. DOI: 10.1080/03906701.2020.1776919

Morrison, K. M. (2014). Animism and a proposal for a post-Cartesian anthropology. In *The handbook of contemporary animism* (pp. 38–52). Routledge.

Nakata, M. (2007). *Disciplining the Savages, Savaging the Disciplines*. Aboriginal Studies Press.

Nasr, S. H. (1964). *Three Muslim Sages: Avicenna, Suhrawardi, Ibn Arabi*. Harvard University Press.

Pels, P. (1997). The anthropology of colonialism: Culture, history, and the emergence of western governmentality. *Annual Review of Anthropology*, 26(1), 163–183. DOI: 10.1146/annurev.anthro.26.1.163

Pels, P. (2008). What has anthropology learned from the anthropology of colonialism? *Social Anthropology*, 16(3), 280–299. DOI: 10.1111/j.1469-8676.2008.00046.x

Perrett, R. W. (1998). *Hindu ethics: A philosophical study* (Vol. 17). University of Hawaii Press. DOI: 10.1515/9780824847043

Ranz, R. (2021). Developing Social Work Students' Awareness of their Spiritual/Religious Identity and Integrating It into Their Professional Identity: Evaluation of a Pilot Course. *British Journal of Social Work*, 51(4), 1. DOI: 10.1093/bjsw/bcab046

Recchiuti, J. L. (2007). *Civic engagement: Social science and progressive-era reform in New York City*. University of Pennsylvania Press.

Rizal, J. (1890). *2011. Events in the Philippine Islands* (Alzona, E., Trans.). National Historical Commission of the Philippines.

Roque, R. (2017). *Headhunting and Colonialism: Anthropology and the Circulation of Human Skulls in the Portuguese Empire, 1870-1930*. Springer.

Russell, B. (1945). *A History of Western Philosophy*. Simon and Schuster.

Russell, B. (1945). *A History of Western Philosophy*. Simon and Schuster.

Russell, B. (1945). *A History of Western Philosophy*. Simon and Schuster.

Sachau, E. C. (2013). *Alberuni's India: An Account of the Religion, Philosophy, Literature, Geography, Chronology, Astronomy, Customs, Laws and Astrology of India* (Vol. I). Routledge.

Said, E. (1993). *Culture and Imperialism*. Vintage Books.

Said, E. W. (1978). *Orientalism*. Pantheon Books.

Sandford, M. (2018). *Kant, Cosmopolitanism, and Human History*. Oxford University Press.

Sanguineti, J. J. (1988). Epistemology and Methodology: A Research Program.

Sanguineti, J. J. (1988). *Logic and gnoseology* (Vol. 9). Pontifical Urban University.

Sanguineti, J. J. (1988). *Logic and gnoseology* (Vol. 9). Pontifical Urban University.

Scheler, M. (2009). *The Phenomenology of Knowledge*. Northwestern University Press.Battiste, M., & Henderson, J. Y. (2000). *Protecting Indigenous Knowledge and Heritage: A Global Challenge*. Purich Publishing.

Scheper-Hughes, N. (1995). The Primacy of the Ethical: Propositions for a Militant Anthropology.

Shaposhnikova, Y. V., & Shipovalova, L. V. (2018). The demarcation problem in the history of Science, or what historical epistemology has to say about cultural identification. *Epistemology & Philosophy of Science*, 55(1), 52–66. DOI: 10.5840/eps20185518

Shulman, L. S. (1987). Knowledge and teaching: Foundations of the new reform. *Harvard Educational Review*, 57(1), 1–22. DOI: 10.17763/haer.57.1.j463w79r56455411

Simpson, L. B. (2014). *Dancing on Our Turtle's Back: Stories of Nishnaabeg Re-Creation, Resurgence, and a New Emergence*. Arbeiter Ring Publishing.

Smith, L. T. (2021). *Decolonising methodologies: Research and indigenous peoples*. Zed Books Ltd. (Original work published 1999) DOI: 10.5040/9781350225282

Smith, L. T. (2023). *Indigenous Storywork: Educating the Heart, Mind, Body, and Spirit*. UBC Press.

Smith, T. (Ed.). (2023). *Animism and Philosophy of Religion*. Springer Nature. DOI: 10.1007/978-3-030-94170-3

Spivak, G. C. (1988). Can the Subaltern Speak? In C. Nelson & L. Grossberg (Eds.), Marxism and the Interpretation of Culture. Macmillan.

Spivak, G. C. (2004). *Critique of Postcolonial Reason: Toward a History of the Vanishing Present*. Harvard University Press.

Steinmetz, G. (2013). A child of the empire: British sociology and colonialism, 1940s–1960s. *Journal of the History of the Behavioral Sciences*, 49(4), 353–378. DOI: 10.1002/jhbs.21628 PMID: 24037899

Studley, J., & Horsley, P. (2018). Spiritual governance as an indigenous behavioural practice. *Cultural and spiritual significance of nature in protected areas: Governance, management and policy*.

Suzuki, D. T. (1953). The Natural Law in the Buddhist Tradition. *Nat. L. Inst. Proc.*, 5, 89.

The Guardian. (2021b, 25 May, 2021). 'Horrific' cuts in pipeline for English universities and students, by Richard Adams Education editorhttps://https://www.theguardian.com/education/2021/may/24/horrific-cuts-in-pipeline-for-english-universities-and-students

The Guardinn. (2021a, 29 March, 2021). war against humanities at Britain's universities, https://www.theguardian.com/education/2015/mar/29/war-against-humanities-at-britains-universities

Todd, Z. (2016). An Indigenous feminist's take on the ontological turn: 'Ontology' is just another word for colonialism. *Journal of Historical Sociology*, 29(1), 4–22. DOI: 10.1111/johs.12124

Tuck, E., & McKenzie, M. (2015). Relational validity and the "where" of inquiry: Place and land in qualitative research. *Qualitative Inquiry*, 21(7), 633–638. DOI: 10.1177/1077800414563809

Tuck, E., & Yang, K. W. (2012). Decolonization is not a metaphor. *Decolonization*, 1(1), 1–40.

Tuck, E., & Yang, K. W. (2012). Decolonization is not a metaphor. *Decolonization*, 1(1), 1–40.

Turner, E. (2008). Exploring the work of Victor Turner: Liminality and its later implications. *Suomen Antropologi. Journal of the Finnish Anthropological Society*, 33(4).

Van Meijl, T. (2019). Doing indigenous epistemology: Internal debates about inside knowledge in Māori society. *Current Anthropology*, 60(2), 155–173. DOI: 10.1086/702538

Van Meijl, T. (2019). *Indigenous Movements and Spirituality: Struggles for Cultural Survival and Self-Determination*. Berghahn Books.

Wilkinson, I., & Kleinman, A. (2016). *A Passion for Society: How We Think about Human Suffering*. University of California Press. DOI: 10.1525/california/9780520287228.001.0001

Wilson, S. (2008). *Research is Ceremony: Indigenous Research Methods*. Fernwood Publishing.

Yannakakis, Y. (2023). *Indigenous Rights and Cultural Revival in Latin America*. Cambridge University Press.

Young, R. J. (2020). *Postcolonialism: A very short introduction*. Oxford University Press. DOI: 10.1093/actrade/9780198856832.001.0001

KEY TERMS AND DEFINITIONS

Archeology of Western Knowledge: Michel Foucault created the term "archaeology of Western knowledge" to describe a strategy for uncovering historical and structural features of knowledge in Western nations. It investigates classification, language, and societal influence, as well as how knowledge forms, institutions, and power intersect over time. It challenges conventional historical narratives by disclosing latent frameworks, demonstrating that knowledge is not neutral but is affected by complex cultural, social, and political factors, ultimately affecting our view of its formation and importance.

Disciple of Discipline: Uncritical social scientists who follow the Eurocentric concepts, methodologies and those who blindly follow of supervisors' advice without knowing the root of the advised theory or method.

Indigenous Gnoseology: This Indigenous Gnoseological stand is an important aspect of vibrant Indigenous life. Without this, a terrifying application, such as other researchers, can be implied in producing knowledge, ultimately reproducing and legalizing the west that we excoriate. Indigenous Cosmology is a separate setting, a different face, an independent science and thus creates another dimension of subjectivity and reflections when it comes to the question of 'data validity.

JPR Self-Repairing Model: The combination of Rakhain Sitama (healers) and Bante (Spiritual leader) shows some eating habits, sleep cycles and some of our generic breathing techniques. Which helps in Esoteric—balanced blood flow, thinner cells, low blood pressure, low heart rate and balanced pulse. With Exoteric techniques—one can keep the blood cells open and keeps the right airflow and obstacles. And, above all, it helps to keep our cognition and consciousness sensual, our body-mind-spirit in a balanced manne.

Indigenous Gnoseology: A working definition of IG is as *Indigenous Gnoseology is the guidelines of being Practical, Reciprocal with academic wisdom and knowledge and Indigenous wholism for intellectual happiness.'*

Chapter 5
Harnessing Pedagogical Content Knowledge for Cross-Disciplinary Innovation in Engineering

H. Kareemullah
https://orcid.org/0009-0000-3045-3834
Department of Electronics and Instrumentation Engineering, B.S.A. Crescent Institute of Science and Technology, Chennai, India

M. D. Mohan Gift
https://orcid.org/0000-0003-4939-8809
Department of Mechanical Engineering, Grace College of Engineering, Tuticorin, India

R. Bhaskaran
https://orcid.org/0000-0003-0680-9006
Department of Information Technology, PSNA College of Engineering and Technology, Dindigul, India

T. Santhana Krishnan
https://orcid.org/0000-0003-4716-8364
Department of Electrical and Electronics Engineering, Rajalakshmi Engineering College, Thandalam, India

S. Senthil kumar
https://orcid.org/0000-0001-5910-1322
Department of Electrical and Electronics Engineering, New Prince Shri Bhavani College of Engineering and Technology, Chennai, India

DOI: 10.4018/979-8-3693-0655-0.ch005

ABSTRACT

The chapter will present the integration of PCK toward the fostering of cross-disciplinary innovation within engineering. Being itself the composite of content expertise with effective teaching strategies, PCK acts as the main ingredient in developing holistic approaches to education that transcend traditional boundaries. On the basis of PCK, educators will be able to design curricula that enhance not only disciplinary-based understanding but also interdisciplinary collaboration. The chapter shares cases on how PCK-driven approaches to engineering education will let learners solve complex problems creatively and think innovatively about a wide range of contexts. It also provides strategies for embedding PCK in engineering programs through collaborative projects, interdisciplinary workshops, and experiential learning opportunities.

INTRODUCTION

The shifting landscape of challenges in engineering demands innovative solutions that exceed conventional boundaries between the disciplines. The more complex and integrated the engineering problems, the more there is a need for educational approaches that can enhance cross-disciplinary collaboration and creative problem-solving. Pedagogical Content Knowledge provides a correspondingly promising framework to match these challenges by bringing together deep subject matter expertise with effective teaching strategies. The chapter explores how harnessed PCK can drive cross-disciplinary innovation in engineering education, equipping students with the skills and competencies to solve multifaceted problems in dynamic collaborative environments(Bogoslowski et al., 2021).

Pedagogical Content Knowledge was a term first brought about by Lee Shulman in the late 1980s, which means exactly what it says: it reflects the nuanced understanding teachers have about how best to teach specific content. Going beyond the content knowledge, which is an essential ingredient in PCK, pedagogical dimensions zero in on how educators make complex concepts accessible and engaging for learners. This definition clearly takes account of the fact that teaching is not solely about making available information; it lays emphasis on knowing how students learn and knowing how to facilitate such learning in meaningful ways(Cima et al., 2021).

PCK assumes a very particular meaning within the framework of engineering education by representing the answer to the question of how to teach technical content in such a way that it simultaneously becomes understandable and useable. Engineering disciplines, and particularly complex product development, are interdisciplinary by nature. They draw upon insights from mathematical, physical, and computer science areas. These conventional educational models do little to help a student integrate the knowledge in the application of real-life problems. It is in this regard that PCK can be used by educators in designing curricula that would fill up these gaps, and consequently provide the right environment for learning in which interdisciplinary thinking and innovation can thrive(Miller et al., 2022).

One of the central aspects of PCK concerns the applicative way in which knowledge is treated. Within engineering education, this would imply that there should be developed ways of teaching that transcend merely teaching something theoretically to also demonstrate how it can be applied in real life. For example, instead of teaching mathematics and physics as subjects on their own, the teacher can integrate these when problems in engineering are given for which their application is needed. The approach allows the students to become aware of how different strands of knowledge interrelate in the understanding and use of collaborative knowledge toward the solution of complex engineering challenges(Wu, 2022).

The integration of PCK into the engineering education curriculum would further foster critical skills for cross-disciplinary innovation: problem-solving, creative thinking, and collaboration—the very competencies that have become ever more important in today's engineering workforce. Learning designs that move these skills to the forefront will help students work efficiently in multidisciplinary teams on complex problems and come up with innovative solutions. With respect to these, applications of PCK can be made through collaborative projects, interdisciplinary workshops, or experiential learning opportunities that help to foster these skills(Yazici et al., 2020).

Another important advantage of PCK lies in the realm of improving relevance and engaging engineering education. Oftentimes, traditional ways of teaching may leave the impression of disconnection from practice, eventually resulting in the disengagement of students. PCK is a tool for the design of curricular relevance, problems, and collaborative projects, which make learning engaging and purposeful. This not only helps students develop an in-depth understanding of the material but also applies the knowledge in real life(Kähkönen & Hölttä-Otto, 2022).

The chapter will discuss practical ways in which PCK can be integrated into the learning environments of engineering education. This includes case studies of successful curriculum innovations for using PCK as a basis for cross-disciplinary collaboration. For example, projects requiring collaboration between engineering students and those majoring in other disciplines could provide some important insights into how PCK allows the bridging of different knowledge fields. These examples shall show just how possible it is to have PCK-driven approaches leading to more effective and innovative practice development within education(Tai & Ting, 2020).

In the final section, this chapter shall deal with common challenges pertaining to the use of PCK in engineering education, such as possible resistance to changing traditional methods of teaching, coordination of the interdisciplinary nature of projects, or professional development that would assist educators in building their PCK. Pointing out these challenges and possibilities for their solution, the chapter will provide a complete view of PCK use in enabling innovation in engineering education effectively(Pyrialakou et al., 2020).

In summary, Pedagogical Content Knowledge is an important framework that helps in developing cross-disciplinary innovation within the context of engineering education. Bringing deep content knowledge into conjunction with teaching practices, PCK helps in establishing learning environments that foster interdisciplinary approaches toward ways of collaboration, problem-solving, and creative thinking. This prepares students to solve complex engineering challenges while offering them a more engaging and relevant educational experience. As engineering problems change, in some cases becoming more interdisciplinary in nature, PCK will become central to the development of future engineers who can work towards technological progress and solve a set of difficult global challenges(Borda et al., 2020).

Background: Pedagogical Content Knowledge is the intersection of knowledge about content and effective teaching practices. First coined in the late 1980s by Lee Shulman, PCK recognizes that teachers need to develop a deep understanding of subject matter and concomitant pedagogical skills in order to communicate complex content effectively. Of particular relevance in engineering education, PCK has been considered to play a very important role in methods for engaging and teaching students about highly technical material.

State-of-the-art solutions to complex, situated problems in engineering today often demand interdisciplinary approaches. More traditional curricula in engineering have focused on expert knowledge that is rooted in different specialist domains and therefore often leave a gap in the possibilities for students to integrate insights from the different fields. By including PCK, instructors can design learning activities that bridge these gaps and support an atmosphere where cross-disciplinary innovation flourishes. The chapter tries to emphasize ways in which PCK can be harnessed to further engineering education in a way that will put the different engineering disciplines and other subjects into closer collaboration. This chapter argues for the insertion of PCK into curriculum development, focusing on experiential learning and projects that require collaboration around various expertise. To understand and apply PCK in this manner is very important for the multi-faceted challenges that modern engineering careers are going to throw at students.

Scope: In this chapter, PCK will be applied to create pedagogical and curricular innovation in the prospect of a cross-disciplinary engineer education. It is concerned with the integration of PCK into the design of curricula to foster interdisciplinary collaboration and skills in problem-solving and creative thinking. Case studies and examples will be highlighted throughout to show precisely how PCK could be used in creating dynamic learning environments. It also discusses the problems of PCK implementation and future directions of PCK's role in advancing engineering education and innovation. An overview is given for the benefit of educators and curriculum designers.

Objectives: The chapter aims to explain how PCK can be used in the pursuit of cross-disciplinary innovation in engineering education. It tries to show how the engineering curricula could be designed and integrated with PCK to promote interdisciplinary collaboration and creative problem-solving. It illustrates practical strategies and case studies as a means to provide educators with actionable insights into designing effective, cross-disciplinary learning experiences. It also aims at underlining the role of experiential learning and helping to resolve common problems related to the use of PCK, all in the interest of development in engineering education and building a foundation for technological innovation.

CONCEPTUAL FRAMEWORK

Defining Pedagogical Content Knowledge

Pedagogical Content Knowledge is the conceptual idea that combines deep knowledge in content and ways of teaching effectively. Proposed by educational psychologist Lee Shulman in the late 1980s, PCK is where one's content knowledge intersects with pedagogical approach; it requires knowing the content and how to make it available for teaching to the students in a way that will yield learning and understanding(Wu, 2022).

PCK is made up of basically the following:

- Content Knowledge: This is the teacher's personal understanding of the subject matter. It includes facts, concepts, theories, and procedures that concern the discipline in general.
- Pedagogical Knowledge: It means the ways and means to teach content effectively, such as techniques of presentation, methods to engage students, or ways to adapt one's teaching to learning needs that are diverse.
- Knowledge of Context: When an educational context is defined—the previous knowledge and learning styles of the students and difficulty issues specific to students—it is called effective teaching.
- Knowledge of Student Understanding: PCK is also an understanding of common forms of explanation in a particular content area. Those explanations

- have inherent problems that students would typically face. This is what helps a teacher tune his teaching to meet those problems effectively.
- Curriculum and Assessment Knowledge: The context of the content within the curriculum will also be a part of the knowledge, as well as ways to assess the learning of students such that an understanding of the concept is assured.

PCK is, therefore, a dynamic and integrated form of knowledge that enables the educator to design and deliver instruction that is content-rich yet pedagogically sound. It helps teachers in translating complex ideas into accessible and engaging lessons, hence an important aspect of effective teaching.

PCK and Its Role in Engineering Education

PCK assumes a very important role to bridge the wide gap between theoretical knowledge and practical application in engineering education. In nature, much of the technical content knowledge goes with engineering, together with the ability to use that knowledge in solving real-life problems. By combining theory and practice, the relevance becomes expressed specifically with PCK(Bogoslowski et al., 2021).

a) Improving Curriculum Design: It can have a significant influence on the design and implementation of curricular activities in engineering education. By integrating PCK, educators can develop curricula that not only cover all the most fundamental concepts of engineering but also place real importance on their practical applications. For example, other than teaching principles of theory in isolation, with PCK, educators could insert real-world problems and case studies to make the content more relevant and engaging to students. Students can directly see an application of what is being taught and be better placed to face professional challenges.

b) Interdisciplinary Learning in Engineering Education: Very often, problems within the discourse of engineering education draw upon knowledge in mathematics, physics, and computer science. PCK will support learning that is interdisciplinary by assisting the teacher in designing lessons that bring together concepts from various disciplines. For example, the project-based learning approach would be very effective in showing students how principles in engineering are linked to concepts in computer programming. Such integration will foster a holistic understanding of complex problems and help students to think outside of traditional class boundaries.

c) Facilitating Active Learning and Problem-Solving: PCK puts forth the message of active learning strategies, including problem-based learning and collaborative projects. In an engineering curriculum, students leverage these skills to develop critical thinking and complex problem-solving. Using PCK, instructors design learning activities which will confront the learner with scenarios requiring application of knowledge, teaming, and innovation. These experiences are critical in the students' preparation to tackle complex, multidisciplinary problems that they will encounter in their professional careers.

d) Getting at Student Misconceptions: One of the essential elements of PCK pertains to determining common misconceptions students hold about a subject and doing something about it. Abstractions and complex approaches to solutions are usual hurdles in the field of engineering that students commonly have to be faced head-on. PCK, hence, empowers teachers to anticipate these types of problems with mechanisms that clearly unravel misconceptions and drive home key concepts. Addressing these in this very open manner leads to increased understanding on the part of the student and allows for the shoring up of principles before progression to more advanced concepts is attempted.

e) Supporting Professional Development: The proper implementation of PCK in engineering education, as described, also needs continuous professional development of educators. That means training teachers to integrate PCK into teaching practices and keeping pace with evolution in both engineering content and pedagogical strategies. Through the support of professional development programs, educators could increase their PCK and better guide students toward learning and innovation.

Concisely, Pedagogical Content Knowledge is among the most important frameworks aimed at improving engineering education. It is through the integration of deep content knowledge with effective practices of teaching that PCK helps teachers derive curricula that are both theoretically robust and practically relevant. Interdisciplinary learning is encouraged, active problem-solving is supported, student misconceptions are addressed, and continuous professional development is underlined. In view of the fact that engineering challenges are changing over time, PCK will become critical in the preparation of students so that they are able to contribute to such innovative solutions in a manner that advances the field.

PCK IN ENGINEERING CURRICULUM DESIGN

Strategies for Integrating PCK into Engineering Courses

The integration of PCK into the engineering curriculum design involves developing educational experiences that combine deep content understanding with pedagogical actions specially tailored to enhance learning(Borda et al., 2020; Perpignan et al., 2020). Examples of strategies to achieve this are as follows:

Figure 1. Strategies to integrate PCK into engineering courses

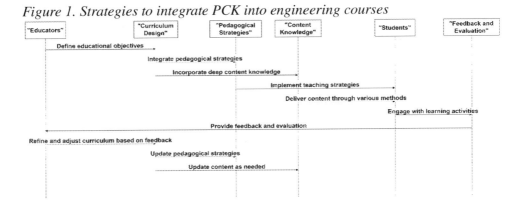

Figure 1 exemplifies the integration of PCK into courses in engineering by portraying this as a cyclic process, thus reinforcing that the design of the curriculum and further improvement is an iterative exercise.

- Contextualized Engineering Learning Experiences: Concepts in engineering could be made more relevant through the design of learning experiences that directly relate to real-world applications. This might be embedded in project-based learning, where students are assigned real engineering problems that span several content areas. For instance, as part of a fluid dynamics course, there could be a project asking students to design a water filtration system where theoretical concepts have to be applied in a practical setting.
- Interdisciplinary Projects: The collaboration between different engineering disciplines or with other disciplines, such as business or environmental science, may further enrich the applications of PCK. One example of an interdisciplinary project could be mechanical engineering students working on a smart wearable device in conjunction with electrical engineering students. Such a project not only expands the breadth of the knowledge and under-

standing of students but also shows how different engineering principles interact with each other.
- Active Learning Techniques: Implementation of active learning strategies, such as flipped classrooms, peer instruction, and problem-based learning, engages students and helps them reinforce their understanding. In a flipped class, theoretical content is studied outside the classroom; the time in class is used for problems and discussions. This creates opportunities for more interactive and hands-on applications of engineering concepts.
- Tailored Pedagogical Approaches: PCK can be utilized by educators in tailoring teaching approaches to address relevant student needs. For instance, the application of formative assessments to check students' understanding of concepts for appropriateness ensures that learning is aligned in relation to their needs; this may involve some change in assignments, offering additional resources, or covering different lecture content dependent upon student progress.

Work through Examples of Realistic Scenarios: Much more engaging and practical material can be included in the course by the educator through the use of case studies and simulations of real engineering challenges. For instance, taking students through a simulation on a bridge design project allows them to apply theoretical knowledge on a realistic engineering problem and thus appreciate the nuances and constraints of actual engineering work.

CASE STUDIES OF PCK-DRIVEN CURRICULUM INNOVATIONS

Case Study 1: MIT Integrated Design & Management Program

The Massachusetts Institute of Technology (MIT) has developed a program, Integrated Design & Management, that embodies the ideology of PCK in engineering studies. The program seamlessly integrates the classic and fundamental principles of engineering design with that of management and entrepreneurship-related studies. Through this, the underlying character of the curriculum implicitly suggests an interdisciplinary approach. This program is designed for conducting projects that involve engineering principles and, at the same time, attempt to see a standpoint in the market requirements or the business strategy that it might fulfill. The curriculum is highly reliant on mutual efforts, collaboration with the industry, and real-world problem solving, which aids in actualization of the potential of technical content knowledge to cultivate both technical content and applicative skills(Venkatasubramanian et al., 2024).

Case Study 2: University of California, Berkeley's Engineering Design Education

University of California, Berkeley relies on engineering knowledge to make PCK, particularly engineering courses, which use work-based studies. Courses such as "Engineering Design for Sustainability" and "Innovative Design for Health" include real-world projects allowing students to work on developing solutions for sustainable energy and healthcare challenges. These courses are multi-disciplinary with content being drawn across different engineering domains, multi-institutional with involvement of industry, and multi-astute since they allow the students to practice theoretical content to solve practical problems. This is the approach that reinforces technical knowledge and infra-engineering teamwork and innovation.

Case Study 3: Georgia Tech's Capstone Design Courses

Another example of PCK-driven curriculum innovation can be seen in the capstone design courses required as part of the curriculum at the Georgia Institute of Technology. These design classes require big engineering projects that often require off-campus clients and address really authentic problems. The students are asked to solve specific needs like enhancing the functionality of a product or improving a process. PCK is undoubtedly incorporated into these courses, which in turn helps the students apply their knowledge in engineering and how to manage projects at the meantime, the way to work in a team, and communicate with the client. This works as a bridge between what is learned theoretically and how to apply it in real life.

Case Study 4: Stanford University's Design Thinking Methodology

At Stanford University, PCK is applied through the design thinking methodology in most courses conducted at the d.school. Design thinking is an approach to engineering in which the emphasis is placed on empathy, ideation, and prototyping in iterations, thereby urging the learner to come up with solutions through an appreciation of user needs and testing of ideas. A case in point through which PCK can enhance creative problem-solving skills and interdisciplinarity in engineering education is that of Stanford, in which it is embedded in the design thinking approach applied in training engineers at an institution. The methodology does more than just teach technical content; it is an embodiment of innovation and user-centered design skills(Singh Madan et al., 2024).

In this view, the incorporation of PCK in the engineering curriculum necessitates strategies for situating learning in practice and fostering interdisciplinary collaborations incorporated through active and real-world learning experiences. The case examples of institutional innovation from MIT, UC Berkeley, Georgia Tech, and Stanford show how PCK could be applied effectively to elicit engaging, relevant, and innovative engineering education. The incorporation of PCK could enable a faculty to better design curricular activities and, thus, better prepare students for typical contemporary engineering practice: complex and interdisciplinary problems.

FACILITATING INTERDISCIPLINARY COLLABORATION

Approaches to Promote Cross-Disciplinary Work

Promotion of interdependence in engineering education requires strategic approaches for meaningful interaction among students and professionals from different disciplines(Verma et al., 2024; Vijaya Lakshmi et al., 2024). Some of the key strategies to facilitate cross-disciplinary work are as follows:

Figure 2. Approaches to promote cross-disciplinary work

Figure 2 shows a classification and visualization of the different approaches for the promotion of cross-disciplinary collaboration in engineering education; it is aimed at presenting an organized view of strategies involved.

- Curriculum Integration: The construction of curricula with aspects of multiple disciplines inherently drives cross-disciplinary approaches of collaboration. For example, the integration of courses that merge engineering principles with business, design, or social sciences empowers students to work on projects involving diversified perspectives and skills. A course in sustainable engineering could contain aspects of environmental science, economics, and policy, encouraging students to look at problems from a multitude of angles.
- Interdisciplinary Projects: This is possible through project-based learning, where students from different disciplines are engaged in solving complex problems. During projects requiring contributions from fields like engineering, computer science, and environmental studies, students will learn from others while applying their own specific knowledge. For instance, the development of a smart irrigation system may require the engineers for the technical design of the system, the computer scientists for the development of software, and the environmental scientists for checking the ecological impacts of the system.

It will further interdisciplinary collaboration by designing collaborative learning environments in the form of physical and virtual spaces that bring students and faculty together across disciplines. Innovation labs, maker spaces, and online collaborative platforms all offer students opportunities to engage in interdisciplinary work. These environments foster the informal interactions, ad hoc brainstorming sessions, and teamwork that are critical to building a collaborative culture.

Seminars and workshops that are cross-disciplinary in nature offer students and researchers the opportunity to get organized. Such seminars and workshops draw experts, researchers, and students not only from the same background but from diverse fields. This chance allows them to share knowledge, discuss current research, and explore potential collaboration. An example is a workshop on emerging technologies where speakers are from the disciplines of engineering, data science, and business. Hosts of the workshop give participants the opportunity to think about how different disciplines come into play with one another.

- Faculty Collaboration: The facilitation of faculty collaboration around research and teaching can model interdisciplinarity for students. Faculty teams, including members from more than one department, may co-design courses, develop joint research projects, and co-supervise student projects. This kind of collaboration will provide for the coherently integrated meshing of diverse perspectives into the curriculum and demonstrate the values of interdisciplinarity.

- Industry Partnerships: Interdisciplinary learning can be brought in through partnerships across industry organizations that are into multi-sector operations. Industry-sponsored projects, internships, and research collaborations provide students with a real-world context in which to apply their knowledge. This may be in the form of a partnership with a technology firm that manufactures wearable health devices, for example. Engineering students would be working with biomedical engineers and data analysts.

Examples of Successful Collaborative Projects

City Science Initiative at MIT— This is an excellent example of interdisciplinary collaboration. Engineers, urban planners, and computer scientists work together with social scientists to find technological and design solutions for problems in cities. Several research projects under this initiative develop smart city solutions coupling data analytics and urban design with social research. In such a process, it combines the expertise of multiple disciplines to bring out comprehensive solutions toward urban sustainability and quality-of-life improvements(Kalaiselvi et al., 2024; Prabhuswamy et al., 2024).

Projects from Stanford's d.school: Stanford University's Hasso Plattner Institute of Design is famously interdisciplinary in its approach to problem-solving. Any given project at the d.school is likely to include students majoring in engineering, design, business, and social sciences. For example, a collaborative process between engineering students, industrial designers, and health professionals produced an inexpensive, easy-to-operate prosthetic limb.

Georgia Tech's IDEaS Program: At Georgia Institute of Technology, the Integrated Design & Engineering Applications program combines students on projects that span across topics in several fields related to engineering and design. One of the most well-known successful projects was the development of an advanced, wearable health monitoring device. Mechanical engineers, software developers, and biomedical experts contributed to the project. This shows how work from cross-disciplinary areas can be combined to find innovative solutions in health technology.

UC Berkeley's Engineering for Sustainability Program: The University of California, Berkeley's program on Engineering for Sustainability focuses on interdisciplinary projects to solve environmental and sustainability challenges. A recent one entailed designing a sustainable energy system for a rural community. Students in the team included engineering students, an environmental scientist, and a policy expert. Students work collaboratively to come up with a technically feasible, environmentally sound, economically viable solution.

MDP University of Michigan's program: At the University of Michigan, students of various majors are brought together to execute real-world projects through its Multidisciplinary Design Program. Take, for example, working on designing a new kind of water purification system where mechanical engineers, chemical engineers, industrial designers, and environmental scientists bring their expertise in to help create an entire solution to solve the problem.

The facilitation of interdisciplinarity in engineering education—through integration of curricula, completion of collaborative projects, design of learning environments, and building faculty and industry partnerships—is set up to be demonstrated by the successful examples from MIT, Stanford, Georgia Tech, UC Berkeley, and the University of Michigan. These instances will help elucidate the strong functions these approaches can take in driving creativity and solving complex problems characterized by differing views and expertise. It is only by promoting cross-disciplinary work that educators can have a better chance of preparing students for the multifaceted challenges lying ahead in the modern engineering landscape.

INNOVATIVE PROBLEM-SOLVING AND CREATIVE THINKING

How PCK Enhances Problem-Solving Skills

PCK enriches problem-solving skills by bringing deep subject matter expertise together with efficient teaching strategies. This puts the learners in a better position to effectively handle problems and come up with creative solutions. Figure 3: How Pedagogical Content Knowledge will enrich problem-solving skills of students undergoing education in engineering(Das et al., 2024; Durairaj et al., 2023).

Figure 3. Integrating PCK principles into engineering education for enhancement

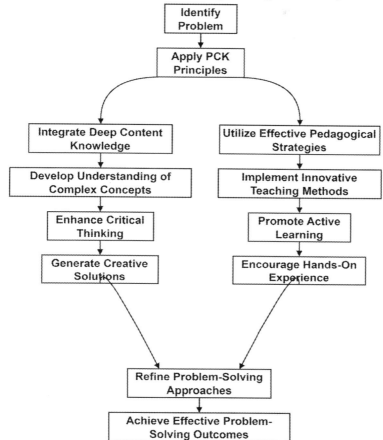

- Understanding the context: PCK allows learners to develop a contextualized understanding of the problems. For these reasons, it is through the integration of content knowledge with pedagogical strategies that teachers will have the ability to design for their students learning experiences that bring as an outcome real-world challenges for the students. For instance, they may be asked to develop a sustainable energy system for a given community in an engineering course. In this way, students will not only learn theoretical concepts but also how these can be used; this later thing develops their problem-solving capabilities.
- Application of Theoretical Knowledge: PCK helps to apply theoretical knowledge to solve practical problems with the student. By employing pedagogical

strategies that place great emphasis on problem-based learning, the teacher encourages learners to practically apply their content knowledge in different contexts. The hands-on practice allows students to experiment with different solutions, test their hypotheses, and repeat the improvements they make to their design. For example, a unit on mechanical engineering with real-world case studies helps students apply their lessons in the principles of thermodynamics and materials science to actual engineering problems.

- Identification of Big Ideas: PCK helps a teacher know the important ideas to underscore and model in order for students to be able to solve complex problems. Therefore, understanding common misconceptions and difficulties that students usually have, a teacher tunes his/her teaching accordingly. For example, in a class on computer science, if one had underscored the core algorithms and data structures, a student would have acquired a sound basis and then gone on to handle tougher problems—from developing efficient software systems to solving optimization challenges.
- Facilitation of Critical Thinking: PCK makes a case for developing critical thinking skills by integrating content knowledge with efficient pedagogical strategies. An educator can design activities for the students to analyze, evaluate, and synthesize information. For example, in a course on engineering ethics, students could be asked to use case studies to analyze some of the ethical dilemmas that have developed in practice. This approach enhances critical thinking and assists the learner in developing the ability to make informed decisions based on content knowledge.
- Collaborative Problem Solving: PCK brings together pedagogical moves that promote collaborative problem-solving. The students work in groups to solve problems collectively through collaborative projects, group discussions, and peer reviews. For instance, in a product design project, students from various majors have to put their different expertise together to come up with an innovative solution.

Fostering Creativity through Interdisciplinary Learning

Interdisciplinary learning doesn't only give an open approach to different perspectives but it cultivates creativity through exposure to different approaches. Exposure to different approaches through melding together different areas of knowledge leads to a way of outward thinking while allowing innovation of coming up with solutions(Durairaj et al., 2023). Now here is how interdisciplinary learning boosts creativity:

- Diverse perspective exposure: With an interdisciplinary learning approach, students are exposed to the multiplicity of points of view and problem-solving. Working with peers of other disciplines fosters the students' exposure to other methods and viewpoints that can help wake up new ideas and methodologies. For example, a project done by a combination of engineering, design, and business students may very creatively present fusion of ideas on the aspects of feasibility, user experience, and market viability.
- Synthesis of Knowledge: By integrating information from different areas of learning, a student learns how to assimilate concepts and methods in a new way and thus identify and develop fresh solutions that combine diverse expertise. For example, a project that combines engineering and environmental science may result in the production of a new kind of eco-friendly material or technology.
- Experimentation Encouragement: Interdisciplinary learning encourages experimentation by providing learners with the freedom to explore different approaches and try out new ideas. Such flexibility in experimenting with methods and concepts breeds creativity and innovativeness. For instance, a design project that pulls elements from engineering, art, and psychology may come up with really unique and creative ways of addressing functionality and aesthetics.
- Collaboration and Teamwork: Many a time, interdisciplinary projects involve teamwork, which enhances creativity with the diverse skills and knowledge within the team. Collaborative environments are rich in brainstorming and idea generation. For example, students are at liberty to build on other ideas to come up with more creative solutions. In this light, if one was working on a healthcare technology project, engineers, medical professionals, and user experience designers can all contribute to creating an innovative product.
- Problem Framing and Reframing: This interdisciplinary learning enables the students to frame and reframe problems from various dimensions. Approaching the problems from multiple angles may assist the student in going deeper into issues at hand and coming up with new solutions. For instance, an interdisciplinary team that is tasked to investigate a problem in transportation could take into account technical, environmental, social, and economic dimensions and hence go on to develop more comprehensive and creative solutions.
- Soft Skills Development: Through such interdisciplinary learning, some of the very important soft skills, like communication, collaboration, and critical thinking in enhancing creativity, are developed. Through different teams, learners will have the ability to communicate ideas, work with others, and think critically about problems.

Summary: PCK enhances a person's problem-solving skills by providing the framework through which to apply content knowledge in practical problems, facilitating critical thinking, and collaborative efforts. Interdisciplinary learning enhances creativity through exposing students to different perspectives, integrating knowledge from various fields, promoting experimentation, and enhancing soft skills. Only with the inclusion of PCK and interdisciplinary approaches can one set their students more towards the ability to fully overcome complex challenges and devise innovative solutions within their professional callings.

EXPERIENTIAL LEARNING AND PCK

Implementing Hands-On Learning Opportunities

One of the most critically important pedagogical approaches is experiential learning, in which students directly engage in experiences enhancing their knowledge and skills. Pedagogical Content Knowledge could make real experiential learning much more effective by ensuring that learning experiences are pedagogically sound and deeply connected with what is being taught(Venkatasubramanian et al., 2024). Figure 4 shows a gradual integration of PCK into the experiential learning process in order to attain real effectiveness and impact from hands-on experiences as a result of these learning experiences. Following is an example of how, through PCK, experiential learning could be effectively carried out:

Figure 4. Implementing hands-on learning opportunities

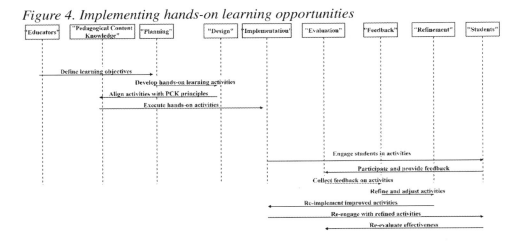

Desiging real-world projects: Embedding real-life projects into the curriculum provides a great opportunity for students to have a practical experience that bridges the gap between theory and practice. PCK is instrumental toward helping a teacher design relevant projects for specific content and attain the pedagogical goals for the same. For instance, in an engineering course, it could be designing how to implement a sustainable energy system for a local community. The project combines knowledge of engineering, environmental science, and economic analyses, thus making it a comprehensive project for student training.

Simulations and prototyping are experiential ways of learning where students can test the concept in a controlled environment. PCK allows teachers to create simulations that accurately mirror real-life situations and problems. For instance, in a mechanical engineering course, this could include a simulation of the performance for various materials under various conditions. In contrast, prototyping allows students to build and test physical models of their designs, offering immediate feedback in ways that create a basis for iterative improvement.

Field experiences and site visits give students an opportunity to see and engage in the actual application. PCK will ensure that such experiences are very well integrated into the curriculum and enlighten the learner with associated valuable insights related to content. For instance, in a course on civil engineering, the site visit may mean visits to construction projects under implementation where they could view design principles and construction techniques put into practice.

Case-Based Learning: This is where learners use cases, either existing or imaginary, to apply their theoretical knowledge in solving complex problems. PCK enables a teacher to choose relevant cases and structure them in ways that best fit their learning objectives and content coverage. For example, students working on a business engineering course will be analyzing a case of a company deciding whether to acquire new technology. In this way, students get to use their knowledge in engineering and business concepts in a real-life situation.

Collaborative Learning Activities: This run of activities, from projects run in groups to team problem activities, uses the PCK to help ensure that students will be able to collaborate appropriately when applying the knowledge that they have gained. For instance, it could be a project in which students at an engineering campus were partnered with design students in developing a process to create a new product. The PCK guides an educator on how to structure these activities to ensure high learning achievements and how to ensure students learn how to apply themselves in both their technical and collaborative skills.

Impact of Experiential Learning on Innovation

Experiential learning is nourishing innovation, as it gives the platform where the learner can apply their knowledge and ideas in a creative and pragmatic manner. Improvement of Problem-Solving Abilities: Experiential learning empowers its pupils to face the real challenges in world scenarios and thereby nurtures the way of thinking and their abilities to solve problems. Hands-on projects help students develop an approach to various complex issues, be creative with solutions, and propose multiple design alternatives. For example, exercising project learning in an engineering course might lead the students to utilize innovation solutions for optimizing a manufacturing process(Agrawal et al., 2023; Das et al., 2024; Durairaj et al., 2023).

- Encouragement of Creativity: Hands-on learning experiences encourage creativity by enabling students to explore different ideas and approaches. The freedom in exploration and prototyping encourages students to think outside the box and develop new solutions. For example, a design challenge in which students are asked to make a new kind of wearable technology could lead to radical breakthroughs in functionality and user experience.
- Relevance to the real world: Experiential learning necessarily relates back to real-world application of academic content, experiences, and therefore highly increases relevance and motivation for students. This relevance may very well be a factor that motivates students to think creatively about how their knowledge can be applied to meet current challenges and opportunities. For instance, a field-based project on environmental sustainment may drive students to develop innovative ways to reduce carbon emission.
- Development of Practical Skills: Through the course of practical activities, learners get to develop practical skills that are helpful in innovation. While working on real projects, learners get to work with tools, techniques, and processes that are relevant to practice in their future careers. For example, students working on the prototyping of a new engineering design acquire relevant experience in testing, iteration, and project management.
- Feedback and Iteration: Experiential learning allows for immediate feedback and iteration, that is critical for innovation. Students who test their ideas and respond to feedback from peers, mentors, and industry professionals can further iterate on the solution and hone their design. For example, building in multiple rounds of prototyping and testing into a product development project enables students to further iterate on their designs from real-world feedback.
- Cultivating a Growth Mindset: Experiential learning nurtures a growth mindset in students due to the emphasis it lays on learning from failures and grit.

Students learning through experience start to view challenges as opportunities for growth and novelty. For instance, design failure in a prototype project is a good learning experience and insight to yield more innovative solutions.

In other words, experiential learning consolidates Pedagogical Content Knowledge to give students hands-on experiences to apply their knowledge in meaningful ways. Such approaches enhance problem-solving skills, creativity, and innovation through a mapping of the academic content to the real world and by encouragement of experimentation, offering feedback that is of great value and practical experience. By using PCK in designing and implementing effective learning opportunities, an educator can set his students up for dynamic and innovative challenges throughout their career.

CHALLENGES AND SOLUTIONS

Challenges that must be faced by applying Pedagogical Content Knowledge effectively can be summed up as the insufficient training of teachers, resistance to change, lack of resources, impossibility of conciliation between content and pedagogy, problems in assessment, and lack of cooperation. Done through investment in professional development, promotion of the culture of innovation, use of technology and partnerships, development of integrated curriculum models, adoption of innovative assessment methods, and collaboration, teachers and educational institutions can negotiate these difficulties and increase the effectiveness of PCK in education(Sharma et al., 2024; Singh Madan et al., 2024; Venkatasubramanian et al., 2024).

Common Obstacles in PCK Application

- Poorly Trained Teachers: Inadequately trained teachers are the paramount problem in the practical use of PCK. Teachers have not been adequately taught how to combine content knowledge with good process knowledge; hence, they haven't been able to effectively design and develop learning experiences.
- Resistance to Change: The resistance of educators and institutions to change may deter PCK-based approaches from adoption. There might be such deep roots of traditional teaching methods and curricula that it becomes difficult to bring in new pedagogical strategies and, at the same time, link them effectively with content knowledge.

- Not Enough Resources: A number of the PCK-dependent strategies require additional resources, whether special materials, technologies, or time for the preparation of curriculum materials. Limited budgets and resources may dampen the effective implementation of PCK in the classroom.
- Content and Pedagogy mismatch: The flux between the depth of content and the pedagogies may always be challenging to resolve. In treatment with hard matter content, it may be pretty tricky to couple complex content with suitable methods to teach them, yielding less efficient or badly matched learning experiences.
- Assessment Challenges: It's a challenge to assess whether and the extent students are applying the things learned through the subject content in bonafide situations. Traditional means of assessment may not be adequate to display how effectively PCK is developed and applied in students.
- Non-collaboration Effectiveness in applying PCK usually requires the collaboration of educators, departments, and institutions. When non-collaboration exists, silo approaches might be underrun, and possibilities for integration of different perspectives and expertise missed.

Strategies for Overcoming Challenges

a) Better Professional Development: Institutions, therefore, need to invest in a complete professional development package with an emphasis on PCK. Training should be offered not only in content knowledge but also in the pedagogical strategies that most effectively integrate such knowledge into teaching. Workshops, seminars, and follow-up assistance have helped many educators in developing and refining their PCK.

b) Innovation Culture: The inertial resistance of educational contexts to this can be overcome only if they acquire the ability to innovate. If educators are encouraged to experiment with new pedagogies and the sharing of successful case studies, and if innovative practices get recognized, the attitude and behavior of people toward the adoption of PCK-based approaches will change.

c) Leveraging Technology and Partnerships: Institutes, in view of the question of limited resources, can utilize technology and foster a network with industry, community organizations, and other educational institutions. Technology might offer access to digital tools and resources that enable PCK-based teaching, while partnerships offer additional resources and expertise. For example, linking up with industry partners can grant access to case studies in real-world scenarios and hands-on experience.

d) Developing Integrated Curriculum Models: The content and pedagogy can be integrated into the curriculum models; the educators work out a model in which an explicit connection between content knowledge and the pedagogical strategies developed exists. While designing the curriculum, it should be done by an interdisciplinary team so that content and pedagogy would be dovetailed. For example, the construction of project-based learning opportunities that integrate disciplines may make a connection between content and pedagogy.

Innovative Assessment Methods: To better determine the effectiveness of teaching based on PCK, teachers should start using innovative assessment methods that capture students' application of knowledge and skills in real-life contexts. These involve performance-based assessments, portfolios, and reflective journals, all of which give a greater overview of the process of students' learning and the effects of the PCK-based approach.

Foster collaboration and communities of practice: Building collaboration among educators, departments, and institutions can enhance the application of PCK. Arranging for communities of practice, where educators share experiences, resources, and best practices in the application of PCK, will diffuse it across different contexts. These may be further supported by collaborative planning sessions and cross-disciplinary projects.

FUTURE DIRECTIONS

The rising trends in engineering education are AI, interdisciplinarity, and sustainability, which are going to configure the future of engineering practice. Pedagogical Content Knowledge will be central in adjusting to these trends for better educational practice and innovation. Through PCK, educators can harness ways of effectively integrating new technologies and approaches to develop a confident engineering student who is ready to tackle complex problems and foster innovation for the future(Das et al., 2024; Durairaj et al., 2023; Kalaiselvi et al., 2024; Prabhuswamy et al., 2024).

Figure 5. Emerging trends and areas of focus within the field of engineering education

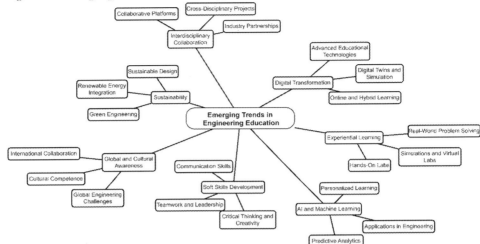

Emerging Trends in Engineering Education

Figure 5 describes the current trends and focus areas in the field of engineering education. This course covers AI and Machine Learning applications in engineering, interdisciplinary collaboration, experiential learning, sustainability, digital transformation, soft skill development, global and cultural awareness, interdisciplinary projects, solution of real-world problems, green engineering, sustainable design, integration of renewable energy, online and hybrid learning, advanced educational technologies, and digital twins/simulation. Communication, teaming, and critical thinking skills are addressed.

a) AI and ML integration: AI and ML in engineering education redesign the way concepts are delivered and applied. Harnessed in the power of the above technologies, construction of intelligent learning tools—like adaptive learning platforms and virtual simulations—can be realized that enable personalized learning experiences with real-time feedback. AI-driven analytics also offer insights into student performance, allowing educators to tailor instruction accordingly.

b) Interdisciplinary and Cross-Disciplinary Approaches: Interdisciplinary and cross-disciplinary approaches are gaining increased traction within the context of engineering education. Knowledge integration from a range of fields, such as computer science, environmental science, and economics, leads to a holistic understanding of problems of high complexity. Projects that combine several disciplines broaden the view of students on the solution space toward completeness and innovation in solving real-life issues that are multifaceted.

c) Emphasis on Soft Skills and Human Factors: More emphasis is given to soft skills, such as communication, teamwork, and ethical reasoning, in today's engineering curriculum. As engineers take up projects that would finally affect diverse communities and the environment, understanding of human factors and societal impacts becomes more crucial. Courses and activities targeting these skills are being integrated into programs to ready students for collaborative and ethical practice.

d) Attention is fast becoming a focus of project-based and experiential learning, with time. The approach focuses more on practical hands-on experience and solution finding in real-life problems. This approach fully satisfies the requirements of the industry and trains students to address the practical challenges of life. Some of the institutions of learning have initiated capstone projects, internships, collaborations with industries, and other such means to provide a student with the opportunity to practically implement their knowledge.

e) Application of Virtual Reality and Augmented Reality: Both are finding places in the curriculum of engineering education because of their capability to make learning very interactive and immersive. In such technologies, students can see the envisioning of complicated systems, run several virtual experiments, and experience abstractions through simulations. VR and AR also make it possible for students to learn remotely and hence enhance opportunities to education through collaboration.

Sustainability and Green Engineering: Ideas of sustainability and green engineering have been increasingly emphasized within undergraduate engineering education. Programs are orienting themselves toward the introduction of principles on environmental stewardship, resource efficiency, and sustainable design into their curriculum. Students are trained to develop solutions that would minimize their impact on the environment and promote sustainable practices in various engineering domains.

Role of PCK in Future Engineering Innovations

a) Interdisciplinary learning support: In the interdisciplinary trend of engineering education, PCK becomes important in the way it should help to amalgamate content from various disciplines harmoniously to achieve meaningful and comprehensible conceptual development. Educators with strong general PCK can embed curricula that develop problem-solving skills through cross-discipline collaboration and innovative practices of solution. For example, integration of mechanical principles, computer science, and environmental science can produce new solutions in the field of renewable energy technologies.

b) Supporting AI-Driven Education: The utility of PCK will be key to maximizing AI and ML technologies for enhancing practices related to education. For the first time in history, educators would be empowered to design a set of truly sophisticated, dynamic, personalized, adaptive AI-driven tools that could be tailored according to their content and pedagogical goals. Educators would use data from AI systems to interpret and adapt teaching styles.

c) Enabling Project-Based Learning: PCK will play a vital role in moving forward with project-based and experiential learning. The educator is going to utilize PCK to create a good project design that meets the aims of learning and real-life applications. Proper use of PCK is going to structure the projects, hence giving relevant experiences, which empower the development of skills vital for innovation: creativity, critical thinking, and problem-solving.

d) Set Up Soft Skills Training: As engineering education increasingly pays attention to soft skills, PCK will be a key means to set them up within the curriculum. Teachers rich in PCK can design the means for teaching the content of communication, teamwork, and ethical reasoning in conjunction with technical content. This will ensure that the graduate is well prepared for sophisticated crossdisciplinary projects, working styles, and functioning within cross-cultural teams.

e) Advancing Sustainability Education: PCK will help advance the incorporation of sustainability principles into the engineering curriculum by reconciling content and effective pedagogies. PCK will help educators design courses to teach students how to design solutions to environmental challenges and practice in sustainable design that prepare students to solve global sustainability challenges. As such, it can help students develop innovative solutions that consider both technical and environmental parameters.

f) Deployment in VR and AR Applications: PCK will thus play a significant role in ensuring that such VR and AR tools are properly aligned in support of pedagogical goals and content. PCK will therefore help educators in designing immersive experiences for enhanced understanding, interactive learning, and feedback creation. This alignment opens up enormous possibilities for the impact of VR and AR on student learning and innovation.

CONCLUSION

This chapter has pushed into the near-revolutionary power of pedagogical content knowledge to reshape engineering education for cross-disciplinary innovation. Built on a blend of deep content knowledge with best-practice pedagogies, PCK offers an exceptionally powerful framework for building educational experiences that are meaningful and impactful.

PCK is an important element in the education of engineers: it ties content and pedagogy together, ensuring rigor on both the technical and pedagogical sides. It will help improve teaching and learning for deeper understanding of complex ideas and applying their knowledge in contexts. Effective curriculum design infuses PCK for engaging, relevant, and aligned CoPs. It is in this way that teachers can provide students with numerous creative opportunities to engage in complex problem-solving through real-world projects, simulations, and hands-on activities. PCK allows for cross-disciplinary collaboration, whereby students will have a chance to deal with different perspectives and expertise, therefore preparing them for modern engineering practice. It builds problem-solving skills, creativity, and gets students to explore and experiment with new ideas. In engineered education of the future, PCK can play a very important role in responding to new emerging trends like AI, interdisciplinarity, and sustainability. If PCK is built into the design, then future educational innovation will better position students for tomorrow.

Thus, Pedagogical Content Knowledge is an indispensable ingredient in quality engineering education. Not only does its application enhance the quality of teaching and learning, but it also innovates and equips students for the dynamic and interdisciplinary nature of modern engineering practice. Moving into the future, PCK will be crucial to creating educational experiences that are transformative yet relevant to changing engineering needs.

ABBREVIATIONS

PCK: Pedagogical Content Knowledge
MIT: Massachusetts Institute of Technology
IDM: Integrated Design and Manufacturing
UC: University of California
IDE: Integrated Development Environment
MDP: Multi-Disciplinary Project or Management Development Program
AI: Artificial Intelligence
ML: Machine Learning
VR: Virtual Reality

AR: Augmented Reality

REFERENCES

Agrawal, A. V., Pitchai, R., Senthamaraikannan, C., Balaji, N. A., Sajithra, S., & Boopathi, S. (2023). Digital Education System During the COVID-19 Pandemic. In *Using Assistive Technology for Inclusive Learning in K-12 Classrooms* (pp. 104–126). IGI Global. DOI: 10.4018/978-1-6684-6424-3.ch005

Bogoslowski, S., Geng, F., Gao, Z., Rajabzadeh, A. R., & Srinivasan, S. (2021). Integrated thinking-a cross-disciplinary project-based engineering education. *Visions and Concepts for Education 4.0: Proceedings of the 9th International Conference on Interactive Collaborative and Blended Learning (ICBL2020)*, 260–267.

Borda, E., Haskell, T., & Boudreaux, A. (2020). Cross-disciplinary learning: A framework for assessing application of concepts across STEM disciplines. *arXiv Preprint arXiv:2012.07906*.

Cima, F., Pazos, P., Kidd, J., Gutierrez, K., Ringleb, S., Ayala, O., & Kaipa, K. (2021). Enhancing preservice teachers' intention to integrate engineering through a cross-disciplinary model. *Journal of Pre-College Engineering Education Research (J-PEER), 11*(2).

Das, S., Lekhya, G., Shreya, K., Shekinah, K. L., Babu, K. K., & Boopathi, S. (2024). Fostering Sustainability Education Through Cross-Disciplinary Collaborations and Research Partnerships: Interdisciplinary Synergy. In *Facilitating Global Collaboration and Knowledge Sharing in Higher Education With Generative AI* (pp. 60–88). IGI Global.

Durairaj, M., Jayakumar, S., Karpagavalli, V., Maheswari, B. U., & Boopathi, S. (2023). Utilization of Digital Tools in the Indian Higher Education System During Health Crises. In *Multidisciplinary Approaches to Organizational Governance During Health Crises* (pp. 1–21). IGI Global. DOI: 10.4018/978-1-7998-9213-7.ch001

Kähkönen, E., & Hölttä-Otto, K. (2022). From crossing chromosomes to crossing curricula–a biomimetic analogy for cross-disciplinary engineering curriculum planning. *European Journal of Engineering Education, 47*(3), 516–534. DOI: 10.1080/03043797.2021.1953446

Kalaiselvi, D., Ramaratnam, M. S., Kokila, S., Sarkar, R., Anandakumar, S., & Boopathi, S. (2024). Future Developments of Higher Education on Social Psychology: Innovation and Changes. In *Advances in Human and Social Aspects of Technology* (pp. 146–169). IGI Global. DOI: 10.4018/979-8-3693-2569-8.ch008

Miller, D. I., Pinerua, I., Margolin, J., & Gerdeman, D. (2022). *Teachers' Pedagogical Content Knowledge in Mathematics and Science: A Cross-Disciplinary Synthesis of Recent DRK-12 Projects*. American Institutes for Research.

Perpignan, C., Baouch, Y., Robin, V., & Eynard, B. (2020). Engineering education perspective for sustainable development: A maturity assessment of cross-disciplinary and advanced technical skills in eco-design. *Procedia CIRP*, 90, 748–753. DOI: 10.1016/j.procir.2020.02.051

Prabhuswamy, M., Tripathi, R., Vijayakumar, M., Thulasimani, T., Sundharesalingam, P., & Sampath, B. (2024). A Study on the Complex Nature of Higher Education Leadership: An Innovative Approach. In *Challenges of Globalization and Inclusivity in Academic Research* (pp. 202–223). IGI Global. DOI: 10.4018/979-8-3693-1371-8.ch013

Pyrialakou, V. D., Dey, K., Martinelli, D., Deskins, J., Fraustino, J. D., Plein, C., Rahman, M. T., Rambo-Hernandez, K. E., & Roy, A. (2020). Holistic engineering: A concept exploration in a cross-disciplinary project course experience. *2020 ASEE North Central Section Conference*. DOI: 10.18260/1-2--35736

Sharma, D. M., Ramana, K. V., Jothilakshmi, R., Verma, R., Maheswari, B. U., & Boopathi, S. (2024). Integrating Generative AI Into K-12 Curriculums and Pedagogies in India: Opportunities and Challenges. *Facilitating Global Collaboration and Knowledge Sharing in Higher Education With Generative AI*, 133–161.

Singh Madan, B., Najma, U., Pande Rana, D., & Kumar, P. K. J., S., S., & Boopathi, S. (2024). Empowering Leadership in Higher Education: Driving Student Performance, Faculty Development, and Institutional Progress. In *Advances in Educational Technologies and Instructional Design* (pp. 191–221). IGI Global. DOI: 10.4018/979-8-3693-0583-6.ch009

Tai, Y., & Ting, Y.-L. (2020). English-learning mobile app designing for engineering students' cross-disciplinary learning and collaboration. *Australasian Journal of Educational Technology*, 36(2), 120–136.

Venkatasubramanian, V., Chitra, M., Sudha, R., Singh, V. P., Jefferson, K., & Boopathi, S. (2024). Examining the Impacts of Course Outcome Analysis in Indian Higher Education: Enhancing Educational Quality. In *Challenges of Globalization and Inclusivity in Academic Research* (pp. 124–145). IGI Global.

Verma, R., Christiana, M. B. V., Maheswari, M., Srinivasan, V., Patro, P., Dari, S. S., & Boopathi, S. (2024). Intelligent Physarum Solver for Profit Maximization in Oligopolistic Supply Chain Networks. In *AI and Machine Learning Impacts in Intelligent Supply Chain* (pp. 156–179). IGI Global. DOI: 10.4018/979-8-3693-1347-3.ch011

Vijaya Lakshmi, V., Mishra, M., Kushwah, J. S., Shajahan, U. S., Mohanasundari, M., & Boopathi, S. (2024). Circular Economy Digital Practices for Ethical Dimensions and Policies for Digital Waste Management. In *Harnessing High-Performance Computing and AI for Environmental Sustainability* (pp. 166–193). IGI Global., DOI: 10.4018/979-8-3693-1794-5.ch008

Wu, Z. (2022). Understanding teachers' cross-disciplinary collaboration for STEAM education: Building a digital community of practice. *Thinking Skills and Creativity*, 46, 101178. DOI: 10.1016/j.tsc.2022.101178

Yazici, H. J., Zidek, L. A., & St. Hill, H. (2020). A study of critical thinking and cross-disciplinary teamwork in engineering education. *Women in Industrial and Systems Engineering: Key Advances and Perspectives on Emerging Topics*, 185–196.

Chapter 6
Mapping the Growth of Pedagogical Content Knowledge Across Teaching Careers

Thangjam Ravichandra
https://orcid.org/0000-0002-9243-2534
Department of Finance and Accounts, Alliance School of Business, Alliance University, Bengaluru, India

M. Mariappan
Department of Civil Engineering, Dr. Mahalingam College of Engineering and Technology, Pollachi, India

C. V. Padmaja
https://orcid.org/0000-0003-0935-0958
Department of English, GITAM University, Visakhapatnam, India

Narasinga Rao Barnikana
https://orcid.org/0000-0001-5443-9850
Department of English, National Law Institute University, Bhopal, India

T. Saravanan
Department of Electronics and Communication Engineering, New Prince Shri Bhavani College of Engineering and Technology, Chennai, India

Sampath Boopathi
https://orcid.org/0000-0002-2065-6539
Department of Mechanical Engineering, Muthayammal Engineering College, Namakkal, India

ABSTRACT

This chapter of the book presents how pedagogical content knowledge among teachers undergoes changes throughout their careers. The authors try to trace how this kind of expertise develops and finally impacts teaching practices. By analyzing data on a longitudinal basis, case studies will be made in order to realize how PCK develops among teachers from the initial VET stage into the entire life

DOI: 10.4018/979-8-3693-0655-0.ch006

career history of a teacher, mainly focusing on key factors that might lead to its development. It discusses how professional development, reflective practice, and classroom experience work to improve PCK and how these are changed with the changes in educational contexts and student needs. The chapter provides insights into the mechanisms by which PCK deepens, offering practical recommendations for educators and policymakers in supporting ongoing professional growth. It thus illuminates the dynamics of teaching expertise and its implications for teacher education and the quality of instruction.

INTRODUCTION

PCK is one of the cornerstones of effective teaching that integrates subject matter knowledge with relevant and applicable instructional strategies, rendered appropriate for student understanding. The concept was first introduced by Lee Shulman in the 1980s and insists on the interaction between teachers' knowledge of their subjects and how to transmit that knowledge to learners. Understanding how PCK develops across teacher careers is important for increasing instruction quality and supporting professional growth with changing educational settings and diversifying student needs(Wu, 2022).

Teaching as a profession is dynamic and transformative. Teachers start their profession with some foundational PCK acquired through initial training, which at all times has to be refined and expanded on. The trajectory of PCK development incorporates a number of stages in the form of the novice phase characterized by learning and adapting and the early and mid-career phases, characterized by growing expertise and innovation. Their PCK deepens with progress, classroom experience, professional development, and reflective practices. Each phase has its own problems and opportunities for growth, strongly influenced by evolving educational standards, technological changes at work, and changes in student demographics(Wei et al., 2022).

This is a period when novice teachers rely mostly on their theoretical pre-service knowledge; in effect, there is a very steep learning curve for the educators experiencing the classroom situations. Here, too, programs for initial professional development serve to help teachers develop their abilities concerning lesson planning, management, and assessment techniques. However, it is not an easy matter to move from theory into practice since teachers need to contextualize and individualize their PCK in their classrooms. Reflecting back from the early years, the establishment of strong PCK is pretty critical since this is the time when most teachers start to grasp hold of what their subject really entails and to know how to teach it properly(Miller et al., 2022).

This meant that the PCK is part of the development of teachers from starting their career through early career and mid-career. Here, teachers further develop their pedagogy, as veteran educators, into more variegated pedagogical strategies and adaptive in their content knowledge to support student diversity on a continuum. Professional learning forms part of the whole, through providing opportunities to teachers to further their learning bases on new methodologies, peer collaboration, and involvement in reflective. This assists teachers in developing their PCK to include their fresher understanding of lifelong learning and the emergent problems in their classrooms(Kähkönen & Hölttä-Otto, 2022).

It is then that teachers, who are in the mid-career stage of their professional life, have been known to exhibit a high level of PCK. Having toiled in classrooms for quite some time, they mostly turn out very conversant and possessing the content and pedagogy knowledge. They will start to develop the ability to be innovative and flexible in their practices based on new educational patterns and the dynamic needs of the students. Experienced educators often mentor less experienced educators, share their expertise within the profession, and make contributions to the educational community. In these ways, experience—combined with ongoing professional development—supports further development of PCK by a teacher partway through his career(Cima et al., 2021).

It is at this later stage of teaching careers that most teachers reflect on their vast experiences and polish their PCK to solve more complex educational challenges. At this stage, there is a mature and subtle view of the teaching-learning process. When they reflect on their immense experiences, they are able to see the wood for the trees. At this mature stage, more experienced teachers usually undertake professional development at higher levels. ´ Endorsed professional development would include aspects of leadership, curriculum development, and even educational research. ´. Their deepened PCK allows them to really make a difference in their schools and the education field at large. That notwithstanding, their PCK remains something to be maintained and evolved as they continue adapting to new educational paradigms and technologies(Bogoslowski et al., 2021).

The growth of PCK is also influenced by a number of other factors during a teaching career: professional development opportunities, reflective practices, and changes in educational contexts. Having professional development programs gives rise to the bringing of current knowledge into the teacher's arena and new pedagogical methods which assist in keeping up with the current state of education. Various reflective practices, such as self-assessment and peer feedback, allow the teachers to reflect on and enhance their PCK critically. Moreover, these educational contextual changes—for example curriculum reform, improvement in information technology, and changing student needs—always demand a modification and an extension of teachers' PCK(Stek, 2023).

Knowledge of the trajectory of the development of PCK across one's teaching career gives insight into the conscientious nature of educators' development. It points out the need to support these teachers with well-targeted professional development, increased possibilities for reflection, and resources for survival in an increasingly changing educational landscape. Mapping the growth of PCK, we engage in a depth of appreciation for the dynamic nature of expertise in teaching and factors that could foster effective instruction(De Back et al., 2023). This knowledge can, therefore, deepen policies and practices in the areas of teacher education reform, instructional improvement, and direct benefits for the students and the educational system at large.

Background

One of the most important constituents in teaching is Pedagogical Content Knowledge (PCK): well-grounded subject matter knowledge intertwined with pedagogical approaches that consider student approaches to learning. It was introduced by Lee Shulman, putting an emphasis on the necessity to understand content knowledge and to know how to teach it effectively. This complex construct is able to exert a huge impact on instructional quality and finally on student achievement. Like the educational environment and learners themselves, teachers' PCK is constantly undergoing a process of change, influenced by these changing conditions. Historically, teacher education programs did focus on the basic PCK of teachers; however, continuous professional development and reflective practices were the real keys to its sustained growth. There is, however, a dearth of comprehensive understanding of how PCK develops across different career stages. How this actually evolves can yield insight into the optimization of teacher training and support, bearing directly on the enhancing of instructional practice and eventually the improvement of educational outcome.

Scope

This chapter takes the teacher's career from training levels through late-career phases. It reviews how teachers initially acquire PCK, the role of ongoing professional development, classroom experience that affects it, and the influence of evolving educational contexts. This research looks at longitudinal data and case studies in attempts to understand the dynamics of PCK development, offering practical insights for improvement in teacher education and instructional practice based on its findings.

Objectives

The aim of this chapter is to describe how PCK develops over a teacher's career, outlining the main phases of development from initial training to experienced practice. Among these are an analysis of how PCK changes with experience, determining those factors that contribute to its growth, and assessing the impact of professional development and reflective practices in this process. It intends to provide practical advice to experts in education and policy advisors on how to make continuous professional growth a reality and make teaching effective through well-focused intervention and support mechanisms.

BASICS OF PEDAGOGICAL CONTENT KNOWLEDGE

Definition and Components of PCK

Pedagogical Content Knowledge is a multi-dimensional construct that Lee Shulman put forward in 1986; it symbolizes the interaction of teachers' knowledge of content and their pedagogical skills(Borda et al., 2020; Perpignan et al., 2020). Key constituents would be:

- Content Knowledge: This includes the deep subject matter understanding by the teacher. It comprises knowledge about facts and conceptual structures in disciplines. In simple terms, good teaching is more than just recalling facts; it also involves knowing how content is structured and its subtleties.
- Pedagogical Knowledge: This is the generic aspect of teaching methods and strategies, comprising lesson planning, classroom management, and assessment techniques.
- Pedagogical Content Knowledge: At the heart of PCK lies the intersection of content knowledge with pedagogical knowledge: knowing how best to teach particular content so it is understandable and engaging to learners, including selection of appropriate teaching strategies, development of effective instructional materials, and anticipation of student misconceptions.
- Students: Effective PCK also rests on knowledge about students, their previous knowledge, learning needs, and the difficulties that may arise. Teachers use this knowledge to adjust their teaching accordingly to meet the diversity in learning styles and challenges.
- Curricular Knowledge: A teacher shall have knowledge of the curriculum and the standards for the subject area he or she teaches. That basically means

a teacher knows how the content fits into a broader educational scheme and how the instruction will be aligned to meet the goals of the curriculum.

Models of PCK Development

There are several models put forward to describe PCK development over time(Tai & Ting, 2020):

- Shulman's Original Model: Shulman postulated PCK evolves as teachers blend content knowledge with pedagogical strategies over time, through practice. It is in this model that PCK is dynamic, with its constant change or development along the continuum of experience.
- The structure of the Knowledge Quartet further extended the work of Shulman by disaggregating PCK into further four interrelated domains: foundation—knowledge of content and pedagogy; transformation—how teachers adapt and transform content for teaching; connection—linking content to students' understanding; and practice—the actual execution of teaching. This model shows the complexity of PCK and, at the same time, the different phases through which it develops during teaching.
- The PCK Framework by Magnusson, Krajcik, and Borko: The PCK was identified by this framework to have several domains which include knowledge of curriculum, knowledge of students, knowledge of instructional strategies, and knowledge of assessment. It focuses on how the interactions of these domains contribute to effective teaching.
- The Dynamic Model of PCK: This view presents the PCK as a dynamic, context-bound entity that keeps changing with the teaching context and the needs of the students, and in changes of general pedagogical understanding. Through the changes, PCK is supposedly continually shaped and reshaped by practice and reflection.

The Role of PCK in Effective Teaching

It performs a fundamental role in effective teaching since subject matter knowledge is condensed and crystallized into teaching practice(Miller et al., 2022). The contributions that PCK makes towards teaching effectiveness include:

- Instructive design: Teachers with well-developed PCK are well placed to plan and implement lessons likely to deliver the subject matter in ways that address students' needs of learning. Experts can select relevant approaches

to instruction, develop relevant resources, and adapt their approaches in response to student reactions.
- Better Engagement of Students: Pre-service teachers with better PCK can prepare lessons in ways that better link their teaching approaches to students' background knowledge and interests. This makes it easier to secure students' interest and keep them motivated to learn.
- IBAction on Misconceptions: Teachers who possess an advanced level of PCK will be better placed to anticipate common misconceptions and challenges to learning. They shall be able to design strategies to explain any complicated concepts and give extra support to students experiencing problems while learning the concepts.
- Curricular Alignment: PCK allows the instructor to align instruction not only with curricular goals and standards but also to see that students acquire proper knowledge and skills. This arrangement shall, therefore, be beneficial in building coherence in the learning experience and shall help students realize educational objectives.
- Reflective Practice: Robust PCK is tied to continuous reflection and acts of adaptation. Teachers with robust PCK regularly reflect on their instructional practices and measure their impact on student learning to see where adjustments are needed to bring about better results.

Hence, PCK represents an important part of good teaching, which includes deep content and pedagogic understanding. It is in perpetual evolution through experience, professional development, and reflective practice. Insight into the understanding and working processes of the enrichment of PCK holds huge potential for instruction quality and student achievement.

STAGES OF PCK DEVELOPMENT

PCK is developmental—it matures over a teaching professional's career as she gains experience and refines her practice in a changing educational landscape. Documents produced by the various stages in this development—from initial teacher training through late-career expertise—help to clarify ways in which educators grow and how their instructional effectiveness improved(Pyrialakou et al., 2020; Tai & Ting, 2020).

Figure 1. Stages of Pedagogical Content Knowledge (PCK) development

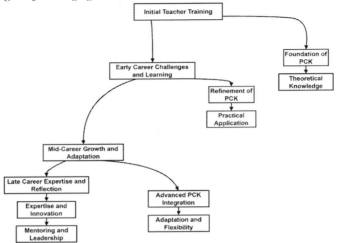

Figure 1 represents the process of professional development in teaching, wherein fall the stages of initial teacher training, early career challenges and learning, mid-career growth and adaptation, late career expertise and reflection, foundation of PCK, refinement of PCK, advanced PCK integration, and expertise and innovation. It starts with the theoretical knowledge gained during initial training and then goes on to include its practical application by adjusting according to the classroom experiences. It leads to attainment of expert status with a contribution to the field through mentoring and leadership.

Initial Teacher Training

PCK finds its initiation during initial teacher training where the aspiring teacher gets induction into the fundamentals of teaching and learning. The importance of this stage lies in laying the ground work for the way a teacher will come to understand and integrate the content knowledge on pedagogical strategies(Tai & Ting, 2020; Yazici et al., 2020).

- Focus on Theoretical Knowledge: A great part of the initial training focuses on the acquisition of theoretical knowledge. The teacher candidates study educational psychology, instructional methods, curriculum design, and assessment techniques. However, their understanding of how to effectively teach specific content areas is still developing. At this point, PCK is usually more

theoretical, and there are fewer opportunities for application in real classroom settings.
- Observation and Practice: Generally, as part of the teacher training programs, there are observation sessions and teaching practicums. In view of this, the quality experiences for the translation of theoretical knowledge to be developed in practice would be where candidates can begin developing PCK. This early PCK, however, is underdeveloped because teacher candidates are still learning how to manage classrooms, engage students, and deliver content effectively.
- Foundational PCK: By the end of their training, teacher candidates know very little about how to teach their subject matter. They know how to lesson plan, manage classrooms, and recognize common student misconceptions. However, their PCK remains only in an embryonic state and needs further nurture by real teaching experiences.

Early Career Challenges and Learning

The leap from teacher training into the classroom is a quantum leap. The induction into practice for early-career teachers brings an associated steep learning curve, moving them from training to meet the realities of teaching, which were far more complex than they had encountered(Sidekerskienė & Damaševičius, 2023; Stek, 2023).

- Application of PCK in the Classroom: The application of PCK in diverse and dynamic classroom environments is something early-career teachers have to master in an extremely short period of time. Classroom management, differentiation of instruction for diverse learners, and adjusting lesson plans to meet the needs of learners are common challenges. It is a time of experimentation; in other words, teachers gain experience through practical applications, which eventually polish their PCK.
- Addressing Student Needs: Early-career teachers begin to become aware that the backgrounds of students, learning styles, and prior knowledge are important aspects to understand. This understanding is extremely important for PCK since it means that teachers can apply better instructional strategies that relate more to the needs of the students. The extent to which the balancing of these demands teaches in an overwhelming way makes the pace of PCK development slow.
- Professional Development and Mentorship: Professional development and mentorship become very important at this stage. In the early years of teaching, teachers benefit from the guidance of more senior peers and help in tid-

ing over difficulties and improving their PCK. At the same time, participation in professional learning communities and attending workshops allow them to learn new strategies and further develop existing ones.

Mid-Career Growth and Adaptation

Their PCK is more sophisticated and refined when they move into their mid-career phase, characterized by deeper subject matter and pedagogic knowledge, with a better ability to adapt to changing educational contexts at this stage(Venkatasubramanian et al., 2024).

Refining PCK: Here, the teachers would already have created a strong base of PCK and further carry on the practice through experience and reflection. Teachers have more confidence in their instructional practices and can better predict student misconceptions more appropriately and respond to them. Mid-career teachers often experiment with new teaching strategies and technologies that they incorporate into their PCK in attempts at enhancing student learning.

Adaptability to changing contexts: Mid-career teachers adjust their PCK more easily in response to changed curriculum standards, education technologies, and student demographics. They are leaders in their schools and help colleagues by sharing their expertise in initiating curriculum development. This flexibility is a prime characteristic of mid-career PCK and enables teachers to be effective throughout a changing educational environment.

Continuous Professional Development: At this stage, professional development is also viewed as important. The mid-career teacher seeks increased training and remains part of a professional learning community with whom he stays updated about current educational research and the best practice techniques. This commitment to continuous learning helps them in keeping the PCK relevant and effective.

Late Career Expertise and Reflection

Later in their careers, teaching professionals achieve a level of expertise that will then enable them to reflect deeply on their practice and contribute to the wider educational community(Singh Madan et al., 2024).

Mastery of PCK: Late-career teachers typically have a very well-developed PCK characterized by deep and nuanced subject matter knowledge and pedagogical knowledge. Instructional techniques have been finely tuned over many years of experience, and the late-career teacher can improvise and modify teaching to better connect diverse learners to subject matter. This enables high quality instruction and mentorship of younger teachers.

Reflection now assumes center stage in the development of PCK. The very late-career teachers more commonly involve themselves with reflective practices, including self-assessment, observing peers, and participating in professional dialogues. Such activities let them look at their teaching critically, make adjustments, and grow as educators.

Leadership and Mentorship: The experienced practicing teachers often assume leadership roles in which they share knowledge and expertise with colleagues through mentoring, professional development workshops, and contributing to educational research. Their now well-developed PCK enables them to influence practices beyond their classrooms, hence contributing much toward the development of the profession as a whole.(Singh Madan et al., 2024; Yadav et al., 2024)

Embracing new trends: Even at this advanced stage, the late-career teacher has to further adapt to new trends in education, new technologies, and changing student needs. It is upon this experience that the changes can be merged into their PCK with greater comfort, ensuring relevance and effectiveness in teaching.

PCK development is related to lifelong learning processes that evolve through experience, reflection, and professional growth. In this respect, each stage of a teaching career exposes a person to the challenge and possibilities for developing PCK. Understanding these stages can help educators and policymakers design focused support systems that can foster teachers' instructional effectiveness and promote student learning. This paper furthers the argument that continuous PCK development will help the teaching profession meet ever-increasing demands within an educational landscape in flux.

FACTORS INFLUENCING PCK GROWTH

PCK means Pedagogical Content Knowledge and is an important attribute associated with teaching effectiveness. This is the process of bridging content knowledge with pedagogical skills so that a teacher can deliver the subject matter comprehensibly and interestingly. Growth in PCK throughout a teacher's career is influenced by different factors. Getting to know them helps answer how educators can develop their PCK and, therefore, enhance teaching practices and subsequent learning by students(Saravanan et al., 2024; Sharma et al., 2024). The factors that lead to the formation of PCK and how they relate to one another are shown below in Figure 2.

Figure 2. Factors Influencing PCK Growth

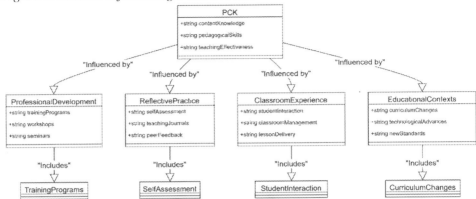

Professional Development Programs

PD programs are vital in the development of PCK because they provide opportunities for teachers to gain knowledge, hone pedagogical skills, and become updated with the newest findings of educational research(Prabhuswamy et al., 2024).

Content-Specific Training: The PD programs focusing on subject-specific content aim at enhancing teachers' knowledge of the subject. With improved subject matter knowledge, it places the teacher in a better position to be able to determine what central ideas must be presented and what student misconceptions are, together with the strategies for presenting material. It is these components that get represented in workshops, seminars, and courses with experts at the helm, arming the teachers with ways of developing PCK.

Pedagogical skill development: Such PD programs also target the pedagogical skills that provide classroom management, instructional strategies, and assessment techniques. If these programs make a crosswalk between content knowledge and pedagogy, then it goes directly to the development of PCK. They learn new strategies that can be applied in their specific subject area and enhance the teaching of complex content(Sharma et al., 2024).

Collaborative Learning Communities: Among all PD programs that put teachers in collaborative work, like Professional Learning Communities, there is a big potential for the enhancement of PCK. Teachers are allowed to share experiences, talk through problems, and plan how they will actually carry out new teaching methods within a common learning environment. This approach enhances an understanding of 'how to teach' certain content effectively, thus helping in the growth of PCK.

Sustained and Ongoing Development: PD programs with sustained, ongoing support will go much deeper into enhancing teachers' PCK than one-shot workshops. Consequently, this provides them with an opportunity to apply the new knowledge obtained within classrooms and experience reflection with iterative improvements in their practices.

Reflective Practice

It is because of reflective practice that PCK grows; it provides the teachers with an opportunity to reflect upon and learn from experiences about teaching(Kalaiselvi et al., 2024).

Self-Assessment: One characteristic of reflective practice is frequent assessment of teaching methods and their results. As an outcome of constant self-assessment, pre-service teachers engaged in reflective practice will be better placed to identify areas where their PCK may be lacking and know what to do to fill the gaps. Self-assessment typically includes questions such as, "What worked well in this lesson?" or "How might I reword my explanation of this?"

Peer Observation and Feedback: Observing others' teaching practices and receiving feedback from peers are similarly powerful tools in reflective practice. One gets insights into how to teach practices that a teacher can apply to their content area. Similarly, peers' good constructive feedback points to areas of improvement and, thus, the continuous development of PCK.

It basically allows teachers to journal any experiences, reflections, and growth noted over some time, hence detecting patterns of success and challenges to teaching particular content. All these therefore contribute to the growth of PCK. Reflective journaling encourages a more deliberate and thoughtful approach to teaching.

Some teachers do action research in the sense that they systematically investigate their own teaching practices with a view to answering some questions that perplex them about the effectiveness of their teaching. The power of impact by such research-driven reflection is very strong on enhancing PCK, which results in evidence-based changes in instructional approaches.

Classroom Experience and Student Interaction

Probably the most key experiences to influence the growth of PCK are direct classroom experience and interaction with the students. In the day-to-day realities of teaching lies a place where teachers would learn and fine-tune their PCK(Das et al., 2024).

- Trial and Error: In the early career, teachers rely much on trial and error to see what goes well in their classrooms. This is an important part of experience while developing PCK, as teachers may try out different instructional strategies, learn from success and failure, and gradually develop a means of teaching the content.
- Matching to Student Needs: Through experience, the teacher acquires an enhanced capability to recognize student needs and act on them. Indeed, one of the defining features of PCK is a flexible ability to adjust teaching in light of student feedback. For example, if some students fail to appreciate a particular point, then the experienced teacher can use their PCK to work out alternative ways of explaining the concept so that better understanding ensues.
- Classroom Dynamics: The continuous interaction with the students makes the teacher understand the impact of different ways of teaching on learning. A teacher, over a period, evolves a better understanding about students' behavior, learning style, and misconceptions that a teacher could use in tuning one's teaching. This continuous interaction would perhaps drive growth in PCK very strongly.
- Continuous Improvement: The practice of classroom experience is such that, year by year, PCK is improved upon. Each year brings new students, new challenges, and new opportunities for a teacher to learn and grow. This iterative process lies at the very heart of long-term PCK development.

Changes in Educational Contexts

Educational contexts never stay the same, and every change in the curriculum standards, technology, and educational policy affects teachers and their development of PCK(Das et al., 2024).

Curricular Reforms: This shift in the standards of the curriculum places a demand on teachers to adapt their PCK so that their practice is in line with these new expectations. Examples are the infusion of more inquiry-based learning or the integration of cross-disciplinary content that would require changes in instructional strategies. Such changes might mean immense growth in PCK, as teachers find their way and learn to throw a new curriculum demand. It is through technology integration that PCK is made evident. The challenge placed on the teachers is to present an awareness of the best ways in which technology can be used as an effective tool in the delivery of content and pedagogy to students. This requires not only the possession of technical skills but also understanding how the technology supports the delivery of content and pedagogy and therefore extends PCK.

Diverse Learning Environments: Demographic changes require increased diversity in classrooms, in turn necessitating the development of culturally responsive teaching strategies. Such ongoing adjustability serves to improve not just PCK as an identity but specifically a PCK that is more universal and effective. Teachers must design their PCK in such a way that it can, from time to time, be adjusted to suit the needs of students from different backgrounds, languages, or abilities.

Policy and Assessment Changes: Policies on education and methods of assessment are always changing over time. Teachers hence should have an updated chronology of events, and their PCK should reflect this fact. For example, new modes of assessment that are likely to put a premium on formative assessment more than summative assessment might call upon teachers to invent newer methods of observing and supporting learning in students, thus augmenting their PCK.

It is the act of professional development, reflective practice, classroom experience, and developmental changes within the educational context jointly that affects the growth of PCK; the four variables are very much interrelated to contribute maximally toward the development of the teacher's capacity and capability to effectively integrate the process of transitioning the content knowledge into pedagogical strategies. Appreciation and leverage on these can enhance a teacher's career continuously, for teachers to be responsive to factors improving their capacity and consequently increasing their students' potential learning.

METHODOLOGY

The next section deals with the data collection and analysis processes for PCK growth during teaching careers. It aims to provide insights into how PCK changes over time and what could possibly influence its development through a systematic collection and analysis of data from different sources(Agrawal et al., 2023; Das et al., 2024; Durairaj et al., 2023). Figure 3 describes systematic approach to data collection and analysis for the study of PCK growth: interaction between the researcher and participants with different methodological stages.

Figure 3. Process of data collection and analysis in the study of Pedagogical Content Knowledge (PCK) growth

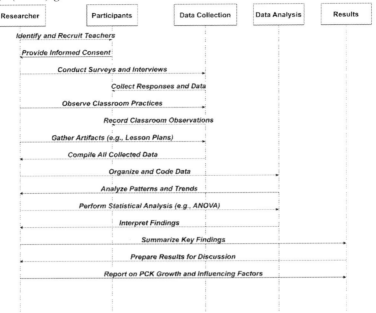

Data Collection

Data collection took the form of a mixed-methods approach, comprising both quantitative and qualitative methods for an in-depth understanding of PCK growth(Sharma et al., 2024; Singh Madan et al., 2024). The steps that ensued in collecting data are summarized as follows:

Survey Instruments: A structured questionnaire was administered to a large sample of teachers representing all career stages, from initial teacher training to those at the end of their careers. It probed teachers' reports of their PCK and experiences and reflections concerning their classroom practices and professional development. The questions are both closed-ended, for example Likert scale ratings, and open-ended, therefore eliciting both quantitative and qualitative insights.

Interviews: In-depth, semi-structured interviews were conducted for a subsample of the teachers to elaborate on their experiences of developing PCK.

Such interviews would help elaborate on the finest details as to how the teachers perceive their growth in PCK, the challenges they face, and the strategies they use to enhance teaching effectiveness. Participants were selected to get a heterogeneous subsample based on the response categories of the survey on career stages, subject areas, and educational contexts.

Observation of Classrooms: Observations of classroom practice were done to directly assess the enactment of teachers' PCK. The instructional strategies employed, the mode of delivery of content, and student engagement—some very central aspects of PCK—were targeted for observation. Systematically recorded and analyzed behaviors observed were captured in detailed field notes and checklists.

Analysis of Documents

Documents, including lesson plans, teaching portfolios, and professional development records, were analyzed to give complementary insights into the teachers' PCK. This analysis served to triangulate data gathered via surveys, interviews, and observations, and thus provided a more robust understanding of PCK growth(Kalaiselvi et al., 2024; Prabhuswamy et al., 2024; Saravanan et al., 2024).

Longitudinal Data: The authors used longitudinal data in tracking the development of PCK over time in one cohort of teachers during a five-year period. It included repeated surveys, interviews, and observations to trace changes in PCK as the teachers progressed through different career stages.

Data Analysis

First and foremost, both quantitative and qualitative analyses were done for better insight on the collected data.

Quantitative Analysis: The data collected using the questionnaires were statistically analyzed to reveal trends and patterns in PCK growth at different career stages. Descriptive statistics, such as means and standard deviations, were used to describe data whereas inferential statistics, like ANOVA and Regression Analysis, were used to test hypotheses about factors that influenced the development of PCK. Longitudinal survey data were analyzed for change in PCK over time using growth curve modeling.

Qualitative Analysis Interview transcripts, observation notes, and responses to open-ended questions in the survey were analyzed for themes related to PCK development. The analysis process involved coding the data to find common themes related to PCK development, including professional development experiences, reflective practices, and the impact of classroom interactions. The thematic analysis identified common patterns across participants but has also explored unique individual experiences.

Triangulation: To extend the validity of the findings, data triangulation was used by comparing and integrating results from multiple data sources: survey responses, interviews, observations, and documents. This corroborated the findings and created a better understanding of what contributed to PCK growth.

Comparative Analysis: Moderate comparisons were made of the development among demographic groups like teaching experience, subject area, educational context, among others. This was done in order to find possible differences in PCK growth among the targeted groups and to realize particular needs where more professional development needed to be targeted.

Narrative Synthesis: The qualitative data was then narratively synthesized to come up with elaborate case studies that help detail the process of PCK development in individual teachers. These case studies gave rich, contextualized accounts of how PCK evolves and provided a depth that complemented the broader trends identified through quantitative analysis.

The methodology of the study corresponds to a rigorous data collection and analysis plan for tracing PCK growth across teaching careers. This will give a comprehensive view of how the development of PCK takes place, what factors its growth is influenced by, and what this has for implications on teacher education and professional development programs. Done in this manner, this methodological approach enables a robust and nuanced understanding of PCK that adds richness to the greater realm of educational research.

FINDINGS AND DISCUSSION

This section presents the findings of the study on the growth of Pedagogical Content Knowledge (PCK) across teaching careers, organized into three key areas: patterns of PCK development, the impact of professional development and reflection, and the influence of classroom experience and contextual changes(Venkatasubramanian et al., 2024).

Patterns of PCK Development

The data reveal distinct patterns of PCK development that align with different stages of a teacher's career(Vaithianathan, Shastri, et al., 2024; Vaithianathan, Subbulakshmi, et al., 2024).

Initial Teacher Training: At this initial training period, the PCK is more at a foundational stage. At this time, teachers heavily rely on theoretical knowledge they had learned through education programs and tend to try and put these into practice. The data from the survey showed that most new teachers' knowledge of content and pedagogical ways of teaching tend to integrate frequently into a rigid adoption of similar teaching approaches.

Early Career: There is lots of growth in PCK during early-career stages when teachers start developing their practice. The interviews revealed that this was the time for experimentation: the teacher is trying to work out what works and how to better adjust the content for the needs of the students. Indeed, early-career teachers still tend to feel swamped with the burden of complex teaching and would appreciate more help in the development of instructional strategies.

Mid-Career: By the middle of careers, teachers have developed more sophisticated understandings of PCK because they represent a balanced integration between content knowledge and pedagogy. Their ability to adjust lessons based on student feedback and other diverse learning needs was observed in classroom observations and Illustrated in survey responses as midcareer teachers were more confident. However, the problem at this point is that some of these teachers begin to plateau in terms of their PCK growth and will need further, focused professional development in order to continue to improve.

Late Career: At the late career stage, most teachers have reached a high level of PCK, matching depth of content knowledge with extensive teaching experience. The interviews with expert teachers revealed some experiences that they do practice reflection. They indeed extend their experience-rich knowledge bases to adapt to novel educational challenges and mentor less-experienced colleagues.

Contrary to high expertise, late-career teachers may struggle with keeping pace in educational technology and swift student demographic changes, which could challenge their PCK if continuous learning opportunities are not made available.

Impact of Professional Development and Reflection

The findings indicated that reflective practice and professional development were the two prime factors influencing PCK growth at all career stages(Herrera-Pavo, 2021).

Professional Development Programs: The research concluded that successful PD programs play a significant role in the growth of PCK. Those who partook in continuous, focused PD showed a significant improvement in being able to combine content knowledge with pedagogical strategies. PD programs that emphasized collaborative learning through workshops and peer observations provided useful opportunities for sharing best practice and gaining constructive feedback. However, the effectiveness of PD varied, with some teachers pointing out that generic or one-size-fits-all programs had lesser impact. It has to be highlighted that PD programs need to be tailored to the needs and career stages of teachers.

Reflective Practice: Throughout all this, one loud message for the mechanisms of PCK growth was reflective practice. Through reflective practice, teachers who reflect frequently on practice show a better understanding of what might be done to better tailor teaching toward improving student learning. Reflection provided a means and avenue for teachers to go through the critical analysis of instructional approaches through problem setting and finding of solutions. This became very instrumental for midand late-career teachers in securing and extending their PCK.

The findings from the data also showed that institutional support in terms of providing time and necessary resources for the reflective activities increased its effectiveness in enhancing the impact of reflection in developing the PCK.

Influence of Classroom Experience and Contextual Changes

The results also showed that development in PCK was powerfully driven by classroom experience and educational context change.

Classroom experience: The gaining of classroom experience was one of the major facilitators of the development of PCK. The more experienced teachers felt better able to know in advance where students would have trouble, extent their practice in differentiated instruction and adapt their instructional methods spontaneously during a lesson.

More experienced teachers were better placed to handle different classroom situations, from accommodating different student abilities to responding to unexpected challenges that enriched their PCK. Their finding revealed that experience alone was not necessarily a sufficient condition to create growth in PCK. That is, growth in teachers without an active approach to professional development or reflective practice was slow. This offers the implication that continuous learning processes must be combined with experience.

Contextual Changes:

PCK development was an extremely deep process influenced by changes in the educational context: curriculum standards, developments in technologies, and changes in student demographics. Such changes were easier to make for some teachers who showed more robust growth in PCK, as they themselves were very adaptable and capable of meeting these challenges. For example, using technology inside the classroom was seen to be a challenge and also an opportunity in that teachers who integrated their pedagogy well with digital tools developed enhanced PCK. On the other hand, those resistant to change or who felt unsupported in traversing new educational landscapes reported challenges in sustaining their PCK, leading to plateaus or even decline in teaching effectiveness.

The research findings support that development of PCK across a teacher's career is complex and dynamic. Although initial education sets the scene, continuous professional development, reflective practice, and adapting to changing educational contexts in general are essential conditions for further PCK growth. These insights illustrate a need for support systems that are tailored to the explicit needs of teachers at different career stages so that these teachers will be in a position to develop and apply PCK with an eye toward better student learning outcomes.

Pedagogical content knowledge (PCK) is a term coined in 1986 by Shulman to explain the specific amalgamation of subject matter and teaching acumen that is demanded from a teacher for effective instruction. PCK is crucial for teachers because it means understanding what it takes to make subject matter meaningful to learners. For the experienced teacher, PCK accrues over time through experiences, professional development, and reflective practice, thus enhancing one's ability to tailor the content to the needs of their students.

CASE STUDY

The case study aimed to trace the development of PCK over a career. It involves a description of how teachers acquire and develop PCK at various stages of teaching experience. Exploring the conditions that influence the growth in PCK, research goes on to open up avenues to support teachers in developing this most critical body of knowledge(Vaithianathan, Shastri, et al., 2024; Vaithianathan, Subbulakshmi, et al., 2024; Venkatasubramanian et al., 2024; Yadav et al., 2024).

Methodology

The study had a longitudinal design, involving three teachers with varying experience levels: either beginner (0-5 years), mid-career (6-15 years), or veteran (15+ years). Information on each teacher's approach in planning, executing, and assessing lessons on a particular subject area was collected using interviews, lesson observations, and self-reflections. Information from student feedback further elucidated the effectiveness of the PCK application for each teacher.

- Early Career Teachers: The early career teacher had extremely poor PCK which was predominantly passed on through the curriculum documents and theory. It was difficult to plan for not knowing that students would not under-

stand and it was not feasible to change strategies mid-instruction. Mentorship support and professional development became a necessity at this stage.
- Mid-career teachers: In this mid-career stage, PCK is now more identifiable from the understanding of teachers. Predictable misconceptions started emerging with accompanying trust to differentiate instruction. Yet the application of PCK was mostly guided by trial-and-error experiences, instead of looking for formal training, rather on reflective practice.
- Veteran Teachers: A veteran teacher, the veteran teacher had demonstrated well-developed PCK, with a profound understanding of either content nuances or students' needs. In fact, one of the most skillful teachers in flexibly adapting lessons at any given moment and bringing reality into the classroom to help students better understand things, he has developed this PCK after decades of iterative practice and continuous learning, including peer collaboration.

Implications for Teacher Preparation

The case study further shows that the growth of PCK is lifelong and development can be fostered through professional development, reflection, and collaborative engagement. In novice teachers, an accelerated development of PCK is achieved through systematic mentorship and carefully organized workshops. Mid-career teachers appreciate collaborative opportunities and reflective practice experiences, while veteran teachers provide mentoring engagements and transmit their developed PCK to colleagues at the other end of the professional ladder.

PCK development is a career that changes at different points as the teacher gains experience and becomes comfortable with various classroom configurations. Timely support throughout the stages of a teacher's career will help increase PCK, which in turn increases the quality of the instruction given, stimulates learning, and fosters interest among the learners. This case study shows that continuous professional learning provides a way to foster the development of PCK over one's teaching career.

IMPLICATIONS FOR PRACTICE

Growth of PCK is basic to the establishment of effective practices in teaching throughout a teacher's career. In this section, implications for practice are synthesised, and based on these, recommendations are made as regards how effectively educators, policymakers in teacher education, and enhancers of PCK might meet the challenge of growing teachers' PCK(Kezar, 2023; Ruben et al., 2023). Figure 4 shows the implications for practice on the growth of Pedagogical Content Knowledge.

Figure 4. Implications for practice regarding the growth of Pedagogical Content Knowledge (PCK)

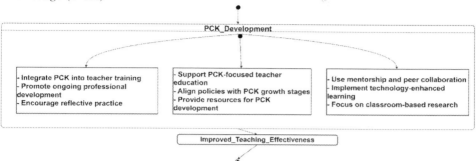

Recommendations for Educators
- Engagement in Reflective Practice: It is essential for educators to view reflective practice as an ongoing process rather than an occasional activity. The reflection on the daily teaching experience helps a teacher measure his technique of imparting information and act on the outcomes of the findings. It involves the use of tools such as teaching journals, peer discussion, and self-assessment frameworks in analyzing one's teaching. Preoccupying oneself with regular reflection would afford a deeper understanding of how to link content knowledge with best practices in pedagogy, consequently enhancing PCK.
- Active Participation in Professional Development: Teachers should seek out and participate in professional development opportunities that focus on their teaching career stage. Effective PD programs should be collaborative in operation so that opportunities for peer learning and sharing of best practices are given to educators. All PD activities, which take the initiative to combine content knowledge with pedagogical skills and bridge gaps created by emerging challenges in education such as technology integration and students' needs' diversity, are encouraged to be taken up by educators.
- Adaptability to Educational Changes: Teachers have to respond to every kind of change in educational contexts: curriculum, technology, and the changing demographics of students. The willingness to adopt a new tool or strategy in teaching enhances PCK and simultaneously aids the teacher in attending to the divergent needs of their students. Constant renewal of knowledge base and practice is a requirement for relevance and effectiveness in teaching.

Policy Implications for Teacher Education
- Tailored Programs of Teacher Education: Programs in the education of teachers should be tailored to meet the needs of teachers at different career stages. Initial training must provide the foundation for PCK, while advanced training will engender a deeper level of exploration and application in varied contexts. High-level policymakers must promote the embedding of reflective practice and continuous professional development within pre-service teacher education. This will further develop the PCK and enhance it throughout one's career.
- Support for Continuous Professional Development: Policymakers should look into advocating continuous funding and support for professional development programs. In this respect, professional development programs should be innovated to cater to the changing challenges facing educators and ensure continuous building of their PCK in return. Policies should give support to creating professional learning communities where educators come together to work collaboratively, sharing knowledge and supporting each other in developing their PCK.
- Incentives for Lifelong Learning: The decision-makers should consider offering certifications, merit-based promotions, and other monetary benefits to the educators practicing reflective work and professional development as a habit. It would motivate teachers towards continuous learning for enhancing PCK, which directly links with their teaching effectiveness.

Strategies for Enhancing PCK

- Integrating Technology in Teaching{: Integrating technology into teaching practices is one clear way of increasing PCK in course content delivery and the engagement of students. In this regard, different technologies and digital platforms should be explored by teachers to add value to their pedagogies, which might include interactive simulations, educational applications, and digital assessment tools. Pre- and in-service teacher training programs might, therefore, integrate modules on how to integrate technology in the classroom, so that teachers know how to effectively combine traditional and digital approaches in their teaching.
- Collaborative Learning and Peer Mentorship: Collaboration and peer mentorship are powerful PCK learning strategies. Guided insights and learning from peers' experiences could occur through collaborative planning sessions, peer class observations, and co-teach opportunities. Faculties and schools need to facilitate the formation of peer mentoring programs so that more ex-

perienced practicing teachers help less experienced fellow teachers in forming their PCK. This is a collaborative approach benefiting individual teachers and, as such, the learning environment within the profession as a whole.
- Focus on Student-Centered Teaching: The improvement in PCK calls for a high sense of student-centered teaching, whereby the needs, interests, and abilities of the learners are at the forefront of instructional planning and delivering. The teacher shall periodically undertake assessment of student learning, and based on the results, modify his approaches to teaching. Such a continuous circle makes a teacher develop a sense of PCK more responsive to student feedback and learning outcome. Educators should also, therefore, use formative assessments and differentiated instruction in their teaching practice to respond more effectively to the differing learning needs of their students.
- Ongoing Reflection and Self-Assessment: In order for growth in PCK to be sustained, ongoing reflection and self-assessment are necessary. Teachers need regularly to review their practice, recognize areas where improvements might be made, and detail particular goals to which to aspire in their professional development. Tools such as teaching portfolios, reflective journals, and self-assessment rubrics can be used to document and analyze PCK over time. They will be able to identify successful strategies and, at the same time, identify areas for further growth by engaging in systematic reflection on practice.

All these things require a multi-dimensional approach: reflective practice, professional development, adaptability to change, and strong student-centered teaching in order to enhance PCK during a teacher's career. It will take collaboration among educators, policymakers, and institutions to create an environment that sustains continuous learning and the development of PCK. Only when these recommendations and strategies are put into practice will the development of PCK be effectively done to ensure better teaching practices and improved student outcomes.

FUTURE DIRECTIONS FOR RESEARCH

PCK research has radically advanced the understanding of effective teaching, yet there are so many future research directions that deepen such knowledge. Further work should account for a changing educational landscape and the need for more sophisticated insights pertaining to PCK development in various contexts, at different stages of career, and across disciplines(Miller et al., 2022; Wei et al., 2022). Figure 5 offers a view on key areas and some of the possible research directions for further inquiry into PCK.

Figure 5. Potential research directions in PCK

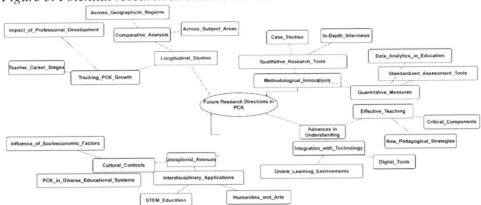

One line of future research might lie in the development of PCK within different educational settings. Whereas much of the previous literature is based on traditional classroom environments, online and blended learning platforms raise a new playing field for PCK research. The way PCK is developed in digital and remote learning settings becomes paramount when these forms of education grow to be such a large proportion of education. Research should examine how teachers modify their pedagogical practices for these new environments and how technology might be harnessed in enhancing PCK. Cultural, socio-economic, and linguistic diversity influencing the development of PCK could be usefully researched in finding out how teachers can respond efficaciously to diverse student populations.

Another very important area for future research is the longitudinal study of PCK development across a teacher's career. While there is a general supposition that PCK changes from initial teacher training to late career, much more detail is needed about the changes which take place over time. Such studies could consider the extent to which different kinds of professional experiences—that is, through induction programs, reflective practices, and/or peer collaboration—contribute to PCK growth. More than this, it would be about the key challenges and opportunities that arise at each career stage and their bearing on the sustained development of PCK. This would help in providing a more complete model of PCK growth, hence guiding initiatives not only in teacher education programs but also in-service training(Boopathi, 2024; Krishnamoorthy et al., 2024).

The role of reflective practice in PCK development, therefore, remains open to further research. Reflection has been widely accepted as a central component of professional development, with numerous questions still to be addressed regarding the most powerful forms of reflective practice and how these might contribute to PCK.

One can look at research about different kinds of reflective tools and approaches, for example, teaching journals, video analysis, and peer feedback, to learn the extent to which they impact teachers' abilities with regard to integrating content knowledge with pedagogical strategies. One may further want to learn how exactly one would systemically embed reflective practice within pre-service and in-service teacher education so as to get practical guidelines on improving PCK.

Finally, future work needs to take into account policy and practice implications of PCK for teacher education. Assessment of the effectiveness of current programs of teacher education in developing teachers' PCK, in view of new educational challenges, is required. It could further elaborate on which curricular approaches to teacher education would need to be changed or modified in order to more successfully promote the development of teachers' PCK. This can be conceived with respect to new trends in education, such as STEM education, interdisciplinary teaching, and technology integration in the classroom. It might also examine how different policy frameworks bear on PCK development, hence providing policy makers with evidence-based recommendations. Although there has been substantial progress in understanding PCK, several areas are yet to be further researched. Addressing these research gaps would contribute to effective practices through future studies and result in better outcomes for students.

CONCLUSION

This chapter provides a Pedagogical Content Knowledge: its definition, components, models of development, and the important role it plays in the construction of efficient teaching practices during the different career stages of a teacher. We investigate the basic aspects of PCK, its definition, components, models of development, and the several phases through which PCK develops: from initial teacher education to late-career expertise. Several factors, such as professional development, reflective practice, classroom experience, and educational context changes, were very prominent in the discussion of PCK growth. These findings underscore the dynamic nature of PCK, emphasizing the fact that it is not just a static body of knowledge but a continuously evolving construct. This growth in experience will therefore have effective teaching dependent on how well content knowledge will be melded with educators' pedagogical strategies in ways responsive to the needs of diverse learners and adaptive to the changing educational environment.

The chapter has clearly pointed out the practice implications in terms of targeted professional development, support of reflective practices, and flexibility toward educational innovation. It is such insights that shall be important in helping teachers, policy-framers, and institutions aiming at high-quality teaching and learning environments.

It is for these reasons that an understanding of, and supports for, the growth in PCK are so important to enhancing teaching effectiveness and improving student outcomes. The chapter sets some foundations for future research and practice that can continue to broaden our understanding of PCK and its key role in education.

ABBREVIATIONS

PCK - Pedagogical Content Knowledge
PD - Professional Development
PLC - Professional Learning Community
ANOVA - Analysis of Variance
STEM - Science, Technology, Engineering, and Mathematics

REFERENCES

Agrawal, A. V., Pitchai, R., Senthamaraikannan, C., Balaji, N. A., Sajithra, S., & Boopathi, S. (2023). Digital Education System During the COVID-19 Pandemic. In *Using Assistive Technology for Inclusive Learning in K-12 Classrooms* (pp. 104–126). IGI Global. DOI: 10.4018/978-1-6684-6424-3.ch005

Bogoslowski, S., Geng, F., Gao, Z., Rajabzadeh, A. R., & Srinivasan, S. (2021). Integrated thinking-a cross-disciplinary project-based engineering education. *Visions and Concepts for Education 4.0:Proceedings of the 9th International Conference on Interactive Collaborative and Blended Learning (ICBL2020)*, 260–267.

Boopathi, S. (2024). Digital HR Implementation for Business Growth in Industrial 5.0. In *Convergence of Human Resources Technologies and Industry 5.0* (pp. 1–22). IGI Global. DOI: 10.4018/979-8-3693-1343-5.ch001

Borda, E., Haskell, T., & Boudreaux, A. (2020). Cross-disciplinary learning: A framework for assessing application of concepts across STEM disciplines. *arXiv Preprint arXiv:2012.07906*.

Cima, F., Pazos, P., Kidd, J., Gutierrez, K., Ringleb, S., Ayala, O., & Kaipa, K. (2021). Enhancing preservice teachers' intention to integrate engineering through a cross-disciplinary model. *Journal of Pre-College Engineering Education Research (J-PEER), 11*(2).

Das, S., Lekhya, G., Shreya, K., Shekinah, K. L., Babu, K. K., & Boopathi, S. (2024). Fostering Sustainability Education Through Cross-Disciplinary Collaborations and Research Partnerships: Interdisciplinary Synergy. In *Facilitating Global Collaboration and Knowledge Sharing in Higher Education With Generative AI* (pp. 60–88). IGI Global.

De Back, T. T., Tinga, A. M., & Louwerse, M. M. (2023). Learning in immersed collaborative virtual environments: Design and implementation. *Interactive Learning Environments, 31*(8), 5364–5382. DOI: 10.1080/10494820.2021.2006238

Durairaj, M., Jayakumar, S., Karpagavalli, V., Maheswari, B. U., & Boopathi, S. (2023). Utilization of Digital Tools in the Indian Higher Education System During Health Crises. In *Multidisciplinary Approaches to Organizational Governance During Health Crises* (pp. 1–21). IGI Global. DOI: 10.4018/978-1-7998-9213-7.ch001

Herrera-Pavo, M. Á. (2021). Collaborative learning for virtual higher education. *Learning, Culture and Social Interaction, 28*, 100437. DOI: 10.1016/j.lcsi.2020.100437

Kähkönen, E., & Hölttä-Otto, K. (2022). From crossing chromosomes to crossing curricula–a biomimetic analogy for cross-disciplinary engineering curriculum planning. *European Journal of Engineering Education*, 47(3), 516–534. DOI: 10.1080/03043797.2021.1953446

Kalaiselvi, D., Ramaratnam, M. S., Kokila, S., Sarkar, R., Anandakumar, S., & Boopathi, S. (2024). Future Developments of Higher Education on Social Psychology: Innovation and Changes. In *Advances in Human and Social Aspects of Technology* (pp. 146–169). IGI Global. DOI: 10.4018/979-8-3693-2569-8.ch008

Kezar, A. J. (2023). *Rethinking leadership in a complex, multicultural, and global environment: New concepts and models for higher education*. Taylor & Francis. DOI: 10.4324/9781003446842

Krishnamoorthy, V., Chandra, S., Rajesha, S., Bhattacharjee, S., Murugan, G., & Sampath, B. (2024). Emerging Startups in the Evolving Industry Landscape by Empowering Entrepreneur Growth: An Agile Marketing Practice. In *Digital Transformation Initiatives for Agile Marketing* (pp. 455–484). IGI Global. DOI: 10.4018/979-8-3693-4466-8.ch017

Miller, D. I., Pinerua, I., Margolin, J., & Gerdeman, D. (2022). *Teachers' Pedagogical Content Knowledge in Mathematics and Science: A Cross-Disciplinary Synthesis of Recent DRK-12 Projects*. American Institutes for Research.

Perpignan, C., Baouch, Y., Robin, V., & Eynard, B. (2020). Engineering education perspective for sustainable development: A maturity assessment of cross-disciplinary and advanced technical skills in eco-design. *Procedia CIRP*, 90, 748–753. DOI: 10.1016/j.procir.2020.02.051

Prabhuswamy, M., Tripathi, R., Vijayakumar, M., Thulasimani, T., Sundharesalingam, P., & Sampath, B. (2024). A Study on the Complex Nature of Higher Education Leadership: An Innovative Approach. In *Challenges of Globalization and Inclusivity in Academic Research* (pp. 202–223). IGI Global. DOI: 10.4018/979-8-3693-1371-8.ch013

Pyrialakou, V. D., Dey, K., Martinelli, D., Deskins, J., Fraustino, J. D., Plein, C., Rahman, M. T., Rambo-Hernandez, K. E., & Roy, A. (2020). Holistic engineering: A concept exploration in a cross-disciplinary project course experience. *2020 ASEE North Central Section Conference*. DOI: 10.18260/1-2--35736

Ruben, B. D., De Lisi, R., & Gigliotti, R. A. (2023). *A guide for leaders in higher education: Concepts, competencies, and tools*. Taylor & Francis.

Saravanan, S., Chandrasekar, J., Satheesh Kumar, S., Patel, P., Maria Shanthi, J., & Boopathi, S. (2024). The Impact of NBA Implementation Across Engineering Disciplines: Innovative Approaches. In *Advances in Higher Education and Professional Development* (pp. 229–252). IGI Global. DOI: 10.4018/979-8-3693-1666-5.ch010

Sharma, D. M., Ramana, K. V., Jothilakshmi, R., Verma, R., Maheswari, B. U., & Boopathi, S. (2024). Integrating Generative AI Into K-12 Curriculums and Pedagogies in India: Opportunities and Challenges. *Facilitating Global Collaboration and Knowledge Sharing in Higher Education With Generative AI*, 133–161.

Sidekerskienė, T., & Damaševičius, R. (2023). Out-of-the-Box Learning: Digital Escape Rooms as a Metaphor for Breaking Down Barriers in STEM Education. *Sustainability (Basel)*, 15(9), 7393. DOI: 10.3390/su15097393

Singh Madan, B., Najma, U., Pande Rana, D., & Kumar, P. K. J., S., S., & Boopathi, S. (2024). Empowering Leadership in Higher Education: Driving Student Performance, Faculty Development, and Institutional Progress. In *Advances in Educational Technologies and Instructional Design* (pp. 191–221). IGI Global. DOI: 10.4018/979-8-3693-0583-6.ch009

Stek, K. (2023). *A Challenge-Based Experiment Aiming to Develop Strategic Thinking an Inquiry into the Role of Stimulating Creativity for out-of-the-Box Thinking*. EasyChair.

Tai, Y., & Ting, Y.-L. (2020). English-learning mobile app designing for engineering students' cross-disciplinary learning and collaboration. *Australasian Journal of Educational Technology*, 36(2), 120–136.

Vaithianathan, V., Shastri, D. S., Nandakumar, V., Misba, M., Kumar, P. S. V. V. S. R., & Boopathi, S. (2024). NEP Policy Implementation Strategies in Education in India. In *Educational Philosophy and Sociological Foundation of Education* (pp. 325–356). IGI Global., DOI: 10.4018/979-8-3693-3587-1.ch013

Vaithianathan, V., Subbulakshmi, N., Boopathi, S., & Mohanraj, M. (2024). Integrating Project-Based and Skills-Based Learning for Enhanced Student Engagement and Success: Transforming Higher Education. In *Adaptive Learning Technologies for Higher Education* (pp. 345–372). IGI Global. DOI: 10.4018/979-8-3693-3641-0.ch015

Venkatasubramanian, V., Chitra, M., Sudha, R., Singh, V. P., Jefferson, K., & Boopathi, S. (2024). Examining the Impacts of Course Outcome Analysis in Indian Higher Education: Enhancing Educational Quality. In *Challenges of Globalization and Inclusivity in Academic Research* (pp. 124–145). IGI Global.

Wei, Y.-Y., Chen, W.-F., Xie, T., & Peng, J.-J. (2022). Cross-disciplinary curriculum integration spaces for emergency management engineering talent cultivation in higher education. *Computer Applications in Engineering Education*, 30(4), 1175–1189. DOI: 10.1002/cae.22513

Wu, Z. (2022). Understanding teachers' cross-disciplinary collaboration for STEAM education: Building a digital community of practice. *Thinking Skills and Creativity*, 46, 101178. DOI: 10.1016/j.tsc.2022.101178

Yadav, U., Pitchai, R., Gopal, V., Kumar, K. R. S., Talukdar, M., & Boopathi, S. (2024). Powers of Higher Education Leadership: Navigating Policy and Management in Academic Institutions. In *Navigating Leadership and Policy Management in Education* (pp. 103–136). IGI Global., DOI: 10.4018/979-8-3693-9215-7.ch004

Yazici, H. J., Zidek, L. A., & St. Hill, H. (2020). A study of critical thinking and cross-disciplinary teamwork in engineering education. *Women in Industrial and Systems Engineering: Key Advances and Perspectives on Emerging Topics*, 185–196.

KEY TERMS AND DEFINITIONS

PCK: Pedagogical Content Knowledge
PD: Professional Development
PLC: Professional Learning Community
ANOVA: Analysis of Variance
STEM: Science, Technology, Engineering, and Mathematics

Chapter 7
Developing Science Pedagogical Content Knowledge (PCK) Among Preservice and Novice Elementary Teachers

Sandy White Watson
https://orcid.org/0000-0002-8885-6203
University of Louisiana at Monroe, USA

ABSTRACT

In this chapter, the author focuses on elementary-level practicing and pre-service teachers' development of pedagogical content knowledge (PCK), beginning with the state of U.S. students' science performance, and science instruction in elementary school settings. The historical development of studies related to teachers' knowledge forms (content, pedagogical, and pedagogical content) are explored individually, along with an investigation of models of PCK, PCK specific to teaching science, and studies on strategies for facilitating PCK development among elementary teacher candidates and in-service teachers.

INTRODUCTION

STEM (science, technology, engineering, mathematics) proficiency in the United States has long been in a state of decline, negatively impacting America's economy and security. Its citizens are not filling U.S. STEM jobs; to keep these positions filled, America relies on immigrants. International students are increasingly coming to

DOI: 10.4018/979-8-3693-0655-0.ch007

the US to be trained in STEM and then remain here to fill vacant STEM positions (Herman, 2019).

American students have been lagging behind other nations' science academic success for years (Santau et al., 2014). While other countries have greatly improved their students' science test scores, the United States' students' science scores have remained stagnant since 2006. The most recent PISA (2015) results indicated that the US ranked 24th out of 71 countries in science and the gap between high and low-performing students in science continues to increase (NCSES, 2019). Of the 35 OECD (Organization for Economic Co-operation and Development) countries, the US ranked 19th. In 2015 (most recent), scores from the National Assessment of Educational Progress revealed that only 35% of U.S. fourth graders were proficient or better in science. And, according to the TIMSS study (Trends in International Mathematics and Science Study) from 2105, of 48 countries, seven outperformed the U.S. in fourth-grade science. Finally, of U.S. high school students planning to attend college, only 20% were prepared to pursue STEM degrees (Committee on STEM Education, 2018). In contrast, U.S. colleges and universities offer some of the best STEM education programs globally, and America continues to be highly attractive to international students, especially those pursuing STEM degrees at both the graduate and undergraduate levels (Herman, 2019). In addition, STEM jobs in the U.S. have grown over four times that of other jobs, yet STEM positions continue to be unfilled by native U.S. citizens (Hossain & Robinson, 2012). This STEM crisis in the United States threatens our national security, economy, and world standings in STEM. We must address the problem where it begins, in the U.S. K-12 educational system, a system failing to motivate students in STEM.

The State of U.S. Science Education in Elementary Schools

U.S. children's first formal experiences with science should take place in the early grades of elementary school, and when they receive these expected experiences, firm foundations in science are established (National Research Council, 2012). Strong and early experiences with science are critical for the development of children's science content knowledge, science positivity, science-confidence, for promoting their science literacy and development as socially responsible citizens (King et al., 2001), and for promoting their interest in STEM fields. Yet, science in elementary schools continues to be either ignored, greatly diminished or taught mostly via direct instruction (Blank, 2012). In fact, instructional time devoted to science in elementary schools has declined since the *No Child Left Behind Act* of 2001, which placed priority on reading and mathematics, by 75 minutes per week (Center for Education Policy, 2008; National Research Council, 2012). By 2018, children were taught science on average, only 18 minutes per day, while they received

89 minutes of English language arts instruction and 57 minutes of math instruction (National Survey of Science and Mathematics Education, 2018) per day. This lack of emphasis on science in elementary schools, a time when children have high science interest, contributes to elementary students' loss of interest in science that begins in fourth grade and continues to high school entrance (Barmby et al., 2008; Devetak et al., 2009; Murphy et al., 2006; Turner & Ireson, 2014). Reasons for this lack of interest in science among elementary students has been tied to teachers' over-reliance on direct instruction (Zinger et al., 2020), lack of time spent on science instruction (Levy et al., 2008), and lack of student confidence in science (O'Dwyer & Childs, 2014). All of these reasons are linked to elementary teachers' limited science content knowledge (SCK) – or knowledge about science as a subject matter. Other similar forms of knowledge include content knowledge (CK) –any subject matter knowledge coupled with knowledge of its organizing structures (Shulman, 1986), pedagogical knowledge (PK) -knowledge of teaching (Schulman, 1986), or pedagogical content knowledge (PCK) – a combination of subject matter knowledge, knowledge of teaching, and knowledge of one's students that together, most positively impacts students' learning gains (Loughran et al., 2006). All of these related forms of knowledge will be examined in this chapter with a focus on the need for the reformation of university teacher preparation/science education programs and how teachers are prepared for teaching science.

Educational researchers have determined that the science content knowledge of elementary and pre-service teachers is significantly lacking (Burgoon et al., 2011; Catalano et al., 2019) and that many of them hold science-related misconceptions (Bursal, 2012). Science content areas of particular difficulty for elementary teachers include the states of matter (Ozden, 2008; Valnides 2000), cell topics (Usak, 2009), buoyancy, (Potvin & Cyr, 2017), forces and motion, gravity, density, energy transformation and conservation, and physical and chemical changes (Akgun, 2009; Anggoro et al., 2017; Dawkins et al., 2003; Papadouris et al., 2014; Stein et al., 2018; Trumper, 2003). When elementary teachers possess limited science content knowledge, their science teaching self-efficacy is low (Anggoro, 2017; Koc & Yager, 2016), and their confidence in, comfort with, and preparedness for teaching science declines (Kind, 2009). All of these factors combined often causes them to avoid science instruction, which in turn negatively impacts students' science learning outcomes (Krall et al., 2009) and science interest levels, which tend to decrease beginning in fourth grade (Mullis & Jenkins, 1988). Researchers further believe that elementary teachers' limited science content knowledge is directly linked to their own negative attitudes toward science, and their reduced ability to teach science (King et al., 2001). All of these issues often result in teachers' avoidance of science instruction (Burgoon et al., 2011; Krall et al., 2009) and over-reliance on textbooks, pre-packaged curricula, and lectures rather than active learning (Abell, 2007).

Content Knowledge

What elementary teachers must know to be able to effectively teach elementary school students has long been a topic of investigation among educational researchers. Earlier expectations focused on content knowledge (CK) alone. Content knowledge refers to subject matter knowledge coupled with knowledge of its organizing structures (Shulman, 1986). CK can also be described as being aware of what actions are and aren't legitimate in a field of study, understanding *why* something is the way it is, and what elements of a discipline are central or peripheral (Shulman, 1986). Content knowledge is specific to disciplines (science CK, mathematics, CK, etc.). In the case of science CK, it is the teacher's knowledge of science content and the process of science inquiry involving evidence collection and interpretation to support conceptual comprehension (Fleer & Pramling, 2015) as well as knowledge of science process skills, such as observing, measuring, inferring, classifying, interpreting data, comparing, etc. (Nyisztor & Marcus, 2008).

Pedagogical Knowledge

The earliest studies of what teachers must know to be able to teach concentrated entirely on CK. Later, pedagogical knowledge (PK- teaching knowledge) was also deemed necessary (Schulman, 1986). Pedagogical knowledge is concerned with the act of teaching and includes multiple components such as planning, implementing, and evaluating a lesson, organizing a sequence of lessons, how to best present the content and ideas of a lesson, and more (Barnett & Hodson, 2001). Most educational researchers agree to a similar set of elements but disagree as to how pedagogical knowledge might be conceptualized. For example, Tardif (2010) described pedagogical knowledge as being composed of five types of knowledge: (1) professional knowledge derived from pedagogical curricula; (2) disciplinary knowledge related to classroom management; (3) curricular knowledge; (4) experiential (practical) knowledge: skills and habits garnered from teaching experiences; and (5) pedagogical knowledge gained from reflective practice. However, Shulman identified two categories of knowledge for teaching: teaching knowledge and sources of acquisition for such teaching knowledge, each containing specific types of knowledge. The first (teaching knowledge) consists of (1) subject matter knowledge; (2) knowledge of teaching in general; (3) curricular knowledge; (4) subject-related pedagogical knowledge; (5) student learner knowledge; (6) knowledge related to the context of education; and (7) knowledge of the philosophical and historical foundations of educational goals, aims and values. The second (sources for the acquisition of these types of knowledge) include (1) knowledge garnered from discipline-specific training that enables teacher candidates to distinguish between essential and peripheral concepts; (2) knowledge of the didactic elements of foundational teaching principles; (3) knowledge of the processes of teaching, learning, and schooling, and (4) knowledge gained from practical teaching experience. To simplify, we can deduce that pedagogical knowledge is "knowledge in use," a dynamic, evolving set of skills and practices that often develop out of a teacher's interactions with their students over time in the classroom environment (Schön, 1998).

Pedagogical Content Knowledge

Shulman (1986) stated that possessing content knowledge (CK) and pedagogical knowledge (PK) as separate entities was insufficient for effective teaching and merged these two knowledge types, calling this expanded type of knowledge pedagogical content knowledge (PCK). Shulman defined this broader PCK as a dramatic shift in which teachers move from being able to comprehend subject matter for themselves, to becoming able to elucidate subject matter in new ways, reorganize and partition it, clothe it in activities and emotions, in metaphors and exercises, and in examples and demonstrations, so that it can be grasped by students. (Shulman, 1987, p. 13)

Others define it as the unique, distinctive and powerful blended knowledge possessed by a teacher related to content, pedagogy, and their students that results in student learning gains (Loughran et al., 2006), and the transformation of a teacher's CK so that it is accessible to all of their students (Abell, 2007). Niess (2005) defined PCK as "the intersection of knowledge of the subject with knowledge of teaching and learning" (p. 510). Lowery (2002) described it as "that domain of teachers' knowledge that combines subject matter knowledge and knowledge of pedagogy" (p. 69), while de Berg & Grieve (1999) conceptualized it as "the product of transforming subject matter into a form that will facilitate student learning" (p. 20). Still others refer to it as CK alone, or mostly pedagogical knowledge, or frame it in such a broad way that it seems to encompass all types of pedagogical knowledge possessed by teachers, with no distinctions for teachers' beliefs, reasoning, actions, and knowledge (Ball et al., 2008).

Further, Chan & Hume (2019) and Park and Chen (2012) maintained that it is the integration of all of these components of PCK that is crucial for effective science instruction, while Gess-Newsome & Lederman (1999) stated that it is not an integration, but rather an amalgamation or transformation. All of these varying conceptions of PCK contribute to a lack of clarity surrounding PCK and its boundaries.

Moreover, Cochran et al. (1993) felt Schulman's perception of PCK was still too compartmentalized and static. They instead posited that PCK should always be growing and changing and thus gave their version of the idea the name pedagogical content knowing (PCKg), which includes four types of teacher knowledge: subject matter knowledge, pedagogical knowledge, knowledge of their students, and knowledge of the educational environment (Shing, et al., 2015). All of these concepts of PCK are embedded in the constructivist learning theoretical framework that posits that learning will occur if the environment is relevant, that learning involves social interaction and collaboration, knowledge is presented in multiple formats, knowledge is constructed and learners are aware that it is constructed, and that learners have ownership in their learning (Woolfolk, 2014).

PCK Effectiveness

Research shows that elementary teachers with higher levels of science PCK are competent at facilitating useful class discussions, pose higher-level questions, and are more likely to connect science content with real-world experience than those with lower PCK (Davis, 2004; Newton & Newton, 2001). In addition, teachers strong in science PCK are more likely to plan and implement inquiry-based instruction and maintain a classroom culture based on investigations (Luera et al., 2005).

An effective science teacher with integrated PCK will make lesson-planning decisions based on the learning needs of their students. For example, such a teacher with a BVI (blind or visually impaired) student in his class might plan to demonstrate the structure of an animal cell to the BVI student with a tactile diagram of the cell and its organelles and to regularly sighted students with a microscope and animal cell slides. This command of integrated PCK correlates to highly effective (Park & Chen, 2012), and more experienced teachers (Akin & Uzuntiryaki-Kondakci, 2018).

Furthermore, pedagogical content knowledge is situated within the constructivist learning theoretical framework, a framework long regarded as the reigning paradigm in US education (Hausfather, 2001). Constructivism as it posits the following: that learning will occur if the environment is relevant, that learning involves social interaction and collaboration, knowledge is presented in multiple formats, knowledge is constructed and learners are aware that it is constructed, and that learners have ownership in their learning (Woolfolk, 2014).

Integrative and Transformative Models of PCK

Since Shulman's introduction of PCK (1986), other scholars have advanced the concept of PCK by creating PCK models from differing perspectives (Hashweh, 2005; Loughran et al., 2006), including two primary models: integrative and transformative. The integrative model (see Figure 1) maintains that PCK is not a stand-alone knowledge domain, but rather it only becomes a knowledge form when "teachers selectively draw upon the independent knowledge bases of subject matter, pedagogy, and context and integrate them as needed to create effective learning opportunities" (Gess-Newsome, 1999, p.11), while the transformative model (see Figure 2) views

PCK as a synthesized knowledge form consisting of subject matter, pedagogical and context knowledge, and that these three types of knowledge are only useful for teaching when they work together (Gess-Newsome, 1999).

Gess-Newsome (1999) distinguished between transformative and integrated PCK by using a simple, but effective, analogy of a mixture versus a compound. Like a mixture, the components of integrated PCK can be separated fairly simply, with each component retaining its original characteristics. There is little interaction among the components of a mixture, just as there is little interaction among the components of integrated PCK. On the other hand, the transformative model of PCK is similar to a compound, where the elements making up the compound are joined together with lots of interaction among them. The components are synthesized and cannot be separated, thus what results in the case of a compound or transformative PCK, is something entirely new. For PCK it is a new type of knowledge.

Figure 1. Integrative Model of PCK

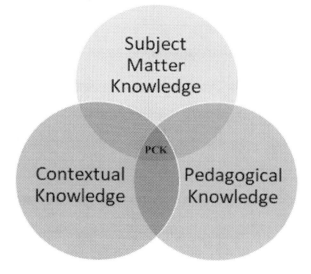

Figure 2. Transformative Model of PCK

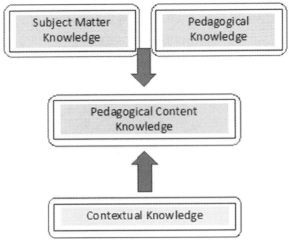

Enacted and Personal Models of PCK

PCK was further analyzed in 2019 by Carlson and Daehler, who determined that it could consist of two distinct domains: *enacted* and *personal,* and that either of the two can influence the other. Enacted PCK refers to knowledge a teacher invokes in the classroom environment, while personal PCK refers to the teacher's own knowledge and experiences, including professional experiences and interactions, whether with other teachers, associated individuals or students. According to Carlson and Daehler, the learning context within which a teacher exists is influenced by both enacted and personal domains. They further identified a *collective* PCK as consisting of the specific knowledge base a teacher holds for teaching a subject to certain students in a specific learning context (to include subject matter knowledge, knowledge of their students, knowledge of pedagogy, knowledge of curricula, and knowledge of assessment), which was validated by Razak et al. 2024). This collective PCK is also shared with other professionals in the specific learning context and can influence a teacher's personal PCK.

Teacher Pedagogical Actions and Reasoning

Baxter and Lederman (1999) added an additional dimension to PCK by including a teacher's pedagogical actions in the classroom setting and their reasoning behind those actions. They stressed the importance of establishing a link between a teacher's pedagogical practices and knowledge, and factors that might encourage or impede their enactment of PCK (Aydeniz & Kirbulut, 2014). Thus, PCK must be examined at both the planned level as well as the enacted level for a better understanding of how it is developed by teachers and how they implement it in practice (Aydeniz & Kirbulut, 2014). At the planned level, PCK refers to the combination of CK and PK needed to effectively explain a particular topic to students (Park & Oliver, 2008), while enacted PCK refers to the metacognitive actions taken by a teacher to meet their students' learning needs. Both espoused/planned PCK and enacted PCK are necessary for effective teaching (Aydeniz & Kirbulut, 2014; Park & Oliver, 2008).

Technological PCK

Finally, a third type of PCK has emerged called Technological Pedagogical Content Knowledge (TPACK) that focuses on the types of technological tools and associated resources used by teachers in their teaching practices. TPACK integrates technology into CK and PK (Arnold et al., 2009) for improving instructional methods and enhancing students' content understanding. Figure 3 depicts the TPACK model. The diagram illustrates the relationships among technological tools/resources, content knowledge, and pedagogical knowledge.

Figure 3. TPACK

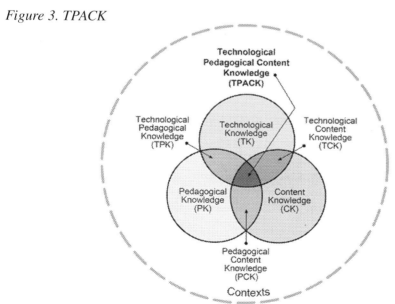

Note. TPACK image illustrating knowledge intersections, used with permission from http://www.tpack.org

Science PCK

Magnusson et al. (1999) created a specific model of PCK for use in the natural sciences. Their model incorporated knowledge of science instructional strategies and knowledge of assessing scientific literacy. This new science-specific PCK model has been widely accepted and utilized in the literature as a model that is helpful for understanding elements of PCK (Kind, 2015). Other work in this area includes that of Loughran et al. (2004), who identified elements of knowledge necessary for effective science teaching. Knowing the specific elements of PCK necessary for teaching science is especially helpful for developing the scientific PCK of pre-service and novice teachers. In fact, to be effective teachers of science, elementary teachers must have advanced espoused and enacted PCK (Mansor et al., 2010). However, teacher education programs have not yet been successful in developing sophisticated PCK among their pre-service teachers (Aydeniz & Kirbulut, 2014). Thus, many new teacher graduates remain ineffective at teaching science.

Elementary Teachers' PCK for Teaching Science

An elementary teacher's command of science PCK is particularly critical for developing science literacy, science content knowledge (SCK), science confidence, and positive attitudes toward science among their students (National Research Council, 2012). Researchers (Kind, 2009; O'Dwyer & Childs, 2014) found a direct correlation between an elementary teacher's SCK and their students' science learning outcomes and between teachers' science instruction and the successful development of students' comprehension of science concepts (Lee & Luykx, 2007).

However, there is some disagreement among scholars on whether or not SCK should be jettisoned for a focus on PCK (Lee et al., 2007; Santau et al., 2014). For example, Santau et al. (2014) found that there is great value in revisiting SCK before an emphasis on PCK occurs because, without strong science content understanding, the development of PCK cannot take place. Specifically, elementary teachers with weak SCK ask lower-level questions and garner lower levels of student participation in discussions than those with stronger SCK (Carlsen, 1987); they are often unable to adequately explain science terms and complex concepts (Carrier, 2013); are more apt to tell students science concepts rather than have them discover such concepts themselves through inquiry-based investigations (Newton & Newton, 2001); often demonstrate a substantial dependence on texts, worksheets, and pre-packaged curricula; prefer direct instruction for teaching science, and avoid students' science-related questions (Abell, 2007). There is also a dearth of hands-on, active learning of science in elementary school classrooms led by teachers with lower levels of SCK (Banilower et al., 2013.)

Many elementary teachers likely possess some SCK, but that knowledge is often "not sufficient to teach rigorous standards-based science content" (Santau, 2014, p. 18). Weak SCK among teachers means they are less likely to be able to identify and correct the science misconceptions of their students (Davis, 2004) and less likely to anticipate their students' science learning directions (Shallcross et al., 2002). Thus, elementary teachers need to have their existing knowledge base in science strengthened (Weiss et al., 2001) and their science misconceptions corrected (Bursal, 2012; Rice & Kaya, 2012) before they will be effective teachers of science.

There are several reasons why a thorough development of science PCK among elementary pre-service teachers has been challenging. First, according to Grossman (1990), teacher candidates enter teacher education programs with a variety of diverse SCK levels, epistemological perspectives, worldviews, and experiences (Aydeniz & Kirbulut, 2014), meaning some candidates might be more apt to develop science PCK than others. Next, science education professors are time-constrained and thus cannot model best practices for every science topic that makes up a typical elementary school science curriculum (Grossman, 1990), so many science topics are not broached in elementary science methods courses. Finally, PCK differs according to science topic and student diversity, thus science methods instructors are not likely to be able to address every possible context. These three variables make the development of sophisticated PCK in pre-service teachers difficult (Ball et al., 2008).

To be effective in PCK, teachers must have a firm command of both PK and CK. If either PK or CK is weak, PCK will also be weak. As previously stated, educational researchers have determined that the SCK of elementary and pre-service teachers is limited (Burgoon et al., 2011; Catalano et al., 2019; Pamintuan, 2024; Sunzuma et al., 2024), especially in chemistry and cell topics (Ozden, 2008; Usak, 2009) and that many of them hold science-related misconceptions (often passed on to their own students) (Bursal, 2012), even though if asked, they will indicate they are teaching science effectively.

When elementary teachers have limited PCK, their confidence in their ability to understand and teach science concepts is also limited, and consequently, they become reluctant to teach science (Kind, 2009). A 2019 National Science Foundation survey found that less than 25% of elementary teachers felt well prepared to teach any science subject and only 3% indicated feeling capable of teaching engineering (Banilower et al., 2013). This lack of science teaching confidence is a significant barrier to the development of PCK among teachers, whether preservice or practicing (Appleton, 2006). Also, a limitation for elementary teachers is their school's ability to provide science-related teaching resources. These two limitations combined with the perception passed by school leaders to teachers that science is not a priority, further contribute to elementary teachers' low science self-efficacy (Goodrum et al., 2001).

Tools for Developing and Measuring Science PCK among Elementary Teachers

The literature admits there is a challenge related to assessing PCK (Lin & Wang, 2024), especially in larger scaled studies. In an attempt to aid pre-service and novice teachers in their development of PCK, "praxis tools" have been created to help them engage in responsive practice discussions (Curry, 2008; Windschitl et al., 2011). According to Windschitl et al. (2011), "Praxis tools embed theory about good teaching into material resources or strategies that guide planning, instruction, analysis of learning, and reflection" (p. 1317). Two such tools are the CoRes (Content Representation) and PaP-eRs (Pedagogical and Professional-experience Repertoires) projects (Loughran et al., 2004). The CoRes was created to better understand the PCK of science teachers by capturing, portraying, and codifying it in such a way that other teachers might access and utilize it. The PaP-eRs is a tool for understanding the decisions teachers make regarding their pedagogical actions. The PaP-eRs tool is also beneficial to educational researchers, helping them better understand how teachers view and classify science content, how they interpret the interactions of science content and science processes, and how they transfer science content to their students in ways students can understand. In addition, these tools are useful for helping teachers build sophisticated PCK through pedagogical experience and reflection (Hume & Berry, 2011).

Aydeniz & Kirbulut (2014) developed an instrument called the Secondary Teachers' Scientific Pedagogical Content Knowledge (STSPCK) specific to measuring science pre-service teachers' electrochemistry PCK and topic-specific PCK using espoused PCK as their reference. This third tool focused on the strengths and weaknesses of teacher candidates who espoused PCK by having them respond to prompts related to curriculum, assessment, and instruction.

In the curriculum category, participants responded to statements such as "the teacher uses an inquiry-based curriculum" or "the teacher uses a problem-based science curriculum" by providing examples of such usage and comments for each statement. The same process was followed for statements in the instruction category (such as "the teacher identifies the limitations and strengths of his/her students' poor conceptions" or "the teacher provides experiences for the students to understand the limitations of their initial ideas") and in the assessment category (examples include "the teacher poses open-ended questions" or "the teacher uses problems that require the students to communicate their understanding of the concept through multiple means") (Aydeniz & Kirbulut, 2014, pp. 164-166). Data analysis of students' responses indicated that the STSPCK was specifically useful for identifying "aspects and nature of content knowledge, curriculum, and assessment relevant to the concept of PCK" (p. 163). While Aydeniz and Kirbulut focused on secondary science teachers in this work, their instrument could easily be adapted for use with elementary teachers by changing the topic to one addressed in elementary science classes.

Finally, Lin and Wang (2024) developed a Rasch-modeled measurement method quantitative instrument to assess each element of PCK of scientific thinking, which allows for a better understanding of the individual elements of PCK on "overall PCK performance" (p. 505), allowing for "investigating teachers' PCK in authentic classroom settings on a large scale" (p. 505). However, they recommend further research surrounding how each PCK element connects and integrates.

Integration of PCK Components in Pre-service Elementary Teachers

Some studies indicate that pre-service elementary teachers are capable of early integration of PCK components (Kaya, 2009; Mavhunga, 2020; Schneider, 2015). Schneider (2015) discovered that pre-service teachers consider students' learning abilities and cognition when planning instructional strategies, delivering a lesson, and reflecting on that lesson, thus they are actively engaged in integrating PCK elements. Additionally, Kaya (2009) found when analyzing pre-service teachers' survey data evidence of PCK integration includes knowledge of specific science curricula, instructional strategies, and their students' levels of understanding. Finally, Mavhunga (2020) found evidence of integrated PCK when analyzing pre-service teachers' science content representation. However, studies focusing on the developing integration of PCK skills among pre-service teachers enrolled in teacher education programs are limited, although the studies that are available stress the importance of teaching experience and reflection for developing PCK integration skills in pre-service teachers (Saeleset & Friedrichsen, 2021).

One study that focused on the development of PCK integration skills in pre-service teachers is that of van Driel et al. (2002), who focused on examining pre-service teachers' knowledge of students' understanding of science (KSU) and their knowledge of instructional strategies (KIS). van Driel et al. (2002) found that both KSU and KIS developed during teaching experiences, a fact later confirmed by Sorge et al. (2019). van Driel et al. also learned that KSU and KIS developed among pre-service teachers while being mentored by a veteran teacher and as a result of university workshops emphasizing PCK development. Moreover, Brown et al. (2013) conducted a related study and found that KSU and KIS develop at the same time during student teaching, and Aydm et al. (2013) noted increased PCK integration among pre-service teachers during a 14-week practicum course focused on PCK integration.

Developing Science PCK in Elementary Teachers

Until fairly recently, educational researchers considered the development of PCK among teachers to involve a similar process, whether they were elementary or secondary. The studies of Appleton (2006), Smith (1999), and Smith and Neale (1991) indicate that the development of PCK occurs differently for elementary teachers as compared to secondary teachers. For example, Bell et al. (1998), when working with secondary physics teachers, observed different levels of PCK situated in a type of hierarchy. The three levels of PCK they identified consisted of a broad knowledge base in science, a more specific discipline-aligned knowledge base (chemistry, for example), and a third level of knowledge related to a specific topic, such as pH. On the other hand, Appleton (2006) found that elementary teachers work with PCK differently than secondary teachers, often starting with an activity or idea for a specific science lesson (the third specific topic level for secondary teachers) and are rarely able to develop disciplinary knowledge (second level for secondary teachers). Moreover, because elementary teachers are trained as generalists in order to teach several subjects, it is difficult for them to have expertise in some of the more challenging subjects such as life, earth, and physical science (Kilic, 2024; Nowicki et al., 2012.). Thus, strategies for developing science PCK among elementary teachers must be specific to their experiences and science learning needs.

Bell and Gilbert (1996) explored what they termed transformative professional development in science. This more effective type of professional development includes social (developing opportunities for teacher collaborations), professional (focus on ideas and actions), and personal (focus on emotions). Teachers participating in this type of transformative professional development demonstrated integrated PCK, which allowed for profound lasting changes in their science teaching practices.

Another method for helping elementary teachers acquire PCK is by providing them with sustained, individual mentoring (Peers et al., 2003). Appleton (2008) described his role as a long-term science mentor for elementary teachers as a subject matter expert whose presence sometimes allowed teachers to hand over class control when their science knowledge faltered, a co-lesson planner in the quest for clearer outcomes, a helper during instruction, a source of alternative teaching and learning viewpoints, and a challenger of their current (and sometimes stagnant) teaching practices. At the end of his experience with his mentees, the mentored teachers described changes in their teaching practices to include a greater focus on outcomes rather than activities (constructivism), an increase in their own use of metacognition, asking more probing questions of students, more effective scaffolding skills, improving the frequency and quality of explanations and modeling, increasing the frequency and quality of hands-on science experiences, relinquishing control of lessons to allow students more freedom to explore, and increasing their ability to correct students' science misconceptions. Mentees also experienced increased confidence in their own science comprehension and ability to teach science.

Aydm et al. (2013) investigated how professional science teaching journals facilitate teachers' PCK growth. Practical professional journals such as *Science and Children* for teachers of elementary students, and *Science Scope,* for teachers of middle grades students, contain many of what Appleton called "activities that work." These well-constructed lessons are often excellent models of good science teaching practice and "contribute to the development of teachers' PCK" for science teaching (Aydm et al., 2013, p. 978). While not all of the articles they examined promoted PCK development in teachers, Aydm et al. felt that most could easily do so if they were enhanced.

Pre-service Elementary Teachers' Science Experiences

The elementary science methods course taken by pre-service teachers is a logical starting point for their development of science PCK in teacher candidates. However, elementary science methods courses are as varied as the universities that offer them, and the primary focus of many of these courses is science pedagogy rather than science content. Moscovici & Osisioma (2008) reviewed the content of multiple elementary science methods courses across the U.S. and found the following topics commonly offered across the courses: inquiry science, learning cycles, active learning, cooperative groups, nature of science, assessment, integration with other subjects, equity and diversity, technology, constructivism, concept mapping, curriculum evaluation, safety, misconceptions, and reflective practice. Even though it is possible that the science methods course is the final opportunity to help teacher candidates learn science content, since it occurs most often toward the end of these students' educational programs of study, no science content appeared in Moscovici & Osisioma's (2008) listing of course topics, a problem also mentioned by Nowicki et al. (2012).

Prior to taking the science methods course, pre-service elementary teachers must take a number of general education natural science courses, however, they are rarely required to take physics or chemistry, two traditionally problematic subjects for these teachers (Trygstad, 2013). In addition, most university general education science courses are taught via traditional lecture methods, strategies long known to be ineffective at improving students' science comprehension (Stains et al., 2018) or mitigating science misconceptions (Carmel & Yezierski, 2013). These courses have long been frustrating to teacher education students because while they are being taught to teach science via active and inquiry-based learning in their science methods course(s), they are experiencing science instruction that is just the opposite in their general education science courses (Kumar & Morris, 2005). These feelings of frustration contribute to pre-service teachers' negative attitudes toward science and avoidance of teaching science (Avard, 2010).

The potential for creating effective elementary science teachers is possible with reimagined science methods courses focused on science education reform in order to build elementary teachers' science confidence and attitudes (Morrell & Carroll, 2003; Tosun, 2000).

Researchers have studied methods for building elementary teacher candidates' PCK within a science methods course. What follows is a review of some of those studies and their results.

Developing Science PCK in Elementary Preservice Teachers

Many researchers espouse that deep science content understanding facilitates the development of PCK in teacher candidates (Nilsson, 2008; Oztay & Boz, 2021; Pamintuan, 2024; Park & Oliver, 2008; van Driel et al., 1998). However, little is understood about how CK impacts PCK.

Appleton (2006) proposed the use of science "activities that work" (p. 38), curricula that not only help elementary students learn science content but also promote the science learning of their teachers. These "educative curriculum materials" (Davis & Kracik, 2005) do not consist of just a set of activities and related pedagogical strategies, like many curricula, but are designed to assist teachers in understanding effective formative and summative assessment strategies that link teaching and learning; help them anticipate, identify and correct students' science misconceptions; provide suggestions for challenging students' thinking, like analogies and different ways to represent content ideas (Hanuscin et al., 2014). Adym (2013) described these activities as "hands-on, interesting and motivating for learners, manageable in the classroom, have clear outcomes or results, draw on equipment that is readily available, and lend themselves toward integration" (p. 979).

The field experiences of pre-service teachers involving interaction with veteran teachers have proven to be fruitful for developing elementary preservice teacher candidates' PCK (Henze et al, 2008; Loughran et al., 2012). Specifically, several researchers have noted the positive impact of the use of the lesson study (LS) method to develop preservice teachers' PCK (Fernandez & Yoshida, 2004). The LS method involves veteran teacher(s) moving through the LS cycle with preservice teachers, as shown in Figure 4. The steps include: (1) creation of overall and particular academic goals; (2) group lesson planning takes place with a focus on pedagogical choices and their impacts on student learning; (3) decisions are made on which preservice teacher will teach the lessons and which will observe and collect student data; (4) lesson plan is reflected upon and revised based on observational data collected; (5) a new teacher is selected who teachers a revision of the same lesson to a new student group while the remaining preservice teachers observe and collect student data; (6) observation results are assessed and disseminated.

Figure 4. Lesson study cycle

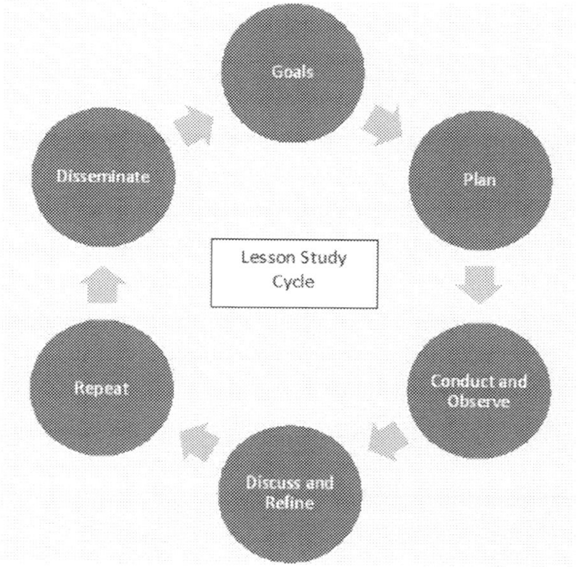

Note: Image credit: Fernandez & Yoshida, 2004.

Using the LS method is particularly effective for the development of PCK because it utilizes the production of research-based knowledge as generated by the observations and their analyses, allows for the focus to be placed on the subject matter being taught during the lesson, and allows for consideration of the perspectives of the students being taught (Fernandez & Yoshida, 2004).

However, the LS method was found to be problematic because teachers spent less time on the planning stage, resulting in a lack of PCK knowledge development in their preservice teachers (Hart et al., 2011). To counteract this problem, the previously mentioned praxis tool (CoRes) was utilized along with the LS method (Loughran et al., 2012; Nilsson & Loughran, 2011; Pongsanon et al., 2011). The CoRes instrument served as a scaffolding tool that served to better help preservice teachers during the planning component. Juhler (2016) conducted one of the only studies on the impact of a combination of the LS method and the CoRes instrument on preservice teachers' PCK. His results revealed that if LS and CoRes are used together, the focus of preservice teachers while planning lessons shifted in significant ways, placing greater emphasis on student's conceptual understanding and assessment of that understanding rather than focusing on instructional strategies. In fact, the preservice teachers in the study had a greater uniform focus on all of the elements of PCK when using LS and CoRes simultaneously (Juhler, 2016).

CONCLUSION

This chapter's author presented an overview of teachers' knowledge types, including content knowledge (CK), pedagogical knowledge (PK), and their combination, pedagogical content knowledge (PCK). Each of these knowledge types was defined and discussed individually and the historical progression of how they came to be merged was covered. In addition, PCK was examined in detail, including an analysis of its transformative and integrative models and its planned and enactive models. A focus on science PCK was also included, followed by a discussion of the development of PCK among preservice and novice teachers using specific models such as the CoRes instrument in concert with Learning Cycles, the use of "activities that work," mentoring, the use of science journals, and more.

REFERENCES

Abell, S. K. (2007). Research on science teacher knowledge. In Abell, S. K., & Lederman, N. G. (Eds.), *Handbook of research on science education* (pp. 1105–1149). Erlbaum., DOI: 10.4324/9780203097267-54

Akgun, A. (2009). The relation between science student teachers' misconceptions about solution, dissolution, diffusion, and their attitudes toward science with their achievement. *Education in Science*, 34(154), 26–36.

Akin, F. N., & Uzuntiryaki-Kondakci, E. (2018). The nature of the interplay among components of pedagogical content knowledge in reaction rate and chemical equilibrium topics of novice and experienced chemistry teachers. *Chemistry Education Research and Practice*, 19(1), 80–105. DOI: 10.1039/C7RP00165G

Anggoro, S., Widodo, A., & Suhandi, A. (2017). Pre-service elementary teachers' understanding of force and motion. *Journal of Physics: Conference Series*, 895, 1–7. DOI: 10.1088/1742-6596/895/1/012151

Appleton, K. (2006). Science pedagogical content knowledge and elementary school leaders. In K. Appleton (Ed.), *Elementary science teacher education: International perspectives in contemporary issues and practice* (pp. 31-54). Lawrence Erlbaum in association with the Association for Science Teacher Education.

Appleton, K. (2008). Developing science pedagogical content knowledge through mentoring elementary teachers. *Journal of Science Teacher Education*, 19(6), 423–545. DOI: 10.1007/s10972-008-9109-4

Arnold, S. R., Padilla, M. J., & Tunhikorn, B. (2009). The development of per-service science teachers' professional knowledge in utilizing ICT to support professional lives. *Eurasia Journal of Mathematics, Science and Technology Education*, 5(2), 91–101. DOI: 10.12973/ejmste/75261

Avard, M. M. (2010). Use of thermochrons in the classroom. *Journal of College Science Teaching*, 38(6), 24–29.

Aydeniz, M., & Kirbulut, Z. (2014). Exploring challenges of assessing pre-service science teachers' pedagogical content knowledge (PCK). *Asia-Pacific Journal of Teacher Education*, 42(2), 146–266. DOI: 10.1080/1359866X.2014.890696

Aydm, S., Demirdogen, B., Muslu, N., & Hanuscin, D. (2013). Professional journals as a source of PCK or teaching nature of science: An examination of articles published in *The Science Teacher (TST)*. *Journal of Science Teacher Education*, 24(6), 977–997. DOI: 10.1007/s10972-013-9345-0

Ball, D. L., Thames, M. H., & Phelps, G. (2008). Content knowledge for teaching: What makes it special? *Journal of Teacher Education*, 59(5), 389–407. DOI: 10.1177/0022487108324554

Banilower, E. R., Smith, P. S., Weiss, I. R., Malzahn, K. A., Campbell, K. M., & Weis, A. M. (2013). *Report of the 2012 National Survey of Science and Mathematics Education*. Horizon Research, Inc.

Barmby, P., Kind, P. M., & Jones, K. (2008). Examining changing attitudes in secondary school science. *International Journal of Science Education*, 30(8), 1075–1093. DOI: 10.1080/09500690701344966

Barnett, J., & Hodson, D. (2001). Pedagogical context knowledge: Toward a fuller understanding of what good science teachers know. *Science Education*, 85(4), 426–453. DOI: 10.1002/sce.1017

Baxter, J. A., & Lederman, N. G. (1999). Assessment and measurement of pedagogical content knowledge. In Gess-Newsome, J., & Lederman, N. G. (Eds.), *Examining pedagogical content knowledge* (pp. 147–161). Kluwer Academic., DOI: 10.1007/0-306-47217-1_6

Bell, B., & Gilbert, J. (1996). Teacher development as personal, professional, and social development. *Teaching and Teacher Education*, 10(5), 483–497. DOI: 10.1016/0742-051X(94)90002-7

Bell, J., Veal, W. R., & Tippins, D. J. (1998, April). The evolution of pedagogical content knowledge in prospective secondary physics teachers. Paper Presented at the *Annual Meeting of the National Association for Research in Science Teaching*, San Diego, CA.

Blank, R. K. (2012). *What is the impact of decline in science instructional time in elementary school?* Paper prepared for the Noyce Foundation.

Brown, P., Friedrichsen, P., & Abell, S. (2013). The development of prospective secondary biology teachers' PCK. *Journal of Science Teacher Education*, 24(1), 133–155. DOI: 10.1007/s10972-012-9312-1

Burgoon, J. N., Heddle, M. L., & Duran, E. (2011). Re-examining the similarities between teacher and student conceptions about physical science. *Journal of Science Teacher Education*, 22(2), 101–114. DOI: 10.1007/s10972-010-9196-x

Bursal, M. (2012). Changes in American pre-service elementary teachers' efficacy beliefs and anxieties during a science methods course. *Science Education International*, 23(1), 40–55.

Carlsen, W. S. (1987). *Why do you ask? The effects of science teacher subject-matter knowledge on teacher questioning and classroom discourse.* Paper presented at the meeting of the American Educational Research Association, Washington DC.

Carlson, J., & Daehler, K. R. (2019). The refined consensus model of pedagogical content knowledge in science education. In Hume, A., Cooper, R., & Borowski, A. (Eds.), *Repositioning pedagogical content knowledge in teachers' knowledge for teaching science* (pp. 77–92). Springer. DOI: 10.1007/978-981-13-5898-2_2

Carmel, J. H., & Yezierski, E. J. (2013). Are we keeping the promise? Investigation of students' critical thinking growth. *Journal of College Science Teaching*, 42, 71–81.

Carrier, S. J. (2013). Elementary preservice teachers' science vocabulary: Knowledge and application. *Journal of Science Teacher Education*, 24(2), 405–425. DOI: 10.1007/s10972-012-9270-7

Catalano, A., Asselta, L., & Durkin, A. (2019). Exploring the relationship between science content knowledge and science teaching self-efficacy among elementary teachers. *IAFOR Journal of Education*, 7(1), 2019. DOI: 10.22492/ije.7.1.04

Center for Education Policy. (2008). *Instructional time in the elementary schools: A closer look at changes for specific subjects.* Center on Education Policy.

Chan, K. K. H., & Hume, A. (2019). Towards a consensus model: Literature review of how science teachers' pedagogical content knowledge is investigated in empirical studies. In Hume, A., Cooper, R., & Borowski, A. (Eds.), *Repositioning Pedagogical Content Knowledge in teachers' knowledge for teaching science* (pp. 3–76). Springer Nature., DOI: 10.1007/978-981-13-5898-2_1

Cochran, K. F., DeRuiter, J. A., & King, R. A. (1993). *Pedagogical content knowing: An integrative model for teacher preparation.* American Educational Research Association.

Curry, M. W. (2008). Critical friends' group: The possibilities and limitations embedded in teacher professional communities aimed at instructional improvement and school reform. *Teachers College Record*, 110(4), 733–774. DOI: 10.1177/016146810811000401

Davis, E. A. (2004). Knowledge integration in science teaching: Analysing teachers' knowledge development. *Research in Science Education, 34,* 21 53. https://doi.org/ DOI: 10.1023/B:RISE.0000021034.01508.b8

Davis, E. A., & Krajcik, J. S. (2005). Designing educative curriculum materials to promote teacher learning. *Educational Researcher*, 34(3), 3–14. DOI: 10.3102/0013189X034003003

Dawkins, K., Dickerson, D., & Butler, S. (2003, April). Pre-service science teachers' pedagogical content knowledge regarding density. *Paper presented at the annual meeting of the American Educational Research Association, Chicago, IL.* https://files.eric.ed.gov/fulltext/ED475827.pdf

de Berg, K. C., & Grieve, C. (1999). Understanding the siphon: An example of the development of pedagogical content knowledge using textbooks and the writings of early scientists. *Australian Science Teachers'. Journal*, 45(4), 19–26.

Devetak, I., Lorber, E. D., Jurisevic, M., & Glazar, S. A. (2009). Comparing Slovenian year 8 and year 9 elementary school pupils' knowledge of electrolyte chemistry and their intrinsic motivation. *Chemistry Education Research and Practice*, 10(4), 281–290. DOI: 10.1039/B920833J

Executive Offices of the President of the United States (2018). *Committee on STEM Education Report.*

Fernandez, C., & Yoshida, M. (2004). *Lesson study: A Japanese approach to improving mathematics teaching and learning.* Lawrence Erlbaum Associates.

Fleer, M., & Pramling, N. (2015). *A cultural-historical study of children learning science: Foregrounding affective imagination in play-based settings.* Springer., DOI: 10.1007/978-94-017-9370-4

Gess-Newsome, J. (1999). Pedagogical content knowledge: An introduction and orientation. In Gess-Newsome, J., & Lederman, N. G. (Eds.), *Examining pedagogical content knowledge: The construct and its implications for science education* (pp. 3–17). Kluwer Academic., DOI: 10.1007/0-306-47217-1_1

Gess-Newsome, J., & Lederman, N. G. (1999). *Examining pedagogical content knowledge: The construct and its implications for science education.* Kluwer Academics.

Goodrum, D., Hackling, M., & Rennie, L. (2001). *The status and quality of teaching and learning of science in Australian schools.* Commonwealth of Australia.

Grossman, P. L. (1990). *The making of a teacher: Teacher knowledge and teacher education.* Teachers College Press.

Hanuscin, D. L., Lee, M. H., & Akerson, V. L. (2014). Elementary teachers' pedagogical content knowledge for teaching the nature of science. *Science Education*, 95(1), 1–190.

Hart, L. C., Alston, A. S., & Murata, A. (Eds.). (2011). *Lesson study research and practice in mathematics education.* Springer., DOI: 10.1007/978-90-481-9941-9

Hashweh, M. Z. (2005). Teacher pedagogical constructions: A reconfiguration of pedagogical content knowledge. *Teachers and Teaching*, 11(3), 273–292. DOI: 10.1080/13450600500105502

Hausfather, S. (2001). Where's the content? The role of content in constructivist teacher education. *Educational Horizons*, 80(1). https://www.jstor.org/stable/42927076

Henze, I., van Driel, J. H., & Verloop, N. (2008). Development of experienced science teachers' pedagogical content knowledge of models of the solar system and the universe. *International Journal of Science Education*, 30(10), 1321–1342. DOI: 10.1080/09500690802187017

Herman, A. (2019). *America's STEM crisis threatens our national security*. American Affairs.

Hossain, M. M., & Robinson, M. G. (2012). *How to motivate U.S. students to pursue STEM (science, technology, engineering, and mathematics) careers*. U.S.-China Education Review.

Hume, A., & Berry, A. (2011). Constructing CoRes- A strategy for building PCK in pre-service science teacher education. *Research in Science Education*, 41(3), 341–355. DOI: 10.1007/s11165-010-9168-3

Juhler, M. V. (2016). The use of lesson study combined with content representation in the planning of physics lessons during field practice to develop pedagogical content knowledge. *Journal of Science Teacher Education*, 27(5), 533–553. DOI: 10.1007/s10972-016-9473-4

Kaya, O. N. (2009). The nature of relationships among the components of pedagogical content knowledge of pre-service science teachers: 'Ozone layer depletion' as an example. *International Journal of Science Education*, 31(7), 961–988. DOI: 10.1080/09500690801911326

Kilic, A. (2024). Examining pre-service science teachers' personal and enacted content knowledge about seasons. *Journal of Theoretical Educational Science*, 17(1), 100–121. DOI: 10.30831/akukeg.1294954

Kind, V. (2009). Pedagogical content knowledge in science education: Perspective and potential for progress. *Studies in Science Education*, 45(2), 169–204. DOI: 10.1080/03057260903142285

Kind, V. (2015). On the beauty of knowing then not knowing: Pinning down the elusive qualities of PCK. In Berry, A., Friedrichsen, P., & Loughran, J. (Eds.), *Re-examining Pedagogical Content Knowledge in Science Education* (pp. 178–195). Routledge., DOI: 10.4324/9781315735665-19

King, K., Shumow, L., & Lietz, S. (2001). Science education in an urban elementary school: Case studies of teacher beliefs and classroom practices. *Science Education*, 85(2), 465–478. DOI: 10.1002/1098-237X(200103)85:2<89::AID-SCE10>3.0.CO;2-H

Koc, I., & Yager, R. (2016). Preservice teachers' alternative conceptions of science. *Cypriot Journal of Science Education*, 11(3), 144–159. DOI: 10.18844/cjes.v11i3.215

Krall, R., Lott, K. H., & Wymer, C. L. (2009). Inservice elementary and middle school teachers' conceptions of photosynthesis and respiration. *Journal of Science Teacher Education*, 20(1), 41–55. DOI: 10.1007/s10972-008-9117-4

Kumar, D. D., & Morris, J. D. (2005). Predicting scientific understanding of prospective elementary teachers: Role of gender, education level, courses in science, and attitudes toward science and mathematics. *Journal of Science Education and Technology*, 14(4), 387–391. DOI: 10.1007/s10956-005-8083-2

Lee, O., Luykx, A., Buxton, C., & Shaver, A. (2007). The challenge of altering elementary school teachers' beliefs and practices regarding linguistic and cultural diversity in science education. *Journal of Research in Science Teaching*, 44(9), 1269–1291. DOI: 10.1002/tea.20198

Lee, O., Luykx, A., Buxton, C., & Shaver, A. (2007). The challenge of altering elementary school teachers' beliefs and practices regarding linguistic and cultural diversity in science instruction. *Journal of Research in Science Teaching*, 44(9), 1269–1291. DOI: 10.1002/tea.20198

Levy, A. J., Pasquale, M. M., & Marco, L. (2008). Models of providing science instruction in the elementary grades: A research agenda to inform decision makers. *Science Educator*, 17(2), 1–18.

Lin, S., & Wang, J. (2024). Development and application of an instrument for assessing upper-secondary school biology teachers' pedagogical content knowledge of scientific thinking. *Journal of Baltic Science Education*, 23(3), 495–517. Advance online publication. DOI: 10.33225/jbse/24.23.495

Loughran, J. J., Berry, A. K., & Mulhall, P. J. (2006). *Understanding and developing science teachers' pedagogical content knowledge*. Sense. DOI: 10.1163/9789087903657

Loughran, J. J., Berry, A. K., & Mulhall, P. J. (2012). *Understanding and developing science teachers pedagogical content knowledge* (2nd ed.). Sense Publishers. DOI: 10.1007/978-94-6091-821-6

Loughran, J. J., Mulhall, P., & Berry, A. (2004). In search of pedagogical content knowledge in science: Developing ways of articulating and documenting professional practice. *Journal of Research in Science Teaching*, 41(4), 370–391. DOI: 10.1002/tea.20007

Lowery, N. V. (2002). Construction of teacher knowledge in context: Preparing elementary teachers to teach mathematics and science. *School Science and Mathematics*, 102(2), 68–83. DOI: 10.1111/j.1949-8594.2002.tb17896.x

Luera, G. R., Moyer, R. H., & Everett, S. A. (2005). What type and level of science content knowledge of elementary education students affect their ability to construct an inquiry- based science lesson? *Journal of Elementary Science Education*, 17(1), 12–25. DOI: 10.1007/BF03174670

Magnusson, S., Krajcik, L., & Borko, H. (1999). Nature, sources and development of pedagogical content knowledge. In Gess-Newsome, J., & Lederman, N. G. (Eds.), *Examining pedagogical content knowledge* (pp. 95–132). Kluwer Academic., DOI: 10.1007/0-306-47217-1_4

Mansor, R., Halim, L., & Osman, K. (2010). Teachers' knowledge that promote students' conceptual understanding. *Procedia: Social and Behavioral Sciences*, 9, 1835–1839. DOI: 10.1016/j.sbspro.2010.12.410

Mavhunga, E. (2020). Revealing the structural complexity of component interactions of topic- specific PCK when planning to teach. *Research in Science Education*, 50(3), 965–986. DOI: 10.1007/s11165-018-9719-6

Morrell, P. D., & Carroll, J. B. (2003). An extended examination of preservice elementary teachers' science teaching self-efficacy. *School Science and Mathematics*, 103(5), 246–251. DOI: 10.1111/j.1949-8594.2003.tb18205.x

Moscovici, H., & Osisioma, I. (2008). Designing the best urban preservice elementary science methods course: Dilemmas and considerations. *Journal of Elementary Science Education*, 20(4), 15–28. DOI: 10.1007/BF03173674

Mullis, I., & Jenkins, L. (1988). *The science report card, elements of risk and recovery*. Educational Testing Service.

Murphy, C., Ambusaid, A., & Beggs, J. (2006). Middle East meets West: Comparing children's attitudes to school science. *International Journal of Science Education*, 28(4), 405–422. DOI: 10.1080/09500690500339696

National Center for Educational Statistics. (2016). *Highlights from TIMSS and TIMSS advanced*, U.S. Department of Education. https://nces.ed.gov/pubsearch/pubsinfo.asp?pubid=2017002

National Center for Science and Engineering Statistics. (2019). https://ncses.nsf.gov/

National Research Council (NRC). (2012). *Framework for K-12 Science Education*. National Academies Press.

National Survey of Science and Mathematics Education. (2018). *Report of the 2018 NSSME+*. https://horizon-research.com/NSSME/2018-nssme/research-products/reports

Newton, D. P., & Newton, L. D. (2001). Subject content knowledge and teacher talk in the primary science classroom. *European Journal of Teacher Education*, 24(3), 369–379. DOI: 10.1080/02619760220128914

Niess, M. L. (2005). Preparing teachers to teach science and mathematics with technology: Developing a technology pedagogical content knowledge. *Teaching and Teacher Education*, 21(5), 509–523. DOI: 10.1016/j.tate.2005.03.006

Nilsson, P. (2008). Teaching for understanding; The complex nature of pedagogical content knowledge in pre-service education. *International Journal of Science Education*, 30(10), 1281–1299. DOI: 10.1080/09500690802186993

Nilsson, P., & Loughran, J. (2011). Exploring the development of pre-service science elementary teachers' pedagogical content knowledge. *Journal of Science Teacher Education*, 23(7), 669–721. DOI: 10.1007/s10972-011-9239-y

Nowicki, B. L., Sullivan-Watts, B., Shim, M. K., Young, B., & Pockalny, R. (2012). Factors influencing science content accuracy in elementary inquiry science lessons. *Research in Science Education*, 43(3), 1135–1154. DOI: 10.1007/s11165-012-9303-4

Nowicki, J., & Bernstein, L. (1994). *Psychometric theory* (3rd ed.). McGraw-Hill.

Nyisztor, D., & Marcus, B. (2008). Concepts and content belong in early childhood education. *Canadian Children*, 33(2), 16–19.

O'Dwyer, A., & Childs, P. (2014). Organic chemistry in action! Developing an intervention program for introductory chemistry to improve learners' understanding, interest, and attitudes. *Journal of Chemical Education*, 91(7), 987–993. DOI: 10.1021/ed400538p

Ozden, M. (2008). The effect of content knowledge on pedagogical content knowledge: The case of teaching phases of matters. *Kuram ve Uygulamada Egitim Bilimleri*, 8, 611–645.

Oztay, E. S., & Boz, Y. (2021). Interaction between pre-service chemistry teachers' pedagogical content knowledge and content knowledge in electrochemistry. *Journal of Pedagogical Research*, 6(1), 1. Advance online publication. DOI: 10.33902/JPR.2022.165

Pamintuan, C. F. (2024). Investigating the classroom implementation of Mandarin teachers' pedagogical content knowledge (PCK): Exploring effective strategies and practices for teaching Chinese as a foreign language in the Philippines. *International Journal of Language Education*, 8(1), 112–126. DOI: 10.26858/ijole.v8i1.60912

Papadouris, N., Hadjigeorgiou, A., & Constantinou, C. P. (2014). Pre-service elementary school teachers' ability to account for the operation of simple physical systems using the energy conservation law. *Journal of Science Teacher Education*, 25(8), 911–933. DOI: 10.1007/s10972-014-9407-y

Park, S., & Chen, Y. C. (2012). Mapping out the integration of the components of pedagogical content knowledge (PCK): Examples from high school biology classrooms. *Journal of Research in Science Teaching*, 49(7), 922–941. DOI: 10.1002/tea.21022

Park, S., & Oliver, J. S. (2008). Revisiting the conceptualization of pedagogical content knowledge (PCK): PCK as a conceptual tool to understand teachers as professionals. *Research in Science Education*, 38(3), 261–284. DOI: 10.1007/s11165-007-9049-6

Peers, C. E., Diezmann, C. M., & Watters, J. J. (2003). Supports and concerns for teacher professional growth during the implantation of a science curriculum innovation. *Research in Science Education*, 33(1), 89–110. DOI: 10.1023/A:1023685113218

Pongsanon, K., Akerson, V., & Rogers, M. (2011). *Exploring the use of lesson study to develop elementary preservice teachers' pedagogical content knowledge for teaching nature of science*. Paper presented at the National Association for Research in Science Teaching, Orlando, Fl.: NARST.

Potvin, P., & Cyr, G. (2017). Toward a durable prevalence of scientific conceptions: Tracking the effects of two interfering misconceptions about buoyancy from preschoolers to science teachers. *Journal of Research in Science Teaching*, 54(9), 1121–1142. Advance online publication. DOI: 10.1002/tea.21396

Programme for International Student Assessment. PISA (2015). *Results, excellence and equity in education, 1* OECD Publishing.

Razak, R. A., Yusoff, S. M., Leng, C. H., & Marzaini, A. F. M. (2023). Evaluating teachers' pedagogical content knowledge in implementing classroom-based assessment: A case study among esl secondary school teachers in Selangor, Malaysia. *PLoS One*, 18(12), e0293325. Advance online publication. DOI: 10.1371/journal.pone.0293325 PMID: 38157377

Rice, D. C., & Kaya, S. (2012). Exploring relations among preservice elementary teachers' ideas about evolution, understanding of relevant science concepts, and college science coursework. *Research in Science Education*, 42(2), 165–179. DOI: 10.1007/s11165-010-9193-2

Saeleset, J., & Friedrichsen, P. (2021). Pre-service science teachers' pedagogical content knowledge integration of students' understanding in science and instructional strategies. *Eurasia Journal of Mathematics, Science and Technology Education*, 17(5), em1965. DOI: 10.29333/ejmste/10859

Santau, A. O., Maerten-Rivera, J. L., Bovis, S., & Orend, J. (2014). Preservice teachers' science content knowledge within the context of a science methods course. *Journal of Science Teachers'. Education*, 25, 953–976. DOI: 10.1007/s10972-014-9402-3

Schneider, R. M. (2015). Pedagogical content knowledge reconsidered: A teacher educator's perspective. In Berry, A., Friedrichsen, P., & Loughran, J. (Eds.), *Re-examining pedagogical content knowledge in science education* (pp. 162–177). Routledge.

Schön, D. (1998). Learning to teach during the practicum experience. *Revista Electrónica de Investigación Educativa*, 21, e27.

Shallcross, T., Spink, E., Stephenon, P., & Warwick, P. (2002). How primary trainee teachers perceive the development of their own scientific knowledge: Links between confidence, content and competence? *International Journal of Science Education*, 24(12), 1293–1312. DOI: 10.1080/09500690110110106

Shing, C. L., Saat, R. M., & Like, S. H. (2015). The knowledge of Teaching – Pedagogical Content Knowledge (PCK). *The Malaysian Online Journal of Educational Science, 3*(3). www.moj-es.netwoo

Shulman, L. S. (1986). Those who understand: Knowledge growth in teaching. *Educational Researcher*, 15(2), 4–14. DOI: 10.3102/0013189X015002004

Shulman, L. S. (1987). Knowledge and teaching: Foundations of the new reform. *Harvard Educational Review*, 57(1), 1–22. DOI: 10.17763/haer.57.1.j463w79r56455411

Smith, D. C. (1999). Changing our teaching: The role of pedagogical content knowledge in elementary science. In Gess-Newsome, J., & Lederman, N. G. (Eds.), *Examining pedagogical content knowledge* (pp. 163–197). Kluwer Academic., DOI: 10.1007/0-306-47217-1_7

Smith, D. C., & Neale, D. C. (1991). The construction of subject matter knowledge in primary science teaching. *Advances in Research on Teaching*, 2, 187–243. DOI: 10.1016/0742-051X(89)90015-2

Sorge, S., Stender, A., & Neumann, K. (2019). The development of science teachers' professional competence. In Hume, A., Cooper, R., & Borowski, A. (Eds.), *Repositioning pedagogical content knowledge in teachers' knowledge for teaching science*. Springer Nature., DOI: 10.1007/978-981-13-5898-2_6

Stains, M., Harshman, J., Barker, M. K., Chasteen, S. V., Cole, R., DeChenne-Peters, S. E., Eagan, M. K., Esson, J. M., Kight, J. K., Laski, F. A., Levis-Fitzgerald, M., Lee, C. J., Lo, S. M., McDonnell, L. M., McKay, T. A., Michelotti, N., Musgrove, A., Parlmer, M. S., Plank, K. M., & Young, A. M. (2018). Anatomy of STEM teaching in North American universities: Lecture is prominent, but practices vary. *Science*, 359(6383), 1468–1470. DOI: 10.1126/science.aap8892 PMID: 29599232

Stein, M., Larrabee, T., & Barman, C. (2018). A study of common beliefs and misconceptions in physical science. *Journal of Elementary Science Education*, 20(2), 1–11. DOI: 10.1007/BF03173666

Sunzuma, G. Z., Zezekwa, N., Chagwiza, C., & Mutambara, T. L. (2024). Examining pre-service mathematics teachers' pedagogical content knowledge (PCK) during a professional development course: A case study. *Mathematics Teaching Research Journal, 16*(1). https://files.eric.ed.gov/fulltext/EJ1427380.pdf

Tardif, M. (2010). *Los Saberes de los Docentes y su Desarrollo Profesional*. Narcea.

Tosun, T. (2000). The beliefs of pre-service elementary teachers toward science and science teaching. *School Science and Mathematics*, 100(7), 374–379. DOI: 10.1111/j.1949-8594.2000.tb18179.x

Trumper, R. (2003). The need for change in elementary school teacher training – a cross-college age study of future teachers' conceptions of basic astronomy concepts. *Teaching and Teacher Education*, 19(3), 309–323. DOI: 10.1016/S0742-051X(03)00017-9

Trygstad, P. J. (2013). *2012 National Survey of Science and Mathematics Education: Status of elementary school science*. Horizon Research. https://eric.ed.gov/?id=ED541798

Turner, S., & Ireson, G. (2014). Fifteen pupils' positive approach to primary school science: When does it decline? *Educational Studies*, 36(2), 119–141. DOI: 10.1080/03055690903148662

United States. National Commission on Excellence in Education (1983). A nation at risk: The imperative for educational reform: A report to the nation and the secretary of education, *United States Department of Education.* https://edreform.com/wp-content/uploads/2013/02/A_Nation_At_Risk_1983.pdf

Usak, M. (2009). Preservice science and technology teachers' pedagogical content knowledge on cell topics. *Kuram ve Uygulamada Egitim Bilimlerim*, 9(4), 2033–2046.

Valnides, N. (2000). Primary student teachers' understanding of the particulate nature of matter and its transformations during dissolving. *Chemistry Education Research and Practice*, 1(2), 355–364. DOI: 10.1039/A9RP90026H

van Driel, J. H., Jong, O. D., & Verloop, N. (2002). The development of preservice chemistry teachers' pedagogical content knowledge. *Science Education*, 86(4), 572–590. DOI: 10.1002/sce.10010

van Driel, J. H., Verloop, N., & de Vos, W. (1998). The development of preservice chemistry teachers' pedagogical content knowledge. *Science Education*, 86(4), 572–590. DOI: 10.1002/sce.10010

Weiss, I. R., Banilower, E. R., McMahon, K. C., & Smith, P. S. (2001). *Report of the 2000 National Survey of Science and Mathematics Education*. Horizon Research.

Windschitl, M., Thompson, J., & Braaten, M. (2011). Fostering ambitious pedagogy in novice teachers: The new role of tool-supported analyses of student work. *Teachers College Record*, 113(7), 1311–1360. DOI: 10.1177/016146811111300702

Woolfolk, A. E. (2014). *Educational psychology: Active learning edition*. Pearson.

Zinger, D., Sandholtz, J. H., & Ringstaff, C. (2020). Teaching science in rural elementary schools: Affordances and constraints in the age of NGSS. *Rural Educator*, 41(2), 14–30. DOI: 10.35608/ruraled.v41i2.558

Chapter 8
Current Trends and Best Practices of How In-Service Teachers Can Develop and Apply PCK in Social Sciences

Deepak Maun
https://orcid.org/0000-0002-9489-9920
O.P. Jindal Global University, India

Parth Sharma
https://orcid.org/0000-0002-1955-9408
University of Petroleum and Energy Studies, India

Ta Huy Hung
https://orcid.org/0009-0008-6835-3036
Vietnam National University, Vietnam

ABSTRACT

Pedagogical Content Knowledge (PCK) is pivotal in advancing social sciences education by combining deep subject expertise with effective teaching practices. This paper explores current trends and best practices in developing and applying PCK, such as project-based learning, flipped classrooms, and service learning. It examines challenges including limited professional development, inadequate resources, and resistance to change, and identifies future directions such as leveraging advanced technology, fostering interdisciplinary approaches, and expanding community partnerships. By addressing these barriers and embracing emerging opportunities,

DOI: 10.4018/979-8-3693-0655-0.ch008

educators can enhance instructional quality and student engagement. This study highlights the importance of continuous refinement and adaptation in teaching strategies to meet diverse student needs and prepare them for a dynamic world.

INTRODUCTION

PCK's concept has over the past two years received wide attention as a most important component in effectively teaching the social sciences. PCK is meant to represent the intersection between a teacher's understanding of the subject matter and their ability to convey that knowledge in ways that are accessible and engaging to students. It will be the in-service teachers who, in most cases, have to balance classroom management with curriculum requirements and continuous professional development and so find developing PCK highly important. The current trends and best practices sustaining its development and implementation of PCK within social sciences education are reviewed in this chapter.

Few areas of teaching are as challenging as the social sciences because the content typically requires a mix of complex conceptual material with critical thinking and diverse perspectives. Good teaching in this field, therefore, requires more than knowledge of the subject to relate it to experiences of students and to be able to foster a learning environment that encourages inquiry and dialogue. It means that teachers in service, exposed constantly to the real dynamics of the classroom, are better placed to continue refining and broadening their PCK. But they do face challenges with respect to limited time, curriculum standards that evolve over time, and continuously adapting to new technologies and methodologies for teaching.

The chapter will focus on some of the strategies and practices that have been efficacious in supporting in-service teachers to develop and apply PCK in their social sciences classrooms. It is the authors' intention that, through an exploration of the theoretical underpinnings and practical applications of PCK, the chapter will offer educators insight into ways to enhance practice. This will not only give information on the development of PCK but also on reflective practice and continuous professional growth. It will underline the fact that the development of PCK is a continuous process which evolves during experience and with the changing educational arena. The intent of this chapter is to provide some useful insights to working teachers who are trying to enhance their efficiency and effectiveness in the teaching of social sciences.

UNDERSTANDING PCK IN SOCIAL SCIENCES

PCK is that form of professional knowledge which goes beyond the mastery of subject matter. It involves knowing how to teach content effectively to students (Julie, 2015), PCK in social sciences, therefore, would not be solely the deep knowledge about historical events, cultural phenomena, or social theories but also the ability to present these concepts in ways that speak to the lives and perspectives of learners. What makes PCK such a powerful tool for social sciences educators is this dual expertise: knowing what to teach and how to teach it (Nind, 2020). Its theoretical base has fundamentally been premised on the fact that teaching is not one glove that fits all. Social sciences are diverse in nature, often abstract, and demand that teachers render complex ideas accessible and engaging. This is about choosing proper instructional strategies, developing meaningful student learning activities, and creating valid assessments that can measure students' understanding. Moreover, in the social sciences, teachers are very often required to address sensitive and controversial topics and face the risk of having to strike a balance between provoking critical thinking and maintaining respect in the atmosphere within a class. PCK empowers teachers with the competencies to project students' misconceptions, accommodate issues emanating from diverse learning needs, and relate curriculum content to current events and lived experiences of students.

Notably, characteristics of the field of social science uniquely influence the development of PCK. Unlike other well-defined subjects, social sciences are interdisciplinary in nature, drawing on history, geography, political science, sociology, among others. This interdisciplinarity puts a demand on teachers to have broad subject knowledge and the understanding of how to integrate different perspectives and approaches within teaching. For example, a lesson concerning the causes of a historical event may include facts about the event itself but also an examination of economic, social, and political contexts that shaped it. It helps a teacher weave these diverse threads into a cohesive learning experience geared toward fostering a deeper understanding. The very nature of the social sciences, in the second place, requires the teacher often to engage students in discussions related to values, ethics, and human behavior, which, by nature, are complicated and emotionally charged. It is here that PCK becomes very important for guiding the teacher on how to facilitate such discussions to sustain critical inquiry while showing respect for diversity of viewpoints. With very high levels of PCK, teachers are much better positioned to establish a classroom culture in which students feel safe to explore and debate different perspectives, deepening their understanding of the material at hand.

In other words, social science PCK pertains to more than the mere transmission of content; it concerns the construction of meaningful and engaging learning experiences that would best suit the interests of students. It requires nuanced understanding of subject matter and pedagogical moves or other pedagogical strategies that support learners best. The PCK in the domain of social sciences is assuming ever greater importance in its role of shaping effective practices amidst changes in society and education.

Current Trends in Developing PCK for Social Sciences

As a review, changes in educational theory and technology, not to mention new societal needs, have impacted the developing nature of **Pedagogical Content Knowledge (PCK)** in social sciences. Among the recent trends, one of the most pronounced is the tendency to **integrate technology** more into the classroom. Interactive simulations, online databases, and multimedia content are but a few examples of digital resources being increasingly harnessed to innovate the teaching of the social sciences (Fox, & Leidig, 2014). These tools allow the teacher to present ideas in ways that are more engaging and accessible for learners, making abstract ideas more concrete. Besides that, technology enables differentiated instruction—making it possible for teachers to adapt their teaching approaches to meet the diverse needs of their students, thus deepening their PCK.

Collaborative learning is another trend influencing the development of PCK in social sciences (Valtonen, 2011). The encouragement being provided to teachers to participate in professional learning communities is increasing, where they can better share strategies, reflect on their practice, and solve collectively pedagogical challenges. In this way, it refinements at the level of individual teaching practices, but it also generates a culture of continuous professional growth. Peer mentorship and team teaching increase in popularity; as a result, it enhances PCK since the teachers get a chance to observe and learn from one another.

Reflective practice stands to gain great recognition as an essential component in developing PCK for social sciences (Abell, 2008). The teachers are asked to reflect on their teaching experience from time to time, including their experiences on the effectiveness of teaching strategies deployed in the classroom. This is enhanced through the keeping of teaching journals, video recordings of lessons, and peer observations. Systematic reflection on their teaching will let educators perceive where they need to change and try new ways of teaching—that is, to continuously evolve their PCK.

Increasingly, **culturally responsive teaching** is also part of PCK development in the social sciences. As schools become increasingly diverse, it is assumed that teachers will have developed the ability to know how to manage and include different cultural perspectives in teaching (Demoiny, 2018). This involves getting to know the students' culture and using it in making relevant instructional decisions to ensure that the curriculum is relevant and inclusive. Culturally responsive teaching deepens the learning process and helps the students bring the subject closer to themselves.

Finally, more than ever, the relation linking the growth of **PCK with its worth in real-life** has to be established. It encourages teachers to work in current events, societal issues, and real-life situations to make the content relevant and more engaging to the learner. Students start to see what they learn has a practical application that enriches higher order thinking, and the ability to apply knowledge in appropriate contexts (Grabinger, & Dunlap,1995). If teaching were aligned to the applications of an existing domain, it would be then more likely that teachers developed and applied PCK in meaningful and impactful ways.

These trends demonstrate a shift in the reconceptualization of PCK in social sciences development as dynamic and responsive. Embracing the aspects of technology, collaboration, reflection, cultural responsiveness, and real-world relevance enables teachers to enhance their content delivery skills effectively for student outcomes that are engaging and very effective in the teaching and learning of social sciences.

Best Practices in Applying PCK in Social Sciences

1. Inquiry-Based Learning

Inquiry-based learning is a powerful way of putting PCK into practice in the social sciences, as it puts learners themselves on the path of exploration and critical thinking (Cuenca, 2021). In this approach, learners have to formulate queries, conduct research, and test for evidence to form conclusions. This makes the act of learning active rather than passive. Teachers are always framing lessons with open-ended questions that would guide the student along the path of discovery so they are able to create knowledge themselves on complex issues within the social sciences. Inquiry-based learning goes very well with the vision of social science education, where multi-faceted and complex issues—social, political, and historical—are reviewed. This approach is particularly good for enriching knowledge content while helping children develop the skills of critical thinking and problem-solving, which are regarded as key aptitudes for functioning in an increasingly complex world.

2. Case Studies

Case studies can act as a fine tool in linking theory to practice in social sciences education. This can be done by applying the theoretical concepts to real-life scenarios or historical times. By performing this, one brings about relevance and proximity to the learners' experiences, thus improving their understanding of the subject. For instance, using a case study related to an individual historical event, students can research and discuss how macro societal, economic, and political dynamics are at work in that particular event, thereby getting deeper knowledge about the content. Case studies offer an area that fosters critical analysis and discussion because students have to consider different perspectives and outcomes of their work (Petticrew, & Roberts, 2008). This approach makes the learning process enriching, and at the same time, it guides students to feel the impact of social science in their surroundings.

3. Differential instruction

The basis of working effectively with PCK is recognizing the needs of students; differentiated instruction plays a very important role in this. Differentiated instruction means modification of teaching methods and materials to suit the various backgrounds, styles, and abilities of all learners (Tomilson, 2014). This may consist of using several instruction strategies—for instance, group assignments, independent projects, and hands-on activities—to match different learning preferences. Differentiated instruction can, therefore, offer teachers opportunities to ensure that all students access content meaningfully and engagingly. This is especially key in the social sciences, where students will have differing levels of previous knowledge and interests in the content. The differentiated instruction allows a teacher to deal with those differences effectively and helps every child be successful.

4. Formative Assessment

Formative assessment can be described as an integral practice when applying PCK because it offers constant feedback to the teacher about student understanding and guides instructional decisions (Bennett, 2011). In contrast to summative assessments, which evaluate student learning at the end of a unit or course, formative assessments are continuous. They could come in the form of quizzes, class discussions, peer review, or even informal check-ins to track student progress and highlight areas where students perhaps need a little more support. Formative assessment processes engage students in their learning and drive them towards reviewing their level of understanding and taking responsibility for progress. The use of formative assessments could permit teachers to respond to student learning more effectively and make adjustments to their instruction in real-time, thus able to catch on to misconceptions as they arise.

5. Collaborative Learning

Collaborative learning is an important way in which PCK can be applied in social sciences because it reflects the discipline nature of the topic itself. Grouping students to work together on projects, discussions, and research assignments encourages deep understanding of content through the action of interactivity with each other. Students learn from one another, rich with multiple perspectives, developing important social skills in the process (Laal & Laal, 2012). For example, group activities in which students have to work together to solve problems or explore topics can enhance collective and individual understanding of subject matter. Not only does collaborative learning enrich the educational experience, but it also gives them a feel for real-world scenarios when they will be asked to work in teams, arriving at answers through collective analysis.

6. Culturally Responsive Teaching

Culturally responsive teaching is an important practice that goes into the application of PCK, especially in diverse classrooms. This involves recognizing and valuing students' cultural backgrounds and integrating those into the curriculum. It makes the content relevant and creates a more inclusive and respectful learning environment (Vavrus, 2008). This might involve, in social sciences, examining historical events from multiple cultural perspectives; discussing how cultural diversity impacts social and political systems; or using examples and case studies that reflect the diverse backgrounds of the students. Through culturally responsive teaching practices, learning is made relevant and meaningful to all students as their concerns of equity and representation are attended to.

7. Linking Content to Issues

Linking content to real-life issues is another potent application of PCK in social sciences through relating content to students' lives and the general world. Social sciences have intrinsic links with contemporary events, social issues, and debates, which make them especially apt for this approach. One gets impact only when the content is taught with links to current problems about climate change, social justice, or economic inequality (Hackman, 2005). Real-world issues can be easily transported into the classroom through news articles, documentaries, and guest speakers. This will provide students with a richer, more dynamic learning experience. That's not all; it will also improve student engagement while exercising critical thinking and preparing a new generation of informed and engaged citizens.

8. Leveraging Technology and Digital Resources

Technology in the classroom is increasingly becoming a best practice to enact PCK with regards to teaching the social sciences. Digital tools, which include interactive simulations, online databases, and multimedia content, could enhance access to and engagement with subtle and complex subject matter in the social sciences (Lundy, 2018). Moreover, technology enables differentiated instruction, whereby the teacher can adapt both methods and strategies to the vastly different needs of their pupils. For example, interactive maps or virtual reality experiences can bring historical events to life, whereas online forums and collaborative platforms can provide support for group work and discussions. More than ever, integrating technology with teaching practices can aid educators in reinforcing the effectiveness of delivery both in an effective and engaging way, improving student outcomes for social sciences education.

Innovative Pedagogies Informed by PCK

1. Project-Based Learning

Project-based learning is yet another innovative pedagogical approach, empowered by PCK, through which a teacher can present subject material in stimulating ways, with complex questions or real-world problems, to engage and interest students (Kokotsaki, Menzies, & Wiggins, 2016). PBL in social sciences entails students participating in the completion of an extended assignment in which they apply knowledge to remedy a problem or address meaningful questions. Through one long-term project, a lot of the concepts in the social sciences can be involved, coupled with several of the skills, such as research, analysis, and critical thinking. PBL provides for deep student exploration of a subject, entails teamwork, and the presentation of results—an integration of content knowledge with its practical application. This strategy helps students understand social sciences and develop basic skills such as problem solving, working in a team, and communication.

2. Flipped Classroom

Another creative strategy is the flipped classroom model, which is a new concept but very well supported by PCK. This model just reverses the whole teaching approach by delivering instructional content outside the class, usually through video lectures or online modules, while using class time for interactive activities and discussions. For social sciences, this could mean that maybe at home students are reviewing the lectures on historical events or social theories to come to class to have debates, do case studies, or organize into groups for projects (Akçayır, & Akçayır, 2018). This would make more time for active learning during class time, using the teachers to sort out any misconceptions and meaning deep into complex topics. Teachers can utilize PCK in deploying the flipped classroom model by making more effective use of their class time with the students for engaging them in hands-on learning activities.

3. Gamification

Gamification refers to the application of game characteristic elements to a non-game setting, commonly through training activities, for purposes of enhancing engrossment and motivation levels (Orosco, 2014). By integrating elements of games into the learning of social sciences – for example, points, badges, and leader boards – teachers are able to create a more engaging space. For instance, the teacher may design simulation games on historical role-playing or competitive quizzes on current events. Gamification then proceeds to use game mechanics to reinforce PCK—content knowledge—and motivate active participation. This process provides students with an avenue from which to learn and possibly remember concepts in social sciences by applying their knowledge in a fun and engaging set-up.

4. Experiential Learning

Experiential learning is the process of learning through experience and reflection. This can be translated to social sciences through field trips, simulations, or role-plays that place learners close to the real world (Kolb, 2018). This could be a mock trial based on historical events or a visit to local government offices to see how theoretical knowledge of the discipline is applied in practice. Experiential learning strategies engage learners in active problem-solving and critical thinking. Rather, learners build a connection between the classroom environment and real life. This approach increases PCK because it combines content knowledge with experience in a way that truly embeds learning and, consequently, students' ability to apply knowledge in social sciences.

5. Socratic Seminars

Socratic seminars are a teaching strategy aimed at stirring critical thinking and dialogue through structured discussions. A Socratic seminar is when students have a dialogue driven by open-ended questions of the subject area of social sciences, under the guidance of a teacher facilitating—but not leading the conversation (Mitchel, 2006). This allows students to look at different perspectives, ask questions, and find evidence to back ideas. Through such seminars, PCK is enhanced by creating an environment of learning prioritizing inquiry and reflection by students. By guiding discussions that require analysis and expression, a teacher can further strengthen the student's knowledge in social sciences and promote critical thinking.

6. Service Learning

It involves the integration of community service and academic instruction in helping the students apply social sciences concept to real-life experiences. When students work on projects that meet community needs, such as organizing a local history event or participating in social advocacy, they get to see the practical impact of their learning. Service learning capitalizes on PCK through the connection of academic content with real applications that deepen students' understanding of social issues and their role in society (Felten, & Clayton,2011). This approach not only strengthens knowledge retention of the academic material presented but also increases civic responsibility and personal growth.

7. Multimodal instruction

Multimodal instruction brings in a number of media and teaching techniques to be responsive to a multiplicity of learning styles and preferences (Stein, 2014). This can then be integrated with visual aids, text-based resources, interactive materials, and digital tools to express material in a number of different ways within the subject area of social sciences. For instance, available resources for illustrating economic theories include infographics, video clips, case studies, and hands-on simulations. Multimodal instruction uses PCK to handle differences in learners, which further increases how much students are engaged with the material. Through such approaches, a teacher can now be in a position to represent any given complex in the social sciences concepts in multiple formats, hence more accessible and impactful for all kinds of learners.

8. Cross-Disciplinary Integration

Cross-disciplinary integration is the incorporation of the social sciences with other disciplines so as to give a learner a whole experience of learning. As such, social sciences can then be blended with language arts when teachers require students to write historical fiction based on events that truly did occur or in relation sciences with the social sciences when teachers require a study into the various environmental issues in society based on the socio-economic aspect. This then guides the use of PCK in realizing that different fields are interrelated with valid application in various settings. It enriches the cross-disciplinary integration of students' learning about the social sciences and helps concepts become relevant across a variety of knowledge domains (Komerath, & Smith, 2001)

The creative pedagogies that are informed by PCK incorporate a range of approaches to functioning teaching and learning in the social sciences. To facilitate learning that encourages both depth of knowledge of the content and application of the concepts in social sciences, the educators can employ project-based learning, flipped classrooms, gamification, experiential learning, Socratic seminars, service learning, multimodal instruction, and cross-disciplinary integration.

Challenges and Barriers in Developing and Applying PCK

The development and application of Pedagogical Content Knowledge (PCK) in the teaching of social sciences are associated with challenges and barriers through which educators have to navigate for effective teaching and learning. These difficulties arise from different sources, including institutional constraints, personal limitations, and wider systemic problems. Understanding these barriers will be important for educators and decision-makers seeking to strengthen PCK and bring about improvements in learning outcomes.

1. In-Service Training Constraints

One major challenge for the development of PCK remains the inability of many teachers to receive adequate professional development (Kind, 2009). Although the development of effective PCK in teachers cannot be completed without training and support, very few teachers are exposed to intensive professional development programs. The very nature of such programs should be able to deal with the intricate difficulties in ensuring the compatibility of pedagogical strategies with content knowledge. Without being constantly given learning opportunities, the teachers will not be able to imbibe insight into new methodologies and best practices in terms of teaching social sciences. Irregular, general or irrelevant professionals' development adversely affects the skills of creating and implementing PCK.

2. Inadequate Resources and Support

There are enough materials, technology, and organizational support in educational environments for the creation and use of appropriate PCK. In fact, schools and other relevant organizations hardly ever offer these facilities in terms of having recently published texts or even using digital tools for which no funding is available to try new methods Nind, M. (2020). Similarly, adequate administrative support is also lacking, which leads to an inability on the part of the teachers to use new strategies or bring modifications in the teaching approaches that they adopt. The absence of all these resources and support systems might hamper the teachers from developing their PCK to attain a goal of providing better social sciences and quality education.

3. Resistance to Change

A significant obstacle can be resistance to change possessing by the most teachers and other educational systems. The habit of teaching traditionally and their reluctance to learn new strategies or new pedagogy could be the examples of reasons contributing to this. This can be caused by a lack of faith in new methods, fear of failure, or satisfaction with the way things are. Such resistance can be overcome only with a change of mindset and through constant support and encouragement from educational leaders . If the support system is not put into place, then, as Greene hypothesizes, if this kind of resistance goes unchecked, the entire development and application of PCK can be held back by the adherence to such outdated practices.

4. Inadequate Time for Planning and Reflection

Effective application of PCK requires a significant amount of planning and reflection time, which most teachers often find hard to come by. Time is required to design and put in place lesson plans that integrate content knowledge with pedagogical strategies and effect time for reflection on teaching practices and student outcomes. However, the demands, such as grading, taking care of administrative tasks, and meeting other obligations, leave such teachers with no time for all this. And without time for planning and reflection, it is hard for these teachers to also develop and change their PCK effectively.

5. Variability in Teacher Preparation Programs

The Variability of teacher preparation programs can also range in the development various differences in PCK. In specific cases, teacher preparation programs do not put enough emphasis on the intertwining of pedagogical strategies with content knowledge, thus creating chasms in the knowledge or PCK of teachers. Indeed, these programs differ sharply in quality and focus, leaving some teachers rather underprepared with the complexities needed to teach various social sciences effectively. In this regard, it is essential to secure really comprehensive teacher preparation programs in relation to the demands placed on educators to foster strong PCK right from the start of teachers' careers.

6. Challenges in Assessing PCK

Assessing PCK effectively is another challenge, as it involves evaluating both pedagogical and content knowledge simultaneously. Apparently, the subtleties called for by PCK cannot be captured by the traditional tools of assessment. Therefore, it is quite difficult to use general assessment tools to establish the ability of a teacher to integrate pedagogical strategies into content knowledge. Measurement tools on a valid and reliable scale are very important in measuring PCK and enabling us to make inferences about understanding and improving the educators' practices. In that regard, yet lacking effective means of assessment, identifying the development and offering relevant support on developing PCK can prove painstakingly challenging.

7. Diverse Student Needs

Among the challenges that come into the radar of putting PCK into application is the need to cater for diverse student needs. Typical social science classrooms contain students with varied backgrounds, learning modes as well as prior knowledge possessed. The teachers must rise to addressing such needs by developing and applying PCK, an exercise that is pretty tasking. For example, teachers have to modify pedagogical methods to make the content both attractive and accessible to students with varying modes of acquiring knowledge: Such will demand that teachers be highly knowledgeable in students and subject matter as well as flexible is selecting most appropriate instruction.

8. Systemic Challenges in Education

Finally, systemic challenges in education can also hinder the construction and implementation of PCK. This wider description includes such systemic considerations as curriculum standards, testing pressures, and educational policies that can operate to constrain how teachers will enact innovative teaching and developing PCK. For instance, rigid curriculum standards or high-stakes testing could come as a constraint on the degree of freedom teachers have in exploring new pedagogical approaches or to integrate the knowledge of content in meaningful ways. Since these are systemic in nature, they warrant a comprehensive approach that takes in the wider context of education and thus allows for teachers to develop and apply PCK appropriately.

Case Studies

Caselet 1: Innovative Social Sciences Curriculum Integration

Background: The Social Studies department at Greenwood High School took the initiative to adopt an innovative curriculum that would assiduously meld project-based learning with real-world applications (Levin, & Greenwood, 2011). The teachers designed projects that would integrate old historical research with current social issues—such as research on historical trends in migration followed by the examination of current immigration policies in place and the impacts brought about.

Implementation: The inputs also comprised of guest lecturers drawn from the local organizations whose lectures provided the students with real-life applications to issues. With these, the students from generation of team works and derived presentations and reports related to their discoveries to the society.

Outcome: Combining real-life issues with historical facts created a scope of much more involvement and enlightenment by all the students. It was also evident that the students got the chance to acquire a new understanding of the magnitude and reach of the applicability of the social sciences and enhanced their skills of conducting research and presenting information.

Caselet 2: Flipped Classroom Model in a Middle School History Class

Background: In Riverdale Middle School, Mr. Thompson applied a flipped classroom model in his history class for 8th graders. He would create video lessons on important and key historical events for the students to view at home as part of their homework (Hemphill, 2008). The classroom time was then used for discussions, debates, and interactive activities on the topic of the video.

Implementation: Mr. Thompson posted video lectures online. He yoked these with a series of interactive exercises and discussion prompts that he had prearranged for that class. He kept track of student participation using online quizzes and facilitated discussions in an effort to clear up any misconceptions that were identified as falling.

Outcome: Flipped classroom model supported the students to be more engaging during class discussions and activity hours The teachers also reported a better participation and command over the important historical background lessons. However, it was very difficult for students to gain self-discipline to complete video work outside the classroom.

Caselet 3: Service-Learning Project at Crestwood High

Background: The social sciences had integrated a service-learning project in Crestwood High School (Welsch, & Heying, 1999). Students were tasked to engage in a community-based project that supports the resolution of local social problems, such as organizing campaigns to conserve the environment or developing outreach programs to various under-served constituencies.

Implementation: Student understanding was demonstrated using real-world problems posed by teachers in collaboration with local community leaders and non-profits. Students identified meaningful social science concepts, employed by social scientists in analyzing, researching, and advocating, in their projects. Projects were shared with local community stakeholders and students reported on their work.

Outcome: The service-learning project developed the students' awareness of social issues and their role in the community. It instilled practical skills in conducting research and communication in the students while also positively impacting their community locale. The challenges were to manage logistics in the projects and to balance academic work with community service.

Joint Analysis

The three caselets bring out different innovative strategies for applying PCK in Social Sciences each with its strengths and challenges.

Real-World Applications: The three case lets each feature how the use of real-world applications in the social sciences curriculum actually worked. By the project-based learning approach adopted at Greenwood High, the flipped classroom model at Riverdale Middle School, and the service-learning project at Crestwood High, the social sciences curriculum is laced with real life, pertinent issues. That will make the experience of learning relevant and will add to the participation of the student.

Engagement and Skill Development: Each strategy engaged the student differently and developed skills appropriately for that engagement. At Greenwood High, students developed a greater appreciation of historical and contemporary issues. In the case of Riverdale Middle School, the flipped classroom method brought participation and understanding to higher priority levels. The service-learning project at Crestwood High developed practical skills along with a sense of civic responsibility among students. These are just but some of the outcomes associated with PCK's objectives towards the creation of an effective and interesting experience of learning.

Challenges and Considerations: As with the benefits of each approach, each approach has its challenges. The project-based learning at Greenwood High was high in its demand for extreme collaboration and resource management of the student. The flipped classroom model at Riverdale Middle School underlined problems related to self-discipline and access to technology. The service-learning project conducted at Crestwood High posited logistical challenges that demanded a mix between academic and community responsibilities. These are challenges that make it important to have support systems and proper planning for successful application of PCK strategies.

The caselets taken as a group depict how innovative teaching strategies, suffused with PCK, can invigorate the teaching of the social sciences. In other words, they make clear a relevance of material to be learned to applications in the real world and they involve active approaches to learning in ways that make for real understanding and capability formation. Concurrently, some deliberate thinking with respect to enactment as well as implications for ongoing support almost always accompany serious attempts at the challenges that such strategies pose. These case lets illuminate an example par excellence of ways in which educators can develop and enact PCK effectively in ways that will advance teaching and learning in the social sciences.

FUTURE DIRECTIONS AND OPPORTUNITIES

Emerging changes in social science education result in new future directions and opportunities for developing and applying Pedagogical Content Knowledge in the discipline. Finally, these directions and opportunities must be responsive to the past challenges, seize upon the advancements in technology, and meet the changing needs of the students and teachers that will be served. In so exploring these opportunities, therefore, the efforts aimed at ensuring that quality and the effectiveness in the achievement of the provision of instruction in social sciences are also duly improved upon by educators and other policymakers.

1. Leveraging Advanced Technology

Incorporation of new or emerging technology into the system has been observed to play a big role in changing social sciences education. New technologies such as artificial intelligence, virtual reality, and augmented reality have proven to be very instrumental in interactive ways to teach and learn while aiding understanding in varied concepts of social sciences for the learners (Daniela, 2020). Invite VR and AR, which have the capability to make the new learning process more representative because activities like analyzing historical events or social phenomena could be able to be immersed in their environment. With AI technology, it is possible to design tools that will provide adaptive learning paths using advanced analytics, adaptive assessment, real-time feedback, and tangible insights for educators to factor in while personalizing instruction standing on student-driven assessment needs. Embracing these technologies can bolster PCK through innovative methods of content presentation and student engagement in active learning by virtue of these techniques.

2. Encouraging Inter-disciplinary Practices

The Vigor of social science education will contribute towards the inter-disciplinary practices which will blend social sciences with other disciplines. This enables educators to connect various aspects of social sciences with those of science, technology, engineering, and mathematics (STEM) to ensure a more comprehensive and relevant learning scope (Mickelson, & Bottia, 2009).. For example, in studying the social consequences of the development of technology, or interpreting historical events into the shoes of a scientist, may help provide some overview to give the students a general impression and insight of the interaction of the disciplines. Improved PCK can take place through interdisciplinarity when teachers are provoked to take pedagogical practices between content areas to new levels of student experiences.

3. Professional Development

Continuous professional development offers a way, as well as means, to support teachers in the development and practice of PCK. A future that is more central will include high-quality professional development opportunities that are systematically provided with relevance to the needs and interests of social science teachers, such as workshops on new teaching strategies or training on new technological applications and even opportunities to work with and share knowledge with their colleagues. Further, models of professional development would also ensure and reinforce the embedding of research-based practices and enable the availability of practical tools and resources to enable the teachers to embed PCK in their classroom practices. Strong investment in professional development will ensure that teachers keep aligned to the best practices and keep refining and evolving the PCK .

4. Building Collaborative Learning Communities

The development and use of PCK can be fueled with the construction of collaborative learning communities (Schuck, Aubusson, Kearney, & Burden, 2013).. Educators may become more confident about their pedagogical practices through the development of collaborative learning communities and the creation of networks whereby social sciences teachers could pool their resources, strategies, and experiences. There are different forms of collaborative learning communities, such as professional learning communities (PLCs), online forums, and teacher workshops. These communities of practice bring teachers together for the sharing of ideas, conversation around problems, and development on innovative projects. This will collectively promote the PCK of educators and the pedagogical quality of social sciences education.

5. Equity and Inclusion

The future of the social sciences education should be predisposed towards equity and inclusion. To ensure that it prevails, it will include focusing on the gaps created in the resources, support, and opportunities afforded to the students. Educator-employed curricula should mirror diverse experiences and views; educations should aim at total inclusivity (Claiborne, 2020). Apart from achieving a balance, professional development should emphasize on strategies of culturally responsive education and the readiness of teachers in supporting various learners. By supporting equity and inclusion, educators can improve their PCK and establish a more level and consequential learning ecosystem for the students.

6. Utilizing Data-Driven Insights

Data-driven insights can be utilized in the development and application of PCK (Riske, 2022). This implies that student performance data can be analyzed to notice specific areas of the strength of that student and the teaching of the same areas can be optimized. Educators can assess the influence of varied teaching strategies and make data-informed choices about pedagogical practices. If embedded into instructional planning and assessment, this would mean valuable feedback and guidance for ensuring the continuous improvement of PCK.

7. Encouraging Student Agency

To be able to learn under their control, empowering students may be the most promising opportunity for the advancing of PCK. The inducement of student agency enables them to accept more responsibility for learning processes, choice of study topics, research projects, and the mode of presentation. Teachers will infuse a sense of interest and engagement in students through ownership responsibility. Student agency also goes along with the principles of PCK since it promotes active learning as well as critical thinking by the students. Allowing the students to lead their very own learning process is likely to have more insight toward the social sciences and subsequently apply them substantially.

8. Global Perspectives tied to Social Sciences

A student, who is entailed with global perspectives in connection to social sciences, will have a broader perspective associated with international issues. Overall, this helps to gain a more rounded understanding of the world, as the perspectives on global problems, historical facts, and social trends can be shared. Integrating the helping professions' international context within the curriculum for PCK lets the teacher extend their knowledge and teaching approach to the international setting, so students can also engage with international issues, having a more worldly and comparatively connected view of the social sciences.

9. Growing Community and Sector Partnerships

A web of community organisations, industry practitioners, and educational institutions will offer resources together in ways that can provide students with greater opportunities for real-life experiences. These will be in the form of guest lectures, field trips, internships, and collaborative work— as a matter of course in the delivery of social science curriculum. External partnerships can further strengthen teachers' PCK with practical insights and resources that can enliven the content. Furthering these partnerships can equally enhance opportunities through which students can explore potential career paths and apply their knowledge in real-world contexts.

In conclusion, future directions and opportunities for developing and applying PCK in social sciences include leveraging advanced technology, promoting interdisciplinary approaches in teaching, improving professional development, fostering collaborative learning communities, addressing processes of equity and inclusion, using data-driven insights on practice, encouraging student agency, embedding global perspectives, and extending community and industry partnerships. If pursued along these directions, the educator will have the ability to keep forging ahead the advances in social sciences education, ascertaining that students receive a rich and meaningful learning experience.

CONCLUSION

Pedagogical Content Knowledge is very crucial in the effectiveness of social science teaching. PCK combines deep subject content knowledge with sound teaching practices. This combination promotes better comprehension and improved engagement from students. The innovative practices include project-based learning, flipped classes, and gamification. These practices play out the possibilities that are available for students and offer them a more relaxed space to study the world.

However, these practices also come with some drawbacks: low professional development, low resources, and lack of resistance to change.

These barriers can be broken down when resources are put into tailor-made professional development and availed through close working among educators within a properly resourced environment. The future for PCK, therefore, lies in the deployment of sophisticated technology, integrated approaches, and community relationships that offer fresh insights. Through the negotiations of these challenges and taking advantage of future opportunities, significant enhancements in the provision of social sciences instruction can be made to prepare students for such a complex world with truly meaningful learning experiences.

REFERENCES

Abell, S. K. (2008). Twenty years later: Does pedagogical content knowledge remain a useful idea? *International Journal of Science Education*, 30(10), 1405–1416. DOI: 10.1080/09500690802187041

Akçayır, G., & Akçayır, M. (2018). The flipped classroom: A review of its advantages and challenges. *Computers & Education*, 126, 334–345. DOI: 10.1016/j.compedu.2018.07.021

Bennett, R. E. (2011). Formative assessment: A critical review. *Assessment in Education: Principles, Policy & Practice*, 18(1), 5–25. DOI: 10.1080/0969594X.2010.513678

Blin, F., & Munro, M. (2008). Why hasn't technology disrupted academics' teaching practices? Understanding resistance to change through the lens of activity theory. *Computers & Education*, 50(2), 475–490. DOI: 10.1016/j.compedu.2007.09.017

Claiborne, L. (2020). Beyond Inclusion/Exclusion in Teaching about Difference: Entanglements at the Edge of Practice. In *Moving Towards Inclusive Education* (pp. 181–201). Brill. DOI: 10.1163/9789004432789_013

Cuenca, A. (2021). Proposing core practices for social studies teacher education: A qualitative content analysis of inquiry-based lessons. *Journal of Teacher Education*, 72(3), 298–313. DOI: 10.1177/0022487120948046

Daniela, L. (2020). New perspectives on virtual and augmented reality. In *New Perspectives on Virtual and Augmented Reality*. Routledge. DOI: 10.4324/9781003001874

Demoiny, S. B. (2018). Social studies teacher educators who do race work: A racial-pedagogical-content-knowledge analysis. *Social Studies Research & Practice*, 13(3), 330–344. DOI: 10.1108/SSRP-04-2018-0017

Felten, P., & Clayton, P. H. (2011). Service-learning. *New Directions for Teaching and Learning*, 2011(128), 75–84. DOI: 10.1002/tl.470

Fox, E. A., & Leidig, J. P. (2014). *Digital Libraries Applications: CBIR, Education, Social Networks, Escience/Simulation, and GIS*. Morgan & Claypool Publishers. DOI: 10.1007/978-3-031-02284-5

Grabinger, R. S., & Dunlap, J. C. (1995). Rich environments for active learning: A definition. *Research in Learning Technology*, 3(2), 5–34. DOI: 10.3402/rlt.v3i2.9606

Hackman, H. W. (2005). Five essential components for social justice education. *Equity & Excellence in Education*, 38(2), 103–109. DOI: 10.1080/10665680590935034

Hemphill, C. (2008). *New York City's Best Public Middle Schools: A Parents' Guide*. Teachers College Press.

Julie, G. N. (2015). A model of teacher professional knowledge and skill including PCK: Results of the thinking from the PCK Summit. In *Re-Examining Pedagogical Content Knowledge in Science Education* (pp. 28–42). Routledge.

Kind, V. (2009). Pedagogical content knowledge in science education: Perspectives and potential for progress. *Studies in Science Education*, 45(2), 169–204. DOI: 10.1080/03057260903142285

Kokotsaki, D., Menzies, V., & Wiggins, A. (2016). Project-based learning: A review of the literature. *Improving Schools*, 19(3), 267–277. DOI: 10.1177/1365480216659733

Kolb, D. A. (2014). *Experiential learning: Experience as the source of learning and development*. FT press.

Komerath, N. M., & Smith, M. J. (2001). Integrated knowledge resources for cross-disciplinary learning. *Session D-7, Proceedings of ICEE*.

Laal, M., & Laal, M. (2012). Collaborative learning: What is it? *Procedia: Social and Behavioral Sciences*, 31, 491–495. DOI: 10.1016/j.sbspro.2011.12.092

Levin, M., & Greenwood, D. (2011). Revitalizing universities by reinventing the social sciences. *Handbook of Qualitative Inquiry*, 27-42.

Lundy, S. E. (2014). *Leveraging digital technology in social studies education* (Doctoral dissertation, Portland State University).

Mickelson, R. A., & Bottia, M. (2009). Integrated education and mathematics outcomes: A synthesis of social science research. *North Carolina Law Review*, 88, 993.

Mitchell, S. (2006). Socratic dialogue, the humanities and the art of the question. *Arts and Humanities in Higher Education*, 5(2), 181–197. DOI: 10.1177/1474022206063653

Nind, M. (2020). A new application for the concept of pedagogical content knowledge: Teaching advanced social science research methods. *Oxford Review of Education*, 46(2), 185–2020. DOI: 10.1080/03054985.2019.1644996

Orosco, J. S. (2014). *Examination of gamification: Understanding performance as it relates to motivation and engagement*. Colorado Technical University.

Petticrew, M., & Roberts, H. (2008). *Systematic reviews in the social sciences: A practical guide*. John Wiley & Sons.

Riske, A. K. (2022). Teacher Professional Knowledge and Pedagogical Practices for Data-Driven Decision-Making (Doctoral dissertation, Arizona State University, USA).

Schuck, S., Aubusson, P., Kearney, M., & Burden, K. (2013). Mobilising teacher education: A study of a professional learning community. *Teacher Development*, 17(1), 1–18. DOI: 10.1080/13664530.2012.752671

Stein, P. (2014). Multimodal instructional practices. In *Handbook of Research on New Literacies* (pp. 871–898). Routledge.

Tomlinson, C. A. (2014). *The differentiated classroom: Responding to the needs of all learners* (2nd ed.). ASCD.

Valtonen, T. (2011). *An insight into collaborative learning with ICT: Teachers' and students' perspectives*. Itä-Suomen yliopisto.

Vavrus, M. (2008). Culturally responsive teaching. In T. L. Good (Ed.), *21st Century Education: A Reference Handbook* (Vol. 1, pp. 519–527), Sage Publications. DOI: 10.4135/9781412964012.n56

Welsch, A., & Heying, C. (1999). Watershed Management and Community Building: A Case Study of Portland's Community Watershed Stewardship Programtitle. *Administrative Theory & Praxis*, 21(1), 88–102. DOI: 10.1080/10841806.1999.11643351

Chapter 9
Unlocking Ms. Inaoka's PCK:
A Case of Grammar Instruction in a Japanese Junior High School

Kunitaro Mizuno
Kobe Women's University, Japan

ABSTRACT

This paper explores the integration of Pedagogical Content Knowledge (PCK) in pre-service English teacher education in Japan. It focuses on the design and delivery of a course using PCK to enhance the preparation of future English teachers. The study centers on an introductory lesson on the "be going to" form by Ms. Inaoka, a renowned teacher, to illustrate the practical application of PCK. Through the analysis of video recordings and a collaborative online platform, students engage with and reflect on teaching strategies, enhancing their understanding of PCK. The paper also discusses the Pedagogical Reasoning and Action model proposed by Shulman, which outlines the transformation process through which teachers develop PCK, emphasizing comprehension, transformation, and instruction. This study contributes to the understanding of how theory and practice are integrated in teacher education and how effective pedagogical strategies are developed through the lens of PCK, thus preparing teachers to be more responsive and effective in diverse classroom settings.

DOI: 10.4018/979-8-3693-0655-0.ch009

BACKGROUND AND OBJECTIVE OF THE STUDY

This paper examines the integration of Pedagogical Content Knowledge (PCK) within the domain of pre-service English teacher education in Japan. Sato (2015) highlighted that the overarching theme in teacher education reforms globally since the 1980s has been the professionalization of teaching. In alignment with international trends, Japanese educational institutions have been urged to cultivate continuous learning capabilities in their teacher candidates, empowering them with sophisticated professional competencies. While comprehensive frameworks for teacher education reform have been conceptualized worldwide for the 21st century, Shulman's (1986, 1987)[1] concept of PCK remains seminal, advocating that core professional knowledge for teachers centers around this concept. Despite its recognized importance, there is a notable scarcity of research in Japan exploring the incorporation of PCK in English teacher education. As an educator involved in pre-service English teacher education at a Japanese university, this study details my approach to designing and delivering a course on English teaching methods through a PCK lens. Additionally, this paper discusses the potential benefits of this approach for pre-service English teachers, specifically how it prepares them for practical teaching scenarios and fosters their development into learning specialists.

1. SHULMAN'S PEDAGOGICAL CONTENT KNOWLEDGE (PCK) AND ITS IMPLICATIONS FOR TEACHER EDUCATION THEORY

The foundational papers by Shulman in 1986 and 1987 marked a significant shift in the theoretical underpinnings of teacher education research, transitioning from a focus on behavioral science prevalent until the 1970s to a concentration on teachers' professional knowledge and thought processes. This paradigm shift, underscored by the rise of cognitive science and learning science, propelled the field towards examining practical knowledge — the knowledge that teachers actively utilize and operationalize in educational settings (Sato, 2015).

In response to this change, Shulman introduced a framework of seven "knowledge bases" essential for teachers to formulate this practical knowledge, significantly impacting educational practices. These bases include:

(1) Content Knowledge
(2) General Pedagogical Knowledge
(3) Curriculum Knowledge
(4) Pedagogical Content Knowledge (PCK)
(5) Knowledge of Learners and Their Characteristics

(6) Knowledge of Educational Contexts
(7) Knowledge of Educational Ends, Purposes, and Values, along with their Philosophical and Historical Grounds

(Shulman, 1987: 8)

Among these, PCK — defined as the unique amalgamation of content and pedagogy—emerges as a central element. This special blend allows teachers to transform their subject matter knowledge into pedagogically effective and adaptable teaching strategies, addressing diverse student needs and backgrounds (Shulman, 1987). Shulman posits that PCK represents a form of professional understanding distinct to teaching, differentiating the knowledge base of teachers from that of subject matter experts in other fields.

Further elaborating on PCK, Shulman emphasizes its role in distinguishing between a subject matter expert (like a math major or a history specialist) and a teacher in those fields. He argues that the essence of teaching lies at the intersection of content knowledge and pedagogical capability, where a teacher's ability to transform content knowledge into teachable material plays a pivotal role in catering to the varied abilities and backgrounds of students (Shulman, 1987).

The practical application of Shulman's PCK framework in teacher education is illustrated through the design of English language teaching methodologies for Japanese junior high school students, implemented in my classes in 2023. This paper will specifically analyze an introductory lesson on the *be going to* form conducted by Ms. Inaoka, using it as a case study to explore the application of PCK in teaching practice and to examine the learning outcomes from a PCK perspective. The subsequent chapter will delve deeper into the evolution of PCK as articulated by Shulman in his seminal works, setting the stage for a detailed reflection on Ms. Inaoka's lesson.

2. PEDAGOGICAL REASONING AND ACTION MODEL

Shulman introduces the transformation process, which teachers undergo to develop PCK, as a fundamental component of the teacher learning process, as depicted in Figure 1. This process is encapsulated within what he terms the "pedagogical reasoning and action model." According to Shulman (1987), this model illustrates that teacher learning involves a cyclical journey through six distinct phases.

Figure 1. Pedagogical Reasoning and Action Model (Shulman, 1987: 15)

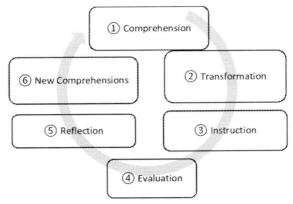

(Diagram created by the author)

① Comprehension

In this initial phase, teachers must grasp the objectives of the subject matter, understand the components of the learning content, and discern the interrelations among these components. This understanding extends to the relationship between the content at hand and other subject areas.

② Transformation

During transformation, teachers engage in a series of non-linear cognitive processes where content comprehension is altered to enhance student understanding. This involves:

(1) **preparation**: Critical examination and interpretation of existing teaching materials through structuring and segmentation.
(2) **representation**: Re-expressing teaching materials in forms more comprehensible to students, utilizing analogies, metaphors, examples, and demonstrations.
(3) **selection**: Choosing appropriate educational methods from a broad array of available teaching strategies.
(4) **adaptation and tailoring**: Customizing content and teaching methods to fit the unique characteristics of the student body, considering factors such as age, interests, prior knowledge, misconceptions, and cognitive abilities.
③ Instruction

This stage involves the enactment of the PCK developed through pedagogical reasoning, transforming the theoretical and preparatory work into practical teaching activities observable within the classroom.

④ Evaluation

The teacher assesses the students' understanding through interactive classroom dynamics, simultaneously evaluating the effectiveness of their own teaching methods in real-time.

⑤ Reflection

Teachers reflect on the teaching session, interpreting the significance and interrelations of student learning outcomes in relation to the classroom events.

⑥ New Comprehension

Through continuous pedagogical reasoning and reflective practice encompassing the previous stages, teachers develop a new, comprehensive understanding, leading to the reformation of PCK.

Thus, Shulman situates the concept of ②Transformation as a pivotal element within the pedagogical reasoning and action model, emphasizing its role in forming PCK through an iterative series of thought processes from comprehension to reflection.

3. INTEGRATING THEORY AND PRACTICE THROUGH THE CASE METHOD

Chapters 1 to 2 explored the concept of teacher education from the perspective of the "knowledge approach" as proposed by Shulman, emphasizing the essence of PCK and its formation processes. To effectively place PCK at the center of the teacher education curriculum, it is crucial for students to understand how English teachers apply and operationalize PCK in real classroom settings. This is achieved through the integration of theory and practice.

To facilitate this integration, I designed a course titled English Language Teaching Methods, centralizing the case method by utilizing video recordings of junior high school English lessons as primary examples. A focal point of this course is to enable students to learn the nexus between practice and PCK through the observation of these recordings, particularly those of Ms. Inaoka.

Ms. Inaoka (1955-2019) was a distinguished English teacher known for her dedication to promoting communicative English education in both public and private schools in Himeji City, Hyogo Prefecture. Her contributions were recognized with several awards, including the Palmer Prize[2] from the Institute for Research in Language Teaching and the Minister of Education, Culture, Sports, Science and Technology's Excellence Award.

Following her passing on September 5, 2019, the "Inaoka Project" was initiated by six volunteer teachers from Himeji City who had collaborated with Ms. Inaoka. This group compiled video recordings of her lessons to preserve and learn from her educational practices. The publication of the book, *Tips for English Teachers: A Message from Ms. Inaoka*, emerged as a critical guide for undergraduate students lacking practical teaching experience, aiming to learn from Ms. Inaoka's instructional approach.

As Sato (2015) articulates, observing video recordings alone does not suffice to comprehend the practical knowledge and reasoning of a teacher. The true educational value of these recordings is unlocked through careful interpretation of the events depicted. Thus, utilizing *Tips for English Teachers*, my students are able to delve into the nuanced dynamics of the classroom that are not immediately apparent through mere observation. This resource helps transform Ms. Inaoka's "invisible practice," or her improvisational thinking and judgments as elements of PCK, into "visible practice."

Leveraging *Tips for English Teachers* as a scaffold, students observed Ms. Inaoka's lessons, uploaded to a campus server. Accessible only during class hours, students controlled playback on their individual PCs and documented their observations and insights on a collaborative website, Padlet. I encouraged them to write comments from dual perspectives—focusing both on the teacher and the students—and to consistently cite specific language used during the lessons.

These Padlet comments facilitated a shared, ongoing dialogue among the class, fostering a collaborative lesson study environment. Before each subsequent class, I reviewed these comments, selecting notable insights for discussion to deepen students' understanding of Ms. Inaoka's PCK and her pedagogical reasoning. Additional materials were provided as needed, and I enriched the dialogue with feedback.

This class design exemplifies how lesson study can evolve into an active participation in the Inaoka Project, a community of learning experts, thereby effectively bridging theoretical knowledge with practical application in teacher education.

4. LESSON STUDY OF MS. INAOKA'S INTRODUCTORY CLASS ON THE *BE GOING TO* FORM

This section utilizes the introductory lesson on the *be going to* form by Ms. Inaoka, aimed at first-year junior high students, to explore its execution within the framework of Shulman's "pedagogical reasoning and action model" (Figure 1). As my students observed the video recording of this lesson, they utilized the platform Padlet to analyze and discuss the design and implementation of PCK by Ms. Inaoka. This analysis focuses on her strategies for introducing students to the *be going to* form for the first time, examining both the planned PCK and its practical application in the classroom.

4.1 Knowledge Necessary for ☐ Comprehension of *be going to* Form

Understanding the *be going to* form requires a comprehensive grasp of its structure and semantic implications, as it is crucial for conveying future intentions grounded in the present. Consider the following analyses:

(1) This meeting *is going to* be longer than I thought.

Here, "is" indicates the present tense, and "is going" signifies a present progressive form. This construction suggests a continuation of the current state into the future, implying that the meeting, currently in progress, will extend beyond initial expectations.

(2) I *am going to* research it this weekend.

In this instance, "am" represents the present tense, and "am going" again uses a present progressive form. The sentence frames a future activity (research this weekend) as a planned action, reflecting preconceived plans and intentions.

(3) I am researching this weekend.

The usage of the "-ing" form directly following "research" indicates that the action has already commenced, suggesting preparations or initial steps (such as buying a plane ticket) might have already been made.

(4) I will research this weekend.

Here, "will" indicates a future intention that is decided at the moment of speaking, not necessarily pre-planned, emphasizing the speaker's immediate decision rather than a pre-arranged schedule.

These distinctions highlight the nuanced use of the English tense system, which lacks a distinct future tense verb form, relying instead on present tense constructions to express future implications. Such an understanding is pivotal for teachers tasked with introducing the *be going to* form, as they must delineate its usage from other future expressions. This comprehension is essential for effectively conveying the subtleties of English tense to learners, particularly in how present perceptions influence the articulation of future events.

4.2. Formation Processes of □ Transformation to Form PCK for Introducing *be going to* Form for Junior High School Students in Japan

(1) Preparation: A critical examination of the traditional introduction of *be going to* form.

This *be going* to form lesson taught by Ms. Inaoka is an introduction lesson before the lesson begins, where *be going to* form appears for the first time in the junior high school English-authorized textbooks. Therefore, in terms of "preparation," it is necessary to critically examine the traditional method of introducing *be going to* form. The problem with the traditional teaching method of *be going to* form was raised in Wakabayashi (1990) as a simple question asked by junior high school students:

After learning "I will visit Mr. Smith," the teacher came up with "I am going to visit Mr. Smith," which also expresses "future," and also said that "will" and "be going to" have the same meaning. I thought it was strange, but it is better not to rebel against what the teacher said, so I kept quiet.
(Wakabayashi, 1990: 150)

This junior high school student's simple question can be rephrased as "Difference in form implies difference in meaning." Therefore, when introducing *be going to* form, it is necessary to set up lessons that reflect the different ways of understanding the future between the previously learned "will" and the new *be going to* form.

(2) Representation: Showing *be going to* form in an expression that is easy for students to understand.

In ① Comprehension we confirmed that there are three ways of understanding and expressing the future in English. To make it easier for junior high school students to understand the essence of the meaning expressed by each expression, they can be reworded and expressed using the following names: will (intention expression), be going to (prospective form), be + -ing + time point expressing the future (preparation completed form) (Lewis, 2002).

Furthermore, the perception of the future in *be going to* form, where the speaker has a plan in mind and the speaker's mind is moving toward that plan, can be expressed in the following diagram.

Figure 2. The mental picture (Image schema) of the speaker's use of be going to form

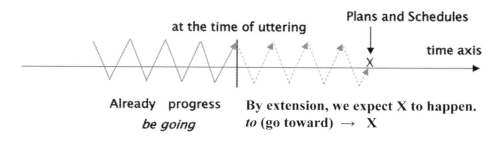

The X on the time axis represents the future plans and schedules that are in mind. As can be seen from the use of the progressive form, *be going to* form is used to expect future events based on facts that are already in progress.

(3) Selection

The third stage in the transformation process involves the selection of appropriate instructional strategies from a diverse array of communicative activities. As documented in *Tips of Lessons for English Teachers*, Ms. Inaoka utilized a comprehensive repertoire of communicative activities in her teaching practices, which included:

Speaking: Interviews, conversations, chats, roles as reporters, skits, presentations, speeches, discussions, show and tell sessions, and debates.

Writing: Conditional writing, free English composition, diary entries, letters, emails, cards, creative writing, reports, and dictation

(INAOKA Project, 2022: 36).

In Section 5.3, we will engage in a detailed exploration of the specific methods selected and integrated into the classes that introduced the *be going to* form, drawing extensively from the aforementioned repertoire of communicative activities.

4.3 Adaptation and Tailoring

In the adaptation and tailoring phase, Ms. Inaoka customized the PCK strategies developed through the stages outlined in (1) to (3) above by incorporating various creative elements to facilitate learning. A key adaptation involved contextualizing the *be going to* form within realistic scenarios familiar to the students, such as: classmates' birthdays, the season of competitive club games, plans for the upcoming weekend, summer vacation plans, a video message discussing plans from Ms. Chelsea, the Assistant English Teacher, a real letter from Ms. Chelsea outlining her plans for the weekend and the summer vacation.

These scenarios were carefully designed to resonate with the students' everyday experiences, thereby enhancing the relevance and applicability of the lessons. Ms. Inaoka's approach to tailoring the content ensured that the PCK was not only theoretically sound but also practically applicable, making the learning experience more engaging and effective. The subsequent section will delve into how Ms. Inaoka seamlessly integrated theory and practice in her pedagogical approach to introducing the *be going to* form.

4.4 Pedagogical Content Knowledge Application in Teaching the *be going to* Form

4.4.1 Sequential Integration of Tenses: Reviewing Past Tense and Introducing Future Form

Ms. Inaoka structured her instructional approach into three cohesive segments: a review of previous grammar, the introduction of new grammatical structures, and engagement in developmental communication activities. The initial phase, "Review," aimed to revisit the past tense, setting a chronological foundation that transitions from past experiences to present circumstances and future plans using the *be going to* form. This review session, lasting approximately 13 minutes, was characterized by its interactive nature, consisting of several distinct activities[3]:

(1) Teacher Talk

Ms. Inaoka initiated the session with a straightforward question-and-answer interaction focused on the past tense. She engaged students with relatable topics, such as recent physical education classes or notable events like the World Cup. Questions like "This morning, did you enjoy swimming?" or "Last night, did you watch soccer on TV?" prompted students to respond in English, incorporating gestures for emphasis. When a student expressed a dislike for swimming, stating, "No, I don't like swimming. It's difficult," Ms. Inaoka countered with a positive remark, "Swimming is fun! You can practice!" This exchange demonstrated her strategic use of dialogue to expand conversation, ensuring it was not merely a one-sided interaction.

(2) Chat

Following the initial Q & A, Ms. Inaoka selected a student to come to the front for a more extended dialogue, or chat. She posed a series of questions employing the past tense, such as "What did you do last night?"/ "Did you study ?"/ "What did you study?"/ "What did you eat for dinner last night?" "What time did you go to bed?" / "What time did you get up this morning?" This method not only reinforced the grammar review but also encouraged students to discuss their daily activities, thus practicing spontaneous English speaking.

(3) Pair Check

After the chat, students paired up to recapitulate the dialogue they had just heard. Each pair discussed what had been said, using "She" as the subject to report on their peer's responses. This activity was designed to enhance listening skills and ensure comprehension, as students were more likely to pay close attention to the interaction in anticipation of this task. These activities collectively aimed to strengthen the students' grasp of the past tense while seamlessly linking it to the present and future constructs, thereby preparing them for the introduction of the *be going to* form in subsequent parts of the lesson.

(4) Impromptu Reporting

After completing the pair work, Ms. Inaoka initiated an impromptu reporting session. She selected a student as "today's reporter" who then stood before the class to report on the conversation held during the pair work, using "she" as the subject of his sentences. Ms. Inaoka positioned herself next to the student in such a way that she did not overshadow him, yet was readily available to provide support as needed. This positioning was adapted based on the student's proficiency in English, demonstrating a tailored approach to individual student needs (INAOKA, 2022: 27).

(5) Self-expression activity in pairs or groups

Subsequently, students engaged in self-expression activities where they exchanged information with different partners from the previous task. To ensure diverse interactions, Ms. Inaoka had a structured system for pairing students: Partner A was the student next to them, Partner B was the student in front or behind, and Partner C was diagonally across. This method prevented repetitive pairing and encouraged a broader range of interaction among students. When initiating these pairings, Ms. Inaoka asked students to choose among Partners A, B, or C, fostering decision-making and collaboration.

(6) Writing Activity

Reflecting on the self-expression activities, students then wrote about "What their friends did and what they did last night" in their notebooks. This brief writing task, lasting about five minutes, was a critical component of the lesson. INAOKA (2022) observes that Ms. Inaoka collected these notebooks each class and provided detailed feedback on grammar, spelling, and sentence connectivity with a red pen. She expressed enthusiasm for reading these entries, indicating a deep commitment to her students' learning progress (INAOKA, 2022: 28).

Through these interconnected activities—speaking, listening, and writing—Ms. Inaoka crafted a comprehensive learning experience that not only reinforced the grammatical focus of the lesson but also promoted a dynamic classroom environment. Observations posted by my students on Padlet revealed their recognition of how these activities facilitated connections among peers and fostered an inclusive educational atmosphere. As one student noted, the interaction was not confined to the student and Ms. Inaoka alone but extended to include the entire classroom, highlighting the collective nature of learning in her approach.

4.4.2 Application of the *be going to* Form Using Contextual Learning

Following a comprehensive review of previous grammar points, Ms. Inaoka introduced the new grammatical structure *be going to* by incorporating scenarios familiar to the students, thereby facilitating an intuitive grasp of its usage. This method effectively bridged conceptual understanding with real-life application, as demonstrated in the structured teaching activities that followed.

The initial context for applying the *be going to* form was a classmate's upcoming birthday, making the learning environment both relevant and engaging for the students. Ms. Inaoka utilized the birthday of a student named Airi, which was to occur the following day on July 1, to integrate the new grammar point. The class celebrated by singing "Happy Birthday," and Ms. Inaoka introduced the sentence, "Airi is going to be fourteen." This practical application not only reinforced the grammatical structure but also enhanced retention through repetitive practice structured as follows: practice as a whole class, practice in pairs (designated as Pair A, B, and

C), and individual presentations (INAOKA, 2022: 30). This sequence ensured that students articulated the sentence multiple times and heard it even more frequently.

Students observing this session noted on Padlet the natural progression from singing to grammatical instruction. When prompted about her birthday, Airi's reply, "Tomorrow," led to a spontaneous and warm birthday celebration, which transitioned seamlessly into the grammar lesson. Ms. Inaoka capitalized on this moment to introduce "Airi is going to be 14 tomorrow," effectively linking the celebration with the teaching of the new form.

Subsequently, Ms. Inaoka expanded the context to include upcoming sports tournaments, another event relevant to the students' current experiences. She introduced the sentence, "The sports tournaments are going to start this weekend," and created additional examples in dialogue with the students, such as, "The volleyball team is going to play games against the Omato team." These examples were juxtaposed on the blackboard to highlight grammatical nuances.

To ensure comprehension, Ms. Inaoka addressed critical grammatical distinctions between "be going to" and "will" (a previously taught future form), and between the uses of "are" and "is" in the sentences, discussing these points in Japanese[4]. This bilingual explanation helped students discern the usage of singular versus plural forms, facilitating a deeper understanding of subject-verb agreement in the context of the *be going to* form.

Through these methodical teaching strategies, Ms. Inaoka not only introduced a new grammatical concept but also reinforced it through contextual learning, making the abstract structure tangible and directly tied to the students' everyday lives and immediate future plans.

4.4.3 Employing Chunk Expression "I'm going to..." for Weekend Plans

Following the introduction of the *be going to* form, Ms. Inaoka implemented a targeted exercise to reinforce this new grammatical structure among her students. She focused on the specific chunk expression "m going to... this weekend" to solidify its usage through both listening and speaking activities.

Initially, Ms. Inaoka presented a series of sentences using the "I'm going to..." structure, each depicting a different weekend activity. She instructed students to listen attentively and raise their hands if they shared the same plans, thus engaging them in a personal connection with each sentence:

"What are you going to do this weekend?"
"*I'm going to*play *baseball this weekend.*"
"*I'm going to*study *English this weekend.*"

"*I'm going to* <u>watch</u> TV *this weekend.*"
"*I'm going to* <u>go</u> cycling *this weekend.*"
"*I'm going to* <u>play</u> computer games *this weekend.*"
"*I'm going to* <u>go</u> to Hawaii *this weekend.*"

Ms. Inaoka repeated these sentences, ensuring that students heard the "I'm going to... this weekend" construction multiple times to enhance their familiarity with the pattern. This method utilized token frequency —the repetition of the same expressions—and type frequency—the introduction of different verbs (play, study, watch, go) following "to." According to usage-based model in cognitive linguistics[5], these frequency measures are crucial for the memorization and mastery of language patterns, effectively demonstrating the "frequency effect" that Ms. Inaoka aimed to maximize.

Subsequently, Ms. Inaoka encouraged students to think about their own upcoming weekend plans and to articulate these thoughts using the "I'm going to..." structure. She facilitated this through a pair activity where students shared their plans with each other, further increasing both token and type frequencies through interactive dialogue. Each student then presented their weekend plans to the class, enhancing retention and confidence in using the new grammatical form.

Observers from my class noted significant improvements in student engagement and language use as a result of these activities. They highlighted that by providing numerous relatable examples of the "I'm going to..." structure, Ms. Inaoka enabled even those students who typically struggled with English expression to participate effectively in the discussions. The structured practice culminated in individual presentations where each student confidently articulated their plans without hesitation.

This sequence of activities not only reinforced the grammatical structure but also promoted active student participation and linguistic confidence, demonstrating a practical application of cognitive linguistic principles in a classroom setting.

4.4.4 Utilization of a Video Letter From an Assistant Language Teacher (ALT) to Reinforce the *be going to* Form

A video letter from the Assistant Language Teacher (ALT) was shown on the TV screen in the classroom, and the following English message from the ALT clearly showed that Ms. Inaoka and the ALT worked together to create the frequency effect so that the students could learn how to use *be going to* form. The "italicized" words relate to token frequency and the "underlined" words relate to type frequency:

What are you going to <u>do</u> *this weekend?*
I am going to <u>go to</u> *the beach with my friends.*

> *We are going to eat a picnic lunch and go swimming.*
> *What are you going to do this summer?*
> *I am going to go to Mt. Fuji with Jason.*
> *We are going to go to the top.*
> Please tell me, *what are you going to do this summer?*

Before the video was played, students engaged in predictive exercises, using the structure "She is going to..." to speculate on the contents of the ALT's message. This preparatory activity primed them for the language patterns they were about to hear, setting a clear expectation and focus. Following the video, Ms. Inaoka facilitated a review in which students verified their understanding and recollection of the content by repeating phrases such as "She is going to..." This repetitive practice not only reinforced the students' grasp of the grammatical structure but also enhanced their ability to comprehend and retain the specific details of the ALT's plans.

Through these structured activities surrounding the video letter, Ms. Inaoka effectively combined audio-visual materials with active learning strategies to deepen the students' understanding and use of the "be going to" form, demonstrating an innovative approach to teaching future expressions in English.

4.4.5. Integration of Skills Through ALT Correspondence

In the educational sequence designed by Ms. Inaoka, she presented the students with letters that contained messages from the ALT corresponding to earlier video presentations. This method effectively bridged listening and speaking exercises with reading activities. By engaging with these letters, students encountered additional instances of the *be going to* grammatical structure, which is posited to enhance language acquisition through repeated exposure—a concept known as the frequency effect.

The letters were strategically used not only as a reading exercise but also as a springboard for writing. They concluded with a prompt asking students, "What will you do this summer?" This question was designed to elicit a written response, thereby fostering a holistic communicative experience that intertwined listening, speaking, reading, and writing skills.

My students who watched the video message from the ALT commented as follows:

Watching the video of their ALT instead of a fictional character excited the students and made them more eager to learn. They watched the video again, listened to their friends, share the messages from the ALT in English, and gradually tried to express the ALT's message in their own English. Through these activities, students not only practiced language skills but also gained confidence and satisfaction from their successful use and understanding of English. This approach exemplifies an effective integration of multiple language skills, promoting a dynamic and interactive learning environment.

4.4.6. Implementation of the *be going to* Form in Summer Vacation Planning

Following the introduction and practice of the *be going to* grammatical structure, a communicative activity was designed as the centerpiece of the class session, lasting approximately seven minutes. This activity employed the structure to articulate summer vacation plans. For instance, the Assistant Language Teacher (ALT) presented their vacation plans through multimedia, including videos and written narratives, serving as a practical model for the students.

Furthermore, Ms. Inaoka exemplified this grammatical form in her speech. She placed particular emphasis on the phrase "I'm going to..." by repeating it frequently and coupling it with expressive gestures to underscore its usage while discussing her own summer vacation plans.

> *What are you going to do this summer?*
> *I'm going to visit my aunt.*
> *I'm going to visit my aunt in Osaka.*
> She is 92. So *I'm going to say* "Hello, Obasan".
> And *we are going to talk* for a long time.
> I like her very much. *I'm going to enjoy* this summer.
> Thank you. OK?
> *What are you going to do this summer?*
> Please say to your partner A. Are you ready?

After listening to Ms. Inaoka's speech, the students began to talk about their summer vacation plans without planning with Partner A using *I'm going to...*. While she was walking in the classroom, she helped the students who were having trouble expressing their summer vacation plans using *I'm going to...*. After the pair activity, Ms. Inaoka chose one student to give an impromptu speech in front of the classroom.

The student sensed that Ms. Inaoka was standing a little closer to him and gently offered him a helping hand when he was in trouble, so he felt at ease and talked about his plans for the summer vacation with Ms. Inaoka in the following exchange:

> S: *I'm going to do* my homework this summer. I'm going to pool with my sister.
> T: Oh, you are going to the swimming pool with your sister, I see.
> S: *I'm going to study* at Juku.
> T: At Juku? Not at home? …At home too. Of course. Thank you.

S: *I'm going to enjoy* this summer. Thank you.

After this, the students presented their "mini speeches" in groups of four. Before starting the mini-speech, Ms.Inaoka asked the students to listen to more examples of "plans" using *be going to* form in the following questions:: Who *is going to watch* high school baseball on TV this summer? *Are you going to watch* a movie? Toy Story? In each group, the speaker stood up, and the remaining three listened with their eyes on the speaker and applauded when the speech was finished.

At the end of the lesson, to conclude the *be going to* lesson, Ms. Inaoka gave the following message to the students, telling them that their homework was to write a letter in response to the ALT:

You are going to study English tonight. Yes?
You are going to study English tomorrow. Yes?
You are going to write sentences about summer vacation using "I'm going to..."

After watching the entire video of Ms. Inaoka's *be going to* lesson, my students commented as follows:

I thought that it was because Ms. Inaoka actively used English that the students were responding in English. It was wonderful that she was able to create an atmosphere in which the students were encouraged to speak as much English as possible on their own initiative.

Everything students learned was connected, making it easy for them to learn without problems. Also, Ms. Inaoka always said "Very good./ Great./ OK." or asked questions when the students talked.

While observing the class, I saw that each student had plenty of chances to be in the spotlight, as they frequently shared ideas with friends, had conversations, and took turns speaking in front of the class. I believed that focusing on student interactions in English class would create a class where every student takes a leading role. By giving students many successful experiences, they would come to love English more.

This chapter has provided a detailed exploration of how Ms. Inaoka transformed the subject content of the *be going to* form into PCK and effectively implemented it in her lesson. The next chapter will discuss how well the "transformation" followed the principles of grammar instruction design.

5. ASSESSMENT OF MS. INAOKA'S *BE GOING TO* GRAMMAR INSTRUCTION

Ms. Inaoka's grammar class, which focuses on the *be going to* construction, adheres to the pedagogical framework suggested by Tanaka and Tanaka (2014). They propose that effective grammar teaching should encompass four stages: introduction, explanation, practice, and activity. Additionally, each stage should fulfill the "three good conditions" for successful grammar instruction. This paper evaluates Ms. Inaoka's methodology in accordance with these guidelines, particularly emphasizing the educational value derived from observing her class recordings for training students to become adept language educators.

5.1 Introduction

The introduction of the *be going to* form by Ms. Inaoka is meticulously documented in Section 5.3.2. Tanaka and Tanaka (2014) articulate three essential conditions for an effective introduction in grammar teaching: 1) demonstration of usage scenarios to enhance student awareness of the function and meaning of the grammar form; 2) cultivation of a perceived need for learning the grammar; and 3) simplicity in presentation.

Ms. Inaoka initiated the introduction by engaging with a student, Airi, asking about her birthday, thereby setting a relatable and specific context (Condition 1). This context naturally led to a demonstration of how to express upcoming events in English, fostering a perceived need among students to learn this specific grammatical structure (Condition 2). Ms. Inaoka then introduced the new phrase "Airi is going to be fourteen" clearly and repetitively, ensuring simplicity and comprehensibility in her delivery (Condition 3). This strategy allowed students to practice the phrase with variations, using different names as subjects, thereby solidifying their understanding through repetition.

The analysis confirms that Ms. Inaoka's introduction of the "be going to" construction meets all three prescribed conditions for an effective grammar lesson introduction. This structured approach not only facilitates grammatical comprehension but also enhances pedagogical effectiveness, making it a valuable model for future educators.

5.2 Explanation of the *be going to* Construction

In accordance with the instructional framework proposed by Tanaka and Tanaka (2014), the explanation stage of the "be going to" construction in Ms. Inaoka's class is discussed in Section 6.3.2. This section delineates the application of the grammatical structure within contexts familiar to the students, meeting the standards set for effective grammar instruction. The criteria for a proficient explanation include: 1) raising student awareness of new grammatical forms, meanings, and functions; 2) delivering explanations in a straightforward manner; and 3) linking the explanation to subsequent practice and activities.

Ms. Inaoka's approach prior to formally explaining the "be going to" form involved crafting sentences about forthcoming weekend plans in interaction with the students, thereby contextualizing the grammar point (Condition 1). She then succinctly wrote these sentences on the blackboard, employing visual aids to reinforce learning. The use of pre-written white cards, arranged on the blackboard, served to emphasize key elements of the grammatical structure (Condition 2).

The Sports tournaments are going to start this weekend.

The volleyball team is going to play games against Omato team.

White cards were used to highlight the new grammatical form of *be going to* and to make the students aware of the meaning that the volleyball team already started to practice and their minds were directed toward the game against their opponents. Ms. Inaoka also helped them grasp the function of the *be going to* form, which is used for talking about plans and schedules. In this way, Ms. Inaoka provided a simple explanation of the "new grammatical form, its meaning, and its use" (satisfying Condition 1 and Condition 2) for students to easily understand and apply.

On the other hand, Ms. Inaoka made the students visually realize the difference between "are" in the first example and "is" in the second example by using white cards to highlight it (Condition 1). With this fundamental understanding of the *be going to* form, the students can progress to the next stage, which is practicing the *be going to* form (Condition 3)."

5.3 Practice of the *be going to* Construction

Tanaka and Tanaka (2014) outline three critical conditions that effective grammatical practice must satisfy: 1) linking the grammatical form to its meaning and ensuring its retention in memory; 2) facilitating the automation of processing this form-meaning connection; and 3) building learner confidence through incremental steps. The practice sessions for the *be going to* form, detailed in Sections 5.3.3 to 5.3.6, are designed to embed this grammatical structure deeply within the students' cognitive frameworks through integrated language skills activities involving listening, speaking, reading, and writing.

These practice activities enabled students to internalize *be going to* as a coherent lexical chunk, enhancing retention and ease of access in memory (Condition 1). By repeatedly applying this structure in various communicative contexts, students progressed toward automaticity in processing the grammatical form in conjunction with its meaning (Condition 2). This automaticity is critical for fluent language use, allowing learners to focus more on communication rather than on the mechanics of language structures. Moreover, the structured design of these activities supported students in taking manageable steps towards mastering the construction, thereby bolstering their confidence in using *be going to* accurately and fluently (Condition 3).

Thus, the practice component of Ms. Inaoka's instruction not only adhered to the pedagogical conditions outlined by Tanaka and Tanaka but also effectively consolidated students' understanding and use of the *be going to* form. This approach demonstrates a comprehensive application of theory to practice, facilitating both cognitive and practical mastery of essential English grammar.

5.4 Activity: Impromptu Presentation on Summer Vacation Plans

The *be going to* activity, designed as an impromptu presentation about summer vacation plans, plays a pivotal role in the practical application of grammar instruction in Ms. Inaoka's class, as outlined in Section 6.3.6. Tanaka and Tanaka (2014) provide a framework for evaluating the effectiveness of such activities, stipulating three conditions: 1) the communicative scene should be natural; 2) the activity should facilitate the exchange of new information; and 3) the activity should be simple and executable within a short duration.

In this educational setting, a natural communicative scene was effectively established by situating the activity in the context of the upcoming summer vacation (Condition 1). This setting encouraged students to engage genuinely and meaningfully as they discussed their plans. Moreover, the activity was structured to ensure the exchange of previously unshared information, as students formed groups to reveal their summer vacation plans to each other (Condition 2). Lastly, the design of the presentation activity was straightforward, allowing for quick and efficient execution without unnecessary complexity (Condition 3).

This analysis of Ms. Inaoka's class through the lens of the four-step grammar instruction model proposed by Tanaka and Tanaka (2014) confirms that each instructional phase met the prescribed "three good conditions." Furthermore, the integration of theory and practice is exemplified through the use of video recordings of Ms. Inaoka's classes. By observing, recording, and critiquing these sessions, students not only engage with concrete examples of effective teaching strategies but also enhance their PCK. This approach underscores the value of Lesson Study as a central element of the curriculum, enabling students to acquire specialized knowledge crucial for their development as proficient educators. This methodological approach prepares students for practical teaching scenarios, where they can apply their learned skills in real-world contexts.

6. ASPIRATIONS AND CHALLENGES FOR FUTURE CLASSES

6.1 Incorporating Stop-Motion Lesson Study

Given the division of each 50-minute lesson into three segments (review, introduction and practice of new grammar points, and developmental communicative activities), this course previously allotted one week per segment for classroom observation. This format allowed for a piecemeal review of Ms. Inaoka's class sessions but did not provide adequate time for comprehensive reflection on her full class structure. To address this issue, the forthcoming academic year will dedicate four weeks to observing a complete 50-minute class. The final week will involve a continuous, uninterrupted viewing, using the "stop-motion method" for lesson study.

This method entails projecting the class video on a single computer, with groups of four students collaboratively watching. Each student has the opportunity to pause the video at moments they deem significant, explain their reasoning, and engage in a detailed discussion with their peers. Fujioka (1991) highlights three advantages of this approach: 1) it allows for discussions to be closely aligned with actual classroom events, preventing deviations from the factual basis of the class; 2) it facilitates a shared viewing experience, even for those not physically present in the class, thereby enhancing the depth of discussion; and 3) it enables participants to contribute their unique insights and experiences.

6.2 Challenges with the Apprenticeship of Observation and PCK Formation

A significant challenge in teaching English language methods pertains to the "apprenticeship of observation," a concept described by Lortie (2002). Aspiring teachers typically spend 12 years passively observing their teachers, during which they form subconscious assumptions about effective teaching and teacher-student interactions. These entrenched preconceptions are brought into teacher education programs, often leading to resistance to learning new methods that do not align with their established beliefs. Additionally, students' perspectives on teaching are inherently limited and subjective. They are usually unaware of the complexities involved in the various phases of teacher development, such as the transformation processes required to form Pedagogical Content Knowledge (PCK) or reflective practices post-teaching. Uchida (2009) criticizes this narrow perspective, likening it to a child attempting to measure the vast diversity of the world with a simple 30-centimeter ruler.

Students' pre-university experiences with education tend to produce shallow and potentially distorted views of teaching. These misconceptions may conflict with established educational research and hinder openness to innovative teaching methods. The primary challenge for future educational development is to reframe these views by merging theoretical knowledge with practical teaching experiences. This will involve critical evaluation of the viewpoints students have developed through years of observational learning, using case methods such as video analyses of exemplary classes like those of Ms. Inaoka. This approach aims to expand students' understanding and appreciation of diverse educational practices and the complexities of teaching.

6.3 Exploration of PCK Transformation Processes and Their Classroom Function

This course serves as an orientation in teacher education for undergraduate students, focusing on the three critical aspects outlined in Figure 1: comprehension, transformation, and classroom practice. The transformation process, pivotal in shaping PCK, involves a sequence of nuanced and complex stages: preparation, expression, selection, and adaptation and tailoring. The concept of the apprenticeship of observation, discussed earlier in section 7.2, plays a significant role in influencing these transformation processes. Given the highly individualized and intricate nature of PCK, it is crucial to study its actual dynamics in the classroom through various case methods, including the analysis of Ms. Inaoka's teaching practices.

Additionally, as depicted in Figure 1, teacher development is conceptualized as a cyclical process comprising six phases. This framework necessitates that future research in teacher education not only address these phases but also connect them comprehensively. To achieve this, it would be beneficial to conduct surveys with students who have completed their teaching practicums and with current teachers to examine how they have developed and utilized PCK across these phases and how they reflect on these experiences post-classroom. Developing a case study methodology for "Lesson Study" based on this cyclical model will be a focus of future investigations. This approach aims to enhance the understanding and application of PCK, thereby contributing to the professional growth of teachers and the effectiveness of teacher education programs.

REFERENCES

Akita, K. (2012). *Psychology of Learning: Designing the Classroom*. Sayusha.

Cowan, R. (2008). *The Teacher's Grammar of English A Course Book and Reference Guide*. Cambridge University Press.

Fujioka, N. (1991). *(1991). The Method of Classroom Research by the Stop Motion Method*. Gakuji-shupan.

Hatta, S. (2008). A Reflection on Shulman's Pedagogical Content Knowledge: Following Analyses of Projects Based on 'Pedagogical Reasoning and Action Model' *Bulletin of the Graduate School of Education. Kyoto University Research Information Repository*, 54, 180–192.

Hatta, S. (2009). The development of Lee Shoman's theory of teacher knowledge and learning process. *Journal of Educational Methodology*, 35, 71–81.

Herring, M., Koehler, M., & Mishra, P. (2016). *Handbook of Technological Pedagogical Content Knowledge (TPCK) for Educators*. Routledge. DOI: 10.4324/9781315771328

INAOKA Project. (2022). *Tips of lessons for English Teachers: A message from Ms. Inaoka*. Hamajima-shoten.

Kawai, C. (2019). From All English to English Rich Classes - Teaching Techniques for Making the Classroom a Communicative Scene. *English Education*, (October), 68–69.

Langacker, R. W. (2008). *Cognitive Grammar: A Basic Introduction*. Oxford University Press. DOI: 10.1093/acprof:oso/9780195331967.001.0001

Lewis, M. (2002). *The English Verb*. Heinle Cengage Learning.

Lortie, D. (2002). *Schoolteacher: a sociological study*. University of Chicago Press. DOI: 10.7208/chicago/9780226773230.001.0001

Mizuno, K. (2020). *Explorations of cultural and educational values of Graded Readers in English education in Japan*. Tokyo: Kuroshio-shupan Ministry of Education, Culture, Sports, Science and Technology. (2017). *Course of Study for Junior High Schools: Foreign Languages – English*. https://www.mext.go.jp/component/a_menu/education/micro_detail/__icsFiles/afieldfile/2019/03/18/1387018_010.pdf (Date of Viewing: October 25, 2023)

Sato, M. (2015). *Educating Teachers as Professionals*. Iwanami-shoten.

Sato M, Akita K, Iwakawa N, & Yoshimura T. (1991). Practical Thinking Styles of Teachers: A Lesson of Descriptive Inquiry on Thought Processes. *Bulletin of the faculty of education, the University of Tokyo*.31: 183-200.

Sato M, Iwakawa N, Akita K. (1990). Practical Thinking Styles of Teachers: Comparing Expert's Monitoring Processes with Novices. *Bulletin of the faculty of education, the University of Tokyo*.30: 177-198.

Shimura, T. (2017). An Educational Study on PCK (Pedagogical Content Knowledge) Theory from the Perspective of Social Studies/ Geography Education. *Bulletin of Joetsu University of Education*, 37(1), 139–148.

Shulman, L. (1986). Those who understand: Knowledge growth in teaching. *Educational Researcher*, 15(2), 4–14. DOI: 10.3102/0013189X015002004

Shulman, L. (1987). Knowledge and teaching: Foundations of the new reform. *Harvard Educational Review*, 57(1), 1–22. DOI: 10.17763/haer.57.1.j463w79r56455411

Tanaka T & Tanaka. (2014). *Designing of English Classrooms and Grammar Teaching*. Tokyo: Taishukan-shoten.

Tokuoka, K. (1995). A Study on the Features of Pedagogical Content Knowledge and its Implications. *Journal of Educational Methodology*, 21, 67–75.

Tomasello, M. (2003). *Constructing a Language: A Usage-Based Theory of Language Acquisition*. Harvard University Press.

Uchida, T. (2009). *Children with No Ambition, Youths Who Don't Study, and Unemployed Young People*. Kodansha.

Wakabayashi, S. (1990). *36 chapters that answer simple English questions*. Japan Times.

Wakamatsu, D. (2020). Rethinking Schulman's Theory of Teacher Knowledge: Process of Theory Development. *Bulletin of the Graduate School of Education. Kyoto University Research Information Repository*, 66, 43–56.

Yano, H. (1998). Review of the Studies on Teacher's Pedagogical Content Knowledge focused on Social Studies. Bulletin of Graduate School of Education. *Tokyo Univ*, 38, 287–295.

ENDNOTES

1. The overview of the PCK concept proposed by Shulman in this paper is based on Shulman (1986, 1987) and the following previous studies: Akita (2012), Hotta (2008, 2009), Sato, Akita, Iwakawa and Yoshimura (1991), Sato, Iwakawa, and Akita (1991). Sato (2015), Shimura (2017), Tokuoka (1995), Yano (1998), Wakamatsu (2020).

2. The Palmer Prize is an award presented by the Institute of Language Education to individuals, schools, and organizations that have achieved outstanding results in improving and developing foreign language education in Japan.

3. Ms. Inaoka uses about 1 to 2 minutes of "chants" (memorizing expressions using rhythm) during review, but this is omitted in this article. I would like to take this opportunity to consider the "Inaoka-style chants" again.

4. Ms. Inaoka spends about 47 minutes of the 50-minute class in English without using Japanese. On the other hand, she effectively uses Japanese to explain the points of newly introduced grammar (be going to) in order to ensure that the students understand the grammar. Ms. Inaoka's classes are not "All English." The term "All English" is not used in the *Course of Study for Junior High Schools: Foreign Languages - English* (Ministry of Education, Culture, Sports, Science and Technology, 2017), which specifies, "English classes shall be conducted in English" (p. 9). With regard to "the basis of teaching in English," this class quotes the following words from Kawai (2019) to highlight "how Ms. Inaoka's classes are not "All English" but "English Rich": The term "All English" is sometimes interpreted to mean that "100% of classes must be conducted in English" or that students are expected to "avoid using Japanese." The current global trend in English education encourages the effective use of the native language, and both teachers and students are more likely to use Japanese if it is deemed more effective (Kawai, 2019: 68).

5. For more information on the "usage-based model," see: Langacker (2008), Mizuno (2020), Tomasello (2003).

Chapter 10
A System Thinking Approach to Pre-Service Teachers' Formation:
An Epistemological Perspective From Europe and USA

Francesco Maiorana
https://orcid.org/0000-0001-7327-2611
IIS G. B. Vaccarini Catania, Italy

Andrew P. Csizmadia
https://orcid.org/0000-0002-9779-055X
Newman University, UK

Gretchen M. Richards
Independent Researcher, USA

Giusy Cristaldi
IIS Concetto Marchesi Mascalucia, Italy

Janet L. Bavonese
Jacksonville University, USA

ABSTRACT

It is acknowledged that it is necessary to introduce computing for a quality education starting from primary education. This can be accomplished by empowering pre-service teachers to become confident in teaching computing. The work will review the literature and compare teacher pre-service formation (PSF) activities in each author's country with an overview of the respective continents. Drawn from direct

DOI: 10.4018/979-8-3693-0655-0.ch010

field experiences, this work will present, discuss, compare, and draw conclusions and best practices, through the lens of system thinking, on the complex process of pre-service computing teacher transformation. Similarities are acknowledged, while differences in approaches are highlighted. Using the lens of systems thinking, a review of research and theory to examine pre-service teacher (PST) formation will include Technological Pedagogical Content Knowledge (TPCK) in the realm of science, technology, engineering, arts, and mathematics (STEAM). Celia (Computer Educators Learning Inclusive Actor) will represent the teaching candidates' professional pathways in each country.

INTRODUCTION

For nearly a decade, there has been a worldwide resurgence to adopt compulsory P12 computing education. This revival shifted focus to computer science, coding and computational thinking to transition learners from consumers to creators of digital artefacts. Different countries are at different stages of adopting computing education with England regarded as an innovator, Italy within the early majority group, and USA as a late adopter. In the USA, the Department of Education can increase resources and guidance to enhance the quality of education through pre-service and leadership (Maiorana, 2022). However, the states remain independently reliant on the federal government's framework of policies and laws but are required to meet the diverse cultural dependencies within each state. By 2018, forty-four states adopted or are in the process of adopting standards in teaching computing education (CSTA K-12, 2017; National Standards, 2019; Richards & Turner, 2019; Code.org, 2018). Most states have blended two or more organizations' recommendations (CSTA K-12, 2017; National Standards, 2019; Richards & Turner, 2019; Code.org, 2018; Maiorana, Csizmadia, & Richards, 2020).

Recently researchers around the world have proposed a systemic approach (Fuller & Kim, 2022; Sengeh, 2022) as a way to achieve a holistic development of students (Datnow, 2022). Research (Maiorana & Cristaldi, 2023) has highlighted the importance of a system-thinking approach to transform schools (Fuller & Kim, 2022), supporting teachers, the mind and heart of the educational system around the world, through adequate policies supporting their continuing professional learning (Boeskens et al., 2020a; (OECD, 2021b; OECD, 2019b), advocating for upskilling and investing in people through bottom-up solutions and insights (Maiorana, 2023; (Maiorana, 2020b; OECD/OPSI, 2020).

A global perspective on teaching is needed for an ample and systemic reform of the educational system involving all the actors of the educational community and in this respect, a wise use of digital technologies can contribute towards a positive digital and green transition of society. According to the European Parliament's decision to establish the Digital Decade Policy Programme 2030[1] "Digital technologies should contribute to achieving broader societal outcomes that are not limited to the digital sphere but have positive effects on the everyday lives and well-being of citizens. If it is to be successful, the digital transformation should go hand-in-hand with improvements as regards democracy, good governance, social inclusion, and more efficient public services". The reader can find reflections for computing curriculum designers and computing educators lessons learned in the application of social science learning theories in computing education curriculum design and delivery (Cristaldi, 2022).

In this regard, this work aims to make a small contribution in this direction by providing, as a proof of concept, a set of strategies to overcome identified problematic areas, along with a set of best practices and resources suitable for teaching computing to prospective teachers, through the lens of system thinking.

This work examines concerted efforts in creating computing education uniformity through various initiatives (Alabama Code Title 16 Education, 2019; Forlizzi, 2018; Klopfenstien, Delpriori, Maldini & Bogliolo, 2019; Maiorana, Csizmadia, & Richards, 2020; Redecker, 2017; Royal Society, 2017). For compulsory computing education renaissance to flourish, sufficient competent, capable, and confident professional computing teachers need to be recruited and trained. In this work the authors, drawing upon their experience and expertise as initial teacher educators in different countries, analyze the complex process of pre-service computing teacher transformation through the lens of system thinking.

Similarities are acknowledged, while differences in approaches are highlighted. Identifiable stages for computing educators include the recruitment of candidates who are trainable to teach computing, and supporting pre-service computing teachers from the classroom to becoming in-service computing teachers. Using the lens of systems thinking, a review of research and theory to examine pre-service teacher (PST) formation will include Technological Pedagogical Content Knowledge (TPCK) in the realm of science, technology, engineering, arts, and mathematics (STEAM). Celia (Computer Educators Learning Inclusive Actor) will represent the teaching candidates' professional pathways in each country. Figure 1 illustrates the key stakeholders at each stage, thus contextualizing the system where the problem may reside.

Figure 1. System Workflow of Computing Teacher Formation

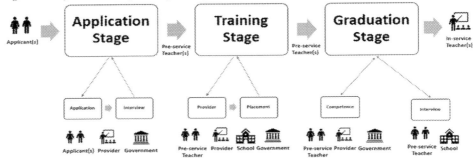

Celia (Computer Educators Learning Inclusive Actor) represents the persona of a pre-service teacher as they transit the different phases during the teacher metamorphosis. When Celia applies for a computing educator program, she may be required to take a national or proprietary examination before the faculty assesses her ability to learn methodologies in teaching and computing education. If Celia is conditionally accepted, she must achieve benchmarks based on Specific Measurable, Attainable, Realistic Timeframe (SMART) targets. Table 1 outlines the number of required hours of curriculum in the respective countries or universities and Table 2 reflects the teaching requirements by grade bands.

Table 1. Curriculum in Authors' Respective Countries or Institutions

Country	Year 1	Year 2	Year 3	Year 4	Year 5	Certification Exams
England Secondary: Postgraduate route	Celia must graduate from an undergraduate computer related program where computing forms 50% of the program's content. This is a compulsory requirement to be considered as an applicant for a postgraduate secondary computing trainee teacher program.		Celia studies a one-year Postgraduate Certificate in Secondary Computing Teaching with Qualified Teacher Status (QTS). This course consists of: School placement 120 days Professional Enquiry and Subject Leadership in Computer Science 200 hours Evidence Informed Learning, Teaching and Assessment in Computing 200 hours Transition and Enhancement Placement 75 hours Subject Knowledge and Professional Practice for Teachers 240 hours Once graduated Celia will complete a further two years in a secondary school being assessed against the Early Career Framework.			Celia presents a portfolio of evidence against the Teachers' Standards and passes the academic postgraduate assignments.
England Primary: Postgraduate route	Celia must graduate from an undergraduate program where 50% of the program's content is that of a national curriculum primary subject. This is a requirement to be considered as an applicant for a postgraduate secondary computing trainee teacher program.		Celia studies a one-year Postgraduate Certificate in Secondary Computing Teaching with Qualified Teacher Status (QTS). This course consists of: School placement 120 days Professional Enquiry and Contemporary, Creative and Innovative Practice in Core Curriculum 200 hours Processes, Application, and Influence of Assessment Practices on Teaching and Learning 200 hours The Core Curriculum 100 hours The Broad Curriculum 100 hours Professional Studies in Education 100 hours Once graduated, Celia will complete a further two years in a secondary school being assessed against the Early Career Framework.			Celia presents a portfolio of evidence against the Teachers' Standards and passes the academic postgraduate assignments.
Italy Primary with CFU	1 CFU = 6 hour for lessons, 19 hours for independent study. In round brackets the CFU for Laboratory activities.					Teaching certificate for primary teachers
	Pedagogy 8 Art 8 Didactic 6 Didactic technologies Physiology for special education 8 Ecology Physics Sport Science Geography History of Education Hygiene		Italian literature Linguistic History and didactic of history 16 Didactics 8 (2) School and Clinical Psychology 16 Educational sociology 8 Mathematical logic 8 (1) Mathematics 12 (1) Music 8 (1) Italian Literature and Linguistics 12 (1) English certification 2 (4) Internship and Practicum 11 Thesis and final exam 9			

continued on following page

Table 1. Continued

Country	Year 1	Year 2	Year 3	Year 4	Year 5	Certification Exams
Italy Secondary	Celia must complete 13 years of school, 3 years of undergraduate courses and two years of master courses in technical domains such as Computing, Engineering, Physics and mathematics according to national laws[2]. With the Master, Celia can start seeking non-tenured teaching contracts. After 3 years of teaching services in an 8-year time span, she acquires the teaching certificates. Celia can also obtain her teaching certificate after completing an annual university course requiring a 1,500 workload and 60 CFU. With her teaching certificate and 24 CFY on Anthropology, Psychology or Pedagogy she can participate in a national competitive exam with available positions identified according to regional needs. If Celia is ranked among the first positions available in the region where she participated, she becomes a tenured teacher.					
USA-Alabama Computer Science Educator (6-12)	In the first 2 years Celia will need to complete: Humanities 9 hours Literature 6 hours Fine Arts 6 hours History 6 hours Social/Behavior Sciences 6 hours Sciences 12 hours Mathematics 6 hours Computer Science 9 hours Total Hours Years 1&2: 60 hours		In the last 2 years Celia will need to complete: Professional Studies 9 hours Teacher Ed. Coursework 24 hours Internship 6 hours CS Courses 21 hours Total Hours Years 3&4: 60 hours Alabama Code § 290-2-2-101(2) outlines the required hours for specified teaching fields.		The initial CSE certification can occur in a bachelor's (Class B) or masters (Alt-A) program. After the teaching certification is received additional degrees could result in a promotion or salary increase.	Praxis 5652 Computer Science Exam and a report in a Case Study format containing Celia's lesson plan(s), activities, a self-reflection, and samples of student assignments to measure her impact and effectiveness on her student's learning.

Table 2. Certifications and Responsibilities for Teaching Computing Education

Country	Grades Pre-K-3	Grades 4-5	Grades 6-8	Grades 9-12
England	Taught by certified primary teachers following the Computing Programme of Study. They may have completed either an undergraduate primary teacher program or a postgraduate teacher training program and have gained a Teach Primary Computing Certificate awarded by the British Computer Society.		Taught by certified secondary teachers following the Computing Programme of Study. These may be certified as PGCE Secondary Computing teachers and have gained a Teach Secondary Computing Certificate awarded by the British Computer Society.	
Italy	Taught by primary teachers with a teaching certificate obtained after 5 years of higher education and after winning a national competitive exam.		When computing is in the curricula it is taught by non-tenured teachers with proper certification or by tenured teachers who won a national competition. To obtain certification teachers must have a master's degree in STEM domain.	
USA-Alabama Computer Science Educator (6-12)	Taught by educators certified in early childhood or elementary education. Digital literacy and fundamental skills are predominantly taught in these grades.	Taught by educators certified in early childhood or elementary education. Digital literacy becomes a lesser topic and building knowledge and skills in computer science begin.	Currently taught by educators with a secondary education field certification. Currently CS is integrated into all curriculums.	When the Computer Science Educator (6-12) teaching certification is standard practice, Celia will be responsible for teaching programming, algorithms, databases, operating systems, AI, HCI, and much more.

Additionally, the institution will provide Celia an academic environment to explore theoretical and pedagogical approaches in teaching computing under a recognized subject matter expert's guidance and the institution's technological infrastructure. For Celia to become successful, she will need access to a learning, teaching, and assessment environment designed and developed by the experience of a computing educator mentor. The governmental agency is not responsible for providing Celia the competence framework that she will be assessed against but specify the compliance framework that educational institutions need to adhere to to be licensed to train teachers (Alabama Code Title 16 Education, 2019; Forlizzi, et al., 2018; Klopfenstien, et al., 2019; Maiorana, et al., 2020; Redecker, 2017; Royal Society, 2017).

Relationship between Systems Thinking and TPCK

The process of envisioning and thinking of problems and solutions using various systematic thinking styles defines systems thinking (Goodman, 2018). This develops an understanding of processes that are not optimized to permit expansion to create satisfying, long-term solutions to chronic problems.

Consequently, systems thinking uses the character traits of curiosity, clarity, compassion, choice, and courage. Because computing relies on systems thinking, Celia must demonstrate the ability and willingness to conduct in-depth situational exploration, recognize interrelated characteristics, identify, and test multiple interventions for resolutions including those that are not popular (DfE, 2020; Alabama Code, 2019). Figure 2, and Table 3 exemplify the relationship between system thinking and the TPCK components.

According to (Koehler, Mishra & Yahya, 2007), "At the heart of TPCK is the dynamic, transactional relationship between content, pedagogy and technology. Good teaching with technology requires understanding the mutually reinforcing relationships between all three elements taken together to develop appropriate, context-specific strategies and representations.". This vision has been embraced, according to (Tokuhama-Espinosa, 2023) by learning science where psychology (mind), neuroscience (brain), and pedagogy (education), but also philosophy, cultural anthropology, linguistics, and artificial intelligence provide support for a better understanding of human learning. From the Learning Sciences emerge transdisciplinary insights into the Science of Learning whose end goal is improved teaching.

Figure 2. TPCK Integration of Systems Thinking Styles

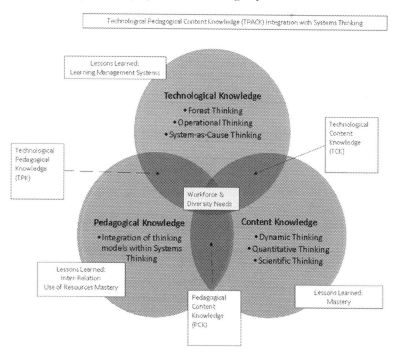

Table 3. System Thinking Styles Relationship to TPCK Categories with Definitions

TK Thinking Style	Definition
Forest Thinking	Sees beyond the details to the context of relationships which are embedded.
Operational Thinking	Thinking in this stage allows logical reasoning
System-as-cause thinking	Known as Endogenous Thinking sees internal actors that manage policies of the system are responsible for the behavior.
CK Thinking Style	**Definition**
Dynamic Thinking	Ability to make optimal decisions in a dynamic or ever-changing environment
Quantitative Thinking	Analysis and interpretation of real-world quantitative information to draw conclusions and resolve issues.
Scientific Thinking	Involves the content of science and the reasoning process such as induction and deduction, or causal reasoning, concept formation or hypothesis testing.

Candidate Selection

Countries differ in the theory and practice of the selection process. The universities are responsible for the assessment of Celia's aptitude and attitude for TPCK, systems thinking, and STEAM-based learning (Alabama Code Title 16 Education, 2019; Forlizzi, et al., 2018; Klopfenstien, et al., 2019; Maiorana, et al., 2020; Redecker, 2017; Royal Society, 2017).

Italy. Table 1 outlines bachelor's and Master's requirements. To be a primary teacher Celia must undertake an admission test administered by each university following national guidelines (Forlizzie, et al., 2018; Ministerial Decree 214, 2020) enacted in computing curricula (Maiorana, 2019) After completing her master's, Celia must secure subject-specific teaching concur to teach either at the primary or secondary level.

England. Celia will apply a maximum of 3 training providers (university-based or school-lead) via an online portal. They are interviewed to determine their potential to train to teach, prior to an offer formally being made. Additionally, the training provider ensures that individual candidates fulfil national compliance requirements prior to commencing their training as part of a rigorous selection process (Royal Society, 2017).

USA. Institutions will vet Celia using multiple measures of scholarly and dispositional suitability (Alabama Code, 2019). Each university bears responsibility for candidates who have a minimum GPA on earned college credit, pass a state-endorsed background check, and demonstrate appropriate ethical dispositions. Candidates are interviewed specific to each university campus, therefore the standards for selection are uniform while the processes differ.

Technological Pedagogical Content Knowledge (TPCK) Framework

Acquisition of TPCK principles aligns with STEAM instruction using systems thinking to better prepare global citizens for the many vocational STEAM opportunities. Emphasis on TPCK and STEAM transitions the traditional rote lesson into experiential learning (ALSDE, 2018; Artworks, and; Culture Learning Alliance, 2017; Di Blas, Fabbri, & Ferrari, 2018; Maiorana, 2019; Nesta, 2014; STEM Learning, 2020; The Big Draw, 2020; Royal Society, 2020). This section explores the introduction, impact, and challenges of TPCK-enhanced STEAM instruction.

Italy. Celia attends training courses for primary education related to the implementation of the TPCK framework (DeRossi & Trevisan, 2018, Maiorana, Richards, Lucarelli, Berry, & Ericson, 2019) and STEAM. European projects offer a wealth of resources related to TPCK (ITELab Project, and; Blamire, Cassells, & Walsh,

2017). A national master and summer school[1] offers Celia updates with technologies (Mandrioli, Torrenbruno, & Marini, 2010). According to Reddecker (2017), STEAM computing is introduced either as a standalone discipline or embedded in the context of other domains (Caspersen, Gal-Ezer, McGettrick & Nardelli, 2018). Proposed Italian national computing guidelines (Forlizzi, et al., 2019) can be used as guidelines for Celia's formation. Recent surveys conclude that pre-and in-service teachers often use informal training (Klopfenstien, et al., 2019).

England. Celia is introduced to the rationale (Culture Learning Alliance, 2017) and TPCK (Nesta, 2014) for developing, supporting, and sustaining a STEAM classroom. National initiatives, such as STEAM Toolkit (Artworks, no date). The Big Draw Festival (2020).

Royal Society's Partnership Grants (2020), support the teaching of STEAM in schools by developing creative and collaborative teaching and learning communities. Impact of STEAM initiatives are articulated by both STEM Learning (2020) and the Royal Society (2020).

USA. Teacher programs adjusted the focus to TPCK and systems thinking content (CSTA K12, 2017; ALSDE, 2018) to address the preparation of college and career-ready students. The adoption of Digital Literacy and Computer Science Standards (2018) meant integration into the different content areas to push TPCK across the curriculum. Now the platform allows faculty to broaden the boundaries of TPCK as Celia negotiates the content knowledge and pedagogy of her discipline (ALSDE, 2018; Richards & Turner, 2019). She is expected to blend STEAM and TPACK initiatives with systems thinking to provide a robust and real-world skillset to her students.

Internship and Practicum

Celia's formation and transformation will be explored through the lens of Kolb's Experiential Learning Cycle (1984) as it relates to systems thinking. Although this is the primary lens, the ability to interweave TPCK and STEAM are relevant in the scoring of Celia's capabilities as a co-instructor.

Italy. During Celia's placement, she will complete an average of 500 hours in different schools. This allows her to be engaged with Kolb's (1984) multiple low-stakes practicum experiences related to TPCK and course goals (Lotter, Singer, & Godley, 2009).

England. Celia is required to complete 120 days of placement in two contrasting school settings (Royal Society, 2017), teaching, generating, and curating competence-based evidence for her Qualified Teacher Status (QTS) certification (DfE (b, c), 2020). Through this process, Celia develops as a critical reflective TPCK practitioner (DfE (c), 2020).

USA. Alabama Code (2019) states clinical experiences occur at least two times during Celia's matriculation using various diversity criteria. Field experiences integrate TPCK with 6-12 standards (Alabama Code, 2019; ALSDE, 2018). Immersing Celia in learning communities to demonstrate competence in STEAM content, she will begin to integrate systems thinking, TPCK, and computing into a comprehensive approach, e.g. the iceberg model, to build competencies as depicted in Figure 3. Successful internship completion requires Celia to integrate TPCK into all instruction including the final computing education instructional unit with interactive activities. She will present her case study with lesson plans, cooperating teacher and university supervisor observations, self-reflection, and student assignments to measure outcomes to ensure all criteria in planning, instruction, and professionalism set forth by the institution and the state are met.

Figure 3. Iceberg Model of Competencies for Teaching Computing

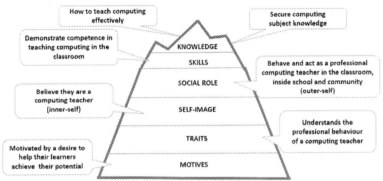

Table 4. Role of TPCK, Systems Thinking and Styles in Computing Education Formation

	Motive *A desire to help learners achieve their potential.*	**Traits** *Understands the professional behavior of a computing teacher.*	**Self-Image** *Believes they are a computing teacher (inner self)*	**Social Role** *Behaves and acts as a professional computing teacher in the classroom, school, and community (outer self).*	**Skills** *Demonstrate competence in teaching computing in the classroom.*	**Knowledge** *How to teach computing effectively.*
Thinking Style	Operational	Systems-as-Cause	Forest	Quantitative	Scientific	Dynamic
Technological Knowledge (TK), Pedagogical KNowledge (PK), and Content Knowledge (CK)						
TK	Does Celia address ethical issues and influence in coding HCI, AI and other current topics in computing education?	Does Celia respond to uncomfortable questions effectively on well versed and topics with less knowledge?	Does Celia project her knowledge and self-confidence to her students during instruction?	Does Celia project a respectful teamwork, collaborative environment?	Does Celia demonstrate competencies with age and grade appropriate exercises and content?	Does Celia effectively promote the integration of systems thinking and computing competencies in students?
CK	Does Celia explain digital literacy and other computing concepts as it relates to the content subject area?	Does Celia address the negative impact of content knowledge when applied inappropriately among her students?	Does Celia constructively guide and praise students as they work throughout their learning path?	Does Celia promote a respectful collaborative teamwork, and acceptance of diverse thinking?	Does Celia assist students in learning content, skill, and competencies effectively through positive reinforcement and empowerment?	Was Celia well prepared in assessing students' overall computing competencies?
PK	Does Celia employ systems thinking and other pedagogical, social, and emotional approaches effectively?	How flexible is Celia in managing the computing classroom of varying degrees of student learning in technology?	Does Celia promote a positive sense of identity & self-worth in her students when they struggle in a content or skill area?	Does Celia empower her students to be a digital leader in a respectful teamwork, collaborative environment?	Does Celia effectively use systems thinking in her pedagogical knowledge to effectively develop students' content, skills, and competencies in computing?	Has Celia acquired the instructional strategies to effectively teach computing during periods of outages?

Transiting to In-Service

Ultimately, Celia's student outcomes will determine her effectiveness as a computing educator. Therefore, the role of systems thinking and TPCK in the realm of STEAM education during Celia's transition to an effective in-service computing educator is discussed (Alabama Code, 2019; Dfe 2020a; DfE 2020b; DfE 2020c; Kolb, 1984; STEM Learning, 2020). If Celia is unable to acquire the specified level of competencies in the processes and styles of systems thinking with TPCK, then she may not be able to effectively transfer the knowledge, skills, and abilities to her P12 students.

Figure 4. Scaffold of Systems Thinking and TPCK in Computing Education and STEAM

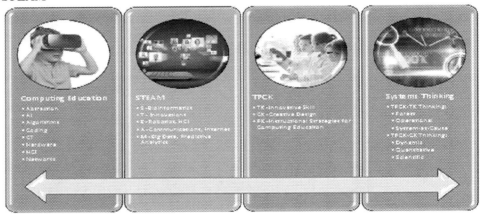

Italy. During the first year of tenured status, Celia is required to attend an induction program (Mangione, Pettanti, & Rosa. 2016). The program consists of preparatory meetings, training workshops in relation to TPCK, group project, professional mentor supervision, and online training aimed at building a digital professional portfolio.

England. Celia will present her competence-based evidence for achieving each of the 8 standards of the Qualified Teachers' Standards (QTS) professional certification (DfE (a), 2020). She is recommended to the Department of Education (DfE) by her training provider. Upon employment, she will undertake the Newly Qualified Teacher (NQT) induction year. This development is underpinned by the early career framework including TPCK. NQTs are supported by her subject-based mentor.

USA. Certification transition includes successful completion of the program, passing the required proprietary exam, Praxis 5652, to demonstrate content knowledge and competence in effective teaching, and two field experiences before internship

(Alabama Code, 2019). Celia can request additional instruction to be successful during her first two years in the classroom. The university is required to assist with technology integration and TPCK skillsets appropriate to the teaching field.

Lessons Learned

Figure 1 Systems Diagram, discussed in the introduction, outlined the key stakeholders and the four key stages in teacher transformation. This diagram illustrates the interaction and interdependence between different stakeholders at each stage of teacher transformation. After Celia becomes an in-service teacher, she may voluntary decide or have the decision made for her to leave the profession, which is a critical failure in the teacher preparation process. Possible reasons for leaving could include academic progress, attitude, aptitude, achievement against teachers' competence standards or a combination of the aforementioned. The potential failures and strategies for resolutions Celia could experience are summarized in Table 5.

Table 5. Dispositional and TPCK Challenges During Computing Educator Formation

Problematic Area	Potential Symptoms	Strategies	Potential Outcomes	
			Positive Outcome	Negative Outcome
Dispositional Challenges				
Low self-efficacy	● Student complains that they are not appreciated by their mentor. ● Student vocalises that they will never be a teacher. ● Student has a negative view of themselves as a teacher.	● Review student's work life balance to ensure sufficient sleep, proper nutrition, regular exercise, and adequate financial resources. ● Review feedback from mentor, identify and learn to celebrate success and learn from failures.	Student has a positive image of themselves as a computing teacher.	Student continues to have low self-esteem issues regarding their self-perception of being a teacher or they leave the program.
Lack of ambition to be a computing teacher	● Student content with marginal performance as a teacher in the classroom. ● Students demonstrates a superficial commitment to be a teacher, exhibited in the comment "I thought I would give teaching a go..." ● Student exhibits a lack of passion regarding teaching computing.	● Recap the concept of marginal gains in teaching to improve a student's performance as a teacher and improve learners' learning in the classroom. ● Review why the student desired to undertake training as a computing teacher. ● Students writes a letter to themselves explaining why they want to be a computing teacher. ● Have student take a career assessment exam to determine best career match.	Student articulates a desire to be a computing teacher which is manifested in the classroom.	Student demonstrates marginal performance as a teacher in the classroom.
Negative attitude to being trained as a teacher	● Poor time management, arriving late to school, leaving early ● Not prepared to teach lessons, for example lesson plan and resources not prepared in sufficient time for mentor to comment on. ● Ignore constructive feedback, advice, and guidance from mentor.	● Review weekly teaching timetable to identify planning sessions ● Ensure that lessons are planned in sufficient time for mentor to provide constructive feedback that can be acted upon. ● Conduct an intervention and developmental plan of action.	Student demonstrates a positive attitude towards being trained as a teacher, by being organized in terms of planning lessons and developing resources.	Student continues to display a negative attitude being trained as a teacher that negatively impacts student learning, which may result in being counselled out of the program.

continued on following page

Table 5. Continued

Problematic Area	Potential Symptoms	Strategies	Potential Outcomes	
			Positive Outcome	**Negative Outcome**
Lack of achievement against teachers' competence standards	• Student failing to achieve against the teachers 'competence standards as reviewed by their mentor.	• Review with student their progress to date against the teachers' competence standards and identify reasons for lack of progress. • Establish SMART targets for student to demonstrate achievement against teachers' competence standards.	Student begins to make progress against the teachers' competence standards.	Student continues to make lack of progress against teachers' competence standards and placed on a support plan. Failure to make any progress may result in termination of their school experience.
Unwillingness to act upon advice and guidance from their mentor	• Student avoids meeting with their mentor. • SMART targets against teacher standards are repeated weekly. • Claims by the student that the mentor is not supportive, harsh towards them and even bullying them.	• Tripartite reconciliation meeting between subject, mentor, and lecturer to discuss issue and identify way forward. • Student is placed on a negotiated support plan with agreed SMART targets for the student to achieve. • Review support plan	Professional relationship between mentor and student restored, student now acting upon advice and guidance and making progress against the teacher standards.	Ultimately, a break down in professional relationship between mentor and student which could result in termination of school experience.
• **TPCK Challenges**				

continued on following page

Table 5. Continued

Problematic Area	Potential Symptoms	Strategies	Potential Outcomes	
			Positive Outcome	Negative Outcome
Poor computing content (subject) knowledge	● Unable to contextualise a specific computing topic. ● Incorrect use and application of computing subject vocabulary. ● Unable to communicate computing concepts, principles, and subject matter. ● Unable to model a computing technique correctly. ● Unable to identify and address students' misconception(s) about a computing topic.	● Review and refresh student's computing subject knowledge audit. ● Review key vocabulary and associated definitions for a specific computing topic. ● Review knowledge organiser for specific computing topic to identify sequence of what needs to be taught, and how identified misconceptions are to be addressed. ● Build a shared resources library ● Devise SMART targets to address student's subject knowledge shortcoming.	The student develops their subject knowledge of a specific computing topic and can confidently teach it clearly and coherently, and address students' misconceptions.	The student continues to demonstrate their poor subject knowledge which may result in negatively impacting learners' learning. Ultimately, this may result in termination of school experience.
Limited pedagogical knowledge for teaching computing	● Not using a range of teaching, learning and assessment strategies in teaching. ● Ineffective modelling of a specific computing topic. ● Lack sufficient application of systems thinking into instructional strategies.	● Review the rationale for student using a limited range of teaching, learning and assessment strategies in a sequence of computing lessons. ● Revisit the pedagogical approaches that were taught and modelled at university. ● Identify pedagogical approaches for a student to adopt and demonstrate on school experience.	The student demonstrates that they can effectively use a range of teaching, learning and assessment strategies in teaching a sequence of computing lessons.	The student is still reliant upon a limited range of teaching, learning and assessment strategies in teaching a sequence of computing lessons. Ultimately, may impact negatively upon learners' experience in the computing classroom and may result in termination of school experience.

continued on following page

Table 5. Continued

Problematic Area	Potential Symptoms	Strategies	Potential Outcomes	
			Positive Outcome	Negative Outcome
Inappropriate technological knowledge for teaching computing.	• Inappropriate modelling and usage of technology for teaching, learning, and assessing a specific computing topic. • Unable to explain and model clearly and concisely to learners how to use the technology to learn a specific computing topic.	• Review with the student the rationale for their usage of technology. • Critique how the student is using technology to teach a computing topic. • Model to student how to appropriately use technology to teach a computing topic.	Student demonstrates that they can effectively use and illustrate appropriate use of technology for teaching computing.	The student continues to use technology either ineffectively or inappropriately which may impact negatively upon the learning of the learners in their computing class and may result in termination of school experience.
Lack of aptitude to be a teacher	• Unwilling to communicate in the classroom by either providing information or giving clear and concise instructions. • Unwilling to lead in the classroom, constantly referring to mentor. • Unwilling to transition into becoming a positive mentor to students.	• Review taught sessions, video case analysis, on how to communicate in the classroom. • Review taught session on leading learning. • Use reflective portfolio • Classroom simulation	The tudentcommunicates clearly and concisely information and instructions and takes initiative for leading in the classroom.	Thestudent neither communicates effectively in the classroom, nor leads learning in the classroom. Negatively impacting the placement school from accepting future teaching candidates.

The previously identified complexities in teacher formation involve complex interpersonal aspects during the short period of metamorphoses from novice to confident, competent, capable, and creative computing teacher. Consequently, success during formation can be viewed from different perspectives. Celia must acknowledge and resolve the intrinsic and extrinsic challenges that they may face (Figure 2). Mastery of computing instruction (pedagogical knowledge), selection of appropriate computing subject knowledge instruction to a specific class (content knowledge) and use the most appropriate tools to teach computing (technological knowledge) will assist Celia to see the interaction and interconnection between pedagogical, content, and technological knowledge. Her professional practice could increase confidence, capability and competence in applying theoretical concepts to systems thinking in the classroom. During placement, Celia must establish a professional relationship with her school-based mentor. The mentor monitors her progress against the required teacher's competences and provides constructive feedback on improving her professional practice before she completes her placement. Other underlying obstacles may include Celia's ambition, attitude, and aptitude, insufficient achievement against teachers' competence standards, and willingness to act upon constructive feedback. The institution is vindicated in recognizing Celia's potential during her application process into the program, investing time and effort in educating Celia. Annual reports on negotiated key performance indicators, such as, number of applicants applying to the institution, number of candidates recruited against negotiated program target, number of successful pre-service teachers completing the program, and percentage of students gaining employment as teachers, are used for both programme and institutional continuous quality assurance and reported to numerous governmental and accreditation agencies.

SUMMARY

Celia's journey through the different stages in each country to become a professional computing educator identified challenges from teacher formation to career placement. The work highlighted the importance of integrating TPCK and systems thinking into the realm of computing and STEAM education. This international case study used a global lens to compare Celia's journey in each country to become an effective and inclusive computing educator framed by systems thinking.

The main benefits for the researcher are:

(1) an epistemological crafted set of problematic areas, the symptom signalling the difficulties, and a set of strategies to overcome these difficulties. This approach, as done in other computing fields, represents the initial seed of a databases of misconceptions and strategies to avoid them ()
(2) A set of best practices in teaching computing crafted according to TPCK and system thinking approach
(3) A set of resources supporting the daily teaching practices along with a set of reflective questions that can be used to frame the end of year analys and next year planning
(4) A multi country comparison of teaching practices and curricula

Allowing researchers and educators to have a research based set of best practices and guidelines to design, develop and assess a computing curricula for pre-service teachers formation and the professional development of the educators workforce.

Table 6. Reflective Questions and Resources

Reflective Questions	
How does your formation compare to Celia's?	Describe how you would increase your knowledge and competencies in computing education after employed as a computing educator?
Which country does your formation closely mirror and why?	What are your strongest attributes, aptitudes, and attitude that would make you an effective computing educator?
Select a computing education topic in STEAM, to describe how your lesson would integrate TPCK and a type of systems thinking?	Which areas do you need to improve to increase your effectiveness as a computing educator?
Explain why the mastery of systems thinking and TPCK would create a positive impact on P12 student learning.	Compile a list of negative attributes, aptitudes, and attitudes of your worst teachers. Do you have or present any of the negative attributes, aptitudes, and attitudes? If you do, how will you change those traits and behaviors?
How would you measure your effectiveness as a computing educator on your students' learning?	Why do you want to become a computing educator?
Resources	
Website	**Description**
https://www.acm.org	Association of Computing Machinery (ACM)
https://code.org	Computing Education Advocacy
https://www.csteachers.org	Computer Science Teachers Association
https://royalsociety.org/topics-policy/projects/computing-education/	England Computing Education
https://ieee-edusociety.org	Institute of Electronic and Electrical Engineers Education Society
https://www.iste.org	International Society for Technology in Education
https://k12cs.org	K-12 Computer Science Framework
https://www.stem.org.uk/audience/secondary-computing	National Centre for Computing Education
http://tpack.org	The TPACK Framework
https://thesystemsthinker.com/introduction-to-systems-thinking/	The Systems Thinker
http://www.eun.org/	European schoolnet
https://www.scientix.eu/	Scientix portal
https://github.com/Code-WvS/awesome-snap	Technological resource: Block based programming environments: App Inventor, Scratch, Snap! and its dialects
https://www.raspberrypi.org/ https://www.arduino.cc/	Technologies: low-cost computer Microcontroller

continued on following page

Table 6. Continued

https://open.umn.edu/opentextbooks/textbooks?term=computer+science&commit=Go https://github.com/EbookFoundation/free-programming-books	Content resources: open book repository
https://diagnosticquestions.com/quantum https://community.computingatschool.org.uk/resources/4382/single	Content resources: assessment resources – Quantum Project
http://peerinstruction4cs.org/	Pedagogical resources: peer instruction
https://cspogil.org/Home	Pedagogical resources: POGIL

REFERENCES

2018State of Computer Science Education. (2018). Retrieved from https://advocacy.code.org/

Alabama Code Title 16. Education § 16-23-3 (2019).

Alabama State Department of Education, (2018). Digital literacy and computer science: Course of study.

Ambrosetti, A., & Dekkers, J. (2010). The interconnectedness of the roles of mentors and mentees in pre-service teacher education mentoring relationships. *The Australian Journal of Teacher Education*, 35(6), 3. DOI: 10.14221/ajte.2010v35n6.3

Artworks (no date). STEAM Toolkit. Retrieved July 9, 2020, from https://artswork.org.uk/wp-content/uploads/2019/09/AW_STEAM_Toolkit_030919_V17_WEB_READY.pdf

Blamire, R., Cassells, D., & Walsh, G. (2017). ITELab monitoring report 1.

Boeskens, L., Nusche, D., & Yurita, M. (2020a). *Policies to support teachers' continuing professional learning: A conceptual framework and mapping of OECD data.*

Caspersen, M. E., Gal-Ezer, J., McGettrick, A., & Nardelli, E. (2018). Informatics for All The strategy.

Computer Science Teachers Association. CSTA K-12 Computer Science Standards, Revised 2017. 2017. Retrieved from http://www.csteachers.org/standards

Cristaldi, G., Quille, K., Csizmadia, A. P., Riedesel, C., Richards, G. M., & Maiorana, F. (2022, March). The intervention, intersection and impact of social sciences theories upon computing education. In *2022 IEEE Global Engineering Education Conference (EDUCON)* (pp. 1561-1570). IEEE. DOI: 10.1109/EDUCON52537.2022.9766704

Culture Learning Alliance [2017] Why STEM can only take us so far? Retrieved July 10, 2020, from https://culturallearningalliance.org.uk/wp-content/uploads/2018/03/CLA-STEAM-Briefing-A4.pdf

Datnow, A., Park, V., Peurach, D. J., & Spillane, J. P. (2022). Research foundation Transforming Education for Holistic Student Development: Learning from Education System (Re) Building around the World.

De Rossi, M., & Trevisan, O. (2018). Technological Pedagogical Content Knowledge in the literature: How TPCK is defined and implemented in initial teacher education. *Italian Journal of Educational Technology*, 26(1), 7–23.

Department of Education [DfE (a)] (2020) Initial teacher training (ITT): criteria and supportingadvice. Retrieved July 9, 2020, from https://www.gov.uk/government/publications/initial-teacher-training-criteria/initial-teacher-training-itt-criteria-and-supporting-advice#c13-suitability

Department of Education [DfE (b)] (2020) Qualified teacher status (QTS): qualified to teach in England. Retrieved July 9, 2020, from https://www.gov.uk/guidance/qualified-teacher-status-qts

Department of Education [DfE (c)] (2020) Early Career Framework. Retrieved July 9, 2020, from https://www.gov.uk/government/publications/early-career-framework

Di Blas, N., Fabbri, M., & Ferrari, L. (2018). Italian teachers and Technology-Knowledge training. Form@re-Open Journal per la formazione in rete, 18(2), 33-47.

Forlizzi, L., Lodi, M., Lonati, V., Mirolo, C., Monga, M., Montresor, A., Morpurgo, A., & Nardelli, E. 2018. A core informatics curriculum for Italian compulsory education. In Int'l. Conf. on Informatics in Schools: Situation, Evolution, and Perspectives. Springer, 141–153. DOI: 10.1007/978-3-030-02750-6_11

Fuller, B., & Kim, H. (2022). *Systems Thinking to Transform Schools: Identifyig Levers That Lift Educational Quality. Policy Brief.* Center for Universal Education at The Brookings Institution.

Goodman, M. (2018). Systems Thinking: What, why, when, where, and how? Online: Leverage Networks https://thesystemsthinker.com/systems-thinking-what-why-when-where-and-how/)

Helleve, I., & Ulvik, M. (2019). Tutors seen through the eyes of mentors assumptions for participation in third space in teacher education. *European Journal of Teacher Education*, 42(2), 1–15. DOI: 10.1080/02619768.2019.1570495

Innovation in Initial Teacher Education: EVIDENCE FROM THE ITELab PROJECT (ND).

Klopfenstein, L. C., Delpriori, S., Maldini, R., & Bogliolo, A. (2019, October). CodyColor: Design of a Massively Multiplayer Online Game to Develop Computational Thinking Skills. In Extended Abstracts of the Annual Symposium on Computer-Human Interaction in Play Companion Extended Abstracts (pp. 453-458).

Koehler, M. J., Mishra, P., & Yahya, K. (2007). Tracing the development of teacher knowledge in a design seminar: Integrating content, pedagogy and technology. *Computers & Education*, 49(3), 740–762. DOI: 10.1016/j.compedu.2005.11.012

Kolb, D. (1984). *Experiential Learning*. Prentice Hall.

Learning, S. T. E. M. (2020). STEM Learning Impact Report 2020. Retrieved July 10, 2020, from https://www.stem.org.uk/impact-and-evaluation/impact

Lotter, C., Singer, J., & Godley, J. (2009). The influence of repeated teaching and reflection on preservice teachers' views of inquiry and nature of science. *Journal of Science Teacher Education*, 20(6), 553–582. DOI: 10.1007/s10972-009-9144-9

Maiorana, F. (2019). Interdisciplinary Computing for STE(A)M: A low Floor high ceiling curriculum. Innovations. *Technologies and Research in Education*, 37, 37–52. Advance online publication. DOI: 10.22364/atee.2019.itre.03

Maiorana, F., Altieri, S., Colli, A., Labbri, M., Nicolini, M., Nazzaro, L., Porta, M., Severi, A., & Guida, M. (2020b). "Scientix teacher ambassadors: A passionate and creative professional community linking research and practice." In *ICERI2020 Proceedings*, pp. 7461-7470. IATED, 2020. DOI: 10.21125/iceri.2020.1610

Maiorana, F., & Cristaldi, G. (2023) From Data to Coding and responsible digital citizenship: the design of a learning journey. VI Seminar "INVALSI data: a tool for teaching and scientific research"

Maiorana, F., Csizmadia, A., & Richards, G. (2020). P12 Computing in Italy, England and Alabama, USA. Proceedings of the 21st Annual Conference on IT Education (SIGITE).

Maiorana, F., Nazzaro, L., Severi, A., Colli, A., Porta, M., Cristaldi, G., & Labbri, M. (2022). Reflections on inclusive leadership education: From professional communities of practices to students. *IUL Research*, 3(5), 324–337.

Maiorana, F., Richards, G., Lucarelli, C., Berry, M., & Ericson, B. (2019, July). Interdisciplinary Computer Science Pre-service Teacher Preparation: Panel. In *Proceedings of the 2019 ACM Conference on Innovation and Technology in Computer Science Education* (pp. 332-333). DOI: 10.1145/3304221.3325543

Maiorana, F. P. (2023). Perspectives on Computer Science Education.

Mandrioli, D., Torrebruno, A., & Marini, L. (2010, April). Computers Foster Education and Education Fosters Computer Science-The Politecnico's Approach. In CSEDU (2) (pp. 289-296).

Mangione, G. R., Pettenati, M. C., & Rosa, A. (2016). Anno di formazione e prova: analisi del modello italiano alla luce della letteratura scientifica e delle esperienze internazionali. Form@ re, 16(2), 47-64.

Ministerial Decree 214 of 12 June 2020 - Modes and contents of the single-cycle degree tests in Primary Education Sciences A.A. 2020/2021 Retrived July 10, 2020 from https://www.miur.gov.it/web/guest/-/decreto-ministeriale-n-214-del-12-giugno-2020-modalita-e-contenuti-delle-prove-di-ammissione-al-corso-di-laurea-a-ciclo-unico-in-scienze-della-formazione

National Standards. (2019). Retrieved May 24, 2019, from https://www.educationworld.com/standards/

Nesta (2014). Fix the pipeline for STEAM talent in the creative economy. Retrieved July 10, 2020, from https://www.nesta.org.uk/blog/fix-the-pipeline-for-steam-talent-in-the-creative-economy/

OECD. (2019b). Teachers' Professional Learning (TPL) Study. https://doi.org/DOI: 10.1787/888934026677

OECD. (2021b). OECD SCHOOLING, TEACHERS AND TEACHING PROJECT. https://www.oecd.org/education/school-resources-review/Schooling,%20Teachers%20and%20Teaching%20Project%20Description.pdf

OECD/OPSI global trend 2020 Upskilling and investing in people—Google Search. (n.d.). Retrieved 4 June 2023, from https://trends.oecd-opsi.org/trend-reports/upskilling-and-investing-in-people/

Redecker, C. European Framework for the Digital Competence of Educators: DigCompEdu. Punie, Y. (ed). EUR 28775 EN. Publications Office of the European Union, Luxembourg, 2017, ISBN 978-92-79-73494-6, , JRC107466DOI: 10.2760/159770

Richards, G., & Turner, T. E. (2019). Infusing Cybersecurity Concepts into PK-12 Education: The Complexity of Integrating Multiple Standards. Retrieved from https://www.nist.gov/itl/applied-cybersecurity/nice/nice-2019-spring-enewsletter #Academic Spotlight 2019

Royal Society. (2017). After the Reboot: computing education in UK schools. Retrieved July 11, 2020, from https://royalsociety.org/~/media/policy/projects/computing-education/computing-education-report.pdf

Royal Society. (2020). Partnership Grants. Retrieved July 10, 2020, from https://royalsociety.org/grants-schemes-awards/grants/partnership-grants/

Sengeh, D., & Winthrop, R. (2022). *Transforming Education Systems: Why, What, and How. Policy Brief*. Center for Universal Education at The Brookings Institution.

The Big Draw. (2020). The Big Draw Festival. Retrieved July 9, 2020, from https://thebigdraw.org/

Tokuhama-Espinosa, T. (2023). A New Science of Teaching. In *New Science of Learning* (pp. 175–209). Brill. DOI: 10.1163/9789004540767_010

ENDNOTES

[1] https://eur-lex.europa.eu/legal-content/EN/TXT/PDF/?uri=CELEX:32022D2481&qid=1687470375262

[2] https://eur-lex.europa.eu/legal-content/EN/TXT/PDF/?uri=CELEX:32022D2481&qid=1687470375262

[3] Coding summer school

Chapter 11
Challenges and Innovations in Developing PCK Among Pre-Service Teachers

Xuan-Hoa Nghiem
https://orcid.org/0000-0003-2292-0257
Vietnam National University, Vietnam

Dhanashree Tharkude
Dr. Vishwanath Karad MIT World Peace University, India

Neeti Goyal
https://orcid.org/0000-0003-0007-4213
University of Petroleum and Energy Studies, Dehradun, India

Ajay Chandel
https://orcid.org/0000-0002-4585-6406
Lovely Professional University, India

Shashank Mittal
O.P. Jindal Global University, India

ABSTRACT

This chapter explores the development of Pedagogical Content Knowledge (PCK) among pre-service teachers, highlighting the challenges and innovations that shape their growth. Through detailed case studies, including the integration of technology, differentiated instruction, and culturally responsive teaching, the chapter examines effective strategies and the role of mentorship in enhancing PCK. It identifies

DOI: 10.4018/979-8-3693-0655-0.ch011

common themes such as the importance of adapting teaching methods to diverse learner needs and the impact of reflective practice. Future directions emphasize the need for incorporating advanced technologies, data-driven instruction, and social-emotional learning into PCK frameworks. The chapter concludes by underscoring the significance of ongoing innovation and support in teacher preparation to improve educational outcomes.

INTRODUCTION

The best way to appreciate the importance of Pedagogical Content Knowledge is to look at where the concept came from, and how it has evolved in terms of its concept. Pedagogical Content Knowledge was a term first coined by Lee Shulman during the 1980s, when discourse about teacher education largely revolved around the issue of a divide between content knowledge and pedagogy (Aydın et al., 2014). It is by this kind of divide that Shulman's conceptualization of PCK was radical, arguing that effective teaching called for not only deep subject matter knowledge but also an understanding of how to convey it in ways comprehensible and engaging to students. The place where the two—content and pedagogy—connect defines PCK and makes it a unique form of knowledge central to the professional practice of teaching.

For Shulman, PCK was more than the simple combination of subject matter knowledge and general pedagogical strategies. It incorporates an understanding of how specific topics, problems, or issues within a particular subject are best taught and understood by students. It involves knowing what makes particular topics easy or hard to learn, how students of different ages and with different experiences form conceptions and preconceptions about the subject matter, and the strategies most likely to prove effective in teaching it (Aydeniz & Kırbulut, 2014). Thus, PCK is highly contextual and does not just differ between subjects but also between topics within a subject area. Thus, PCK development is complex, making this a challenging but very essential component of teacher education. The contribution of PCK to teacher education cannot be underrated. As part of their education, pre-service teachers have to learn how to navigate this intricate balance between the mastering of content knowledge and the pedagogical skills to deliver such content. PCK offers a framework in which such balance may be achieved. It equips the pre-service teacher with the wherewithal to translate the subject matter into teachable content and attune it to the diverse needs of their students. This is the transformative process underlying any act of effective teaching, what really makes the difference between the novice and the expert teacher (Sen & Demirdöğen, 2023). Expert teachers not only possess subject matter knowledge but are also able to make, with remarkable acuity, sense of the learning needs of their students through deep understanding of PCK in guiding instructional decisions. As far as pre-service teacher education goes, the development of PCK is very important. Pre-service teachers are located in a unique place in their professional journey, transitionally moving from student to educator. This shift includes acquiring knowledge about teaching along with the ability to apply the acquired knowledge in actual classrooms. PCK provides a bridge in this transition by helping pre-service teachers integrate academic learning with practical teaching experience (Wiyarsi, 2018). This integration, however, is not without its challenges. Developing PCK requires pre-service teachers to engage in reflective practice: that is, to continually assess and adjust their teaching approaches according to their experiences and the feedback they obtain. This iterative process of reflection and adaptation underlying the growth of PCK can be difficult to attain, especially with novice teachers still building their confidence and competence.

Issues related to the development of PCK in pre-service teachers are extremely complicated. First and foremost, the PCK per se is very complex in itself. Being a deeply contextual and situated form of knowledge, it cannot be codified and taught easily. It requires pre-service teachers to develop deep content knowledge and pedagogical strategies that are most effective in conveying particular content (Can-Kucuk et al., 2022). The double focus can sometimes feel overwhelming, especially if the pre-service teachers are confident about their abilities in one area more than another. Also, PCK development depends strongly on the context in which pre-service teachers learn and practice. These differences in school settings, resources, and support systems could produce very large opportunity differences in developing PCK among pre-service teachers. For instance, pre-service teachers who are placed in well-resourced schools with effective mentoring programs may have more opportunities to develop their PCK as compared to those in less supportive environments.

Another major challenge of developing PCK in preservice teachers is difficulty in assessment and evaluation of PCK. Unlike other more explicit types of knowledge, such as content knowledge or general pedagogical skills, PCK is deeply embedded in teaching practices and often tacit. This makes it very hard to measure and grade in a valid and reliable way (Ekiz-Kiran et al., 2021). Traditional tools for assessment, such as written exams or generic multiple-choice tests, are normally inadequate to capture the complexities of PCK. Whereas PCK calls for finer approaches, such as performance-based assessments, teaching practice observations, and reflective journals. More appropriate to assess PCK, these methods, however, also carry their challenges, specifically on time and resources required to implement them.

Given these challenges, interest has grown in exploring innovative ways to support the development of pre-service teachers' PCK. This chapter considers some such innovations, including case-based learning, microteaching, collaborative learning communities, and technology-enhanced learning. Each of these strategies represents a fundamentally different approach to the problem of developing PCK and shows some possible routes to more effective practice in pre-service teacher education programs (Große-Heilmann et al., 2022).

For example, case-based learning allows pre-service teachers to engage in the wrestle of real-life teaching situations, which can assist in developing their PCK in a very practical and applied way. On the other hand, microteaching provides the pre-service teacher with multiple opportunities to practice teaching skills in a controlled environment that receives feedback from peers and mentors, which can inform continuous development of the PCK. It is in collaborative learning communities—professional learning communities, in this case—that pre-service teachers have a chance to reflect collaboratively with peers on practice and engage in problem-solving for the growth of PCK through shared experiences and collective learning (Mazibe et al., 2023). Technology-enhanced learning takes advantage of digital tools and resources to aid the development of PCK by offering pre-service teachers a great variety of instructional strategies, resources, and simulations that can be used to enhance their teaching practice.

The chapter is then concluded by stating the aims of the introduction, one of which is to explore such and other innovative ways for developing pre-service teachers' PCK. On the other hand, the chapter attempts to bring forth a richer view of the problems and innovations in this field to gain insight into the actual state of development of PCK in teacher education, offering insights and recommendations for educators, policymakers, and researchers seeking to improve preservice teacher-education programs (Ratnaningsih et al., 2019). As such, the chapter aims to add its voice to the continuous teacher education discourses around the instrumental role of PCK in teaching, with innovation and continued support needed in its development as a critical component of effective teaching.

THEORETICAL FRAMEWORK

Historical Evolution of PCK

Pedagogical Content Knowledge was a term introduced by Lee Shulman in 1986 against the background of reigning views that teaching had its orientation either in the mastering of content knowledge or in the development of general pedagogical skills. For Shulman, this dualism did not explain enough about what effective teachers do in the classroom. He recommended that effective teaching called for a unique type of knowledge, one that blended subject matter knowledge with pedagogical moves tailored especially to the teaching of that content. That integration is what

Shulman called PCK, and it contributed to a sea change in the understanding of teacher knowledge (Schiering et al., 2022).

Shulman's conceptualization of PCK was quite ground-breaking because it accepted the fact that teaching is not only about knowing content or pedagogy in a vacuum; rather, it is about knowing how to make content accessible and meaningful to students. This realization essentially includes what makes particular topics easy or hard to learn, what kinds of conceptions and misconceptions would have already been developed by learners about such topics, and what teaching approaches might be more powerful in effectively addressing such challenges. Over time, a number of scholars have expanded and further refined Shulman's concept of PCK, offering greater insight into its constituent components and ways through which it can be developed (Lee et al., 2007).

Models and Conceptualizations of PCK

Since it was first introduced, different models with respect to PCK have developed. Different models present different views with respect to how such knowledge is structured and how it can be applied within teaching practice. Probably the most influential of these models is the "Knowledge-in-Pieces" model, which describes PCK as a dynamic and context-dependent construct made up of a variety of knowledge pieces that interact. In other words, PCK, according to this view, is not something like a static mass of knowledge but very flexible and adaptive in its makeup—a framework that teachers are constantly refining through experiences and reflective practice (DiSessa, 2019).

Another major model is that of the "Integrative Model," in which PCK comes as a result of the integration of three major knowledge domains: content knowledge, pedagogical knowledge, and contextual knowledge. This model emphasizes the understanding of how these domains interact with each other in PCK development. It means that effective teaching involves more than mere deep understanding of the subject matter but must also entail adjustment in strategies applied to the context in which teaching is done, including students' needs, background, and prior knowledge.

The "Nested Model" of PCK takes this idea a step further and argues that PCK is situated within a broader framework of teacher knowledge, one which encompasses general pedagogical knowledge, curriculum knowledge, and knowledge of educational contexts and students. In this model, PCK is the most specialized and contextual form of teacher knowledge in relation to its being directly linked to teaching certain content to certain students under certain circumstances (Chazbeck & Ayoubi, 2024). It places PCK at the center of the teacher knowledge landscape and explains how it works with other forms of knowledge in the process of teaching.

PCK in the Context of Pre-Service Teacher Education

Within pre-service teacher education, the role of PCK assumes a great deal of significance since it represents the knowledge that preservice teachers should develop to become effective educators. The growth of PCK during the pre-service phase is uniquely challenging because, at this stage, the pre-service teachers themselves are still developing both the content knowledge and the pedagogical skills (Agyei & Voogt, 2012). In the present section, a review of how PCK is fostered within teacher education programs and some of the different factors that influence its growth is undertaken.

Certainly, one of the greater challenges to developing PCK among pre-service teachers is that they enter the classroom with very little teaching experience themselves. Whereas experienced teachers, who have spent years in the classroom developing their practice of PCK, may well have learned much of their content and pedagogy separately, pre-service teachers often learn about content and pedagogy at the same time as ways to integrate the two. This makes it hard for a deep, context-specific understanding, as characterized by PCK, to develop (Koyunkaya, 2017).

This challenge has seen a lot of programs in teacher education incorporate explicit approaches toward supporting its development. These include microteaching sessions where pre-service teachers get opportunities to practice teaching small groups of peers or students and case-based learning, which involves the solving of real teaching cases. Approaches like these offer numerous opportunities to exercise content knowledge and pedagogical skills in diverse practical settings for pre-service teachers, hence fostering PCK development.

Another major factor in the development of PCK in pre-service teachers is the role of reflection. According to most, reflective practice is an essential component in the making of a teacher, for this allows pre-service teachers to take a step back from teaching practices and experiences, reflect on them critically, spot what is wrong, and link theory with practice (Agarwal & Sengupta-Irving, 2019). Reflection helps pre-service teachers develop a better understanding of how content knowledge is applied in pedagogically effective ways; hence, their PCK improves.

The educational context in which pre-service teachers are trained also goes on to influence the development of PCK. For instance, the curriculum and assessment practices in teacher education programs form a significant basis for the opportunities available to pre-service teachers in developing their PCK (Koyunkaya, 2017). Programs strong in the integration of content and pedagogy, practices that afford opportunities to enact and reflect on these practices, and support through mentoring and feedback are more likely to foster strong PCK development in pre-service teachers.

Moreover, the creation of PCK requires the guidance and support of mentors and teacher educators. Experienced mentors can model practices that aid pre-service teachers in developing their teaching skills and make suggestions about how to plan and present lessons effectively. This mentorship becomes especially important in guiding pre-service teachers through the complex issues involved in PCK and developing confidence and competence for its application in teaching.

The Dynamic Nature of PCK

One should also realize that PCK is not a body of knowledge and rather dynamic and continually changing thing in itself. As pre-service teachers mature with more experience and engage in professional enhancement at a continuous level, so does their PCK keep growing and changing from one context and problem to the other. This implies that the dynamic nature of PCK expects teacher education programs not only to help pre-service teachers develop PCK during their initial training but also to equip them with the ability to learn throughout life and grow professionally (Koyunkaya, 2017).

The theoretical framework offers a proper conceptual background to PCK and its role in the education of pre-service teachers and the factors that influence its development. Grounding the discussion in these theoretical perspectives, this chapter attempts a deeper understanding of the challenges and innovations in developing PCK among pre-service teachers and sets the stage for later sections that explore these issues in greater detail.

CHALLENGES OF PCK DEVELOPMENT

PCK is a form of complex, context-specific teacher knowledge that brings together deep content knowledge with effective pedagogical strategies adapted to the unique needs of learners. It is not easy to develop PCK, and there are many challenges that come with it, especially for pre-service teachers still in the early years of their profession. However, knowledge gaps raise the question of striking a balance between content and pedagogy above all.

Knowledge Gaps: Balancing Content and Pedagogy

One of the major challenges in developing PCK is gaps in knowledge, particularly the one that stays between balancing content knowledge with pedagogical knowledge. Often, as it is observed, the pre-service teachers join teacher education programs with a different level of expertise in the subject matter, some strong in certain subject disciplines and others less so (Agyei & Voogt, 2012). This variability may limit the ability of pre-service teachers to balance content integration with pedagogical aspects effectively. The problem is not only deepening their subject matter knowledge, but it is also in how to teach that content to students for it to be accessible and meaningful.

In many pre-service teachers' experiences, the content knowledge can be more familiar and concrete, while the pedagogical knowledge may seem more abstract and context-dependent. Such development requires them to know more than just the content; they must move to understanding how the content is taught, considering student misconceptions and learning difficulties and the best instructional strategies for varying topics. In so doing, a duality of focus is created that may become overwhelming, especially when pre-service teachers still have limited confidence in their own understanding of the content. The challenge gets further confounded by the requirement to adjust their teaching strategies according to the different student populations and their unique learning needs.

Contextual Factors: Variability in Learning Environments

The other major challenge to the development of PCK faced by pre-service teachers is the variability of the learning environments they encounter. The context within which teaching and learning takes place plays a very important role in the development of PCK. However, much of their practice is done, for example, through student teaching placements or field experiences, in which they are put into environments which they may have little control. The enacted resources, support systems, and demographics can vary a great deal between environments in which pre-service teachers participate in PCK development opportunities and application (Agyei & Voogt, 2012).

For example, a pre-service teacher who is placed in a school that is well-resourced with expert mentors and administrators who are supportive may have all the time and freedom to try out several teaching strategies and obtain constructive feedback, thus enhancing their PCK. On the other hand, another pre-service teacher who may be placed in an environment less than helpful may not have such resources or mentoring needed to develop their PCK as would be expected. The differences between student populations that exist in schools raise concerns about the applicability of pedagogical strategies in ways that meet the needs of all students. Therefore, pre-service teachers should be taught how to negotiate these contextual differences and how to apply their PCK in varying contexts. For those with limited experience, this could be an overwhelming task.

Assessment and Evaluation: Measuring Development of PCK

One of the significant challenges is the assessment and evaluation of the development of PCK. Unlike content knowledge or general pedagogical skills, PCK is deeply embedded in practices of teaching and often tacit in nature. This makes it very hard to measure and assess in a valid and reliable way. Traditional assessment techniques, such as paper-and-pencil tests or multiple-choice questions, may not really capture this complexity, since they tend to emphasize a discrete, fragmented piece of knowledge rather than the integration of content and pedagogy in specific teaching contexts.

Therefore, subtle and contextual approaches are needed in assessing PCK. Assessment tools that test the application of pre-service teachers' PCK in practice therefore manifest in the form of teaching demonstration tools, lesson plans, and classroom observations. Techniques in this category also pose challenges in terms of time, resources, and expertise required (Agyei & Voogt, 2012). Furthermore, these are techniques of assessment that bear subjective dimensions, which may lead to inconsistencies at the stage of evaluation and hence eventually affect fairness and accuracy. Also, pre-service teachers may struggle to accept feedback on PCK development as this often involves complex, context-dependent interactions, very difficult to assess uniquely.

Mentoring and Supervision: The Role of the Mentor

Two most important elements of PCK development are mentoring and supervision. These are also challenging. Effective mentorship puts the experienced teacher in a position to model PCK in one's own teaching and provides the pre-service teacher with guidance, feedback, and opportunities to reflect on practice. However, it is not necessarily true that mentors have all been adequately prepared to assist the development of PCK; in fact, such mentorship varies in quality. In some cases, mentors may focus more on general classroom management and pedagogical techniques and not be able to provide the kind of subject-specific guidance that would help to develop strong PCK.

Furthermore, the mentor-mentee relationship itself might prove to be a challenge. If the pre-service teachers find their mentors being too busy or unapproachable at times, then they might feel hesitant asking questions or asking for help. Again, mentors could struggle finding the time to give in-depth feedback, especially in schools where mentors take a full teaching load. This PCK may not have a chance to develop because of inconsistent, quality mentorship. Without proper mentoring, pre-service teachers do not get the opportunity to practice any strategies regarding teaching. They are not able to build a deeper understanding of how to teach particular content effectively.

Technology Integration: Challenges in Using Technology

In the current educational scene, the integration of technology into teaching is becoming increasingly important. However, the use of technology in supporting the development of PCK is not without challenges. In a word, even if digital tools and resources put forth wonderful opportunities for pre-service teachers to play around with different teaching strategies, gain access to diverse content, and simulate classroom scenarios, effectively integrating these very tools into teaching practice requires sophisticated understanding of both technology and pedagogy (Agarwal & Sengupta-Irving, 2019).

Pre-service teachers may struggle to choose and apply appropriate technology to meet pedagogical aims and content teaching. They have to master, at the same time, the challenges of technology use—that is, learning how to hold back when using digital tools so they do not get in the way of face-to-face teacher-student interactions, and averting practices that further deepen inequities among students with innumerable differences in the availability of digital technologies. There is the need for pre-service teachers developing PCK in a technologically rich environment to understand how to use technology and how to integrate it in manners that promote rather than hinder student learning. This can be a complex task, especially for those who may not be extensively experienced in the domain of educational technology.

Emotional and Cognitive Demands: The Pressure of Becoming a Teacher

Of particular significance are the emotional and cognitive demands in becoming a teacher. The processes of transition from student to teacher entail much more than the relearning of knowledge and skills; rather, they involve the development of professional identity and confidence in one's teaching abilities. This process can be frustrating and overwhelming in light of the fact that pre-service teachers are met with a huge responsibility regarding managing classrooms, lesson planning, and meeting students' diverse needs.

These may put pressure on performing well in teaching practice, and challenges in integrating content knowledge with pedagogical strategies can result in a significant cognitive load for pre-service teachers. Such cognitive load could make it hard for them to engage in deep reflection and critical thinking to develop PCK. The cognitive load can make it difficult for them to engage in deep reflection and critical thinking, therefore developing PCK. Another challenge in developing PCK comes from the emotional difficulties of teaching, which pertain to classroom behavior management, relationship development with students, and coping with unpredictability in the classroom environment. Therefore, pre-service teachers should take control of these emotional and cognitive demands, but also pay attention to continuous development of their PCK, which requires the attributes of resilience, perseverance, and support (Agarwal & Sengupta-Irving, 2019).

The development of PCK in the pre-service teacher is a complex, multi-dimensional process that is affected by a large array of challenges. Those challenges range from content-pedagogy balancing knowledge gaps due to the variability of learning environments, the difficulty in assessment and evaluation of PCK, the critical role of mentorship and supervision, integrating technology, and emotional and cognitive demands to become a teacher. Dealing with such challenges requires a joint effort between teacher education programs, mentors, and the pre-service teachers themselves, besides a serious commitment to continuous reflection, adaptation, and innovation in teaching practice.

INNOVATIVE APPROACHES TO PCK DEVELOPMENT

Since PCK is challenging and contextual, traditional approaches to teacher education may be inadequate to meet the demands of preservice teachers seeking to integrate content knowledge with effective pedagogical strategies. Therefore, innovative approaches have been invented to fill this gap, making provisions for tools and experiences that a preservice teacher requires to build robust PCK. This chapter explores some of these approaches: case-based learning, microteaching, collaborative learning communities, technology-enhanced learning, and reflective practice (Agarwal & Sengupta-Irving, 2019).

Case-Based Learning: Applying Theory to Real-World Scenarios

Case-based learning is an instructional approach using real-world cases to apply theoretical knowledge to practical teaching situations for pre-service teachers. The technique puts pre-service teachers into the complex and genuine cases, simulating some of the challenges that they will encounter in the classroom. Through the analysis and discussion of the cases, pre-service teachers can delve into the intricacies of teaching particular content; consider various strategies for teaching it effectively; and reflect on possible consequences of different teaching decisions.

Case-based learning enhances PCK because it provides an immediate context within which pre-service teachers consider how content knowledge and pedagogy come together in real teaching situations (Agarwal & Sengupta-Irving, 2019). In the process, pre-service teachers begin to understand deeper how to use knowledge in practice but also how to approach common challenges and dilemmas that are part of teaching. Enhanced are the developments of critical thinking and problem-solving skills because pre-service teachers have to appraise different instructional strategies and make a justified decision on how to meet the needs of students. This is an important reflective process for developing PCK because it encourages PSTs to engage in deeper thinking than theory and to consider practical issues in teaching.

Microteaching: Practicing and Refining Teaching Skills

Microteaching is one such innovative strategy that has already gained wide acceptance in teacher education programs for helping in PCK development. This microteaching approach would mean that preservice teachers deliver short, focused lessons to a small group of peers or pupils, followed by feedback and reflection (Agarwal & Sengupta-Irving, 2019). Hence, this enables preservice teachers to practice specific teaching skills in a controlled, low-stakes environment where one can experiment with different instructional strategies and get immediate feedback on performance.

Microteaching enforces one of the major strengths in breaking down this very complex task of teaching into manageable bits. This enables pre-service teachers to center on specific elements of their teaching, for instance, how to present a new concept, or how to use questioning skills, or how to handle classroom discussions. At the same time, doing so will allow pre-service teachers to develop and further enhance PCK (Oberdörfer et al., 2021). Moreover, the iteracy attribute of microteaching allows for its repetition and improvement of lessons to entail continuous improvement and deeper learning. The feedback from peers and mentors is a small portion of the treasure that will enable pre-service teachers to identify their growth areas and have different perspectives on their teaching practice.

Collaborative Learning Communities: Creating Collective PCK

Other innovative settings for the development of PCK include communities of practice, such as professional learning communities or study groups. Pre-service teachers will come together with their peers, mentors, and experienced educators to engage in collective reflection, discussion, and problem-finding in general. In that collaboration, pre-service teachers can share experiences, exchange ideas, and learn one from another in ways that will enrich their own PCK while building a collective knowledge base.

This is more useful in the creating of PCK, because the number of people within the group provides pre-service teachers access to tapped-in expertise. In discussions and collaborative inquiry, pre-service teachers explore different pedagogical approaches, learn to analyze student learning, and reflect on the effectiveness of different teaching strategies (Agarwal & Sengupta-Irving, 2019). Such collective reflection practices act as a step toward the deepening of the individual PCK and the growth of a culture of lifelong professional learning. Working in a collaborative learning community of practice offers a unique experience for the pre-service teacher to try out new ideas, solicit advice, and provide feedback—all elements essential for continuous development of individual PCK.

Technology-Enhanced Learning: Leveraging Digital Tools for PCK Development

With the digital era and technology-enriched learning, it is considered that one of the major ways through which PCK can be generated is via digital tools and resources that seem to open up a set of new possibilities for engaging with content, trialing pedagogical strategies, and simulating classroom situations in teacher education. Interactive simulations, online discussion boards, video analysis tools, and digital lesson planning platforms help deepen the PCK of preservice teachers more than was possible in traditional teacher education programs.

For instance, through interactive simulations, a preservice teacher can be better engaged in an almost real classroom setting, actually learning how to teach content as well as manage classroom activities complete with student and instructor feedback. These simulations create a safe space for experimentation, wherein pre-service teachers can be exposed to different pedagogical approaches without any pitfalls that may harm real classroom settings (Oberdörfer et al., 2021). Correspondingly, with the use of video analysis tools, pre-service teachers can record and analyze how they practice teaching; that is, to identify their strengths and areas for improvement. Reflection on teaching practice using video analysis allows pre-service teachers to gain much deeper insight into their PCK and to build strategies with the aim of increasing instructional effectiveness.

Forums of online discussion and digital learning communities are likewise vital means in development of technology-enhanced PCK. These comprise platforms through which preservice teachers, mentor educators, and educators could extend their dialogue and continue collaboratively thereby achieving solutions by sharing resources and ideas about teaching, discussing strategies, reflecting on experiences

(Agarwal & Sengupta-Irving, 2019). Since the forums are asynchronous, this means flexibility is automatically there among preservice teachers, for conducting the reflective practices more personalized or self-directed towards PCK development.

Reflective Practice: Cultivating Critical Reflection for PCK Growth

Reflection is an important dimension in the development of PCK, which fosters a pre-service teacher critically reflecting on accumulated teaching experience to identify what could be improved and to make the connection between theory and practice (Oberdörfer et al., 2021). In reflecting, preservice teachers increase understanding of guiding knowledge about how to use content knowledge in pedagogically effective ways, particularly with respect to addressing student needs, and the context in which they are teaching.

Innovative approaches to reflective practice include the use of reflective journals, video reflections, and guided reflection protocols. For pre-service teachers, reflective journals provide a structured way to document their teaching experiences, analyze their instructional decisions, and set goals for future improvements. Video reflections—where pre-service teachers videotape and review their teaching practice—form a powerful basis for self-assessment and critical reflection (Speed et al., 2014). By watching their own teaching, pre-service teachers are provided new insights into instructional strategies, student engagement, and classroom management that might manifest in more informed, purposeful PCK development.

Guiding protocols for reflection, which are typically provided by mentors or teacher educators, present the possibility of structured reflection approaches such that an undergirding depth of analysis is achieved and a genuinely critical assessment of teaching is established on the part of the pre-service teachers (Weinberg & McMeeking, 2017). These protocols typically consist of a series of prompts or questions that focus pre-service teachers in reflection, enabling them to pay attention to identified aspects of their PCK while considering how their practice might be improved. Guided reflection enables pre-service teachers to achieve more concealment and discreet ideas concerning their PCK, producing teaching that is more efficient and adaptable.

Integration of Interdisciplinary Approaches: Broadening PCK through Cross-Disciplinary Learning

Another really innovative approach to developing PCK is through interdisciplinary learning opportunities where the content and pedagogical strategies used enable the PST to learn from multiple disciplines in order to broaden personal teaching knowledge through developing a more holistic understanding of teaching and learning. This means that interdisciplinary approaches encourage links to be made between different subject areas and to explore the interfaces of content and pedagogy across the disciplines and apply this in other contexts (Rogers et al., 2021).

For example, one pre-service teacher in science education might interact with other pre-service teachers in mathematics and language arts to design an interdisciplinary lesson that would contain the concepts from all subject areas. It would ensure subject knowledge in each pre-service teacher for his or her respective areas of interest as well an exploration of pedagogical strategies across the subjects. Interdisciplinary learning allows for creativity, critical thinking, and a deeper understanding of how to teach complex, real-world problems that do not fit squarely within the boundaries of a single discipline (Schiering et al., 2022).

Each of these approaches addresses a different aspect of the challenges involved in developing PCK and, as a result, provides opportunities for PSTs to apply their knowledge in a situated and contextual manner, collaboratively reflect, make use of technology, and engage in interdisciplinary learning towards a deeper understanding. Such alternative, innovative approaches in programs could not only prepare preservice teachers with the kind of PCK to become effective, responsive, and reflective practitioners but even make them pioneers for such initiatives in practice.

CASE STUDIES

Case Study 1: Integrating Technology in Science Education

A group of preservice science teachers—Jessica Martinez, Priya Patel, and Daniel Lee—from Riverside University designed a unit plan for middle school students at Greenfield Middle School. Their work was oriented to incorporate technology in teaching concepts such as the water cycle and climate change (Fariyani et al., 2020). Digital simulations and data visualization approaches were used in the study to aid students in understanding abstract concepts more easily. They sought expert advice from Dr. Ellen Hughes for revising their lessons. Used in the live classrooms. The delivered lessons were full of technology and their students' performance changed greatly. This indicated that the pre-service teachers were gaining their sense of technology with pedagogical approach (Lee et al., 2007; Evens et al., 2017).

Case Study 2: Differentiated Instruction in Mathematics

Math pre-service teachers, namely Emily Thompson and Michael Rodriguez, were trained in Village State College of Education. They developed math lessons differentiated for the heterogeneous population of students spanning Lincoln Middle School. They administered data over which they differentiate instructions by tiered assignments and flexible grouping strategies. With the help of Ms. Laura Kim the mentor, they altered their practices to handle differentiated classrooms effectively (Schiering et al., 2022). The lessons were effectively taught and student's confidence, as well as student engagement, was improved. This was an end result of growth of the preservice teachers have had toward changing the content for diverse learning needs.

Case Study 3: Inquiry-Based Learning in Social Studies

At Crestview University, preservice social studies teachers Aisha Khan and Thomas Nguyen designed and wrote an inquiry-based unit of instruction for high school students attending Highland High School. Specifically, the unit was to focus on civil rights and immigration, working in a primary source analysis, open-ended questions, debates, and under the mentorship of Dr. Brian Smith (Can-Kucuk et al., 2022). They further refined this approach and facilitated these lessons in classrooms. The inquiry-based approach promoted deep understanding, and critical discourse, created a foundation for the developing PCK of prospective teachers involved in the progress of student learning stemming from inquiry-based lessons.

Case Study 4: Collaborative Learning in Language Arts

A collaborative learning plan was implemented to the middle school students in the Oakwood Academy with preservice language arts teachers Sarah Johnson and Ahmed El-Sayed from Westfield University (Wiyarsi, 2018; Aydeniz & Kırbulut, 2014; Sen & Demirdöğen, 2023). Their plan involved Literature Circles and Peer Editing as implicit processes to reach students with varied needs, particularly the English language learners. With the help of Dr. Mary Wilson, they executed the unit very efficiently, which not only resulted in students taking more interest but also in becoming more literate. This case study facilitated collaborative learning on their part and also an assistance to the diverse learners; thus, it also revealed their PCK in an emerging phase.

Case Study 5: Culturally Responsive Teaching in Elementary Education

Laura Green and Carlos Ramirez, two early education specialists at North City College, developed culturally responsive curriculum for the students of Bright Horizons Elementary. These lessons contained culturally relevant content and integrated student cultural experiences. In a mentoring relationship under Professor Alicia Roberts, the pacees modeled these strategies and fostered a classroom environment of support. The outcomes of their culturally responsive lessons reflected that pre-service teachers can alter instruction to include and affirm students' cultures, thus showing growth in PCK (Fariyani et al., 2020).

The effectiveness of the different approaches in fostering pedagogical content knowledge is illustrated in the joint analysis of the case studies among pre-service teachers.

Common Themes

Integration of Innovative Pedagogical Strategies: All the reviewed case studies integrate innovative pedagogical strategies to foster pre-service teachers' PCK. For instance, Jessica Martinez and a team of teachers from Greenfield Middle School utilized technology to make the abstract scientific principles more concrete and simplifies it, whereas Emily Thompson and Michael Rodriguez effectively implemented differentiated instruction thereby catering to multiple intelligences. While Aisha Khan and Thomas Nguyen embraced Inquiry-Based learning of social studies, Sarah Johnson with Ahmed El-Sayed utilized Collaborative learning in language arts. These approaches all demonstrate a commitment toward teaching's alterations to maximize the learning and interest of students (Lee et al., 2007; Evens et al., 2017).

2. **Role of Mentorship:** One of the key elements identified in each case study was the use of mentorship. Dr. Ellen Hughes, Ms. Laura Kim, Dr. Brian Smith, Dr. Mary Wilson, and Professor Alicia Roberts contributed quite a deal of wisdom through recommendations and assessments to get these prospective teachers to alter their approaches. All this support made it possible for the pre-service teachers to apply the right strategies and adjust their teaching to meet their students' needs. Such involvement of experienced coaches illustratively represents how important expert guidance can be in the building of solid PCK (Fariyani et al., 2020).

3. **Focus on Student-Centered Learning:** Every case study had something to do with being more student-centered in teaching, whether that be technology-infused lesson design, techniques of differentiation, inquiry-based learning techniques, cooperative learning activities, or culturally responsive teaching methods. The concern for the individual needs of the students and for engagement in the learning processes

was clear for all cases. For example, the use of digital simulations in science perfumed and literature circles in language arts were both used to create engaging and meaning making experiences for students (Koyunkaya, 2017).

4. **Adaptation to Diverse Learner Needs:** Case studies reveal strong sentiments towards the need to adapt teaching to suit diverse learner needs. The differentiated math lessons at Lincoln Middle School and the culturally responsive teaching at Bright Horizons Elementary School become the prominent examples of how pre-service teachers can adapt their teaching to suit a variety of abilities and cultural backgrounds. This adaptability is a very important component of PCK to assure the inclusivity and effectiveness of all students (Wiyarsi, 2018; Aydeniz & Kırbulut, 2014; Sen & Demirdöğen, 2023).

5. **Development of Reflective Practice:** Use of reflective practice was another common outcome for the cases. Pre-service teachers participated effectively in the critical reflection of the instructional strategy adopted, supported often through mentor and peer feedback. This reflective process supported the assessment of the effectiveness of their approach to instruction, making specific necessary adjustments and deeper professional growth in how to apply PCK within varied instructional contexts (Schiering et al., 2022).

INSIGHTS AND IMPLICATIONS

1. **Effective Technology Integration**: An example of successful integration in this case study at Greenfield Middle School was by showing digital tools as a set of media with a lot of potential for the enhancement of PCK. From that, what can hence be inferred is the fact that technologies on their own do not help to make concepts more accessible and engaging; their incorporation with pedagogic goals is what really matters. Based on such a successful outcome, it can be inferred that students greatly benefit from learning how to leverage technology to support content delivery and student interaction (Lee et al., 2007; Evens et al., 2017).
2. **Differentiation:** The article on differentiated instruction at Lincoln Middle School shows how differentiated teaching strategies are a must in the classroom to cater to its heterogeneous mix of students. Good differentiation requires good subject matter and pedagogical content knowledge, a teacher who can design lessons that attend to student readiness and learning profiles (Wiyarsi, 2018; Aydeniz & Kırbulut, 2014; Sen & Demirdöğen, 2023). This article points to ways in which the field experience can serve as a context not only for learning about differentiated instruction but also for developing and practicing PCK on the part of the pre-service teacher (Koyunkaya, 2017).

3. **Value of Inquiry-Based Learning:** The teaching model implemented in social studies at Highland High School provides an excellent example of the value in stimulating critical thinking and engagement by students through the use of open-ended questions and analysis of primary source documents. Inquiry-based learning will encourage student exploration, and through this top practice method of PCK, pre-service teachers will realize an increased learned ability for designing lesson plans that support higher-order thinking and student exploration of the world around them.
4. **Benefits of Collaborative Learning:** Collaborative learning within the instructional unit at Oakwood Academy demonstrates the benefits of interactions with peers and the process of working together in the development of language arts skills. Collaborative learning caters to diverse learners, but it also benefits students by engaging them in content more meaningfully. Pre-service teachers can develop their PCK by implementing some of the effective collaborative activities. They provide ways to approach content with students to promote learning while establishing a supportive, interactive classroom environment (Fariyani et al., 2020).
5. **Significance of Culturally Responsive Teaching:** This case study at Bright Horizons Elementary School further brings to the fore the fact that a fundamental attribute of such an inclusive learning setup is culturally responsive teaching. A pre-service teacher should use students' culture in their studies to build a strong relationship with the students. Consequently, any teaching that is done should be relevant and informed by the different representations of students, something that is encompassed in PCK (Koyunkaya, 2017).

The combined analysis shows how several innovative approaches contribute to the development of PCK among pre-service teachers, from the use of technology to differentiating instructions, employing inquiry and collaboration to practicing culturally responsive teaching—pre-service teachers can learn to be better pedagogues in a position to help their students (Fariyani et al., 2020). Mentorship and reflective practice, in this process, play another big importance in providing guidance and feedback that beget further changes for improvement. On the other hand, overall, these case studies represent valuable sources for grasping effective strategies in developing PCK and underlining the importance of adaptation in teaching practice to meet different educational needs (Wiyarsi, 2018; Aydeniz & Kırbulut, 2014; Sen & Demirdöğen, 2023).

FUTURE DIRECTIONS

Based on the progress made in teacher education and the development of Pedagogical Content Knowledge, a number of emerging trends and focus areas are bound to influence future practices and research. Some of the important directions of future exploration and development in the area of PCK of preservice teachers have been outlined in the sections that follow.

1. Increased Infusion of Technology and Digital Tools

Integration of technology in the classroom transformed educational practices, which continue to evolve in a way that, in the future, it should cope with developing PCK with advanced digital tools and educational technologies. This includes an examination of the application of artificial intelligence, virtual reality, and augmented reality towards greater immersive learning for students (Schiering et al., 2022). Research should investigate how to integrate these technologies with the content-specific pedagogy so that pre-service teachers learn to use these portfolios effectively to optimize learning outcomes. How much becomes too much, how to integrate when teaching in a more traditional manner, and ensuring that use has a clear pedagogical purpose will be important to discover (Fariyani et al., 2020).

2. Incorporation of Data-Driven Instruction

Certainly, with the increase in the body of educational data that is now becoming available, comes also the increased potential of using data-driven instruction to improve PCK. How pre-service teachers can harness data analytics to bring about changes in instructional practices, including analysis of student performance data for learning gaps, adjustment of instructional stratification to bridge these gaps and result in more personalized learning experiences, would be considered in future studies. Professional development programs ought to include training on how data gets interpreted and utilized so that beforehand teachers are suitably prepared to use data effectively for teaching practice improvements, and in supporting students' performance (Can-Kucuk et al., 2022)

3. Focus on Culturally and Linguistically Responsive Teaching

Under the current trends in the classroom setting, the trend is towards becoming more diverse. Future directions should look at how pre-service teachers can, through their curricula, prepare themselves for PCK while focusing on the issues of diverse student populations; this includes teaching strategies for English language learners, addressing cultural differences, and creating inclusive learning environments (Schiering et al., 2022). For this purpose, comprehensive instruction about and real practicing experience with students in diverse settings are needed on culturally responsive pedagogy to ensure that pre-service teachers are able to create inclusive education.

4. Emphasis on Social-Emotional Learning (SEL) Integration

Integrating Social-Emotional Learning within a curriculum has been acknowledged to have a big influence on the success and well-being of students. Future research should explore how pre-service teachers can be helped to integrate SEL into their PCK, with an understanding of how to integrate SEL strategies into content instruction, how to create supportive learning environments, and how to address students' emotional and social needs. Professional development has to accept the fact that pre-service teachers do have tools for the integration of SEL practices in their teaching in order to whole student's approach (Ratnaningsih et al., 2019).

5. Strengthening Connections Between Theory and Practice

One of the most critical issues concerning teacher education is the gap that exists between theory and practice. Based on this view, directions for the future should encompass ways that can enhance the relationship between theory in PCK and actual practice in class. This would facilitate more practice-based experience through teaching simulations, micro-teaching sessions, and sustained classroom placements (Ekiz-Kiran et al., 2021). From these, school partnerships would be developed to give pre-service teachers teaching experience, integrated with reflective practices that will contribute to the proper application of the theory by pre-service teachers into different classroom settings.

6. Exploring the Impact of Collaborative Professional Development

First investigations in collaborative professional development appeared promising for developing teaching practices and fostering PCK. There is a need for additional research on how to use collaborative models to develop PCK for pre-service teachers, such as professional learning communities and co-teaching arrangements (Große-Heilmann et al., 2022). Such collaborative approaches should become known in program design for professional development for a culture of continuous learning and growth through sharing knowledge and the support of peers.

7. Evaluating the Long-Term Impact of PCK Development

Understanding the value of different instructional strategies means that studies on how long-term development affects teaching efficacy and student performance are critical. It requires longitudinal studies that are focused on tracking growth in PCK for pre-service teachers over time and how this impacts their teaching practices and the achievements of pupils (Schiering et al., 2022). Thus, it shall be possible to evaluate efforts in the long-term development of PCK and evaluate some factors that contribute to success over time, thus eluding clues toward the effective strategies for continuous professional growth.

8. Advancing Equity and Access in Teacher Education

Equity in teacher education is the most fundamental clause of building a teacher force that is diverse and effective (Wiyarsi, 2018; Aydeniz & Kırbulut, 2014; Sen & Demirdöğen, 2023). Continuing in the future, some practices should be that way, leading to a reduction in inequities in access—high-quality teacher education, mainly for underrepresented groups. That includes examining and enhancing admissions equity, financial aid, and targeted supports within diverse candidates. Ensuring that all pre-service teachers have the resources and opportunities they need to develop strong PCK will ensure that the education system is more equitable and inclusive.

9. Innovating Assessment Methods for PCK

Developing innovative tools for the assessment of PCK is nonetheless important for understanding and improving teacher preparation. Future research in this regard shall also take into account the assessment of pre-service teachers' PCK through the performance-based assessment approach, portfolios, and self-assessment tools (Große-Heilmann et al., 2022). Each of these approaches should be well designed to provide views that are complete by themselves, giving an insight into the competence of pre-service teachers in implementing content knowledge and pedagogy effectively. Therefore, in order to ensure that a meaningful measurement and effective support are possible for growing PCK in teacher preparation programs, reliable and valid assessment tools need to be developed (Wiyarsi, 2018; Aydeniz & Kırbulut, 2014; Sen & Demirdöğen, 2023).

Direction for future PCK development among preservice teachers reflects changing time and discovery in the face of continuous changes in improving educational procedure application. By narrowing the focus down to effective technology integration, data-driven decisions, culturally responsive practices, SEL, theory–practice connections, professional learning communities, long-term impact analyses, equity and access, and more innovative systems of assessment, we can bring teacher education further and prepare more professional educators (Schiering et al., 2022). Meaningful engagement with these areas will result in a better understanding of PCK and, consequently, better teaching and learning outcomes for all students.

CONCLUSION

The development of PCK in pre-service teachers becomes greatly enhanced when a clear focus of innovation and strategies is in place. The below-mentioned case studies explain how the need for PCK development can be appropriately achieved by different methodologies such as integrating technology, differentiating instruction, using inquiry-based learning, collaborative settings, and culturally responsive teaching. The examples provide evidence that pre-service teachers need to be optimally trained on employing a balanced mix of content knowledge and a wide repertoire of pedagogical practices.

The studies show that the development of successful PCK cannot be achieved in one single manner. It is a subtle move requiring one to consider the various requirements of different students and the particular contexts of teaching. Technology integration is one such example, where it shows the enriching potency of digital tools in handling complicated ideas, yet it is careful and focused on the alignment of its pedagogical goals. Differentiated instruction and culturally responsive teaching show the same practice in the adaptation of methods for the differentiated needs and learner background, thereby indicating that the same attention to approaches may not work for all.

Central to this process are the conditions of mentorship and reflective practice. Case studies show that on-going reflection, when guided or mentored by experience, helps pre-service teachers improve their practices in instruction and their depth of PCK. Such guidance closes the gap between theory and practice—enabling pre-service teachers to be far more effective in the application of strategies in classroom enactment.

The future orientation of PCK development will orient toward continuous innovation and adaptability. The PCK frameworks for the future will have to align with technologies, data-driven instruction, and social and emotional learning. Second, it will create room for stronger links between theory and practice, professional development collaboration, and ways to seek new forms of assessment.

Such efforts focus on questions of equity and access because ensuring all the pre-service teachers stand an equal opportunity to develop strong PCK is the true avenue to establishing a diverse and capable teaching force. In this way, by mitigating inequities and enhancing supports, we will continue our journey toward a more socially inclusive education system that leads to better results for all students.

This being the case, it opens up one to the fact that the development of PCK in a pre-service teacher is not static yet never completed and calls for a multi-dimensional approach. Insights from current practices and future directions provide the way forward in advancing teacher education for teaching practice, guaranteeing enhanced quality education with positive student learning outcomes if we continue to innovate, reflect, and support pre-service teachers in their development. The redefinition of the strategies for PCK development will ultimately mean a more effective and responsive education system, as Pre-Service Teachers will graduate with confidence and skills in meeting diverse needs for their students in time ahead.

REFERENCES

Agarwal, P., & Sengupta-Irving, T. (2019). Integrating power to advance the study of connective and productive disciplinary engagement in mathematics and science. *Cognition and Instruction*, 37(3), 349–366. DOI: 10.1080/07370008.2019.1624544

Agyei, D., & Voogt, J. (2012). Developing technological pedagogical content knowledge in pre-service mathematics teachers through collaborative design. *Australasian Journal of Educational Technology*, 28(4), 547–564. DOI: 10.14742/ajet.827

Aydeniz, M., & Kırbulut, Z. (2014). Exploring challenges of assessing pre-service science teachers' pedagogical content knowledge (pck). *Asia-Pacific Journal of Teacher Education*, 42(2), 147–166. DOI: 10.1080/1359866X.2014.890696

Aydın, M., Friedrichsen, P., Boz, Y., & Hanuscin, D. (2014). Examination of the topic-specific nature of pedagogical content knowledge in teaching electrochemical cells and nuclear reactions. *Chemistry Education Research and Practice*, 15(4), 658–674. DOI: 10.1039/C4RP00105B

Can-Kucuk, D., Gencer, S., & Akkuş, H. (2022). Development of pre-service chemistry teachers' pedagogical content knowledge through mentoring. *Chemistry Education Research and Practice*, 23(3), 599–615. DOI: 10.1039/D2RP00033D

Chazbeck, B., & Ayoubi, Z. (2024). The nested knowledge system of TPACK: A case study on physics teachers' educational resource selection and integration. *Journal of Education in Science, Environment and Health*, •••, 245–260. DOI: 10.55549/jeseh.707

Conceição, T., Baptista, M., & Ponte, J. (2021). Examining pre-service science teachers' pedagogical content knowledge through lesson study. *Eurasia Journal of Mathematics, Science and Technology Education*, 18(1), em2060. Advance online publication. DOI: 10.29333/ejmste/11442

DiSessa, A. A. (2019). A friendly introduction to "Knowledge in pieces": Modeling types of knowledge and their roles in learning. ICME-13 Monographs, 245-264. https://doi.org/DOI: 10.1007/978-3-030-15636-7_11

Ekiz-Kiran, B., Boz, Y., & Alemdar, M. (2021). Development of pre-service teachers' pedagogical content knowledge through a pck-based school experience course. *Chemistry Education Research and Practice*, 22(2), 415–430. DOI: 10.1039/D0RP00225A

Evens, M., Elen, J., & Depaepe, F. (2017). Effects of opportunities to learn in teacher education on the development of teachers' professional knowledge of french as a foreign language. *Journal of Advances in Education Research*, 2(4), 265–279. DOI: 10.22606/jaer.2017.24007

Fariyani, Q., Mubarok, F., Masfuah, S., & Syukur, F. (2020). Pedagogical content knowledge of pre-service physics teachers. *Jurnal Ilmiah Pendidikan Fisika Al-Biruni*, 9(1), 99–107. DOI: 10.24042/jipfalbiruni.v9i1.3409

Große-Heilmann, R., Riese, J., Burde, J., Schubatzky, T., & Weiler, D. (2022). Fostering pre-service physics teachers' pedagogical content knowledge regarding digital media. *Education Sciences*, 12(7), 440. DOI: 10.3390/educsci12070440

Lee, E., Brown, M., Luft, J., & Roehrig, G. (2007). Assessing beginning secondary science teachers' pck: Pilot year results. *School Science and Mathematics*, 107(2), 52–60. DOI: 10.1111/j.1949-8594.2007.tb17768.x

Mazibe, E. N., Gaigher, E., & Coetzee, C. (2023). Exploring dynamic pedagogical content knowledge across fundamental concepts of electrostatics. *Eurasia Journal of Mathematics, Science and Technology Education*, 19(3), em2241. Advance online publication. DOI: 10.29333/ejmste/13023

Oberdörfer, S., Birnstiel, S., Latoschik, M., & Grafe, S. (2021). Mutual benefits: Interdisciplinary education of pre-service teachers and hci students in vr/ar learning environment design. *Frontiers in Education*, 6, 693012. Advance online publication. DOI: 10.3389/feduc.2021.693012

Ratnaningsih, N., Solihat, A., & Santika, S. (2019). The1analysis of2pre- service teachers' pedagogical content knowledge (pck) in terms of grade point average (gpa).. https://doi.org/DOI: 10.2991/iclick-18.2019.85

Rogers, M., Berry, A., Krainer, K., & Even, R. (2021). Finding common ground: A synthesis of science and mathematics teacher educators' experiences with professional growth. *International Journal of Science and Mathematics Education*, 19(S1), 167–180. DOI: 10.1007/s10763-021-10188-9

Schiering, D., Sorge, S., Keller, M., & Neumann, K. (2022). A proficiency model for pre-service physics teachers' pedagogical content knowledge (pck)—What constitutes high-level pck? *Journal of Research in Science Teaching*, 60(1), 136–163. DOI: 10.1002/tea.21793

Sen, M., & Demirdöğen, B. (2023). Seeking traces of filters and amplifiers as pre-service teachers perform their pedagogical content knowledge. *Science Education International*, 34(1), 58–68. DOI: 10.33828/sei.v34.i1.8

Speed, C., Kleiner, A., & Macaulay, J. (2014). Broadening student learning experiences via a novel cross-disciplinary art and anatomy education program - a case study. *International Journal of Higher Education*, 4(1). Advance online publication. DOI: 10.5430/ijhe.v4n1p86

Weinberg, A., & McMeeking, L. (2017). Toward meaningful interdisciplinary education: High school teachers' views of mathematics and science integration. *School Science and Mathematics*, 117(5), 204–213. DOI: 10.1111/ssm.12224

Wiyarsi, A. (2018). Enhancing of preservice chemistry teachers' self-efficacy through the preparation of pedagogical content knowledge in vocational context. *Jurnal Pendidikan Sains (Jps)*, 6(1), 14. DOI: 10.26714/jps.6.1.2018.14-23

Yiğit Koyunkaya, M. (2017). A teaching experiment methodology that aims to develop pre-service mathematics teachers' technological pedagogical and content knowledge. [TURCOMAT]. *Turkish Journal of Computer and Mathematics Education*, 8(2), 284–322. DOI: 10.16949/turkbilmat.293220

Chapter 12
Training Teachers in Pedagogical Content Knowledge:
A Bridging Method Between University and School

Pasquale Gallo
https://orcid.org/0009-0002-3089-1820
University Magna Grecia Catanzaro, Italy

Rosa Iaquinta
https://orcid.org/0000-0001-7771-4050
Independent Researcher, Italy

ABSTRACT

The teaching needs expressed by new generations require teachers to have various skills: pedagogical, didactic, communicative and design. The work is the result of an experimental project conducted in the academic field, which involved two teachers with extensive professional experience both as teachers in schools and universities. The interest of the research was to demonstrate the validity of Shulman's PCK method through classroom instruction and, at the same time, to promote in future teachers the ability to assess, through direct experience, the importance of the design and implementation of teaching and the significant role of the choice of didactic method.

INTRODUCTION

The motivation behind this work is that the teachers who have produced it are aware of their desire to make the university lecture a place where they can disseminate good practices for the benefit of the professionalism of the teachers in training. In particular, the experience of many years of academic experience has given us an opportunity to see how much knowledge of the new conditions which characterize individuals must be fostered and, above all, enhanced; so that the needs of postmodern man, who needs greater chances for progress, well-being, productive capacity and personal awareness can be satisfied. Educational practice, traditionally based on the pedagogy of teaching (Chiosso, 2018), is now benefiting from the transfer of attention from procedures to processes, from results intended in terms of content to the promotion of subjective learning capacity. The processes accompanying the educational path are currently understood as a transformational and generative route for personal change. The role of the teacher also changes accordingly: no longer a planner of predefined knowledge, but an expert guide who puts students in open situations to stimulate exploratory and creative activity. This awareness, combined with an innate interest in the narrative dimension of knowledge and knowledge, led to thinking and building a training and research route that could constitute a model for future teachers, benefiting, meanwhile, their learning as university students. In particular, the present action research work, theoretical and epistemological, aims to focus attention and reflect on the potential of Pedagogical Content Knowledge (PCK), a model developed by Shulman in 1986 to promote the integration between the subject content and the pedagogical dimension of teaching, which too often remain separate and unconnected in learning processes.

FRAMEWORK

The scientific literature, with reference to epistemology and the hermeneutic dimension of pedagogical science, in recent decades, calls on the academic community and teachers of schools of all levels to focus their teaching on the subject they are learning about, not just on content. What Decroly, in the 1970s, posed as a question, is now a true certainty: we must live the learning dimension as a possibility for school and life through life (Decroly, 1962). Teaching methods change, knowledge becomes widespread and the school is understood, increasingly, as a community in which to share good practices and reflective teacher action that is reflected in cooperation between students and learning by insight (1992). Learning by insight means going deep, literally "seeing inside" the contents and methods of knowledge and not in a discontinuous and fragmented way. This awareness has not always been accepted by the academic community as a possibility for improving teaching and ensuring that the perspective of lifelong learning, and its developments, are given real support. It is evident, however, the need to hook interest, motivation, self-awareness of students, even in academic context, through an approach that leaves room for the purely pedagogical dimension of teaching: configuration of the environment, good practices, educational care and relationship of help, use of methodological strategies and teaching cooperative mold, conscious use of new digital technologies to build a context capable of supporting all. This does not mean to set aside the contents of the discipline taught, reduce or simplify them, but to validate their scope through a methodological framework that is constantly integrated with theoretical knowledge and makes it useful for future life. Especially in the field of teacher training, universities are called upon to adopt special teaching strategies which will train students capable of transferring these same strategies into their own professional activities. Starting from the PCK, it is felt that such a consideration can be made concrete in both university and school classrooms because, since the design phase, it is possible to anticipate the correct combination of theory and practice, content and strategies, The need to encourage better competence of future teachers. In the following pages you can deepen your knowledge of the specific literature of PCK with references to contemporary psychopedagogy and two conceptual frameworks that are compelling: the Universal Design for Learning, to ensure a universal design capable of supporting all and adapting to the needs of individual students and the Episode of Learning Located, to break down the teaching action and promote the active and inclusive participation of all students. In addition, a spark will be offered on the state of the art of academic teaching processes that want to put at the center the theoretical dimension always associated with the laboratory practice to reflect on the need to have to precede the transmission of the practical application of what has been learned. In addition, a research work carried out in the academic year 2023/2024 at the University Mediterranea of Reggio Calabria (Italy) will be presented, which involved 500 students from a specialization course in activities carried out with PCK. The students themselves have had the opportunity to experience PCK in their own work or on-the-job training at school. Research results show that students have been able to shift the focus of their learning from purely cultural and disciplinary content, the methodological dimension and that this has benefited their own learning and training, also in relation to the future teaching profession. The research activities were designed and implemented by two experienced teachers who have been working in the school and academic field for many years, whose professional profile has been built within the framework of general pedagogy, special pedagogy and experimental, General and special education. The two teachers' many years of academic experience, which sees them involved in teaching and laboratory activities, has been the added value to combine in the best way the epistemological dimension of their disciplines, pertaining to general, special and experimental pedagogy and didactics, with the methodological dimension that they have experienced over time in the two professional fields. Empirical research, carried out considering the best scientific evidence in this field, has been decision-oriented and therefore never separated from educational action (Trinchero, 2002). This allowed the students not only to recognize the significance of the example in relation to the concepts illustrated, but to live a real immersive experience within the framework of educational research methodology, Functional to understand general organizing principles of the research process - action that distinguish expert from profane knowledge. During the teaching and research activities, therefore, conceptual frameworks were provided with which to compare and from which to derive models of teaching that are functional in building up one's own skills, Implementing the social and collaborative aspect of the experience. To ensure that the activities take on the canons of scientific research, the controllability and criticality of the choices and operations made by the teaching staff has been considered. This was possible thanks to the accurate description of the various stages and documentation that ensured continuous maximum transparency in the theoretical framework, represented by the PCK, which guided each activity. The results of the research, presented in the last paragraph of this work, show that the activities have been fruitful and leave room for future developments for international scientific literature which will be able to deepen the possibility of training future teachers by creating a bridge between University and School, considering the principles of PCK.

THE LITERATURE OF THE SECTOR

Teacher training has traditionally been focused on the transmission of content that is mostly specific to a subject area, rather than on the pedagogical and methodological dimension necessary for promoting quality learning (Chiappetta Cajola, 2014). However, in recent decades, thanks also to developments in psycho-pedagogy, university and post university training has allowed a certain implementation of the competences of future teachers, paying attention to the importance of the educational relationship, educational strategies, the use of new digital technologies and the inclusive dimension for students with and without special educational needs (Cottini, 2017). The content and pedagogic dimensions have unfortunately remained separate and independent for a long time. Often a good disciplinary training was not followed by a careful implementation of transversal skills (Utgé, Mazzer, Pagliara, & De Anna, 2017), with significant and unprofitable impacts on student learning. Shulman (1987) first introduced the concept of "pedagogical knowledge", which is the correct integration between content and methodological strategies. It also felt that effective teachers needed both the knowledge of content, traditionally identified in the subjects taught, and pedagogical knowledge, related to methodological and teaching strategies. The integration of subject matter and strategies involves understanding how certain topics, problems or issues are organized, represented and adapted to the different interests and abilities of students, as well as presented for teaching. Shulman's interest was primarily to understand the transition from learning to teaching and a reorganization of content that considered activities, emotions, metaphors, exercises, Examples and demonstrations which can arouse the interest and motivation of students. Pedagogical Content Knowledge (PCK) is a model that involves, equally, reasoning and action and provides for the implementation of six pedagogical operations or progressive phases:

1. Understanding. Teaching is, first and foremost, understanding in different ways and being able to relate ideas that relate to the same thematic area or to the transversality of the contents. Understanding refers to educational purposes which go beyond the comprehension of contents.
2. Transformation. The teacher, starting from his own expertise, prepares to make others understand. The forms of transformation involve an innate pedagogical reasoning about the reflective and design capacity on teaching performance. The forms of transformation described by Shulman are related to preparation, representation, selection of teaching tools and adaptation of content.
3. Education. Teacher performance is observable. He organizes and manages the class, presents and explains content, assigns and monitors work as students interact. This phase allows the teacher to understand his teaching style.
4. Evaluation. Learning is monitored on the way and at the end of the course to verify the validity and effectiveness of the teaching process.
5. Reflection. The teacher reflects a posteriori, reconstructs the sequences of design and learning, revisits the act of teaching in relation to the objectives that he had previously proposed to achieve.
6. New understanding. The reflection carried out in the previous phase promotes a new understanding of the aims, the subjects to be covered, but also a better knowledge of the students and the pedagogical processes.

Cochran, DeRuiter and King (1993) have revised Shulman's original model to make it more consistent with the constructivist developments in teaching and learning that have taken hold in education. Their knowledge model involves the integration of four main components:

1. knowledge of the discipline;
2. pedagogical knowledge;

3. knowledge by teachers of the learning skills and strategies of students in relation to age and levels of development, attitudes and motivations, past ideas;
4. knowledge by the teachers of the social, political, cultural and physical environments in which students are called to learn.

The PCK, also briefly outlined in its revision, thus implements the organization of teaching content and meaningful learning (Ausubel, 1963) by students and provides teachers with the possibility of operating forms ofReflect on the educational practices to be introduced to improve the quality of their teaching. Contemporary psychopedagogy is inclusive for all, especially if understood as a way of being of the science of education (Bocci, 2021), provides numerous theoretical points to be redone to give greater value to PCK, to understand how the pedagogical knowledge of the contents constitutes the keystone for the success of training, and how cognitive, behavioral and adaptive processes promote, in a harmonious integration, a better quality of teaching. The expertise of the teacher, therefore, ensures a greater motivation to learn by the students, and a significant educational proposal, not only limited to the subject but functional to the whole course. The PCK, present as a model in the field of teaching for many years now, leads us to consider or reconsider the best evidence from the scientific literature of the '900, that is considered the century of pedagogical activism and the centrality of the student in relation to the transmission of learning until then only track in teaching processes.

The main evidence from scientific research referring to the major representatives of modern and contemporary psychopedagogy, which with their contributions reinforce the postulates of the PCK are briefly recalled. Studies by Lev Vygotskij (2006) show that language is a fundamental component of education. Concepts must therefore be broken down and appropriate, well-articulated and discipline-specific vocabulary must be used for learning to be effective. With reference to the PCK, Vygotskij refers, therefore, to the importance of vocabulary and language in teaching-learning processes, which allow an adequate integration between the subject-specific vocabulary and the teacher's language, that it must be able to adapt and simplify the content. In the same vein as Vygotsky, Benjamin Bloom (1956), in defining the stages of the learning process for the construction of the educational process, refers to the need to standardize contents to support multiple modes of understanding. In particular, Bloom represents through a pyramid the construction of the educational process, identifying six cognitive skills at the basis of learning - evaluation, synthesis, analysis, application, understanding, knowledge - of increasing complexity, Employed for learning. The different modes of understanding by students must be supported by using PCK, through a multiplicity of materials, strategies, and methods for verification and evaluation that go into the content. Jean Piaget, in defining the learning process as being characterized by assimilation and accommodation (1936), also envisages the decomposition of content into progressive phases which allow ever more complex ideas to be understood. In the planning phase, therefore, the teacher who intends to use PCK must provide for a significant integration of content with the methodologies used, so as to promote assimilation and accommodation processes and make them reasonable (Cottini, 2019). Jerome Bruner, using a spiral teaching model, prefigures the possibility of revisiting and revising each learning component for students' understanding and mastery according to individual skill levels. The so-called spiral teaching (Bruner, 1968) refers, as in PCK, to active learning, according to which every knowledge moves from familiar concepts to students and then proceed towards more abstract levels of knowledge. John Sweller's theory of cognitive load (1988) suggests that learning is best under conditions favourable to human cognitive architecture. The cognitive load must be related to the amount of information that the working memory can store at the same time. Because working memory is limited, teaching methodologies must avoid overloading with activities that do not contribute to learning. Sweller, thus, defines a theory, conforming to the PCK, which deals with patterns, or combinations of elements to foster the knowledge base through educational planning. The new alphabets (Rivoltella, 2020) of Media Education are well suited to the original model of Shulman which, moreover, has been examined several times considering the presence of digital technologies. In an era characterized by the pervasive presence of technologies, PCK can use digital to implement the integration between content and methodologies, since the numerous devices present in the educational field favor the process of personalization, rapid access to knowledge and the implementation of inclusive strategies that promote learning by discovery (Bruner, 1961), which is able to better systematize previous ideas and merge them with new ones. In particular, the EAS model (Rivoltella, 2013), with its anticipatory, preparatory and operational phase, allows to decompose the contents and integrate them, also through the support of technologies, proceduralizing knowledge. The Episode of Located Learning is a teaching and learning activity that through a limited content, a reduced temporal development and a contextualized action proposes itself as a form of effective teaching and meaningful learning opportunities. Situated learning is an experience that takes place in a community of practice, in the very context in which it occurs (Lave and Wenger, 1991). The EAS is based on a laboratory teaching method which puts the student in an active and operational way to face the problem, The reversal of the lesson that anticipates the work of students at home by proposing challenging tasks and metacognition that causes the student to reflect on the actions taken. Technological Pedagogical Content Knowledge (TPACK), developed by Mishra and Koehler (2006), is a conceptual model describing the knowledge and skills that the teacher possesses and uses in his teaching practice when using technology mediators. This opportunity is an extension of the Shulman model and proposes a synthesis in complex form with an additional model related to specific technological area skills based on the distinction between technological knowledge of a specific discipline (TCK-Technological Content Knowledge) and pedagogical technological knowledge (TPK). The synthesis of the different areas gives the complex knowledge of Technological Pedagogical Content Knowledge that necessary for the teacher to translate the subject contents according to pedagogical and technological criteria (Mishra, Koehler & Henriksen, 2011). The extension of PCK to new technologies leads to a reflection which effectively combines the model in question with the Universal Design for Learning (UDL), which represents one of the most promising approaches for the breadth and capillarity of the interventions it promotes (Murawski & Scott, 2019). By transferring the principles of Universal Design from architectural and product design to education, it promotes a fair and flexible use of learning materials and tools, ensuring a high level of accessibility of environments (Meyer, Rose & Gordon, 2014). The model is the product of studies in neuroscience on interindividual variability in learning processes (Mangiatordi, 2017). Studies that have highlighted the role of three main interrelated brain networks: recognition networks, related to information acquisition; strategic networks, responsible for knowledge organization and application; The emotional networks, through which the subject gives personal meaning to the information processed. Based on these assumptions, the model seeks to secure individual learning pathways by providing numerous and flexible options in three areas, mirroring brain networks:

1. multiple means of representation, for the perception and understanding of new information;
2. multiple means of action and expression, to express and demonstrate what has been learned;
3. multiple means of involvement, to support the motivation and interest of the student (Cottini, 2019).

These perspectives, theoretical and methodological, are the essential source from which to move to make the best use of PCK and allow, also, the development of Lifewide and Lifedeep Learning. Lifewide Learning is about the spatial dimension of learning places that are increasingly becoming macro contexts as evolutionary laboratories for non-formal and informal experiences of knowledge. Lifedeep Learning, also called deep learning, promotes knowledge as an inner education in a respectful perspective of the person, his experience and the meaning that he attributes to it. the idea of a surface training is surpassed in favor of recovering the fullness of the historical meaning of education as an accompaniment to the development of the person (Mariani, 2021).

THE PCK AT UNIVERSITY FOR TEACHER TRAINING

Academic teaching is historically centered on the frontal lesson (Stains et al, 2018). The teacher explains the contents of the subject, in recent years, using also new technologies, students take notes useful for individual study that is referred to the reference of manuals and textbooks present in the study program. This is followed by a written or oral examination which tests and evaluates the students' knowledge and skills, without regard to the learning process. The many dimensions of pedagogy (Parricchi, 2021), however, impose a paradigm shift to university teachers who must, as much as possible, Integrate the content of your own discipline with innovative and inclusive methodological strategies to encourage greater motivation for study, more careful reflection, and more effective long-term learning outcomes. Research on the professional development of teachers is based mainly on constructivist theory which shares the assumption of knowledge sharing (Fox, 2001). The theory of located learning offers a further insight to the fact that a teacher, collaborating and sharing, becomes more experienced (Fabbri, 2007). Considering this perspective, we have been led to consider how new knowledge is built through the gradual participation in a community of practice (Wenger, 1998) engaged in innovative learning (Hagenauer & Violet, 2014). Especially when we refer to the training of future teachers, it is worth bearing in mind that among the many skills that characterize the figure of the teacher as a professional, the central role is reflexivity. The general concept of reflective practice, developed by Dewey (1933) and reworked by Schon (1993), states that people constantly reflect on their actions while acting and try to give meaning to their actions, choosing how to behave in the different situations they encounter. In the specific case of teaching, reflexivity leads teachers to make choices based on what they observe, being increasingly aware of the models underlying their beliefs about teaching and learning (Crotti, 2017). From this perspective, a new vision of teaching emerges, since whereas the traditional didactics was based on a rigid relationship, in which the action derived from theory and the task of the teacher was purely managerial, There is now a discursive relationship between theory and action (Castoldi, 2015), where theory can become an instrument for the interpretation of practice and practice can contribute to the redefinition of theory.

These insights, already widely taken in the USA in the 1980s, led to the emergence of certain constructs such as that of the PCK, which has become a theoretical framework of fundamental reference for sector studies. The debate on teacher training focuses on practical knowledge and the scientific recognition of this the professional knowledge that led to the creation of the Pedagogical Content Knowledge construct, which aims to model the professional knowledge of the teacher, fundamental also for implementing the transition from scientific knowledge to experiential knowledge and on the explicit of its constituents. Regarding academic teaching, Shulman's construction is to be considered relevant since it directs the attention of the didactic research also on non-formalized qualities of a knowledge specifically teaching (Perla, 2010). In fact, everything that is defined as implicit in the didactic action underlies the subjectivity of the teacher and for this reason it is necessary to work carefully training in the university.

The PCK is a useful framework for educational research (Goodyear, 2001), as it can provide tools to think about the complex system of learning contexts. The reference is to the principles of Dewey's Human Inquiry (1916), where the purpose of education and learning is to instill ability and desire for change through experience. This orientation is also based on the concept of learning, encouraging students to work together in an interdependent and collaborative way (Bruffee, 1987). Numerous studies demonstrate the importance of implementing an active learning approach in professional development programmes for future teachers to improve teaching strategies and learning processes (Fedeli, 2019). To define active learning we can refer to the definition of Prince (2004) which means that method, or methods, involves students in learning processes. When active, these processes become intentional from the design and planning stages, later also effective and facilitating. Active learning becomes, in the long term, transformative (Bracci, 2017) and suitable for all. In fact, if we want to apply the principles of Universal Design for Learning to academic teaching, we can certainly say that what is necessary for someone, becomes useful for everyone in perspective one size fits all (Ianes, 2023). Meeting the needs of all students ensures that motivation and self-control are constantly activated, which promotes interest, performance, personal development, perseverance. Expert learning becomes a significant advantage because it is linked to long-term planning, genuine and meaningful goals. Universities, as the main centres of research and training activities, must be able to offer a professional profile in which theory and practice, knowledge and action co-exist in an equal and synergistic manner and are the promoters of continuous improvement of the effectiveness of the education system. If, in general, the mission of the teacher consists in forming plural minds and hearts of solidarity (Frabboni, 2009) and providing the young generations with the most suitable tools to face society in times of transition, The main and institutional task of universities is to seek the right opportunities to train teachers who are equal to this task and in their turn possess specific cultural tools. Starting from these assumptions, the universities have developed within them that educational materiality that calls into question dimensions of context, culture, symbolic and organizational scenario, institutional and professional subculture (Laneve, 2003). The influence of social processes, to the detriment of an individualistic attitude or negative interdependence, is significant for the acquisition of social and relational competences as well as for the construction of contextualized knowledge to be shared in an intersubjective way. In this direction, with the theory of situated learning (Lave, Wenger, 2006), it was emphasized the important role played by contexts where participants are involved in concrete actions, they confront themselves with peers for problem-solving situations.

The training of future teachers should aim to combine opposite polarity in order to promote a circular vision between knowledge and good practice, rejecting a structured logic and the process of building methodological-didactic, relational and communicative skills, Being significant during the course of university, in becoming theoretical and experiential activities that have the function of mediate and interconnect the knowledge belonging to the teachings provided for in the study plan, among themselves and with practical workshops. The laboratory also represents an authentic life gym (Dewey, 1902), becomes the training space in which the subject can implement, through practice, the dialogue between disciplinary skills and technical and professional skills. The student, in this context, acts, proposes, experiments, applies techniques and implements the process of identity transformation through active experience. The laboratory, place of doing/learning by operating and design (Paparella, 2011), contributes to merge declarative and procedural knowledge, transforming them into intelligent skills, equipped with a reflective profile (Baldacci, 2014). Operationalizing scientific knowledge means creating spaces for the training, in which internal social situations from outside are shaped to guarantee everyone the right of citizenship, the possibility of manifesting one's potential (Dewey, 1899). In these places, which are intended for the simulation, we experience situations very close to the real everyday life of "a school day". There is, therefore, the possibility of negotiating solutions linked to the varied topography of professional practice where there is a stable ground, at a high level, where professionals can make effective use of research-based theories and techniques, and there is a marshy plain where situations are misleading tangles that do not lend themselves to technical solutions. In laboratory teaching, the cognitive apprenticeship model is rightly evoked (Collins, Brown, Newman, 1995). Like a craft workshop, the laboratory is marked by the times of doing: initial phase destined for design, intermediate phase entirely dedicated to production and final phase that coincides with the realization/ sharing of the product. The expert, in this case the teacher, outlines the structure of the activity, defines the objectives and materials to be used to solve a given task, while the novices, students, they acquire greater responsibility through experience and action in problem solving. In the national context, Paparella (2006) and Zanniello (2012) recognize the polymorphic and multifunctional nature of the laboratory, aimed at promoting scientific research activities, design and verification site in which to simulate actions to be activated in real environments. A common methodological reference is also found in the principles of Evidence-Based Research in Education (Atlet, 2010; Higgins, Xiao, Katsipataki, 2012) which have shown that the most effective models for increasing these skills include laboratory activities using experience-focused and contextualized methodologies, Aimed at the development of knowledge and skills in critical and reflective learning processes.

The workshop is an educational system (Bronfenbrenner, 1979) in which the subject is put in a position to experience and redefine his own action through activities, designed roles and interpersonal relationships, typical traits of teacher Farsi. Not so much to physical production spaces as to communities of practice (Wenger, 2006) The aim of this study is to take on board the abilities and actions of different individuals through a social process based on intersubjective dynamics that place the individual and the group in relation to the cultural object. In communities of practice, interaction and participation motivate those involved to seek common answers to situated problems; true knowledge, in other words, is the one that the individual develops by attributing personal and social meanings from the chaotic pile of sensations that have neither order nor structure (Marzano, 2013). The workshop is the appropriate place to establish a collaborative and participatory climate in which peer relationships are linked to the common interest and not to individual interests, reason why in making the communicative exchange and action are to be innate those self-regulating processes and transformations that call on the metacognitive function (Pinto Minerva, 2005). The collaborative dimension and practical thinking are therefore decisive in the professional development of future teachers (Perla, 2014). Teaching mediation requires future teachers and university lecturers to be not only knowledgeable of the alphabet, but to master the teaching methodologies, assessing their potential and criticality, to introduce them appropriately into the training setting (Laurirllard, 2014). For these and many other reasons, the active and participatory use of methodological tools means promoting learning environments where knowledge, The know-how and the knowledge of how to do represent the necessary premises for the subsequent adaptive processes linked to the transition from university to class, from simulation to action (Margiotta, 2014).

Being a teacher is not the result of spontaneous evolution or personal vocation but represents the outcome of an elaborate and complex training process (Bottani, 1994). There is, therefore, the inevitable need to raise the quality of the supply through a training project capable of proposing itself as a network of opportunities diffused in space-time terms. From these reflections arises the need to research new organizational models and emerged the need to experiment and live with students a learning path in which the teaching approach was implemented using a model, the PCK, which would guarantee a correct and harmonious approach to the study. The activities are therefore organized and proposed, trying to structure the training setting as a space for dialectical interaction between theory and practice (Damiano, 1999) for the development of generative learning (Margiotta 2007). In this framework, the university class becomes a place of comparison and active construction of knowledge, the privileged place where the student in training is called to play different roles, typical of his future profession: "designer" responsible for training (Santoni Rugiu, 2006). In this space of action, the playful/ creative sphere stimulates the practice of professional practices and techniques, putting students in a position to manage difficulties and unforeseen events that may arise in the future in a school classroom, identifying decisive actions (Perrenoud, 1994). Students experience the activities, they are gratified by them, they have fun. They study the "theory" and experience the "effects" of it. University teachers also need to promote a culture that allows them to understand the current situation to prepare them for the world of work and life (Morin, 2000). Paraphrasing the title of a work by Gardner (1991), it can be said that it is intended to open students' minds, The challenge also lies in the ability to ensure experiences aimed at mastering procedures and good practices which can then be used by future teachers to meet the needs of their pupils.

PCK: AN EPISTEMOLOGICAL EXPERIENCE

The Framework for Experimentation

Pedagogical Content Knowledge is a teaching model that combines knowledge and teaching, as Shulman uses in his 1987 work. Through its structure, the PCK allows to delineate the meeting point of the pedagogical action with the disciplinary content, this intersection confers continuity to the themes and topics, and the possible problems that may arise in knowledge transfer, allowing the teacher to organize them to present them to the students after appropriate adaptations resulting from their different interests and abilities (Shulman, 1986, 1987).

The importance of adopting the PCK model in the academic field lies in the need to provide future teachers in training with the opportunity to experience first-hand the variety of teaching. So that once the experimental system has been tested, they can verify its effectiveness, identify any strengths and/ or weaknesses and arrive at a conscious and critical assessment about its pedagogical-didactic value. Once they have come to recognize the validity of the Shulman design system, teachers will be able to prepare a valid design and use it in school classes, so as to promote their personal growth, professional development, generating a renewal of the action in class, possibly by adding PCK to other teaching methodologies more known, widespread and used.

The decision to bring PCK into university classrooms is linked to a considerable amount of attention that experts in the field have long devoted to teaching methodologies used by teachers, and the ways in which knowledge is passed on to future generations. Teachers' awareness of how the methods adopted help or hinder students' access to knowledge has grown considerably since the past. However, there are still many school environments in which the teaching and structure of teaching is not the subject of reflection and subsequent comparison between teachers (Gage, 1978).

In the academic field, then, the recurrent model adopted in teaching is that which favors the transmission mode, especially for some disciplines of a purely theoretical nature, without offering students the opportunity to take advantage of facilities that other settings may offer (Bloom, 1976). The use of participatory teaching methods would enable young people to be an active part in building their own knowledge from the moment they hear the lesson in class, so that the essential acquisition is not deferred to a moment separate from that in which the comparison with the teacher and with the peers can take place, so that the phase of deepening, broadening and consolidating knowledge can be more easily (Bonaiuti & Calvani, 2016).

In the university course, students who undertake study paths whose employment opportunities are mainly those of teaching, are trained to be essentially disciplinarists, experts on what is taught rather than on how (Dangeli, 2024) The British Journal of Economic Research.

The use of Pedagogical Content Knowledge with its sequential structure is effective in allowing students to return to contents that may present a greater degree of complexity, whose effectiveness records, also, a greater participation of university students in the teaching of the disciplines and, on the other hand, promotes the acquisition of knowledge through a critical approach to knowledge that expresses its value both in an objective sense (therefore common and shared), as subjective, for the ability to implement an individual path that allows the skills possessed emerge, which, gradually, turn into a variety of competences, not necessarily resulting from specific disciplinary acquisitions (Tombolato, 2021) The Swiss Post. It is useful to reflect on how knowledge and skills are concepts that belong to the same field of knowledge, the distinction between the two constructs is determined by the greater extent of knowledge, in comparison with the competence that can be considered, The specific nature of that knowledge. On their part, since knowledge is distinguished in "know how" (know-how) and "know that" (know-what), the latter of declarative type, even within the scope of competences can generate distinctions. It should be borne in mind, however, that when knowledge and skills are consequential the former refer only to declarative knowledge, to constitute a sort of distinction between theoretical knowledge and practical knowledge (Cooper, Levin & Campbell, 2009).

The PCK developed by Shulman through work with teachers is suitable for use in education, because it responds to the needs of teachers whose type of professional performance leads them to have to resort simultaneously to reasoning and action. Because of these intrinsic characteristics of the dynamics and sequentiality of phases that characterize the PCK model, It was considered suitable to be tested in some lessons within a university teaching for teachers of the second grade secondary school, engaged in a post-graduate course. The aim of adopting classroom teaching structures in line with Shulman's model was to investigate whether the presentation of the content of lectures through the six phases provided for in the PCK led to a greater acquisition of knowledge and, At the same time, promote the assimilation of a design structure to which teachers could resort for each discipline and in any school grade in which they would operate. The use of the model in teaching and the subsequent reflection on its pedagogical system also served to encourage teachers to access their tacit knowledge through a critical reflection on practices that guide teaching unconsciously. The experiment aimed to demonstrate how the PCK implant can make the teacher's actions even more meaningful when it is designed in such a way as to promote the transformation of learning into teaching skills. A transformative passage that cannot be considered an automatism, since the holder of disciplinary knowledge does not possess in itself the ability to know how to transmit it, It is rather necessary that a meta-reflective action be implemented, which investigates the personal modus operandi up to the identification of the mechanisms that lead to adopting a certain mode of operation rather than another, considering the advantages and disadvantages for teachers and learners (Rivoltella, Rossi, 2017). To this end, the six operations indicated by Shulman can be considered fundamental for the teacher who designs the teaching system and translates it into actions and for students who deal with content that remains usable in the long term. It is evident that the different phases of PCK are characterized by a dynamism which crosses the design of the teacher and mobilizes his personal knowledge, spending it on transferring a given content structured so that it can be translated into effective sequences, Thus, interest the students. The transformative dimension of knowledge can become such provided that the knowledge in the hands of the teacher is not considered as granite, the transmission of which takes place according to established and standardized procedures, opens to a transformation fruit of the continuous rethinking inherent in the same knowledge that is enriched through new acquisitions that allow its continuous redefinition (Cardini, 2023).

The unstoppable changes have led to the need to adopt teaching methods capable of mobilizing different skills in students, an objective that arises from the loss of meaning of knowledge for young people, Those who do not recognize the significance of the knowledge imparted can be exposed to the risk of school drop-out and illiteracy, especially for those whose socio-economic and cultural conditions are more fragile (Giancola & Salmieri, 2024).

Method

The academic activities were aimed at teachers from different degree courses and engaged in a post-graduate specialization path to access teaching in secondary schools. The total duration of the course in which the experiment was carried out was ten months, while the teaching in which the experiment was carried out was six months, and each lesson lasted 2.5 hours per week. The students were given a total of 30 hours of teaching, of which 10 hours were structured according to the PCK. The students were also given a full-time course. During the lesson blocks designed on this method were addressed two of the central topics of the teaching "Integrated management of the class group", which represent the cornerstones of knowledge that every teacher should possess to perform his or her activity. The topics organized and according to Shulman's indications were: "The pedagogical importance of the classroom space" and "Models of group-class management". The two groups of students were presented with content using two different methods and designs for the same content. While group 1 followed the first topic following the PCK scheme, group 2 followed it through a traditional teaching of a transmitting type. For the presentation of the second topic, the methods were reversed: for group 1 of students the lesson was delivered through traditional teaching and to group 2 according to the Shulman model. The first data that teachers recorded during the lessons was the level of participation and interaction of students, who interacted with teachers for the entire duration of the lessons according to the PCK, for those held in a transmissible pattern their attitude was passive, limited to some notes while the teacher explained. To detect the impact of lessons at the end of each of the two meetings, the students were subjected to a multiple-choice test using Google modules. The questionnaire contained 50 questions, of which: 20 items on the content being taught; 10 on the level of personal involvement; 10 on the method of delivery of the contents; 5 on awareness of the different phases that characterized the lesson; 5 on the strengths and/or weaknesses they had identified during the presentation of the topics following a traditional teaching approach or structured according to the Pedagogical Content Knowledge method.

Target

The reference sample is adults returning to university to specialise in teaching activities. The geographical origin is varied, they belong to different Italian regions. Cultural education and teaching disciplines are also varied, and they are included in the curriculum of primary and secondary schools.

The students involved in the trial, aged between 30 and 55, were a total of 500, of whom 299 were female and 201 males, and for reasons of participant management they were alphabetically divided into two groups of 250 people and two different classrooms group 1: A/L; group 2: M/Z. Therefore the lessons were not taken by everyone at the same time, the lesson taken on the first day from group 1 was taken by group 2 the next day. The cultural background of the participants was identified before teaching began through the administration of tests which revealed the course of studies, any subsequent specializations; work experience and sector; They also asked whether they had already been involved in teaching and in which school order, to see if they already had the mental patterns that guided their actions. Each of the groups, through alternation in the teaching method of the lessons that had been identified by the teachers responsible for teaching, performed the function of control group for the other group. About cultural background, students came from different fields of study, of which 20% were in the technological area; 30% in the scientific area; 43% in the linguistic area-Literature; 2% of teachers in technical secondary schools providing access to teaching in technical subjects practical and 5% of teachers in service in schools as teachers for support activities for students with disabilities.

Analysis of Data

The data from the analysis of the two multiple-choice questionnaires, administered at the end of the first and second topic, showed the validity of the PCK approach. For the lessons on "The pedagogical importance of classroom space" the test results, to which all 250 students answered, showed that group 1 - A/L (PCK method) recorded that 225 students answered 19 questions out of 20 correctly, and 25 students answered with 18 out of 20 incorrect questions, concerning the content of the course; 90% of the students reported a high level of personal involvement throughout the course; 87% expressed appreciation for the type of content delivery; 60% replied that they were fully aware of the different phases that occurred during the lessons; 60% of the students said they recognized the strengths of the method, while 40% said they did not know. In the case of group 2 - M/Z (traditional teaching method) on "The pedagogical importance of classroom space" the test results, which were answered by 250 students, showed that 130 students answered 17 questions out of 20 correctly, related to the teaching content and 120 answered incorrectly 18 questions out of 20; the level of involvement was 56%; 30% said they appreciated the teaching method used; 30% said that the delivery of the content was acceptable; 70% said they could not follow the structure of the content and 90% said that the method used had several weaknesses. With regard to the second content of the lesson on "Group management models for class groups", the test in group 1 - A/L, which was traditionally didactic, recorded the following percentages: out of 20 answers concerning the content, 190 students gave correct answers (18 out of 20 questions) and 60 students answered incorrectly (17 out of 20 questions); the level of involvement was 20%; 20% found the teaching method acceptable; 20% found the content delivery acceptable; 20% said they were able to follow the content structure and 80% found that there were a number of weaknesses in the method.

FUTURE RESEARCH DIRECTIONS

In the design that the teacher predisposes the focus of his work has been replaced, it is no longer as in the past represented by the cultural object, made of disciplinary contents, but the center around which all role has become the subject in learning and its world. A design idea that focuses on added value, understood as the valorization of each student through the improvement of his or her learning and considering the role played by the context.

For this reason, the teacher must develop the ability to mobilize all his personal and professional resources.

The profile of the teacher that the school needs is that of a professional who is able to harmonize and integrate skills essential to be able to perform better its role as educator and meanwhile form cultural and disciplinary competence, which is rooted in knowledge and mastery of the epistemological structure of the teaching discipline and with a view to research developments; competences of a historical nature pedagogical, based on knowledge of the history of the school and the processes of change which have affected it, as well as the didactic skills that inspire and guide the teaching process; Curriculum skills that guide the training of students so that they can develop a critical approach and interpret the social, intercultural and economic complexity of our time in order to be able to direct their choices; pedagogical competence; Useful for understanding the phases of growth and development of pupils, in order to identify appropriate ways of intervening and supporting the process of growth; psychological competence; based on knowledge and mastery of learning processes concerning the attentive, perceptual-motor, memory and language functions.

By integrating the different skills, the teacher plans his didactic-disciplinary action, giving a kind of flexibility to his design idea, so that his didactic action can respond to needs, educative, formative and ethical questions which he cannot in any way evade. It is the educational responsibility to allow all students to achieve the best possible results, therefore the teacher must necessarily prepare teaching-Personalized education consistent with the learning rhythms and attitudes of students. Flexibility is therefore the key element, the tool that the teacher must use to better promote the educational growth processes of all young people, valuing diversity and promoting the potential of each.

CONCLUSION

For many years, initial and continuing teacher training has been an element of reflection and development in most Western countries, with the aim of matching the role of teachers to the needs of contemporary society, The dynamics are increasingly complex and follow each other rapidly. There is a proliferation of initiatives to monitor this sensitive aspect of the education system, in an attempt to put a halt to the loss of meaning of school, which no longer represents the reference point for youth training. Therefore, the subject of teacher training assumes an essential significance, which, although with different nuances in different contexts, is increasingly considered a priority for the development of human capital in each country. The opportunity for teachers to take advantage of the design and implementation opportunities offered by Shulman's method is in the training and professional growth opportunities that are offered to them. Knowledge can be acquired only through the dissemination of new knowledge, capable of generating in teachers a new design mentality, about the structuring of teaching work, the reflection generated by the exchange of new approaches and the comparison of knowledge between what has been acquired and what has not yet been acquired, To overcome outdated methodological approaches and to renew one's knowledge about the role and function of the teacher and his relationship with teaching. The insufficient dissemination of Pedagogical Content Knowledge in schools is certainly a source of difficulty, partly because of the lack of links between universities and schools. The need to put new theories and data from experimental research into circulation are two inseparable factors in generating a new vision of pedagogical knowledge. The reluctance of teachers to use design and teaching methods within schools and universities stems mainly from their lack of knowledge of many methodologies, which is reflected in a limited range of choice of methods, thus ending with the privileged ones already known.

For reasons of scientific responsibility, it is specified that Pasquale Gallo is the author of the paragraphs: The literature in this field and PCK in the academic field for the training of future teachers; Rosa Iaquinta is the author of the paragraphs: PCK: an epistemological experience and Future research directions. The introduction and conclusions are to be attributed to both authors.

REFERENCES

Altet, M. (2010). La relation dialectique entre pratique et théorie dans une formation professionnalisante des enseignants en IUFM: D'une opposition à uné necessaire articulation. *Education Sciences & Society*, 1(1), 117–141.

Ausubel, D. P. (1963). *Psychology of Meaningful Learning*. Grune & Stratton.

Baldacci, M. (2014). *La formazione dei docenti e il tirocinio*. University Press.

Bloom, B. S. (1956). *Taxonomy of Educational Objectives, Handbook: The Cognitive Domain*. David McKay.

Bloom, B. S. (1976). *Human characteristics and school learning*. Mc Graw Hill.

Bocci, F. (2021). *Pedagogia speciale come pedagogia inclusiva. Itinerari istituenti di un modo di essere della scienza dell'educazione*. Guerini.

Bonaiuti, G., & Calvani, A. (2016). *Fondamenti di didattica. Teoria e prassi dei dispositivi formativi*. Carocci.

Bottani, N. (1994). *Professoressa, addio*. Il Mulino.

Bracci, F. (2017). L'apprendimento adulto. Metodologie didattiche ed esperienze trasformative. Unicopli.

Bronfenbrenner, U. (1979). *The Ecology of Human Development: Experiments by Nature and Design*. Harvard University Press. DOI: 10.4159/9780674028845

Bruffee, K. A. (1987). The art of collaborative learning. Change. *Change*, 19(2), 42–47. DOI: 10.1080/00091383.1987.9939136

Bruner, J. S. (1961). The act of discovery. *Harvard Educational Review*.

Bruner, J. S. (1968). *Processes of Cognitive Growth: Infancy*. Clark University Press.

Cardini, F. (2023). *Le vie del sapere*. Il Mulino.

Castoldi, M. (2015). *Didattica generale*. Mondadori Education.

Chiappetta Cajola, L. (2014). *Didattica inclusiva. Quali competenze per gli insegnanti?* Armando.

Chiosso, G. (2018). *Studiare Pedagogia. Introduzione ai significati dell'educazione*. Mondadori.

Cochran, K., King, R., & DeRuiter, J. (1993). Pedagogical Content Knowledge: A Tentative for Teacher preparation. *Journal of Teacher Education*, 44(4), 263–277. DOI: 10.1177/0022487193044004004

Collins, A., Brown, S. J., & Newman, S. E. (1995). *L'apprendistato cognitivo. Per insegnare a leggere, scrivere e far di conto*. Ambrosiana.

Cooper, A., Levin, B., & Campbell, C. (2009). The growing (but still limited) importance of evidence in education and policy and practice. *Journal of Educational Change*, 10(2-3), 159–171. DOI: 10.1007/s10833-009-9107-0

Cottini, L. (2017). *Didattica speciale e inclusione scolastica*. Carocci.

Cottini, L. (2019). *Universal Design for Learning e curricolo inclusivo. Imparare a progettare una didattica funzionale ai bisogni della classe e dei singoli*. Giunti EDU.

Crotti, M. (2017). La riflessività nella formazione alla professione docente. *Edetania*, (52), 85–106.

Damiano, E. (1999). *L'azione didattica: per una teoria dell'insegnamento*. Armando.

Deangeli, G. (2024). *La facoltà di scegliere*. Mondadori.

Decroly, O. (1971). *Una scuola per la vita attraverso la vita*. Loescher.

Dewey, J. (1899). *The School and Society*. University Press.

Dewey, J. (1902). *The Child and the Curriculum*. University of Chicago Press.

Dewey, J. (1916). *Democracy and education: An introduction to the philosophy of education*. Macmillan.

Dewey, J. (1933). *How We Think: A Restatement of the Relation of Reflective Thinking to the Educative Process*. D.C. Heath & Co Publishers.

Fabbri, L. (2007). *Comunità di pratiche e apprendimento riflessivo. Per una formazione situata*. Carocci.

Fedeli, M. (2019). *Linking Faculty to Organization Development and Change*. Springer.

Fox, R. (2001). Constructivism examined. *Oxford Review of Education*, 27(1), 23–35. DOI: 10.1080/03054980125310

Frabboni, F. (2009). *Un concerto a più voci in onore di un mestiere difficile*. Franco Angeli.

Gage, N. L. (1978). *The scientific basic of the art of teaching*. Teachers College Press.

Gardner, H. (1991). *Aprire le menti. La creatività e i dilemmi dell'educazione*. Feltrinelli.

Giancola, O., & Salmieri, L. (2024). *Disuguaglianze educative e scelte scolastiche. Teorie, processi e contesti*. Franco Angeli.

Goodyear, P. (2001). *Effective networked learning in higher education: notes and guidelines*. Sidney University Press.

Hagenauer, G., & Volet, S. E. (2014). Teacher-student relationship at university: An important yet under-researched field. *Oxford Review of Education*, 40(3), 370–388. DOI: 10.1080/03054985.2014.921613 PMID: 27226693

Higgins, S., Xiao, Z., & Katsipataki, M. (2012). *The Impact of Digital Technology on Learning: A Summary for the Education Endowment Foundation*. EEF.

Ianes, D. (2023). *Specialità e normalità? Affrontare il dilemma per una scuola equa e inclusiva per tutt*. Erickson.

Kolher, W. (1992). *Gestalt Psychology: An Introduction to New Concepts in Modern Psychology*. Liveright Publishing Corporation.

Laneve, C. (2003). *La didattica tra teoria e pratica*. La Scuola.

Laurillard, D. (2014). *Insegnamento come scienza della progettazione. Costruire modelli pedagogici per apprendere con le tecnologie*. Franco Angeli.

Lave, J., & Wenger, E. (1991). *Situated learning: Legitimate peripheral participation*. Cambridge University Press. DOI: 10.1017/CBO9780511815355

Lave, J., & Wenger, E. (2006). *L'apprendimento situato, Dall'osservazione alla partecipazione attiva nei contesti sociali*. Erickson.

Mangiatordi, A. (2017). *Didattica senza barriere. Universal Design, tecnologie e risorse sostenibili*. ETS.

Margiotta, U. (2007). *Insegnare nella società della conoscenza*. Pensa Multimedia.

Margiotta, U. (2014). Insegnare oggi all'Università. Un master per la didattica universitaria, Formazione e insegnamento. *XII*, 1, 89–106.

Mariani, A. (2021). *La relazione educativa. Prospettive contemporanee*. Carocci.

Marzano, A. (2013). *L'azione d'insegnamento per lo sviluppo di competenze*. Pensa Multimedia.

Meyer, A., Rose, D. H., & Gordon, D. (2014). *Universal Design for Learning: theory and practice*. CAST.

Mishra, P., & Koehler, M. J. (2006). Technological Pedagogical Content. Knowledge: A Framework for Teacher Knowledge. *Teachers College Record*, 108(6), 1017–1054. DOI: 10.1111/j.1467-9620.2006.00684.x

Mishra, P., Koehler, M. J., & Henriksen, D. (2011). The Seven Trans-Disciplinary Habits of Mind: Extending the TPACK Framework towards 21st Century Learning. *Educational Technology*, 51(2), 22–28.

Morin, E. (2001). *I sette saperi necessari all'educazione del futuro*. Raffaello Cortina.

Murawski, W. W., & Scott, K. L. (2019). *What really works with Universal Design for Learning*. Corwin.

Paparella, N. (2011). *Insegnare per competenze in università. Modelli, procedure, metodi*. Pensa Multimedia.

Parricchi, M. (2021). *Tempi e spazi della vita e dell'educazione. Cesare Scurati. Sguardi sull'educazione*. FrancoAngeli.

Perla, L. (2010). *Didattica dell'implicito. Ciò che l'insegnante non sa*. La Scuola.

Perla, L. (2014). *I nuovi Licei alla prova delle competenze. Guida alla progettazione nel primo biennio*. Pensa Multimedia.

Perrenoud, P. (1994). *La formation des enseignants entre theorie et pratique*. L'Harmattan.

Piaget, J. (1936). *Origins of intelligence in the child*. Routledge & Kegan Paul.

Rivoltella, P. C. (2013). Fare didattica con gli EAS. *Schole*.

Rivoltella, P. C. & Ross,i P. G. (2017). L'agire didattico. Manuale per l'insegnante. La Scuola.

Rivoltella, P. C. (2020). Nuovi Alfabeti. Educazione e culture nella società postmediale. *Schole*.

Sánchez Utgé, M., Mazzer, M., Pagliara, S. M. & de Anna, L. (2017). La formazione degli insegnanti di sostegno sulle TIC. Italian Journal of Special Education for Inclusion, anno V, n.1, 133-146.

Santoni Rugiu, A. (2006). *Maestre e maestri. La difficile storia degli insegnanti elementari*. Carocci.

Schon, D. A. (1993). *Il professionista riflessivo. Per una nuova epistemologia della pratica professionale*. Dedalo.

Shulman, L. S. (1986). Paradigms and research programs for the study of teaching. In Wittrock, M. C. (Ed.), *Handbook of Research on Teaching* (3rd ed., pp. 3–36). Macmilla.

Shulman, S. L. (1987). Knowledge and Teaching: Foundations of the New Reform. *Harvard Educational Review*, 57(1), 1–21. DOI: 10.17763/haer.57.1.j463w79r56455411

Stains, M., Harshman, J., Barker, M. K., Chasteen, S. V., Cole, R., DeChenne-Peters, S. E., Eagan, M. K.Jr, Esson, J. M., Knight, J. K., Laski, F. A., Levis-Fitzgerald, M., Lee, C. J., Lo, S. M., McDonnell, L. M., McKay, T. A., Michelotti, N., Musgrove, A., Palmer, M. S., Plank, K. M., & Young, A. M. (2018). Anatomy of STEM teaching in North American universities. *Science*, 359(6383), 1468–1470. DOI: 10.1126/science.aap8892 PMID: 29599232

Sweller, J. (1988). Cognitive load during problem solving: Effects on learning. *Cognitive Science*, 12(2), 257–285. DOI: 10.1207/s15516709cog1202_4

Tombolato, M. (2021). *La conoscenza della conoscenza scientifica. Problemi didattici*. Franco Angeli.

Trinchero, R. (2002). *Manuale di ricerca educativa*. Franco Angeli.

Vygotskij, L. (2006). *Psicologia Pedagogica*. Erickson.

Wenger, E. (1998). Communities of practice: Learning as a social system. *The Systems Thinker*, 9(5), 2–3.

Wenger, E. (2006). Comunità di pratica. Apprendimento, significato e identità. Cortina.

Zanniello, G. (2012). *La didattica nel corso di laurea in scienze della formazione primaria*. Armando.

ADDITIONAL READING

Abell, S. K. (2007) Research on Science Teacher Knowledge In: Handbook of Research on Science Education Eds: Abell, S.K. and Lederman, N.G. New Jersey, USA: Lawrence Erlbaum Associates Inc.

Ball, D. L. (2000). Bridging practices: Intertwining content and pedagogy in teaching and learning to teach. *Journal of Teacher Education*, 51(3), 241–247. DOI: 10.1177/0022487100051003013

Borkowski, J., & Muthukrishna, N. (2011). *Didattica metacognitiva. Come insegnare strategie efficaci di apprendimento*. Erickson.

Borzaga, C., Fazzi, L., & Rosignoli, A. (2023). *Guida pratica alla co-programmazione e co-progettazione. Strategie e strumenti per costruire agende collaborative*. Erickson.

Childs, A., & McNicholl, J. (2007). Investigating the relationship between subject content knowledge and pedagogical practice through the analysis of classroom discourse. *International Journal of Science Education*, 29(13), 1629–1653. DOI: 10.1080/09500690601180817

Cochran, K. F., De Ruiter, J. A., & King, R. A. (1993). Pedagogical content knowledge: An Integrative model for teacher preparation. *Journal of Teacher Education*, 44(4), 263–272. DOI: 10.1177/0022487193044004004

Gravells, A. (2017). *Principles and Practices of Teaching and Training: A guide for teachers and trainers in the FE and skills sector*. Sage Pubblications Ltd.

Maccario, D. (2015). *Insegnare a insegnare. Il tirocinio nella formazione dei docenti*. Franco Angeli.

Segall, A. (2004). Revisiting pedagogical content knowledge: the pedagogy of content/ the content

KEY TERMS AND DEFINITIONS

Competence: a characteristic that an individual develops through the transformation of knowledge, it is manifested through performance in the accomplishment of a task or job.

Episode of Located Learning (EAS): teaching and learning activities that through a limited content, a reduced temporal development and an action contextualized proposes itself as a form of effective teaching and meaningful learning opportunities.

Localised Learning: an experience that takes place in a community of practice or in the context itself where it occurs.

MetaCognitive: MetaCognitive knowledge involves the knowledge about cognition in general, as well as the awareness of and knowledge about one's own cognition.

Teaching Design: process of planning and organizing the activities and resources needed to guide students' learning.

Tacit Knowledge: a type of knowledge that is not learned from books but comes from the experience and insight of the person.

Universal Design for Learning (UDL): is a framework to improve and optimize teaching and learning for all people based on scientific insights into how humans learn.

Chapter 13
Pedagogical Content Knowledge (PCK) and Assessment Practices:
Teachers' PCK and Their Assessment Practices and Their Influences on Student Learning Outcomes

Mohit Yadav
https://orcid.org/0000-0002-9341-2527
O.P. Jindal Global University, India

Ashutosh Pandey
https://orcid.org/0000-0002-8255-8459
FORE School of Management, India

Ajay Chandel
https://orcid.org/0000-0002-4585-6406
Lovely Professional University, India

Ta Huy Hung
https://orcid.org/0009-0008-6835-3036
Vietnam National University, Hanoi, Vietnam

ABSTRACT

This study explores the impact of Pedagogical Content Knowledge (PCK) on assessment practices and their subsequent influence on student learning outcomes. Through case studies of three educators—Ms. Sarah Thompson at Lincoln Middle

DOI: 10.4018/979-8-3693-0655-0.ch013

School, Mr. David Martinez at Crestwood High School, and Ms. Emily Chen at Brookfield Elementary School—the research examines how deep subject matter expertise and pedagogical strategies shape both formative and summative assessments. The findings reveal that effective integration of PCK into assessment practices enhances student performance, engagement, and feedback quality. Despite these insights, the study acknowledges limitations such as context-specific findings and qualitative data reliance, suggesting the need for further research across diverse settings and methodologies. The study highlights the importance of PCK in creating equitable and effective assessments and provides implications for educational practice, professional development, and policy.

INTRODUCTION

Background and Rationale

In an emerging paradigm in education, quality teaching and assessment practice forms the most essential factor that determines the outcomes of student learning. Among the numerous factors that can help in fostering the desired effectiveness in teaching, Pedagogical Content Knowledge (PCK) has emerged to be a crucial factor (Razak, 2023). PCK relates to the interaction between content within which teachers engage students in the course of learning. This concept by Lee Shulman in the late 1980s points out that good teaching is not just about mastering subject matter but is essentially about knowing what to teach and knowing how to give it to the students in a way that it is not only accessible but engaging (Mapulanga et al., 2022).

Practices of assessments become equally important in this context since they provide a mechanism to evaluate student comprehension, guide instructions, and improve learning outcomes. Good practices of assessment are those that harmonize with the instructional intentions, provide meaningful feedback, and support the learning process (Can-Kucuk et al., 2022). The confluence of PCK and the assessment practices is a rich area to explore, since it looks at how teachers' understanding of content and how the implementation of the pedagogical strategies affect their approach toward assessment and hence student achievement.

Purpose of the Study

This research will investigate, directly or indirectly, the relationship between a teacher's PCK and their assessment approach and how both aspects affect the performance and learning achievement of students (Tröbst et al., 2018). Within the context of this convergence, the study is informed by a number of key areas of enquiry:

1. What aspects of teachers' PCK guide their decisions and enactment of assessment practices? This question seeks to unravel how teachers' undertakings of content and pedagogical strategies in their understanding influence their assessment decisions.
2. What results can be ascribed to these assessment practices in terms of student learning outcomes? What direct effects different assessment practices have on students' academic performance and overall learning experience.
3. How might findings from this relationship inform educational practice and policy? This thus offers recommendations to improve teaching and assessment strategies based on the findings.

Significance of the Study

There is an obvious need for understanding the dynamics that exist between PCK and assessment practices. This first reason is that literature has been lacking sufficient research on the complex relationships between these two components of teaching. While there is quite some research with regard to PCK and assessment as discrete entities, few studies have discussed the direct linkages between PCK and assessment practices that in turn s yield better student outcomes (Mapulanga et al., 2022).

Further, the research is important for teacher professional development. Through the identification of these ways, therefore, in which PCK can influence assessment practices, the study can be sure to inform training programs into these ways in which effective assessments can be constituted and implemented with corresponding influence on instructional quality and enhanced student learning.

4. Educational policy implications. The current study holds the promise of helping to provide a clear policy for the policymakers on designing the right framework to implement the right practices on assessment along with the appropriate program of professional development that could be aligned with teachers' PCK.

Research Objectives and Questions

The objective of the study are:

1. To study and find the relationship between teachers' PCK and their method of classroom-based assessment.
2. To determine the outcomes related to learning based on the assessment practice.
3. To get informed suggestions applicable from the research findings for the teachers and also the policymakers.

To achieve these objectives, the research will address the following questions:

1. What are the major factors of the teachers' PCK that affect the assessment practices?
2. How the teachers' assessment practices manifest their PCK?
3. How did the diverse assessment practice in diverse educational contexts affect the student'?
4. What strategies would best promote better alignment between PCK and assessment practice?

THEORETICAL FRAMEWORK

It is very important to frame clearly the theory surrounding both PCK and, more importantly, assessment practices. PCK, as postulated by Shulman (1986), merges content knowledge with pedagogical knowledge in order to have a framework for effective teaching. This theoretical framework has emphasized that being an effective teacher means much more than just the knowledge of the subject matter, but rather how to teach the content pedagogically.

On the contrary, assessment practices are based on the theories both of formative and summative assessment. Formative assessment is based on the monitoring of the student learning as it offers sensitive feedback to better the teaching as well as the learning (Can-Kucuk et al., 2022). Summative learning is based on the gauge of the student learning attainment at the end of a learning period to determine whether the learning aim is achieved.

These theories are applied to the present research in such a way that the study investigated how the teachers' PCK influences their formative and summative assessment and how the assessment further influences the outcomes of the students (Mapulanga et al., 2022).

Research Design and Methodology

In this research, through the case study method, it is possible to realize in-depth insights relating to the relationship between PCK and assessment practices. This method of case study makes it feasible to elaborate on particular examples at the juncture of PCK and assessment practices, thereby having rich and context-based data with informative potential that can identify any hidden patterns or dynamics.

The case studies will be selected according to criteria to ensure that cases with a broad and diverse representation of various educational contexts and assessment practices are available. The collection of data will be conducted in the form of structured interviews with teachers, observation while teaching, as well as an analysis of assessment materials. This multi-methods approach will allow an in-depth understanding of how PCK influences assessment practices and practices that have effects on student learning.

Structure of the Chapter

The development of this chapter is in the following order. The literature review projects a general picture regarding past research on PCK and assessment practices, along with the gaps to be dealt with in the current study. The section on methodology gives an account of the research design, case study selections, and the methods of data collection. This chapter presents the results from the case studies and relates these results to existing international and national literature; at the end of the chapter, it provides suggestions for practice and policy based on the study findings.

In summary, such research shall contribute to educational knowledge as far as ways that teachers' PCK guides their assessment practices and how such said practices inform the student learning outcomes. The findings will be useful for educators, policymakers, and other researchers in devising productive ways of teaching and assessing students.

Theoretical Framework

The theoretical underpinning of this study is based on Pedagogical Content Knowledge and theories of assessment, which form the concord to understand how PCK goes a long way in shaping teachers' knowledge along with their assessment practices, which finally affect the learning of students.

Pedagogical Content Knowledge was put forward by Lee Shulman in the year 1986. When Schuman said, good teaching cannot be well done by subject-matter knowledge only; such teaching entails more than that; it involves knowledge of hoe to comminute the subject content to the learners in an interesting and meaningful way.

PCK consists of the combination of SMK, PK, and the intersection of both, which is a reserve precedence for the teaching professionals. SMK refers to deep subject matter understanding, while PK refers to strategies and approaches to teach this content effectively. By mixing the two, one comes up with the Professional Common Knowledge wherein the teacher is instructed on teaching proper strategies and ways of approaching pertaining to students' misconceptions. This theoretical framework lays the foundation of discussion on how PCK informs practice of assessment. For example, high PCK teacher will utilize the PCK to make more relevant, appropriate assessments that genuinely test student understanding and cater to their learning.

The other key component of the theoretical framework is the assessment theories. The assessment practices applied in teaching can be classified in two categories of; formative and summative assessments (Mecoli, 2013). **Formative assessment** is, therefore, collecting and analyzing data relative to student understanding for the purpose of informing instruction and giving feedback in such a way further learning can be supported. Theories on formative assessment underline the part it plays in the learning process by pinpointing its learning needs and, therefore, altering strategies set for that teaching (Yigit, 2014). Unlike this assessment type, **summative assessment** is assessment done at a specified time to determine whether objectives of learning are achieved or not. Summative assessment is basically used for grading and forming student report. Theories related to summative assessment are concentrated to the theoretical quality of the models in terms of its validity and reliability in measurement of learning outcomes (Aydın et al., 2014).

PCK combined with the theory of assessment form an area of interdisciplinary that covers details on how to teachers' knowledge depicts their assessment practices. Teachers with high levels of PCK tend to design assessments, which are implemented and are beneficial in measuring students' learning outcome. This is quite closely related to their ability to predict and deal with student misconceptions, modify the assessment to students' diverse learning needs, and provide meaningful feedback (Chai et al., 2013).

Apart from Shulman's views on PCK, there are also the likes of **Curricular Knowledge** and **Assessment for Learning (AfL)** that add value to the framework. Curricular knowledge suggests that a teacher has an understanding of the curriculum's structure and contents—how that impacts the kind of assessment teachers create and perform in the classrooms compatible with the goals of the curricula. The theories of AfL focus on the role of assessment in promoting students' learning through feedback to teachers and alterations of teaching strategies (Stajcic, 2023).

By examining how PCK influences assessment practices, this study posits to understand how integrated knowledge of content and pedagogy by teachers affects their approach to the design and use of assessments. The theory necessitates the importance of the relationship between them for both effective teaching and improvement in student learning outcome (Sancar-Tokmak & Yelken, 2015). This lens will analyze teachers' PCK influence over their assessment practices and provide insights into improving PCK that yields improvements in assessments and enhanced educational outcomes.

LITERATURE REVIEW

A number of studies have taken a critical examination of this intersection between PCK and assessment practices, where it is being discovered how teachers' knowledge of content and pedagogy leads to their approach toward assessment. Hill, Rowan, and Ball (2005) found that high-PCK teachers are better in designing assessment tasks to match instructional goals and provide a true measure of student learning. Their findings showed that teachers' ability to anticipate and emend student misconceptions, coupled with knowledge of effective assessment strategies, has a huge impact on both the quality of assessments and the effectiveness of their measurement (Li, 2016).

A more recent experiment by Kiefer, Ellerbrock, and Krey in 2012 reported on how teachers' PCK skills affected their use of formative assessment. The general trend or outcome of the study suggested that teachers with strong PCK were more able to use the formative assessments for directed feedback and for modifying their instructional delivery based on student performance. The extent to which such assessment can be used in this way has a very strong interaction with the teacher's deeper knowledge of content and pedagogical subjects and their ability to interpret and act on the assessment data.

Whereas individual studies have been conducted, a number of comprehensive reviews have placed the general relationship between PCK and assessment practices under close scrutiny. For instance, Ainsworth's (2010) work on curriculum-based assessment stresses the importance of integrating assessment practices with curriculum goals and instructional strategies. As Ainsworth describes, effective assessment relies on the deep knowledge of the content that is taught and the instructional methods that are employed to teach the content. It will ensure that the assessments present a real reflection of the learners and offer useful feedback that can help the improvement of instructions (Ginting & Linarsih, 2022).

The literature also points it out that teacher development is critical to improving PCK and assessment practices. Desimone's study (2009) regarding teacher professional improvement argues that appropriate training and such supports could raise the level of PCK understanding in the teachers and that they can develop proper assessment methods. Her study demonstrated that professional development programs aiming at both knowledge of content and pedagogical strategies are more promising in terms of enhancing teachers' assessment practices and, ultimately, thus improving student learning outcomes.

Notwithstanding the huge amount of research undertaken about PCK and assessment practices, there are literature gaps. For example, further studies need to investigate how PCK precisely effects assessment practices in terms of design and implementation within the cross-cutting learning area. Finally, since most of the research study findings report the impact of PCK on standalone formative or summative assessments, precious little information is available regarding implementations of both types of assessment in combination. More research in these regards is required in order to further flesh out these intersections and create a more comprehensive understanding of how PCK and assessment practices interact to yield student learning outcomes (Ginting & Linarsih, 2022).

Overall, this shows an interrelation between PCK and assessment practices and the role of teachers' understanding about content and pedagogy in shaping their assessment practices. The two associated theoretical frameworks with PCK and assessment contribute to the understanding of how these elements may have an impact on teaching and learning (Kıray, 2016). There exists research evidence for the necessity to align assessment practices with instructional goals, and for how professional development may be a way for enhancing teachers' PCK and related assessment skills. Further research is required to fill the gaps that exist and to give subtlety to the interpretation of the relationship between PCK, assessment practices, and student learning outcomes.

RESEARCH METHODOLOGY

In this regard, the research methodology for this study is purposed at delving deeper into the complex relationship between teachers' Pedagogical Content Knowledge and their assessment practices and how this relationship eventually impacts the learning outcomes of students. The reason the case study method has been adopted for this research is to provide an in-depth, qualitative insight into these complex, contextualised dynamics. This will therefore allow for the examination of detailed specific incidences where PCK and assessment practices intersect, hence richly defining how these factors interact in real-life educational settings.

Case Study Design: Given this research purpose, the facts established would only be interpreted clearly by pointing out just how the relationship between Pedagogical Content Knowledge and assessment practices pans out within specific contexts of educational settings. Individual cases can capture the subtlety of the influence of teachers' knowledge on their own assessment strategies and therefore student outcomes. The approach of case studies allows in-depth investigation of many interrelated variables associated with their natural settings and provides a comprehensive view of how PCK influences assessment practices in different teaching environments.

Case Selection: Cases for this study will be selected based on several criteria to ensure a diverse and representative sample. In particular, teachers will be targeted from different levels of education, such as elementary, middle, and high school, and from subject areas like mathematics, science, and language arts. This kind of diversity is intended to capture a broad range of experiences and practices that will enable the research to gain a more generalizable understanding of how PCK impacts assessment practices. Above all, the sample cases will be chosen based on teachers' ability to volunteer as well as the level to which they exhibit forward-looking assessment procedures.

Data Collection Methods: The study will collect data through interviews, classroom observations, and document analysis. In this respect, it will be achieved through interviews with teachers relative to collecting their views and perceptions characteristic of the PCK and their methods of assessment. These semi-structured interviews will be actualized in order to examine teachers' experiences, beliefs, and practices related to PCK and assessment. Classroom observations will provide an overview of how teachers incorporate assessment practices into their teaching. This study will determine how teachers use formative and summative assessments, instructional strategies, and their interactions with the children. Document analysis proceeded through the assessment tools, lesson plans, and other data that proved relevant in understanding the embedding of PCK in assessment practice.

Data Analysis Procedures: The data analysis approach of conducting a thematic and coding analysis will identify data patterns and themes relating to PCK and practice of assessment. Coding will be considered to be the categorization of data into meaningful units that make it easy for analysis to be done in detail how the PCK of teachers impacts their assessment strategy. Thematic analysis will be used in order to notice the appearance of the same themes or insights across more than one case. This should help in illustrating commonalities and differences regarding how PCK has affected assessment practices and therefore impacted student learning outcomes.

Ethical Considerations: Considerations relating to ethics are very important in pursuance of any study that concerns human subjects. This would be upheld by the study to protect the confidentiality and privacy of its participants. Each participant would undergo an informed consent process, and it will be guaranteed to them at that point that their response and observation would be anonymous in the final report. In addition, the participants have the right to withdraw from the study at any point without any negative consequences.

The case study design has the following **limitations**: it gives useful insights into selected cases, but generalizing results from them to all educational contexts becomes near-impossible. Besides, since the research design is focused on the qualitative domain, the results are strictly based on the self-reports of the participants and data that are observed, which may have biases. This will be done through maintaining stringent data collection and data analysis procedures within the study and by placing findings within the wider literature on PCK and assessment practices.

The research methodology is crafted to yield insight into how teachers' PCKs relate to their assessment practice in a holistic way. This is a case study focusing on the chance that PCK information gives to the assessment practices and how the practices can make a difference in the students' learning outcomes. The current research, therefore, contributes to an insight into the interplay of PCK and assessment, intending to arrive at some practical recommendations related to the improvement of strategies for teaching and assessment.

CASE STUDIES

Case Study: Impact of PCK on Assessment Practices at Lincoln Middle School

In this section, we will operationalize how PCK might influence assessment practices at Lincoln Middle School in Austin, Texas, through the experiences of Ms. Sarah Thompson, an eighth-grade mathematics teacher. Ms. Thompson, with experience of more than eight years at Lincoln Middle School, is said to be a preservice and in-service mathematics educator with high mathematics content knowledge and regarded as an innovative mathematics teacher.

Ms. Thompson's PCK is evident in her approach to both instruction and assessment. She possesses knowledge of the subject and, more specifically, has mastery in the subjects of algebra and geometry, which enables her to bring material to students in ways that both relate to students' past experiences and fill their intellectual needs. For example, when teaching the topic of algebraic expressions, she makes use of a number of visual aids and real-life examples, things she has found to be very effective in turning abstractions into things students can understand (Chen & Chen, 2017).

Ms. Thompson performs her assessment duties among her students through formative and summative types of assessments. She uses the following formative kinds of assessments: regular quizzes, exit tickets, and interactive assignments that offer instant feedback regarding student understanding. The formative assessments that she uses are designed not only to test student progress but also to inform her about her teaching (Ginting & Linarsih, 2022). "For example, if it comes out from a quiz that students are really having problems with a certain concept, Ms. Thompson adjusts instruction by providing more practice problems and creating mini-lessons that really give them the space to fill those gaps.".

Her summative assessments have unit tests and projects structured in alignment with the objectives. She ensures such assessments to be comprehensive of everything that has been taught within the unit. She had developed rubrics, guided by her personal understanding of the prioritized concepts and skills that students need to demonstrate. They are very detailed so as to give clear criteria for evaluating student performance, helping in the provision of constructive feedback (Kıray, 2016).

Her PCK, therefore, is believed to impact the assessment practices and hence learning outcomes of her students. Aggregated data from the standardized tests and classroom assessments together suggest that Ms. Thompson's students have a successful record of performing above average compared to their peers in other classrooms. Furthermore, student and parent feedback affirm that these tools measure but also take the ownership of student learning support. Students now feel confident in doing math, and students appreciate explicit and actionable feedback (Lee & Tsai, 2008).

So, to essentially argue that PCK plays a significant role in the assessment practices as evident in the case of Ms. Sarah Thompson at the Lincoln Middle School can be stated. Deeper knowledge in mathematics and pedagogy will enable her to frame and undertake such assessments, which could facilitate learning and measurement among the students (Charles, 2018). Success with such an approach argues for the incorporation of PCK in assessment practices if the ultimate benefit is to be realized: the process of improvement in educational delivery.

Case Study: Enhancing Assessment Practices Through PCK at Crestwood High School

At Crestwood High School in Denver, Colorado, we turn to an examination of how Pedagogical Content Knowledge influences assessment practices through the lens of Mr. David Martinez, a chemistry teacher at the high school level. With fifteen years of teaching experience, Mr. Martinez has a solid reputation for his command of chemistry subject matter and his classroom assessment practices.

This can be seen in the PCK of Mr. Martinez, which has focused both on content mastery and pedagogical techniques (Chen & Chen, 2017). Deep understanding of how chemical reactions really work and laboratory techniques goes along with the understanding of the way these have to be taught in a high school classroom. This integration between content and pedagogy is reflected in how he approaches formative and summative assessments.

He uses assessment tools such as concept maps, peer review, and interactive simulations for formative assessments. These serve to estimate in real time the level of student understanding and further plan his teaching accordingly. For instance, if he finds that too many students are failing to grasp the reaction mechanism, he introduces targeted quizzes and hands-on experiments that explain the concepts clearly. His formative assessments provide immediate feedback, so the student has a way to learn from mistakes so as not to develop any misconceptions (Lucenario et al., 2016).

Mr. Martinez makes use of comprehensive unit tests and project assignments for his summative assessments. His unit tests are constructed to ensure that there is full topic coverage, from theoretical concepts down to practical applications. He designs very detailed rubrics that duplicate the learning targets of each unit so that students can be graded on their ability to apply knowledge in different contexts. In addition, Mr. Martinez incorporates laboratory reports and group projects as methods of summative assessment so as to allow students a chance to express their understanding through application and collaboration (McDonald et al., 2009).

Beginning with the impact of Mr. Martinez's PCK on his assessment practices, the outcome is instantly noticeable in his students' achievements and engagement. Analyzing the data from recent standardized test scores reveals year-after-year, better performance compared to peer groups in other chemistry classes. Student surveys reveal a high satisfaction rate with respect to assessments, citing that feedback is clear, constructive, and therefore helpful to better their understanding of the subject (Melka & Jatta, 2022).

It also reveals Mr. Martinez's commitment to continuous improvement. He engages in frequent scrutiny of assessment data and elicits student feedback to guide a process of continual refinement of his practices. For example, when he found that students consistently had difficulty with the understanding of laboratory procedures, he revised his lab assignments to have more guided practice and explicit instructions; this improved students' performance (McDonald et al., 2009; Melka & Jatta, 2022).

In sum, what has happened in Crestwood High School is a perfect example of how a teacher's PCK can enhance his or her assessment practices. His integration of content knowledge with pedagogical strategies enables him to design and implement assessment instruments that substantially evaluate and further student learning. Such desirable student performance and engagement outcomes underline the importance of PCK in shaping effective assessment practices at the secondary level.

Case Study: Moving PCK Forward into the Assessment Practices of Brookfield Elementary School

At Brookfield Elementary School in Seattle, Washington, the focus will be on how Pedagogical Content Knowledge influences assessment practices through the experiences of Ms. Emily Chen, a fourth-grade teacher with a very strong background in both elementary education and literacy. With over ten years of experience at Brookfield, Ms. Chen is striking for her innovative approaches toward integrating PCK into her assessment strategies.

Ms. Chen's PCK is found in her deep understanding of elementary literacy and the extent to which she can adjust her teaching methods based on the wide-ranging needs of learners. Her deep knowledge about reading and writing development will help her design assessments that not only measure the literacy skills of students but also develop them.

On the other hand, Ms. Chen uses strategies of formative assessment, which include reading journals, interactive read-alouds, and student self-assessments for monitoring students' progress. Reading journals give students an opportunity to reflect on their reading experiences and translate into writing what they have understood from the texts. This way of assessing student progress helps Ms. Chen make out the comprehension and critical thinking abilities of each student (McDonald et al., 2009; Melka & Jatta, 2022). Through interactive read-alouds, where students are engaged in discussions and answering text-related questions, Ms. Chen can continually assess student understanding to make adjustments to her instruction as needed. Student self-assessments involve students' reflection on their own progress and goals and taking personal responsibility for their learning. Summative assessments provide the measure of whether students have achieved the targeted reading and writing skills through literacy tests and created such products as book reports or projects that determine a student's ability to apply their reading and writing skills. Her literacy tests are designed to cover a range of skills, from decoding and fluency to comprehension and analysis. Book reports and projects allow students to express their understanding of the texts through creative presentations and written responses. She then evaluates these assignments by using very detailed rubrics, which ensures that her assessments match the learning targets and generate constructive feedback to the learners (Aydın et al., 2014).

How Ms. Chen's PCK played out in her assessment practices is noted in the progress and achievements of her students. Both school assessment and standard test data reveal that her students have consistently done well in literacy. Reading fluency and comprehension seem to have made huge improvements during the course of the academic year. Parents and students are also very appreciative of the fact that her assessments have helped in the growth of the students. Parents are now pleased with the clarity of their children's progress, and students themselves feel much more confident in reading and writing due to this carefully focused feedback (Aydın et al., 2014).

Ms. Chen keeps her assessment practice current. She goes to many workshops and collaborates with colleagues about the best practices of literacy teaching and assessment. For instance, after having gone through a workshop on differentiated instruction, Ms. Chen integrated some more strategies on how to meet the diverse needs of students into her assessment, and her assessment practice became more effective and inclusive.

The case of Ms. Emily Chen at Brookfield Elementary School illustrates how PCK can make a big difference in assessment practices at the elementary level. Her deep content knowledge about literacy, together with careful and diversified assessment strategies, has served both measurement and developmental functions in students' literacy skills. Student performance and increased engagement are positive indications of the need to combine PCK in assessment practices to ensure effective and responsive teaching (Yigit, 2014; Aydın et al., 2014).

COMBINED ANALYSIS OF CASE STUDIES ON PCK AND ASSESSMENT PRACTICES

The shared case studies—Ms. Sarah Thompson's at Lincoln Middle School, Mr. David Martinez's at Crestwood High School, and Ms. Chen's at Brookfield Elementary School—give an inclusive view of the way Pedagogical Content Knowledge affects assessment practices in different educational contexts. Each case highlights unique aspects about PCK and its impact on the strategies of assessment, while at the same time, they underline common themes and insights.

Content and Pedagogy Integration

A core element of PCK and a central theme across all three cases is the effective integration of content knowledge with pedagogical strategies. In Assessment, Ms. Sarah Thompson of Lincoln Middle School demonstrates mathematics content knowledge in the way she aligns her formative and summative assessments to instructional goals. This is evident in how she utilizes quizzes, exit tickets, and interactive activities to get at a nuanced understanding of how to measure and support student learning in a very dynamic way through the assessment (Aydın et al., 2014). Finally, Mr. David Martinez commands great knowledge of chemistry at Crestwood High School, putting it to use in the planning of comprehensive unit tests and project-based assessments that give a glimpse into the theoretical and practical approaches toward the subject of chemistry. In his use of detailed rubrics and variation in assessment methods, he gives a very fine illustration of how PCK enables, or better still facilitates, the development of rigorous and supportive assessments (Yigit, 2014; Aydın et al., 2014).

The case of Ms. Emily Chen at Brookfield Elementary School again illustrates how PCK in designing the assessments is applied. With her knowledge about literacy development, she is able to provide continuous feedback and support through reading journals, interactive read-alouds, and student self-assessments. Such formative assessments are attuned to the students' order of development, thus demonstrating how PCK can be applied in establishing appropriate ages and effective assessment practices.

Formative and Summative Assessments

Cases also include a clearly detectable and persistent pattern of formative and summative assessment. All three educators use formative assessment to get immediate feedback and to tweek instruction. Ms. Thompson uses quizzes and interactive activities, Mr. Martinez uses concept maps and peer reviews, and Ms. Chen uses reading journals and self-assessments to check student understanding in real time and offer support where needed. Such practices demonstrate a commitment to the on-going use of assessment as an improvement tool rather than a final evaluation technique (Yigit, 2014; Aydın et al., 2014).

Summative assessments in the cases evaluate comprehensive learning and performance. Ms. Thompson's unit tests, projects, Mr. Martinez's comprehensive tests and lab reports, Ms. Chen's literacy tests, and book reports all agree with the instructional objectives in assessment details about student achievement. This happens, first, because of the deep understanding by educators regarding the subject matter and, second, because of an equally deep understanding of the needs of their students—the hallmark of effective PCK (Mecoli, 2013; Yigit, 2014).

Impact on Student Learning Outcomes

The cases of PCK working on its objective—impact on student learning outcomes—can be seen in each case study. At Lincoln Middle School, assessments presented by Ms. Thompson contribute to above-average student performance and positive feedback from both the students and the parents (Yigit, 2014; Aydın et al., 2014). In Crestwood High School, students taught by Mr. Martinez show a consistently high achievement record in class and an increased understanding of some really complex concepts. Ms. Chen's assessments at Brookfield Elementary School measure up for sustained growth in literacy and feedback from students and parents. Results like this give some indication of the enhancement in student learning and progress that can happen in light of PCK-informed assessment practices across subjects and grade levels (Yigit, 2014).

Professional Development and Continuous Improvement

Another shared element is the commitment of educators to professional growth and improvement. Ms. Thompson adjusts based on the formative assessment data, Mr. Martinez refines his assessments by continuous feedback and professional development, and Ms. Chen takes back strategies learnt from workshops into her assessment practices. That is, in very strong terms, an example of how continuing professional growth underpins the effective application of PCK in assessment.

The collective study of these cases emerges with the strong function of PCK in framing quality assessment practices. In-depth knowledge that exists for each educator in terms of their field and pedagogical approaches gives them the opportunity to design and facilitate assessment opportunities that become meaningful for student learning (Mecoli, 2013; Yigit, 2014). If key messages are consistent in terms of the integration of content knowledge with pedagogic techniques, in using both formative and summative evaluation tools, and the positive effects on student outcomes arising thereof, the stronger the enablers there are for PCK to enhance teaching practice. In addition, professional development that is promised and followed through on as part of continuous improvement reflects a larger trend in the use of PCK to develop responsive teaching for effectiveness. These insights could, therefore, help educators and policymakers learn important lessons that would tighten the noose on the improvement of assessment practices in schools and, therefore, student learning outcomes (Mecoli, 2013).

IMPLICATIONS

The findings of the case studies relating to the function of PCK in influencing assessment practices have a few main implications which span several domains: theoretical implications, practical implications, social implications, and managerial implications. The implications lend insight into how PCK might enhance educational practices and provide a meaningful contribution to the larger field of educational systems.

Theoretical Implications

The theoretical implications follow from the extended knowledge of how PCK becomes relevant to assessment practices. The practical implications are rather explicit: the case studies refine Shulman's [10] original framework of PCK and illustrate it in operational use in real classroom practice. They point to a need for a theoretical extension of the nature of those elements of PCK that deal with the interaction between teachers' content and pedagogical approaches, reflected in and impacting assessment (Melka & Jatta, 2022).. These findings mean that PCK should not be viewed simply as a static concept but rather a dynamic interplay of the knowledge that is continually evolving with classroom experience and professional development. Moreover, embedding formative and summative assessment into these PCK frameworks highlight the need for theoretical consistency between the assessment methods with instructional methods in order to enable deep student learning (Kıray, 2016).

Practical Implications

These case studies help to describe important strategies for putting effective assessment practices, underpinned by PCK, into use. It is the development of deep understanding of both the subject matter and pedagogical methods that will position educators to design effective assessments that will be responsive to the learners' needs. Ms Thompson, Mr Martinez, and Ms Chen have illustrated how formative assessment use for perpetual feedback and adjustment of instruction increases student learning and continuous improvement in schools (McDonald et al., 2009). Thus, schools and all educational institutions should invest more in professional development in the integration of PCK to assessment practices so that all teachers are fully equipped to fine-tune these approaches and bring about better educational outcomes. Moreover, this can be guaranteed by the creation of articulate rubrics and the alignment of assessments to learning objectives. Therefore, this would eventually transform assessments into tools that would also be used to provide students with meaningful feedback, thus essentially assessing student success (McDonald et al., 2009; Melka & Jatta, 2022).

Societal Implications

The implication of the results on society extends to insert a nuance in the teacher preparation and assessment practices in the education system. The case studies show a positive impact of PCK on students' results. Therefore, investments in teacher education and professional development will bring about improvement in educational equity and quality. By putting PCK at the top of the agenda in teacher education programs, education policy-makers will contribute to an education system much more effective and fairer (Kıray, 2016). Additionally, the focus on formative assessment and individualized feedback plays a supportive role in achieving the purpose of meeting different learning needs to bring about congruence in structural inequality under which more students stand chances of achieving greater academic success.

Managerial Implications

From a managerial perspective, the cases proffer several actions that school heads and educational administrators can take to support entrenched complementarities between PCK and other elements of assessment practice. For instance, managers at all levels should provide environmental conditions that are appropriate for teachers in their stride towards continuous professional development as they try to enhance their PCK and assessment skills (Kıray, 2016). A way of doing this can be, for example, running workshops, mentoring systems, and collaborative meetings in which teachers can share best practices. School leaders, on their part, must support the development and implementation of tools and rubrics used for assessment purposes that reflect the instructional goals and the teachers' PCK. The leaders need to offer a culture for a reflective practice through which the teachers, as a routine matter, will review and fine-tune their assessment strategies in the light of student achievement data and feedback. In such efforts to be made, the educational manager can make the practice of assessment more effective and thereby can work towards better learning results of students (Razak, 2023).

The implications drawn from the above case studies identify significant roles that PCK can play towards effective assessment practices while calling for a holistic approach to teacher development and assessment design. The theoretical developments, practical strategies, benefits accruing socially, and managerial actions all contribute to the greater cause of enhancing educational practice and its output (Can-Kucuk et al., 2022). Based on this consideration, the embedding of PCK in assessment practices would empower educators, policy makers, and administrators to establish a more effective and equitable educational system, enabling student success in the process of continued professional development.

LIMITATIONS AND SCOPE OF FUTURE RESEARCH

Limitations

Insights drawn from the case studies despite the fact that valuable information was drawn, there are some major limitations that have to be considered. Firstly, findings are contextual in nature. The studies were cases, thus conducted in specific schools, with specific educators. Therefore, the results might not generalize to all educational settings. There will be unique characteristics to every teacher's PCK, subject area, and student demographics that might influence the applicability to different contexts or educational levels (Can-Kucuk et al., 2022).

Other than that, another limitation has to do with the qualitative nature of the data: Even though subjective reports from interviews, observations, and document analysis are useful for drawing in-depth and nuanced insights with case studies, qualitatively, such subjectivity can introduce some bias into the findings and limit objectivity (Tröbst et al., 2018). Besides, heavy reliance on self-reporting by teachers and feedback from student and parents may not necessarily tell the real impact of PCK on the practices of assessment.

Therefore, the case study scope of these studies was limited in terms of time that was available and depth of data that was collected. While these case studies add invaluable snapshots of practice, they cannot represent long-term trends or the myriads of factors that may shape assessment practices (Tröbst et al., 2018; Can-Kucuk et al., 2022). That is, findings cannot control for all possible variables that could impact the relationship between PCK and assessment practices over an extended period of time.

Future Research Scope

These limitations can be overcome by the future research work, which has an expanded scope and methodology of studies in relation to PCK and assessment practices. Longitudinal studies in this respect can also be undertaken to understand the development and impact of PCK in assessment practices over time. In this light, such studies help in settling on the changes and influence PCK has on assessment practice over time. Studies of this type will be able to provide much deeper insights into the ways in which PCK develops and bears upon assessment strategies and student outcomes at the different educational phases (Razak, 2023).

It would also be important for future research to target a broader range of educational contexts and settings. With diverse schools, subject areas, and grade levels included, researchers may attempt to explore how PCK influences assessment practices within diverse environments and thus reveal similar and different features. It would also be beneficial to carry out comparative studies among different education systems, regions, and countries in order to understand how cultural and institutional factors could be mediating the link between PCK and assessment practices (Sancar-Tokmak & Yelken, 2015; Mapulanga et al., 2022).

Wider extensions could also include mixed-methods approaches in the research methodology, which would enhance the strength of the findings. The results will also be bolstered by combining qualitative data with quantitative measures, like for instance standardized test scores or any types of performance metrics that would provide a more comprehensive understanding of the working of PCK on assessment practices and students' learning outcomes. These findings can also be further validated and generalized by large-scale data collection and surveys to support insights of the case study (Sancar-Tokmak & Yelken, 2015; Razak, 2023).

Research on the role of PCK development and assessment practices of teachers in professional development and teacher training constitutes a rich ground for further follow-up study. In fact, examining different professional development programs and their effectiveness in developing teachers' PCK and assessment may really provide significant input into practices and structures of training programs (Sancar-Tokmak & Yelken, 2015; Ginting & Linarsih, 2022).

In outline, while the case studies provide useful insights about the relationship between PCK and assessment practices, by addressing the limitations of these studies and taking up further research opportunities, a fuller and more generalizable conception about how PCK may become manifest and influential in educational practice and outcomes would be possible.

CONCLUSION

The case studies of the impact of PCK on assessment practices reflect in essence the close relationship that exists between deep subject matter knowledge by the educators and their potential to design and implement appropriate assessments. Experience with Ms. Sarah Thompson at Lincoln Middle School, Mr. David Martinez at Crestwood High School, and Ms. Emily Chen at Brookfield Elementary School all suggest PCK to have a very important role to play in both formative and summative assessment practices that are important in the influencing of the learning outcome of any student. In other words, every potential synthesis by an educator of content knowledge with pedagogical strategies pays testimony to the fact that PCK plays a significant role in the making of assessments not only aligned with instructional goals but also responsive to students' needs.

Dry-run studies show that applying PCK to create a learning assessment really works. Overall, these results highlight the role of investing in professional development opportunities to enhance teachers' PCK, along with the continuous support and resources to be availed to educators in the ongoing fine-tuning of the assessment strategies. The studies elaborately show that with a deeper understanding of PCK, more equitable educational practices could become realities, attend to diverse learning needs, and promote academic success across different contexts.

As illuminating as the findings from the case studies above may be, their dual failings in terms of context specificity and reliance on qualitative data clearly suggest that further research is in order. Longitudinal studies and different educational contexts, using a mixed-method design, can give a broader view of how PCK shapes approaches to assessment and influences student results. Through research in this area, it will not only confirm findings to date but also be of assistance in developing a more useful way for training teachers and assessing their work.

This integration of PCK within the classroom and educational context can have positive implications for the practitioner, the policymaker, and the school administrator, impacting work and educational practice in general. PCK, in terms of assessment design and implementation, can contribute toward improving teaching effectiveness and student learning related to the final aim of a more valid and fair learning environment. Future research into and development of PCK-informed assessment practices are needed.

REFERENCES

Abdul Razak, R., Mat Yusoff, S., Hai Leng, C., & Mohamadd Marzaini, A. F. (2023). Evaluating teachers' pedagogical content knowledge in implementing classroom-based assessment: A case study among esl secondary school teachers in selangor, malaysia. *PLoS One*, 18(12), e0293325. DOI: 10.1371/journal.pone.0293325 PMID: 38157377

Ainsworth, L. (2010). *Rigorous curriculum design: How to create curricular units of study that align standards, instruction, and assessment.* Lead+ Learn Press.

Aydın, M., Friedrichsen, P., Boz, Y., & Hanuscin, D. (2014). Examination of the topic-specific nature of pedagogical content knowledge in teaching electrochemical cells and nuclear reactions. *Chemistry Education Research and Practice*, 15(4), 658–674. DOI: 10.1039/C4RP00105B

Can-Kucuk, D., Gencer, S., & Akkuş, H. (2022). Development of pre-service chemistry teachers' pedagogical content knowledge through mentoring. *Chemistry Education Research and Practice*, 23(3), 599–615. DOI: 10.1039/D2RP00033D

Can-Kucuk, D., Gencer, S., & Akkuş, H. (2022). Development of pre-service chemistry teachers' pedagogical content knowledge through mentoring. *Chemistry Education Research and Practice*, 23(3), 599–615. DOI: 10.1039/D2RP00033D

Chai, C., Ng, E., Li, W., Hong, H., & Koh, J. (2013). Validating and modelling technological pedagogical content knowledge framework among asian preservice teachers. *Australasian Journal of Educational Technology*, 29(1). Advance online publication. DOI: 10.14742/ajet.174

Charles, L. (2018). Middle school teachers' perception of differentiated instruction on lower third student achievement. *Teacher Education and Curriculum Studies*, 3(3), 20. DOI: 10.11648/j.tecs.20180303.11

Chen, J., & Chen, Y. (2017). Differentiated instruction in a calculus curriculum for college students in taiwan. *Journal of Education and Learning*, 7(1), 88. DOI: 10.5539/jel.v7n1p88

Desimone, L. M. (2009). Improving impact studies of teachers' professional development: Toward better conceptualizations and measures. *Educational Researcher*, 38(3), 181–199. DOI: 10.3102/0013189X08331140

Ginting, D., & Linarsih, A. (2022). Teacher professional development in the perspective of technology pedagogical content knowledge theoretical framework. *Jurnal Visi Ilmu Pendidikan*, 14(1), 1. DOI: 10.26418/jvip.v14i1.49334

Ginting, D., & Linarsih, A. (2022). Teacher professional development in the perspective of technology pedagogical content knowledge theoretical framework. *Jurnal Visi Ilmu Pendidikan*, 14(1), 1. DOI: 10.26418/jvip.v14i1.49334

Hill, H. C., Rowan, B., & Ball, D. L. (2005). Effects of teachers' mathematical knowledge for teaching on student achievement. *American Educational Research Journal*, 42(2), 371–406. DOI: 10.3102/00028312042002371

Kiefer, S. M., & Ellerbrock, C. R. (2012). Fostering an Adolescent-Centered Community Within an Interdisciplinary Team. *Middle Grades Research Journal*, 7(3), 1–17.

Lee, M., & Tsai, C. (2008). Exploring teachers' perceived self efficacy and technological pedagogical content knowledge with respect to educational use of the world wide web. *Instructional Science*, 38(1), 1–21. DOI: 10.1007/s11251-008-9075-4

Li, G. X. W. (2016). An empirical study on college english teacher's tpack: theory and application. IOSR Journal of Engineering, 06(04), 01-04. https://doi.org/DOI: 10.9790/3021-06410104

Lucenario, J., Yangco, R., Punzalan, A., & Espinosa, A. (2016). Pedagogical content knowledge-guided lesson study: Effects on teacher competence and students' achievement in chemistry. *Education Research International*, 2016, 1–9. DOI: 10.1155/2016/6068930

Mapulanga, T., Nshogoza, G., & Ameyaw, Y. (2022). Teachers' perceived enacted pedagogical content knowledge in biology at selected secondary schools in lusaka. International Journal of Learning. *Teaching and Educational Research*, 21(10), 418–435. DOI: 10.26803/ijlter.21.10.23

Mapulanga, T., Nshogoza, G., & Ameyaw, Y. (2022). Teachers' perceived enacted pedagogical content knowledge in biology at selected secondary schools in lusaka. International Journal of Learning. *Teaching and Educational Research*, 21(10), 418–435. DOI: 10.26803/ijlter.21.10.23

McDonald Connor, C., Piasta, S. B., Fishman, B., Glasney, S., Schatschneider, C., Crowe, E., Underwood, P., & Morrison, F. J. (2009). Individualizing student instruction precisely: Effects of child× instruction interactions on first graders' literacy development. *Child Development*, 80(1), 77–100. DOI: 10.1111/j.1467-8624.2008.01247.x PMID: 19236394

Mecoli, S. (2013). The influence of the pedagogical content knowledge theoretical framework on research on preservice teacher education. *Journal of Education*, 193(3), 21–27. DOI: 10.1177/002205741319300304

Melka, Y., & Jatta, I. (2022). High school students' perceptions towards efl teachers' differentiated instructional practices at higher 23 secondary school, addis ababa, ethiopia. *Education Journal*, 11(2), 75. DOI: 10.11648/j.edu.20221102.14

Papantonis Stajcic, M., & Nilsson, P. (2023). Teachers' considerations for a digitalised learning context of preschool science. *Research in Science Education*, 54(3), 499–521. DOI: 10.1007/s11165-023-10150-5

Sancar-Tokmak, H., & Yelken, T. Y. (2015). Effects of creating digital stories on foreign language education pre-service teachers' tpack self-confidence. *Educational Studies*, 41(4), 444–461. DOI: 10.1080/03055698.2015.1043978

Shulman, L. S. (1986). Those who understand: Knowledge growth in teaching. *Educational Researcher*, 15(4), 4–14. DOI: 10.3102/0013189X015002004

Tröbst, S., Kleickmann, T., Heinze, A., Bernholt, A., Rink, R., & Kunter, M. (2018). Teacher knowledge experiment: Testing mechanisms underlying the formation of preservice elementary school teachers' pedagogical content knowledge concerning fractions and fractional arithmetic. *Journal of Educational Psychology*, 110(8), 1049–1065. DOI: 10.1037/edu0000260

Yigit, M. (2014). A review of the literature: How pre-service mathematics teachers develop their technological, pedagogical, and content knowledge. *International Journal of Education in Mathematics Science and Technology*, 2(1). Advance online publication. DOI: 10.18404/ijemst.96390

Compilation of References

Abdul Razak, R., Mat Yusoff, S., Hai Leng, C., & Mohamadd Marzaini, A. F. (2023). Evaluating teachers' pedagogical content knowledge in implementing classroom-based assessment: A case study among esl secondary school teachers in selangor, malaysia. *PLoS One*, 18(12), e0293325. DOI: 10.1371/journal.pone.0293325 PMID: 38157377

Abell, S. K. (2007). Research on science teacher knowledge. In Abell, S. K., & Lederman, N. G. (Eds.), *Handbook of research on science education* (pp. 1105–1149). Erlbaum., DOI: 10.4324/9780203097267-54

Abell, S. K. (2008). Twenty years later: Does pedagogical content knowledge remain a useful idea? *International Journal of Science Education*, 30(10), 1405–1416. DOI: 10.1080/09500690802187041

Adarkwah, M. (2021). The power of assessment feedback in teaching and learning: A narrative review and synthesis of the literature. *SN Social Sciences*, 1(3), 75. DOI: 10.1007/s43545-021-00086-w

Adelson, L., Culp, R., & Bunn, S.. (2009). Teaching evolution concepts to early elementary school students. *Evolution (New York)*, 2(4), 458–473. DOI: 10.1007/s12052-009-0148-x

Adewumi, T. M., Mosito, C., & Agosto, V. (2019). Experiences of teachers in implementing inclusion of learners with special education needs in selected Fort Beaufort District primary schools, South Africa. *Cogent Education*, 6(1), 1703446. Advance online publication. DOI: 10.1080/2331186X.2019.1703446

Agarwal, P., & Sengupta-Irving, T. (2019). Integrating power to advance the study of connective and productive disciplinary engagement in mathematics and science. *Cognition and Instruction*, 37(3), 349–366. DOI: 10.1080/07370008.2019.1624544

Agrawal, A. V., Pitchai, R., Senthamaraikannan, C., Balaji, N. A., Sajithra, S., & Boopathi, S. (2023). Digital Education System During the COVID-19 Pandemic. In *Using Assistive Technology for Inclusive Learning in K-12 Classrooms* (pp. 104–126). IGI Global. DOI: 10.4018/978-1-6684-6424-3.ch005

Aguilar, S. J. (2018). Learning analytics: At the nexus of big data, digital innovation, and social justice in education. *TechTrends*, 62(1), 37–45. DOI: 10.1007/s11528-017-0226-9

Agyei, D., & Voogt, J. (2012). Developing technological pedagogical content knowledge in pre-service mathematics teachers through collaborative design. *Australasian Journal of Educational Technology*, 28(4), 547–564. DOI: 10.14742/ajet.827

Ainsworth, L. (2010). *Rigorous curriculum design: How to create curricular units of study that align standards, instruction, and assessment*. Lead+ Learn Press.

Ainsworth, S. (2006). DeFT: A conceptual framework for learning with multiple representations. *Learning and Instruction*, 16(3), 183–198. DOI: 10.1016/j.learninstruc.2006.03.001

Akçayır, G., & Akçayır, M. (2018). The flipped classroom: A review of its advantages and challenges. *Computers & Education*, 126, 334–345. DOI: 10.1016/j.compedu.2018.07.021

Akgun, A. (2009). The relation between science student teachers' misconceptions about solution, dissolution, diffusion, and their attitudes toward science with their achievement. *Education in Science*, 34(154), 26–36.

Akin, F. N., & Uzuntiryaki-Kondakci, E. (2018). The nature of the interplay among components of pedagogical content knowledge in reaction rate and chemical equilibrium topics of novice and experienced chemistry teachers. *Chemistry Education Research and Practice*, 19(1), 80–105. DOI: 10.1039/C7RP00165G

Akita, K. (2012). *Psychology of Learning: Designing the Classroom*. Sayusha.

Alabama Code Title 16. Education § 16-23-3 (2019).

Alabama State Department of Education, (2018). Digital literacy and computer science: Course of study.

Al-Ansi, A. M., Jaboob, M., Garad, A., & Al-Ansi, A. (2023). Analyzing augmented reality (AR) and virtual reality (VR) recent development in education. *Social Sciences & Humanities Open*, 8(1), 100532. DOI: 10.1016/j.ssaho.2023.100532

Alatas, F. (2018). *Applying Ibn Khaldun: The Recovery of a Lost Tradition in Sociology*. Routledge.

Alatas, F. (2018). *Silencing as method: Leaving Malay studies out*. Department of Malay Studies, National University of Singapore.

Alatas, S. H. (1972). Captive Mind in Development Studies. *International Social Science Journal*, 24(1), 9–25.

Al-Bīrūnī, A. R. (2020). *The Yoga Sutras of Patañjali*. New York University Press.

Almonacid-Fierro, A., Sepúlveda-Vallejos, S., Valdebenito, K., & Aguilar-Valdés, M. (2023). Analysis of pedagogical content knowledge in science teacher education: A systematic review 2011-2021. *International Journal of Educational Methodology*, 9(3), 525–534. DOI: 10.12973/ijem.9.3.525

Alonso-Amo, R., et al. (1992). an attempt at understanding the nature of the world and a subsequent endeavour to understand the nature of knowledge itself. This is the step from a purely epistemological approach to a gnoseological one.

Alonso-Amo, F., Mate, J. L., Morant, J. L., & Pazos, J. (1992). From epistemology to Gnoseology: Foundations of the knowledge industry. *AI & Society*, 6(2), 140–165. DOI: 10.1007/BF02472778

Alonzo, A. C. (2011). Learning progressions that support formative assessment practices. *Measurement: Interdisciplinary Research and Perspectives*, 9(2–3), 124–129. DOI: 10.1080/15366367.2011.599629

Alonzo, A. C., & Elby, A. (2019). Beyond empirical adequacy: Learning progressions as models and their value for teachers. *Cognition and Instruction*, 37(1), 1–37. DOI: 10.1080/07370008.2018.1539735

Alrawashdeh, G. S., Fyffe, S., Azevedo, R. F. L., & Castillo, N. M. (2024). Exploring the impact of personalized and adaptive learning technologies on reading literacy: A global meta-analysis. *Educational Research Review*, 42, 100587. Advance online publication. DOI: 10.1016/j.edurev.2023.100587

Altet, M. (2010). La relation dialectique entre pratique et théorie dans une formation professionnalisante des enseignants en IUFM: D'une opposition à uné necessaire articulation. *Education Sciences & Society*, 1(1), 117–141.

Ambrosetti, A., & Dekkers, J. (2010). The interconnectedness of the roles of mentors and mentees in pre-service teacher education mentoring relationships. *The Australian Journal of Teacher Education*, 35(6), 3. DOI: 10.14221/ajte.2010v35n6.3

Anggoro, S., Widodo, A., & Suhandi, A. (2017). Pre-service elementary teachers' understanding of force and motion. *Journal of Physics: Conference Series*, 895, 1–7. DOI: 10.1088/1742-6596/895/1/012151

Appleman, D. (2015). *Critical literacy in the classroom: The art of argument*. Guilford Press.

Appleton, K. (2006). Science pedagogical content knowledge and elementary school leaders. In K. Appleton (Ed.), *Elementary science teacher education: International perspectives in contemporary issues and practice* (pp. 31-54). Lawrence Erlbaum in association with the Association for Science Teacher Education.

Appleton, K. (2008). Developing science pedagogical content knowledge through mentoring elementary teachers. *Journal of Science Teacher Education*, 19(6), 423–545. DOI: 10.1007/s10972-008-9109-4

Aristotle, . (2004). *The Nicomachean Ethics* (Thomson, J. A. K., Trans.). Penguin Books. (Original work published 350 BCE)

Arnold, S. R., Padilla, M. J., & Tunhikorn, B. (2009). The development of per-service science teachers' professional knowledge in utilizing ICT to support professional lives. *Eurasia Journal of Mathematics, Science and Technology Education*, 5(2), 91–101. DOI: 10.12973/ejmste/75261

Artworks (no date). STEAM Toolkit. Retrieved July 9, 2020, from https://artswork.org.uk/wp-content/uploads/2019/09/AW_STEAM_Toolkit_030919_V17_WEB_READY.pdf

Audi, R. (2010). *Epistemology: A Contemporary Introduction to the Theory of Knowledge* (3rd ed.). Routledge. DOI: 10.4324/9780203846469

Ausubel, D. P. (1963). *Psychology of Meaningful Learning*. Grune & Stratton.

Avard, M. M. (2010). Use of thermochrons in the classroom. *Journal of College Science Teaching*, 38(6), 24–29.

Aydeniz, M., & Kırbulut, Z. (2014). Exploring challenges of assessing pre-service science teachers' pedagogical content knowledge (pck). *Asia-Pacific Journal of Teacher Education*, 42(2), 147–166. DOI: 10.1080/1359866X.2014.890696

Aydın, M., Friedrichsen, P., Boz, Y., & Hanuscin, D. (2014). Examination of the topic-specific nature of pedagogical content knowledge in teaching electrochemical cells and nuclear reactions. *Chemistry Education Research and Practice*, 15(4), 658–674. DOI: 10.1039/C4RP00105B

Aydm, S., Demirdogen, B., Muslu, N., & Hanuscin, D. (2013). Professional journals as a source of PCK or teaching nature of science: An examination of articles published in *The Science Teacher (TST)*. *Journal of Science Teacher Education*, 24(6), 977–997. DOI: 10.1007/s10972-013-9345-0

Bacon, F. (2008). *The New Organon* (Jardine, L., & Silverthorne, M., Trans.). Cambridge University Press. (Original work published 1620)

Baldacci, M. (2014). *La formazione dei docenti e il tirocinio*. University Press.

Ball, D. L. (2018). The complexity of teaching mathematics: Navigating the terrain of pedagogical content knowledge. *Journal of Mathematics Teacher Education*, 21(1), 29–48. DOI: 10.1007/s10857-017-9398-3

Ball, D. L., Thames, M. H., & Phelps, G. (2008). Content knowledge for teaching: What makes it special? *Journal of Teacher Education*, 59(5), 389–407. DOI: 10.1177/0022487108324554

Banihashem, S. K., Noroozi, O., van Ginkel, S., Macfadyen, L. P., & Biemans, H. J. A. (2022). A systematic review of the role of learning analytics in enhancing feedback practices in higher education. *Educational Research Review*, 37, 100489. Advance online publication. DOI: 10.1016/j.edurev.2022.100489

Banilower, E. R., Smith, P. S., Weiss, I. R., Malzahn, K. A., Campbell, K. M., & Weis, A. M. (2013). *Report of the 2012 National Survey of Science and Mathematics Education*. Horizon Research, Inc.

Banks, J. A., & Banks, C. A. M. (2019). *Teaching strategies for the social studies: Decision-making and citizenship education*. Longman.

Barmby, P., Kind, P. M., & Jones, K. (2008). Examining changing attitudes in secondary school science. *International Journal of Science Education*, 30(8), 1075–1093. DOI: 10.1080/09500690701344966

Barnett, J., & Hodson, D. (2001). Pedagogical context knowledge: Toward a fuller understanding of what good science teachers know. *Science Education*, 85(4), 426–453. DOI: 10.1002/sce.1017

Barton, K. C., & Levstik, L. S. (2015). *Teaching history for the common good*. Routledge.

Battiste, M. (2011). *Reclaiming Indigenous Voice and Vision*. UBC Press.

Battiste, M., & Henderson, J. Y. (2000). *Protecting Indigenous Knowledge and Heritage: A Global Challenge*. Purich Publishing. DOI: 10.59962/9781895830439

Baxter, J. A., & Lederman, N. G. (1999). Assessment and measurement of pedagogical content knowledge. In Gess-Newsome, J., & Lederman, N. G. (Eds.), *Examining pedagogical content knowledge* (pp. 147–161). Kluwer Academic., DOI: 10.1007/0-306-47217-1_6

Bell, B., & Gilbert, J. (1996). Teacher development as personal, professional, and social development. *Teaching and Teacher Education*, 10(5), 483–497. DOI: 10.1016/0742-051X(94)90002-7

Bell, J., Veal, W. R., & Tippins, D. J. (1998, April). The evolution of pedagogical content knowledge in prospective secondary physics teachers. Paper Presented at the *Annual Meeting of the National Association for Research in Science Teaching*, San Diego, CA.

Bell, R. L., Smetana, L., & Binns, I. (2005). Simplifying inquiry instruction. *Science Teacher (Normal, Ill.)*, 72(7), 30–33.

Benecke, K., & Kaiser, G. (2023). Teachers' approaches to handling student errors in mathematics classes. *Asian Journal for Mathematics Education*, 2(2), 161–182. DOI: 10.1177/27527263231184642

Benjamin, A. S., & Pashler, H. (2015). The value of standardized testing: A perspective from cognitive psychology. *Policy Insights from the Behavioral and Brain Sciences*, 2(1), 13–23. DOI: 10.1177/2372732215601116

Bennett, R. E. (2011). Formative assessment: A critical review. *Assessment in Education: Principles, Policy & Practice*, 18(1), 5–25. DOI: 10.1080/0969594X.2010.513678

Bhabha, H. K. (1994). *The Location of Culture*. Routledge.

Bhambra, G., Krabbe, J. S., Shilliam, R., Boatcă, M., Rutazibwa, O., Hansen, P., & Popal, M. (2020). Intermezzo I–Knowledge Orders. *Beyond the Master's Tools?: Decolonizing Knowledge Orders, Research Methods and Teaching*, 63.

Bhatt, M. J., Durani, H., Tanna, P., & Lathigara, A. (2024). Enhancing Real-World Applications Learning In Industrial Engineering: Integrating Out-of-Classroom Experiences for Optimal Skill Development. *Journal of Engineering Education Transformations*, 37(Special Issue 2).

Black, P., & Wiliam, D. (2009). Developing the theory of formative assessment. *Educational Assessment, Evaluation and Accountability*, 21(1), 5–31. DOI: 10.1007/s11092-008-9068-5

Black, P., & Wiliam, D. (2018). Classroom assessment and pedagogy. *Assessment in Education: Principles, Policy & Practice*, 25(6), 1–25. DOI: 10.1080/0969594X.2018.1441807

Blamire, R., Cassells, D., & Walsh, G. (2017). ITELab monitoring report 1.

Blank, R. K. (2012). *What is the impact of decline in science instructional time in elementary school?* Paper prepared for the Noyce Foundation.

Blin, F., & Munro, M. (2008). Why hasn't technology disrupted academics' teaching practices? Understanding resistance to change through the lens of activity theory. *Computers & Education*, 50(2), 475–490. DOI: 10.1016/j.compedu.2007.09.017

Bloom, B. S. (1956). *Taxonomy of Educational Objectives, Handbook: The Cognitive Domain*. David McKay.

Bloom, B. S. (1956). Taxonomy of educational objectives: the classification of educational goals; Handbook I: Cognitive domain. In Engelhart, M. D., Furst, E. J., Hill, W. H., & Krathwohl, D. R. (Eds.), *Taxonomy of educational objectives: the classification of educational goals; Handbook I: Cognitive domain*. David McKay.

Bloom, B. S. (1976). *Human characteristics and school learning*. Mc Graw Hill.

Blumenbach, J. F. (1775). *On the Natural Varieties of Mankind*. T. Cadell.

Boaler, J. (2016). *Mathematical mindsets: Unleashing students' potential through creative math, inspiring messages, and innovative teaching*. Jossey-Bass.

Bocci, F. (2021). *Pedagogia speciale come pedagogia inclusiva. Itinerari istituenti di un modo di essere della scienza dell'educazione*. Guerini.

Boeskens, L., Nusche, D., & Yurita, M. (2020a). *Policies to support teachers' continuing professional learning: A conceptual framework and mapping of OECD data*.

Bogoslowski, S., Geng, F., Gao, Z., Rajabzadeh, A. R., & Srinivasan, S. (2021). Integrated thinking-a cross-disciplinary project-based engineering education. *Visions and Concepts for Education 4.0: Proceedings of the 9th International Conference on Interactive Collaborative and Blended Learning (ICBL2020)*, 260–267.

Bo, N. S. W. (2024). *OECD digital education outlook 2023: Towards an effective education ecosystem*. Hungarian Educational Research Journal.

Bonaiuti, G., & Calvani, A. (2016). *Fondamenti di didattica. Teoria e prassi dei dispositivi formativi*. Carocci.

Boopathi, S. (2024). Digital HR Implementation for Business Growth in Industrial 5.0. In *Convergence of Human Resources Technologies and Industry 5.0* (pp. 1–22). IGI Global. DOI: 10.4018/979-8-3693-1343-5.ch001

Borda, E., Haskell, T., & Boudreaux, A. (2020). Cross-disciplinary learning: A framework for assessing application of concepts across STEM disciplines. *arXiv Preprint arXiv:2012.07906*.

Borko, H., Jacobs, J., & Koellner, K. (2010). Sustaining professional development in the context of teaching reform. *Teachers College Record*, 112(2), 519–548.

Bottani, N. (1994). *Professoressa, addio*. Il Mulino.

Bracci, F. (2017). L'apprendimento adulto. Metodologie didattiche ed esperienze trasformative. Unicopli.

Brass, J., & Webb, A. (2015). *Reclaiming English language arts methods courses: Critical issues and challenges for teacher educators in top-down times*. Routledge.

Bronfenbrenner, U. (1979). *The Ecology of Human Development: Experiments by Nature and Design*. Harvard University Press. DOI: 10.4159/9780674028845

Brown, P., Friedrichsen, P., & Abell, S. (2013). The development of prospective secondary biology teachers' PCK. *Journal of Science Teacher Education*, 24(1), 133–155. DOI: 10.1007/s10972-012-9312-1

Bruffee, K. A. (1987). The art of collaborative learning. Change. *Change*, 19(2), 42–47. DOI: 10.1080/00091383.1987.9939136

Bruner, J. S. (1961). The act of discovery. *Harvard Educational Review*.

Bruner, J. S. (1968). *Processes of Cognitive Growth: Infancy*. Clark University Press.

Buçinca, Z., Malaya, M. B., & Gajos, K. Z. (2021). To trust or to think: Cognitive forcing functions can reduce overreliance on AI in AI-assisted decision-making. Proceedings of the ACM on Human-Computer Interaction, 5(CSCW1), 1–21. https://doi.org/DOI: 10.1145/3449287

Bunch, G. C. (2013). Pedagogical language knowledge: Preparing mainstream teachers for English learners in the new standards era. *Review of Research in Education*, 37(1), 298–341. DOI: 10.3102/0091732X12461772

Burgoon, J. N., Heddle, M. L., & Duran, E. (2011). Re-examining the similarities between teacher and student conceptions about physical science. *Journal of Science Teacher Education*, 22(2), 101–114. DOI: 10.1007/s10972-010-9196-x

Burns, M. (2020). *Formative assessment in the classroom: An introduction*. Routledge.

Bursal, M. (2012). Changes in American pre-service elementary teachers' efficacy beliefs and anxieties during a science methods course. *Science Education International*, 23(1), 40–55.

Bybee, R. W. (2014). The BSCS 5E instructional model: Creating teachable moments. *Science and Children*, 51(8), 10–13. DOI: 10.2505/4/sc14_051_08_10

Caingcoy, M. E. (2023). Culturally responsive pedagogy: A systematic overview. *Diversitas Journal*, 8(4), 3203-3212. DOI: 10.48017/dj.v8i4.2780

Cajete, G. (1994). *Look to the mountain: An ecology of indigenous education.* Kivaki Press, Cajete, G. (2000). *Native Science: Natural Laws of Interdependence.* Clear Light Publishers.

Can, H. B., & Boz, Y. (2022). Development of pre-service teachers' pedagogical content knowledge and the factors affecting that development: A longitudinal study. *Chemistry Education Research and Practice*, 23(4), 980–997. DOI: 10.1039/D2RP00106C

Can-Kucuk, D., Gencer, S., & Akkuş, H. (2022). Development of pre-service chemistry teachers' pedagogical content knowledge through mentoring. *Chemistry Education Research and Practice*, 23(3), 599–615. DOI: 10.1039/D2RP00033D

Capps, D. K., Crawford, B. A., & Constas, M. A. (2012). A review of empirical literature on inquiry professional development: Alignment with best practices and a critique of the findings. *Journal of Science Teacher Education*, 23(3), 291–318. DOI: 10.1007/s10972-012-9275-2

Cardini, F. (2023). *Le vie del sapere.* Il Mulino.

Carlsen, W. S. (1987). *Why do you ask? The effects of science teacher subject-matter knowledge on teacher questioning and classroom discourse.* Paper presented at the meeting of the American Educational Research Association, Washington DC.

Carlson, D., & Daehler, K. (2019). Context-specific PCK: Adapting teaching practices to diverse educational settings. *Journal of Science Teacher Education*, 30(4), 517–532. DOI: 10.1080/1046560X.2019.1624267

Carlson, J., & Daehler, K. R. (2019). The refined consensus model of pedagogical content knowledge in science education. In Hume, A., Cooper, R., & Borowski, A. (Eds.), *Repositioning pedagogical content knowledge in teachers' knowledge for teaching science* (pp. 77–92). Springer. DOI: 10.1007/978-981-13-5898-2_2

Carmel, J. H., & Yezierski, E. J. (2013). Are we keeping the promise? Investigation of students' critical thinking growth. *Journal of College Science Teaching*, 42, 71–81.

Carrier, S. J. (2013). Elementary preservice teachers' science vocabulary: Knowledge and application. *Journal of Science Teacher Education*, 24(2), 405–425. DOI: 10.1007/s10972-012-9270-7

Carter, A. (2021). *Culturally responsive teaching in the social studies classroom: Empowering students through critical inquiry.* Teachers College Press.

Caspersen, M. E., Gal-Ezer, J., McGettrick, A., & Nardelli, E. (2018). Informatics for All The strategy.

Castoldi, M. (2015). *Didattica generale*. Mondadori Education.

Catalano, A., Asselta, L., & Durkin, A. (2019). Exploring the relationship between science content knowledge and science teaching self-efficacy among elementary teachers. *IAFOR Journal of Education*, 7(1), 2019. DOI: 10.22492/ije.7.1.04

Center for Education Policy. (2008). *Instructional time in the elementary schools: A closer look at changes for specific subjects*. Center on Education Policy.

Chai, C., Ng, E., Li, W., Hong, H., & Koh, J. (2013). Validating and modelling technological pedagogical content knowledge framework among asian preservice teachers. *Australasian Journal of Educational Technology*, 29(1). Advance online publication. DOI: 10.14742/ajet.174

Chand, S. P. (2024). Constructivism in education: Exploring the contributions of Piaget, Vygotsky, and Bruner. [IJSR]. *International Journal of Science and Research (Raipur, India)*, 12(7), 274–278. DOI: 10.21275/SR23630021800

Chan, K. K. H., & Hume, A. (2019). Towards a consensus model: Literature review of how science teachers' pedagogical content knowledge is investigated in empirical studies. In Hume, A., Cooper, R., & Borowski, A. (Eds.), *Repositioning Pedagogical Content Knowledge in teachers' knowledge for teaching science* (pp. 3–76). Springer Nature., DOI: 10.1007/978-981-13-5898-2_1

Chao, S. (2020). A tree of many lives: Vegetal teleontologies in West Papua. *HAU*, 10(2), 514–529. DOI: 10.1086/709505

Charles, L. (2018). Middle school teachers' perception of differentiated instruction on lower third student achievement. *Teacher Education and Curriculum Studies*, 3(3), 20. DOI: 10.11648/j.tecs.20180303.11

Chazbeck, B., & Ayoubi, Z. (2024). The nested knowledge system of TPACK: A case study on physics teachers' educational resource selection and integration. *Journal of Education in Science, Environment and Health*, •••, 245–260. DOI: 10.55549/jeseh.707

Chen, J., & Chen, Y. (2017). Differentiated instruction in a calculus curriculum for college students in taiwan. *Journal of Education and Learning*, 7(1), 88. DOI: 10.5539/jel.v7n1p88

Chew, S., & Cerbin, W. (2020). The cognitive challenges of effective teaching. *The Journal of Economic Education*, 52(1), 1–24. DOI: 10.1080/00220485.2020.1845266

Chiappetta Cajola, L. (2014). *Didattica inclusiva. Quali competenze per gli insegnanti?* Armando.

Chilisa, B. (2012). *Indigenous Research Methodologies*. SAGE Publications.

Chiosso, G. (2018). *Studiare Pedagogia. Introduzione ai significati dell'educazione*. Mondadori.

Cho, K., Ward, P., Chey, W. S., Tsuda, E., Atkinson, O. J., & Oh, D. (2023). An Assessment of Preservice Teachers' Volleyball Content Knowledge in Physical Education Teacher Education. *International Journal of Kinesiology in Higher Education*, 7(4), 335–345. DOI: 10.1080/24711616.2022.2163726

Chowdhury, J. S. (2023a). Voice and Photovoice of the Bangladeshi Migrant Workers in Malaysia: An Ethnography of the 3rd Space With Reciprocity. In *Handbook of Research on Implications of Sustainable Development in Higher Education* (pp. 314-336). IGI Global.

Chowdhury, J. S., Abd Wahab, H., Saad, M. R. M., Mathbor, G. M., & Hamidi, M. (2023a). *Ubuntu Philosophy for the New Normalcy*. Springer Nature. DOI: 10.1007/978-981-19-7818-0

Chowdhury, J. S., & Roy, P. K. (2023). A Philosophical Reflection of SDG 4 and Our Education Policy: Justified Self-Interest vs. Common Interest. In *Positive and Constructive Contributions for Sustainable Development Goals* (pp. 200–219). IGI Global.

Chowdhury, J. S., Saad, M. R. M., Abd Wahab, H., & Roy, P. K. (2023b). An Introduction to the Critique of Critical Paradigm: Jürgen Habermas and Social Justice. In *Implications of Marginalization and Critical Race Theory on Social Justice* (pp. 49–67). IGI Global. DOI: 10.4018/978-1-6684-3615-8.ch003

Chowdhury, J. S., Wahab, H. A., Saad, R. M., Reza, H., & Ahmad, M. M. (Eds.). (2022). *Reciprocity and its practice in social research*. IGI Global. DOI: 10.4018/978-1-7998-9602-9

Cima, F., Pazos, P., Kidd, J., Gutierrez, K., Ringleb, S., Ayala, O., & Kaipa, K. (2021). Enhancing preservice teachers' intention to integrate engineering through a cross-disciplinary model. *Journal of Pre-College Engineering Education Research (J-PEER), 11*(2).

Claiborne, L. (2020). Beyond Inclusion/Exclusion in Teaching about Difference: Entanglements at the Edge of Practice. In *Moving Towards Inclusive Education* (pp. 181–201). Brill. DOI: 10.1163/9789004432789_013

Clammer, J., & Giri, A. K. (2013). *Philosophy and Anthropology in Dialogues and Conversations. Philosophy and Anthropology. Border Crossing and Transformations*. Anthem Press.

Clark, A. M., Zhan, M., Dellinger, J. T., & Semingson, P. L. (2023). Innovating teaching practice through professional learning communities: Determining knowledge sharing and program value. *SAGE Open*, 13(4), 21582440231200983. Advance online publication. DOI: 10.1177/21582440231200983

Clarke, D., & Hollingsworth, H. (2020). Building teacher professional development in the age of remote learning. *Teaching and Teacher Education*, 95, 103160. DOI: 10.1016/j.tate.2020.103160

Clifford, J., & Marcus, G. E. (1986). *Writing Culture: The Poetics and Politics of Ethnography*. University of California Press. DOI: 10.1525/9780520946286

Cochran, K. F., DeRuiter, J. A., & King, R. A. (1993). *Pedagogical content knowing: An integrative model for teacher preparation*. American Educational Research Association.

Cochran, K., King, R., & DeRuiter, J. (1993). Pedagogical Content Knowledge: A Tentative for Teacher preparation. *Journal of Teacher Education*, 44(4), 263–277. DOI: 10.1177/0022487193044004004

Collins, A., Brown, S. J., & Newman, S. E. (1995). *L'apprendistato cognitivo. Per insegnare a leggere, scrivere e far di conto*. Ambrosiana.

Computer Science Teachers Association. CSTA K-12 Computer Science Standards, Revised 2017. 2017. Retrieved from http://www.csteachers.org/standards

Comstock, M., Litke, E., Hill, K. L., & Desimone, L. M. (2023). A culturally responsive disposition: How professional learning and teachers' beliefs

Conceição, T., Baptista, M., & Ponte, J. (2021). Examining pre-service science teachers' pedagogical content knowledge through lesson study. *Eurasia Journal of Mathematics, Science and Technology Education*, 18(1), em2060. Advance online publication. DOI: 10.29333/ejmste/11442

Cong-Lem, N. (2024). Teacher agency for change and development in higher education: A scoping literature review. *International Journal of Educational Reform*, 0(0), 10567879231224744. Advance online publication. DOI: 10.1177/10567879231224744

Cooper, A., Levin, B., & Campbell, C. (2009). The growing (but still limited) importance of evidence in education and policy and practice. *Journal of Educational Change*, 10(2-3), 159–171. DOI: 10.1007/s10833-009-9107-0

Corntassel, J.. (2018). *Everyday Acts of Resurgence: People, Places, Practices*. Daykeeper Press.

Corven, J., DiNapoli, J., Willoughby, L., & Hiebert, J. (2022). Long-Term relationships between Mathematics instructional time during teacher preparation and specialized content knowledge. *Journal for Research in Mathematics Education*, 53(4), 277–306. DOI: 10.5951/jresematheduc-2020-0036

Cottini, L. (2017). *Didattica speciale e inclusione scolastica*. Carocci.

Cottini, L. (2019). *Universal Design for Learning e curricolo inclusivo. Imparare a progettare una didattica funzionale ai bisogni della classe e dei singoli*. Giunti EDU.

Cowan, R. (2008). *The Teacher's Grammar of English A Course Book and Reference Guide*. Cambridge University Press.

Cristaldi, G., Quille, K., Csizmadia, A. P., Riedesel, C., Richards, G. M., & Maiorana, F. (2022, March). The intervention, intersection and impact of social sciences theories upon computing education. In *2022 IEEE Global Engineering Education Conference (EDUCON)* (pp. 1561-1570). IEEE. DOI: 10.1109/EDUCON52537.2022.9766704

Crotti, M. (2017). La riflessività nella formazione alla professione docente. *Edetania*, (52), 85–106.

Crotty, M. (1998). The Foundations of Social Research: Meaning and Perspective in the Research Process. *Sage (Atlanta, Ga.)*.

Cuenca, A. (2021). Proposing core practices for social studies teacher education: A qualitative content analysis of inquiry-based lessons. *Journal of Teacher Education*, 72(3), 298–313. DOI: 10.1177/0022487120948046

Culture Learning Alliance [2017] Why STEM can only take us so far? Retrieved July 10, 2020, from https://culturallearningalliance.org.uk/wp-content/uploads/2018/03/CLA-STEAM-Briefing-A4.pdf

Cunningham, J. (2019). Missing the mark: Standardized testing as epistemological erasure in U.S. schooling. *Power and Education*, 11(1), 111–120. DOI: 10.1177/1757743818812093

Curry, M. W. (2008). Critical friends' group: The possibilities and limitations embedded in teacher professional communities aimed at instructional improvement and school reform. *Teachers College Record*, 110(4), 733–774. DOI: 10.1177/016146810811000401

Daly, J. (2019). *How Europe Made the Modern World: Creating the Great Divergence*. Bloomsbury Publishing.

Damiano, E. (1999). *L'azione didattica: per una teoria dell'insegnamento*. Armando.

Daniela, L. (2020). New perspectives on virtual and augmented reality. In *New Perspectives on Virtual and Augmented Reality*. Routledge. DOI: 10.4324/9781003001874

Darling-Hammond, L. (2017). Teacher education and the opportunity gap. *Journal of Teacher Education*, 68(3), 231–245. DOI: 10.1177/0022487117692564

Darling-Hammond, L. (2020). Learning to teach: The role of practice-based teacher education. *Harvard Educational Review*.

Darling-Hammond, L., Schachner, A. C. W., Wojcikiewicz, S. K., & Flook, L. (2023). Educating teachers to enact the science of learning and development. *Applied Developmental Science*, 28(1), 1–21. DOI: 10.1080/10888691.2022.2130506 PMID: 36704361

Das, S., Lekhya, G., Shreya, K., Shekinah, K. L., Babu, K. K., & Boopathi, S. (2024). Fostering Sustainability Education Through Cross-Disciplinary Collaborations and Research Partnerships: Interdisciplinary Synergy. In *Facilitating Global Collaboration and Knowledge Sharing in Higher Education With Generative AI* (pp. 60–88). IGI Global.

Datnow, A., Park, V., Peurach, D. J., & Spillane, J. P. (2022). Research foundation Transforming Education for Holistic Student Development: Learning from Education System (Re) Building around the World.

Datta, D. M. (1997). *The six ways of knowing: A critical study of the Advaita theory of knowledge*. Motilal Banarsidass.

Davis, E. A. (2004). Knowledge integration in science teaching: Analysing teachers' knowledge development. *Research in Science Education, 34,* 21 53. https://doi.org/ DOI: 10.1023/B:RISE.0000021034.01508.b8

Davis, E. A., & Krajcik, J. S. (2005). Designing educative curriculum materials to promote teacher learning. *Educational Researcher*, 34(3), 3–14. DOI: 10.3102/0013189X034003003

Dawkins, K., Dickerson, D., & Butler, S. (2003, April). Pre-service science teachers' pedagogical content knowledge regarding density. *Paper presented at the annual meeting of the American Educational Research Association, Chicago, IL.* https://files.eric.ed.gov/fulltext/ED475827.pdf

De Back, T. T., Tinga, A. M., & Louwerse, M. M. (2023). Learning in immersed collaborative virtual environments: Design and implementation. *Interactive Learning Environments*, 31(8), 5364–5382. DOI: 10.1080/10494820.2021.2006238 de Berg, K. C., & Grieve, C. (1999). Understanding the siphon: An example of the development of pedagogical content knowledge using textbooks and the writings of early scientists. *Australian Science Teachers'. Journal*, 45(4), 19–26.

De Rossi, M., & Trevisan, O. (2018). Technological Pedagogical Content Knowledge in the literature: How TPCK is defined and implemented in initial teacher education. *Italian Journal of Educational Technology*, 26(1), 7–23.

de Sousa Santos, B. (2018). *The end of the cognitive empire: the coming of age of epistemologies of the south*. Duke University Press. DOI: 10.1215/9781478002000

De Wet, C. H. (2021). *The science of Public Administration: a theoretical and meta-theoretical enquiry* (Doctoral dissertation, North-West University (South Africa)).

Deangeli, G. (2024). *La facoltà di scegliere*. Mondadori.

Decroly, O. (1971). *Una scuola per la vita attraverso la vita*. Loescher.

Dei, G. J. S. (2000). *Indigenous Knowledge in Global Contexts: Multiple Readings of Our World*. University of Toronto Press.

Deloria, V. (1969). *Custer died for your sins: An Indian manifesto*. University of Oklahoma Press.

Deloria, V.Jr. (1999). *Spirit and Reason: The Vine Deloria Jr. Reader*. Fulcrum Publishing.

Deloria, V.Jr. (2001). *Power and Place: Indian Education in America*. Fulcrum Publishing.

Demeulenaere, E.. (2021). *Animism and Indigenous Epistemology*. Routledge.

Demeulenaere, E., Yamin-Pasternak, S., Rubinstein, D. H., Lovecraft, A. L., & Ickert-Bond, S. M. (2021). Indigenous spirituality surrounding Serianthes trees in Micronesia: Traditional practice, conservation, and resistance. *Social Compass*, 68(4), 548–561. DOI: 10.1177/00377686211032769

Demoiny, S. B. (2018). Social studies teacher educators who do race work: A racial-pedagogical-content-knowledge analysis. *Social Studies Research & Practice*, 13(3), 330–344. DOI: 10.1108/SSRP-04-2018-0017

Deng, Z. (2018). Pedagogical content knowledge reconceived: Bringing curriculum thinking into the conversation on teachers' content knowledge. *Teaching and Teacher Education*, 72, 155–164. DOI: 10.1016/j.tate.2017.11.021

Depaepe, F., Verschaffel, L., & Kelchtermans, G. (2013). Pedagogical content knowledge: A systematic review of the way in which the concept has pervaded mathematics educational research. *Teaching and Teacher Education*, 34, 12–25. DOI: 10.1016/j.tate.2013.03.001

Department of Education [DfE (a)] (2020) Initial teacher training (ITT): criteria and supporting advice. Retrieved July 9, 2020, from https://www.gov.uk/government/publications/initial-teacher-training-criteria/initial-teacher-training-itt-criteria-and-supporting-advice#c13-suitability

Department of Education [DfE (b)] (2020) Qualified teacher status (QTS): qualified to teach in England. Retrieved July 9, 2020, from https://www.gov.uk/guidance/qualified-teacher-status-qts

Department of Education [DfE (c)] (2020) Early Career Framework. Retrieved July 9, 2020, from https://www.gov.uk/government/publications/early-career-framework

Descartes, R. (1985). *The Philosophical Writings of Descartes* (Vol. I). Cambridge University Press.

Desimone, L. M. (2009). Improving impact studies of teachers' professional development: Toward better conceptualizations and measures. *Educational Researcher*, 38(3), 181–199. DOI: 10.3102/0013189X08331140

Desimone, L. M., & Garet, M. S. (2015). Best practices in professional development: Findings from recent research. *American Educational Research Journal*, 52(3), 375–402. DOI: 10.3102/0002831215577481

Devetak, I., Lorber, E. D., Jurisevic, M., & Glazar, S. A. (2009). Comparing Slovenian year 8 and year 9 elementary school pupils' knowledge of electrolyte chemistry and their intrinsic motivation. *Chemistry Education Research and Practice*, 10(4), 281–290. DOI: 10.1039/B920833J

Dewey, J. (1899). *The School and Society*. University Press.

Dewey, J. (1902). *The Child and the Curriculum*. University of Chicago Press.

Dewey, J. (1916). *Democracy and education: An introduction to the philosophy of education*. Macmillan.

Dewey, J. (1933). *How We Think: A Restatement of the Relation of Reflective Thinking to the Educative Process*. D.C. Heath & Co Publishers.

Di Blas, N., Fabbri, M., & Ferrari, L. (2018). Italian teachers and Technology-Knowledge training. Form@re-Open Journal per la formazione in rete, 18(2), 33-47.

Di Martino, P., & Zan, R. (2010). 'Me and maths': Towards a definition of attitude grounded on students' narratives. *Journal of Mathematics Teacher Education*, 13(1), 27–48. DOI: 10.1007/s10857-009-9134-z

Dieste, J. (2017). *Praise of Historical Anthropology*. Routledge.

Dilley, R. (2010). [Title of the work if available].

Dilley, R. (2010). Reflections on knowledge practices and the problem of ignorance. *Journal of the Royal Anthropological Institute*, 16(s1), S176–S192. DOI: 10.1111/j.1467-9655.2010.01616.x

DiSessa, A. A. (2019). A friendly introduction to "Knowledge in pieces": Modeling types of knowledge and their roles in learning. ICME-13 Monographs, 245-264. https://doi.org/DOI: 10.1007/978-3-030-15636-7_11

Dudley, J. R. (2016). *Spirituality matters in social work: Connecting spirituality, religion, and practice*. Routledge. https://socialwork.uncc.edu/news/2016-08-04/why-spirituality-matters-social-work

Dunn, K. E., & Mulvenon, S. W. (2020). Formative assessment and the role of feedback in educational practice. *Journal of Educational Measurement*, 57(3), 483–501. DOI: 10.1111/jedm.12270

Durairaj, M., Jayakumar, S., Karpagavalli, V., Maheswari, B. U., & Boopathi, S. (2023). Utilization of Digital Tools in the Indian Higher Education System During Health Crises. In *Multidisciplinary Approaches to Organizational Governance During Health Crises* (pp. 1–21). IGI Global. DOI: 10.4018/978-1-7998-9213-7.ch001

Durkheim, E. (1982). *The Rules of Sociological Method* (Halls, W. D., Trans.). Free Press. (Original work published 1895) DOI: 10.1007/978-1-349-16939-9

Duschl, R. (2019). Learning progressions: Framing and designing coherent sequences for STEM education. *Disciplinary and Interdisciplinary Science Education Research*, 1(1), 4. DOI: 10.1186/s43031-019-0005-x

Duschl, R., Maeng, S., & Sezen-Barrie, A. (2011). Learning progressions and teaching sequences: A review and analysis. *Studies in Science Education*, 47(2), 123–182. DOI: 10.1080/03057267.2011.604476

Efros, I. (1942). Saadia's Theory of Knowledge. *Jewish Quarterly Review (Philadelphia, Pa.)*, 33(2), 133–170. DOI: 10.2307/1451990

Eikeland, O. (2006a). Condescending ethics and action research: Extended review article. *Action Research*, 4(1), 37–47. DOI: 10.1177/1476750306060541

Eikeland, O. (2006b). Phrónêsis, Aristotle, and action research. *International Journal of Action Research*, 2(1), 5–53.

Eikeland, O. (2007). From epistemology to Gnoseology–understanding the knowledge claims of action research. *Management Research News*, 30(5), 344–358. DOI: 10.1108/01409170710746346

Ekiz-Kiran, B., Boz, Y., & Alemdar, M. (2021). Development of pre-service teachers' pedagogical content knowledge through a pck-based school experience course. *Chemistry Education Research and Practice*, 22(2), 415–430. DOI: 10.1039/D0RP00225A

Emon, A. M., Levering, M., & Novak, D. (2014). *Natural Law: A Jewish, Christian, and Islamic Trialogue*. Oxford University Press. DOI: 10.1093/acprof:oso/9780198706601.001.0001

Evans, L. (2019). Professional development and reflective teaching: Exploring the intersection of pedagogy and content. *Educational Research Review*, 28, 100–110. DOI: 10.1016/j.edurev.2019.01.002

Evens, M., Elen, J., & Depaepe, F. (2016). Pedagogical content knowledge in the context of foreign and second language teaching: A review of the research literature. *Porta Linguarum*, 26, 187–200. DOI: 10.30827/Digibug.53944

Evens, M., Elen, J., & Depaepe, F. (2017). Effects of opportunities to learn in teacher education on the development of teachers' professional knowledge of french as a foreign language. *Journal of Advances in Education Research*, 2(4), 265–279. DOI: 10.22606/jaer.2017.24007

Evens, R., Hoefler, M., Biber, K., & Lueken, U. (2016). The Iowa Gambling Task in Parkinson's disease: A meta-analysis on effects of disease and medication. *Neuropsychologia*, 91, 163–172. DOI: 10.1016/j.neuropsychologia.2016.07.032 PMID: 27475264

Executive Offices of the President of the United States (2018). *Committee on STEM Education Report*.

Fabbri, L. (2007). *Comunità di pratiche e apprendimento riflessivo. Per una formazione situata*. Carocci.

Fakhry, M. (2002). *Alfarabi, founder of Islamic Neoplatonism: His life, works and influence*. Oneworld.

Fanon, F. (1967). *White skin, black masks*. Grove Press.

Farabi, A. (2001). *The Political Regime* (Mahdi, F., Trans.). University of Chicago Press.

Fariyani, Q., Mubarok, F., Masfuah, S., & Syukur, F. (2020). Pedagogical content knowledge of pre-service physics teachers. *Jurnal Ilmiah Pendidikan Fisika Al-Biruni*, 9(1), 99–107. DOI: 10.24042/jipfalbiruni.v9i1.3409

Fedeli, M. (2019). *Linking Faculty to Organization Development and Change*. Springer.

Felten, P., & Clayton, P. H. (2011). Service-learning. *New Directions for Teaching and Learning*, 2011(128), 75–84. DOI: 10.1002/tl.470

Fernandez, C., & Yoshida, M. (2004). *Lesson study: A Japanese approach to improving mathematics teaching and learning*. Lawrence Erlbaum Associates.

Ferrier, J. F. (1856). *Institutes of metaphysic: the theory of knowing and being*. W. Blackwood and sons.

Fleer, M., & Pramling, N. (2015). *A cultural-historical study of children learning science: Foregrounding affective imagination in play-based settings*. Springer., DOI: 10.1007/978-94-017-9370-4

Fonger, N. L., Stephens, A., Blanton, M., Isler, I., Knuth, E., & Gardiner, A. M. (2017). Developing a learning progression for curriculum, instruction, and student learning: An example from mathematics education. *Cognition and Instruction*, 36(1), 30–55. DOI: 10.1080/07370008.2017.1392965

Forlizzi, L., Lodi, M., Lonati, V., Mirolo, C., Monga, M., Montresor, A., Morpurgo, A., & Nardelli, E. 2018. A core informatics curriculum for Italian compulsory education. In Int'l. Conf. on Informatics in Schools: Situation, Evolution, and Perspectives. Springer, 141–153. DOI: 10.1007/978-3-030-02750-6_11

Fortus, D., & Krajcik, J. (2012). Curriculum coherence and learning progressions. In Fraser, B., Tobin, K., & McRobbie, C. (Eds.), *Second international handbook of science education* (pp. 783–798). Springer., DOI: 10.1007/978-1-4020-9041-7_52

Fortus, D., Shwartz, Y., & Rosenfeld, S. (2016). High school students' meta-modelling knowledge. *Research in Science Education*, 46(4), 787–810. DOI: 10.1007/s11165-015-9480-z

Foucault, M. (1972). *The Archaeology of Knowledge*. Pantheon Books.

Fox, E. A., & Leidig, J. P. (2014). *Digital Libraries Applications: CBIR, Education, Social Networks, Escience/Simulation, and GIS*. Morgan & Claypool Publishers. DOI: 10.1007/978-3-031-02284-5

Fox, R. (2001). Constructivism examined. *Oxford Review of Education*, 27(1), 23–35. DOI: 10.1080/03054980125310

Frabboni, F. (2009). *Un concerto a più voci in onore di un mestiere difficile*. Franco Angeli.

Fraser, S. P. (2016). Pedagogical content knowledge (PCK): Exploring its usefulness for science lecturers in higher education. *Research in Science Education*, 46(1), 141–161. DOI: 10.1007/s11165-014-9459-1

Freeman-Green, S., Williamson, P., & Cornelius, K. E. (2023). Promoting inclusive practices in education: Bridging gaps and fostering independence. *Teaching Exceptional Children*, 56(2), 68–69. DOI: 10.1177/00400599231223785

Fujioka, N. (1991). *(1991). The Method of Classroom Research by the Stop Motion Method*. Gakuji-shupan.

Fuller, B., & Kim, H. (2022). *Systems Thinking to Transform Schools: Identifyig Levers That Lift Educational Quality. Policy Brief*. Center for Universal Education at The Brookings Institution.

Gadamer, H. G. (1975). Truth and Method. *Continuum: an Interdisciplinary Journal on Continuity of Care*.

Gage, N. L. (1978). *The scientific basic of the art of teaching*. Teachers College Press.

Gallagher, K. T. (2021). The philosophy of knowledge. In *The Philosophy of Knowledge*. Fordham University Press. (Original work published 1964)

Gardner, H. (1991). *Aprire le menti. La creatività e i dilemmi dell'educazione*. Feltrinelli.

Garza, R., Alejandro, E. A., Blythe, T., & Fite, K. (2014). Caring for students: What teachers have to say. *ISRN Education*, 2014(4), 1–7. DOI: 10.1155/2014/425856

Gasteiger, H., Bruns, J., Benz, C., Brunner, E., & Sprenger, P. (2020). Mathematical pedagogical content knowledge of early childhood teachers: A standardized situation-related measurement approach. *ZDM Mathematics Education*, 52(2), 193–205. DOI: 10.1007/s11858-019-01103-2

Gebre, E. H., & Polman, J. L. (2020). From "context" to "active contextualization": Fostering learner agency in contextualizing learning through science news reporting. *Learning, Culture and Social Interaction*, 24, 100374. Advance online publication. DOI: 10.1016/j.lcsi.2019.100374

Gess-Newsome, J. (1999). Pedagogical content knowledge: An introduction and orientation. In Gess-Newsome, J., & Lederman, N. G. (Eds.), *Examining pedagogical content knowledge: The construct and its implications for science education* (pp. 3–17). Kluwer Academic., DOI: 10.1007/0-306-47217-1_1

Gess-Newsome, J. (2015). A model of teacher knowledge and its implications for science education research and practice. *Science Education*, 99(1), 50–75. DOI: 10.1002/sce.21125

Gess-Newsome, J., & Carlson, J. (2020). The PCK summit and its aftermath: The growth and impact of the PCK research community. *Journal of Science Teacher Education*, 31(8), 903–911. DOI: 10.1080/1046560X.2020.1832555

Giancola, O., & Salmieri, L. (2024). *Disuguaglianze educative e scelte scolastiche. Teorie, processi e contesti*. Franco Angeli.

Gill, A. (2006). *In search of intuitive knowledge: A comparison of eastern and western epistemology* (Doctoral dissertation, Faculty of Education-Simon Fraser University).

Ginting, D., & Linarsih, A. (2022). Teacher professional development in the perspective of technology pedagogical content knowledge theoretical framework. *Jurnal Visi Ilmu Pendidikan*, 14(1), 1. DOI: 10.26418/jvip.v14i1.49334

Giri, A. K. (2013). Kant and Anthropology. Philosophy and Anthropology: Border Crossing and Transformations, 141.

Godor, B. P. (2021). The many faces of teacher differentiation: Using Q methodology to explore teachers' preferences for differentiated instruction. *Teacher Educator*, 56(1), 43–60. DOI: 10.1080/08878730.2020.1785068

Goldstone, R. L., & Landy, D. H. (2012). The Goldilocks effect: Human infants allocate attention to visual sequences that are neither too simple nor too complex. *PLoS One*, 7(5), e36399. DOI: 10.1371/journal.pone.0036399 PMID: 22649492

Gomez, J. C. (2020). Development of EFL teachers pedagogical content knowledge through action research in a master's program. *Problems of Education in the 21st Century*, 78(4), 533–552.

Goodman, M. (2018). Systems Thinking: What, why, when, where, and how? Online: Leverage Networks https://thesystemsthinker.com/systems-thinking-what-why-when-where-and-how/)

Goodrum, D., Hackling, M., & Rennie, L. (2001). *The status and quality of teaching and learning of science in Australian schools*. Commonwealth of Australia.

Goodyear, P. (2001). *Effective networked learning in higher education: notes and guidelines*. Sidney University Press.

Gordon, H. S. (2002). *The history and philosophy of social Science*. Routledge. DOI: 10.4324/9780203423226

Gore, J., Lloyd, A., & Smith, M. (2014). Professional learning and development in schools. *Review of Educational Research*, 84(1), 1–40. DOI: 10.3102/0034654313496870

Gore, J., Lloyd, A., & Smith, M. (2020). Collaborative practices and professional learning communities: Enhancing teacher practice. *Professional Development in Education*, 46(1), 50–68. DOI: 10.1080/19415257.2019.1601326

Gotwals, A. W., & Cisterna, D. (2022). Formative assessment practice progressions for teacher preparation: A framework and illustrative case. *Teaching and Teacher Education*, 110, 103601. Advance online publication. DOI: 10.1016/j.tate.2021.103601

Gould, S. J. (1994). The Geometer of Race. Discover governmentality. *Annual Review of Anthropology*, 26(1), 163–183.

Grabinger, R. S., & Dunlap, J. C. (1995). Rich environments for active learning: A definition. *Research in Learning Technology*, 3(2), 5–34. DOI: 10.3402/rlt.v3i2.9606

Graham, S. (2019). *The writing workshop: A practical guide*. Heinemann.

Grosfoguel, R. (2013). The structure of knowledge in westernized universities: Epistemic racism/sexism and the four genocides/epistemicides of the long 16th century. *Human Architecture*, 11(1), 73–90.

Große-Heilmann, R., Riese, J., Burde, J., Schubatzky, T., & Weiler, D. (2022). Fostering pre-service physics teachers' pedagogical content knowledge regarding digital media. *Education Sciences*, 12(7), 440. DOI: 10.3390/educsci12070440

Grossman, P. (1990). *The Making of a Teacher: Teacher Knowledge and Teacher Education*. Teachers College Press.

Grossman, P. L. (1990). *The making of a teacher: Teacher knowledge and teacher education*. Teachers College Press.

Grossman, P., Compton, C., Igra, D., Ronfeldt, M., Shahan, E., & Williamson, P. (2018). Teaching practice: A cross-disciplinary perspective. *Teachers College Record*, 120(6), 1–29. DOI: 10.1177/016146811812000601

Grove, J. (2015). Social sciences and humanities faculties 'to close' in Japan after ministerial intervention Universities to scale back liberal arts and social science courses. https://www.timeshighereducation.com/news/social-sciences-and-humanities-faculties-close-japan-after-ministerial-decree

Habermas, J. (1984). The Theory of Communicative Action, Vol. 1: Reason and the Rationalization of Society. Beacon Press.

Hackman, H. W. (2005). Five essential components for social justice education. *Equity & Excellence in Education*, 38(2), 103–109. DOI: 10.1080/10665680590935034

Hagenauer, G., & Volet, S. E. (2014). Teacher-student relationship at university: An important yet under-researched field. *Oxford Review of Education*, 40(3), 370–388. DOI: 10.1080/03054985.2014.921613 PMID: 27226693

Haleem, A., Javaid, M., Qadri, M. A., & Suman, R. (2022). Understanding the role of digital technologies in education: A review. *Sustainable Operations and Computers*, 3, 275–285. DOI: 10.1016/j.susoc.2022.05.004

Hanson, N. R. (1984). *Patterns of Discovery: An Inquiry into the Conceptual Foundations of Science*. Cambridge University Press.

Hanuscin, D. L., Lee, M. H., & Akerson, V. L. (2014). Elementary teachers' pedagogical content knowledge for teaching the nature of science. *Science Education*, 95(1), 1–190.

Harris, J., Mishra, P., & Koehler, M. J. (2009). Teachers' technological pedagogical content knowledge and learning activity types: Curriculum-based technology integration reframed. *Journal of Research on Technology in Education*, 41(4), 393–416. DOI: 10.1080/15391523.2009.10782536

Harris, L. R., Adie, L., & Wyatt-Smith, C. (2022). Learning progression–based assessments: A systematic review of student and teacher uses. *Review of Educational Research*, 92(6), 996–1040. DOI: 10.3102/00346543221081552

Hart, L. C., Alston, A. S., & Murata, A. (Eds.). (2011). *Lesson study research and practice in mathematics education*. Springer., DOI: 10.1007/978-90-481-9941-9

Hashweh, M. Z. (2005). Teacher pedagogical constructions: A reconfiguration of pedagogical content knowledge. *Teachers and Teaching*, 11(3), 273–292. DOI: 10.1080/13450600500105502

Hassel, H., Launius, C., & Rensing, S. (2021). Student learning and principles for assessment. In *A guide to teaching introductory women's and gender studies* (pp. 83–106). Palgrave Macmillan., DOI: 10.1007/978-3-030-71785-8_4

Hatch, L., & Clark, S. K. (2021). A study of the instructional decisions and lesson planning strategies of highly effective rural elementary school teachers. *Teaching and Teacher Education*, 108, 103505. DOI: 10.1016/j.tate.2021.103505

Hatfield, G. (2014). *Descartes and the Meditations*. Routledge.

Hatta, S. (2008). A Reflection on Shulman's Pedagogical Content Knowledge: Following Analyses of Projects Based on 'Pedagogical Reasoning and Action Model' *Bulletin of the Graduate School of Education. Kyoto University Research Information Repository*, 54, 180–192.

Hatta, S. (2009). The development of Lee Shoman's theory of teacher knowledge and learning process. *Journal of Educational Methodology*, 35, 71–81.

Hattie, J. (2020). *Visible learning: Feedback*. Routledge.

Hausfather, S. (2001). Where's the content? The role of content in constructivist teacher education. *Educational Horizons*, 80(1). https://www.jstor.org/stable/42927076

Hegel, G. W. F. (2001). *The Phenomenology of Spirit* (Miller, A. V., Trans.). Oxford University Press. (Original work published 1807)

Heidegger, M. (1962). *Being and Time* (Macquarrie, J., & Robinson, E., Trans.). Harper & Row.

Heissel, J. A., Levy, D. J., & Adam, E. K. (2017). Stress, sleep, and performance on standardized tests: Understudied pathways to the achievement gap. *AERA Open*, 3(3), 2332858417713488. Advance online publication. DOI: 10.1177/2332858417713488

Helleve, I., & Ulvik, M. (2019). Tutors seen through the eyes of mentors assumptions for participation in third space in teacher education. *European Journal of Teacher Education*, 42(2), 1–15. DOI: 10.1080/02619768.2019.1570495

Hemphill, C. (2008). *New York City's Best Public Middle Schools: A Parents' Guide*. Teachers College Press.

Henze, I., van Driel, J. H., & Verloop, N. (2008). Development of experienced science teachers' pedagogical content knowledge of models of the solar system and the universe. *International Journal of Science Education*, 30(10), 1321–1342. DOI: 10.1080/09500690802187017

Herman, A. (2019). *America's STEM crisis threatens our national security*. American Affairs.

Herrera-Pavo, M. Á. (2021). Collaborative learning for virtual higher education. *Learning, Culture and Social Interaction*, 28, 100437. DOI: 10.1016/j.lcsi.2020.100437

Herring, M., Koehler, M., & Mishra, P. (2016). *Handbook of Technological Pedagogical Content Knowledge (TPCK) for Educators*. Routledge. DOI: 10.4324/9781315771328

Hess, D. E. (2009). *Controversy in the classroom: The democratic power of discussion*. Routledge. DOI: 10.4324/9780203878880

Higgins, S., Xiao, Z., & Katsipataki, M. (2012). *The Impact of Digital Technology on Learning: A Summary for the Education Endowment Foundation*. EEF.

Hill, H. C., Ball, D. L., & Schilling, S. G. (2008). Unpacking pedagogical content knowledge: Conceptualizing and measuring teachers' topic-specific knowledge of students. *Journal for Research in Mathematics Education*, 39(4), 372–400. DOI: 10.5951/jresematheduc.39.4.0372

Hill, H. C., Rowan, B., & Ball, D. L. (2005). Effects of teachers' mathematical knowledge for teaching on student achievement. *American Educational Research Journal*, 42(2), 371–406. DOI: 10.3102/00028312042002371

Hobson, A. J., & Malderez, A. (2013). Mentoring and coaching for new teachers. *Teacher Education Quarterly*, 40(4), 1–20.

Hofstein, A., & Lunetta, V. N. (2004). The laboratory in science education: Foundations for the twenty-first century. *Science Education*, 88(1), 28–54. DOI: 10.1002/sce.10106

Honi Soit. (2021, July 13, 2021). Anthropology and Sociology dissolved at UWA as nationwide job losses continue, https://honisoit.com/2021/07/anthropology-and-sociology-dissolved-at-uwa-as-nationwide-job-losses-continue/

Horrigan, P. G. (2007). *Epistemology: An introduction to the philosophy of knowledge*. IUniverse.

Hossain, K. I. (2024). Reviewing the role of culture in English language learning: Challenges and opportunities for educators. *Social Sciences & Humanities Open*, 9, 100781. DOI: 10.1016/j.ssaho.2023.100781

Hossain, M. M., & Robinson, M. G. (2012). *How to motivate U.S. students to pursue STEM (science, technology, engineering, and mathematics) careers*. U.S.-China Education Review.

Huber, S. G., & Skedsmo, G. (2017). Standardization and assessment practices. *Educational Assessment, Evaluation and Accountability*, 29(1), 1–3. DOI: 10.1007/s11092-017-9257-1

Hume, A., & Berry, A. (2011). Constructing CoRes- A strategy for building PCK in pre-service science teacher education. *Research in Science Education*, 41(3), 341–355. DOI: 10.1007/s11165-010-9168-3

Ianes, D. (2023). *Specialità e normalità? Affrontare il dilemma per una scuola equa e inclusiva per tutt*. Erickson.

INAOKA Project. (2022). *Tips of lessons for English Teachers: A message from Ms. Inaoka*. Hamajima-shoten.

Innovation in Initial Teacher Education: EVIDENCE FROM THE ITELab PROJECT (ND).

Jain, J., Ling, L. Y., & Jin, M. S. (2024). A Systematic Review of Pedagogical Content Knowledge for Teaching Nature of Science. *Asian Journal of University Education*, 20(1), 138–151. DOI: 10.24191/ajue.v20i1.25738

Jeff, B., & Vencovská, A. (2016, December). Ancient Indian Logic and Analogy. In *Logic and Its Applications: 7th Indian Conference, ICLA 2017, Kanpur, India, January 5-7, 2017* []). Springer.]. *Proceedings*, 10119, 198.

Jin, H., Mikeska, J., Hokayem, H., & Mavronikolas, E. (2019). Toward coherence in curriculum, instruction, and assessment: A review of learning progression literature. *Science Education*, 103(5), 1206–1234. Advance online publication. DOI: 10.1002/sce.21525

Journell, W. (2016). Teaching politics in secondary education: Engaging with controversial issues in the classroom. *Social Studies*, 107(1), 24–30. DOI: 10.1080/00377996.2015.1132366

Juhler, M. V. (2016). The use of lesson study combined with content representation in the planning of physics lessons during field practice to develop pedagogical content knowledge. *Journal of Science Teacher Education*, 27(5), 533–553. DOI: 10.1007/s10972-016-9473-4

Julie, G. N. (2015). A model of teacher professional knowledge and skill including PCK: Results of the thinking from the PCK Summit. In *Re-Examining Pedagogical Content Knowledge in Science Education* (pp. 28–42). Routledge.

Kähkönen, E., & Hölttä-Otto, K. (2022). From crossing chromosomes to crossing curricula–a biomimetic analogy for cross-disciplinary engineering curriculum planning. *European Journal of Engineering Education*, 47(3), 516–534. DOI: 10.1080/03043797.2021.1953446

Kalaiselvi, D., Ramaratnam, M. S., Kokila, S., Sarkar, R., Anandakumar, S., & Boopathi, S. (2024). Future Developments of Higher Education on Social Psychology: Innovation and Changes. In *Advances in Human and Social Aspects of Technology* (pp. 146–169). IGI Global. DOI: 10.4018/979-8-3693-2569-8.ch008

Kant, I. (1847). The Critique of Pure Reason. (Original work published 1781).

Kant, I. (2013). *Toward Perpetual Peace and Other Writings on Politics, Peace, and History*. Yale University Press.

Kapila, S. (2007). Race matters: Orientalism and religion, India and beyond c. 1770-1880. *Modern Asian Studies*, 41(3), 471–513. DOI: 10.1017/S0026749X06002526

Kawai, C. (2019). From All English to English Rich Classes - Teaching Techniques for Making the Classroom a Communicative Scene. *English Education*, (October), 68–69.

Kaya, O. N. (2009). The nature of relationships among the components of pedagogical content knowledge of pre-service science teachers: 'Ozone layer depletion' as an example. *International Journal of Science Education*, 31(7), 961–988. DOI: 10.1080/09500690801911326

Kelly, K. J., Kast, D. J., Schiksnis, C. A., & Thrash, J. C. (2023). Hands-on Hypoxia: Engaging High School Educators in the science behind Marine Microbial Dynamics in Hypoxic Coastal Areas Through Field and Classroom Experiences. *Current. Journal of Marketing Education*, 38(1).

Kezar, A. J. (2023). *Rethinking leadership in a complex, multicultural, and global environment: New concepts and models for higher education*. Taylor & Francis. DOI: 10.4324/9781003446842

Khan, A., Li, M., & Hu, X. (2021). Action research in education: A review of current practices and future directions. *The Journal of Educational Research*, 114(2), 230–246. DOI: 10.1080/00220671.2020.1833581

Kholid, M. N., Hendriyanto, A., Sahara, S., Muhaimin, L. H., Juandi, D., Sujadi, I., Kuncoro, K. S., & Adnan, M. (2023). A systematic literature review of Technological, Pedagogical and Content Knowledge (TPACK) in mathematics education: Future challenges for educational practice and research. *Cogent Education*, 10(2), 2269047. DOI: 10.1080/2331186X.2023.2269047

Kidd, I. J., Medina, J., & Pohlhaus, G. (2017). *Introduction to the Routledge handbook of epistemic injustice*. Routledge. DOI: 10.4324/9781315212043-1

Kiefer, S. M., & Ellerbrock, C. R. (2012). Fostering an Adolescent-Centered Community Within an Interdisciplinary Team. *Middle Grades Research Journal*, 7(3), 1–17.

Kilic, A. (2024). Examining pre-service science teachers' personal and enacted content knowledge about seasons. *Journal of Theoretical Educational Science*, 17(1), 100–121. DOI: 10.30831/akukeg.1294954

Kilpatrick, J., Swafford, J., & Findell, B. (Eds.). (2001). *Adding it up: Helping children learn mathematics*. National Academy Press.

Kimmerer, R. W. (2013). *Braiding Sweetgrass: Indigenous Wisdom, Scientific Knowledge, and the Teachings of Plants*. Milkweed Editions.

Kind, V. (2009). Pedagogical content knowledge in science education: Perspective and potential for progress. *Studies in Science Education*, 45(2), 169–204. DOI: 10.1080/03057260903142285

Kind, V. (2015). On the beauty of knowing then not knowing: Pinning down the elusive qualities of PCK. In Berry, A., Friedrichsen, P., & Loughran, J. (Eds.), *Re-examining Pedagogical Content Knowledge in Science Education* (pp. 178–195). Routledge., DOI: 10.4324/9781315735665-19

Kind, V. (2015). Preservice science teachers' PCK development during an extended practicum. *Research in Science Education*, 45(5), 851–873. DOI: 10.1007/s11165-014-9444-5

Kind, V. (2019). Science education and inquiry-based learning: Striving for balance. *International Journal of Science Education*, 41(6), 735–752. DOI: 10.1080/09500693.2019.1573466

Kind, V. (2021). The role of pedagogical content knowledge in science education: New perspectives and developments. *Research in Science Education*, 51, 569–586. DOI: 10.1007/s11165-019-09848-3

King, K., Shumow, L., & Lietz, S. (2001). Science education in an urban elementary school: Case studies of teacher beliefs and classroom practices. *Science Education*, 85(2), 465–478. DOI: 10.1002/1098-237X(200103)85:2<89::AID-SCE10>3.0.CO;2-H

King, M. (2016). The Epistemology of Spiritual Happiness. *Journal for the Study of Spirituality*, 6(2), 142–154. DOI: 10.1080/20440243.2016.1235169

King, T. (2016). *The Inconvenient Indian: A Curious Account of Native People in North America*. University of Minnesota Press.

Kleickmann, T., Richter, D., Kunter, M., Elsner, J., Besser, M., Krauss, S., & Baumert, J. (2013). Teachers' content knowledge and pedagogical content knowledge: The role of structural differences in teacher education. *Journal of Teacher Education*, 64(1), 90–106. DOI: 10.1177/0022487112460398

Kleingeld, P. (2014). *Kant and Cosmopolitanism: The Philosophical Ideal of World Citizenship*. Cambridge University Press.

Klopfenstein, L. C., Delpriori, S., Maldini, R., & Bogliolo, A. (2019, October). CodyColor: Design of a Massively Multiplayer Online Game to Develop Computational Thinking Skills. In Extended Abstracts of the Annual Symposium on Computer-Human Interaction in Play Companion Extended Abstracts (pp. 453-458).

Koc, I., & Yager, R. (2016). Preservice teachers' alternative conceptions of science. *Cypriot Journal of Science Education*, 11(3), 144–159. DOI: 10.18844/cjes.v11i3.215

Koehler, M. J., & Mishra, P. (2009). Technological pedagogical content knowledge: A framework for teacher knowledge. *Teachers College Record*, 111(6), 1017–1054. DOI: 10.1177/016146810911100611

Koehler, M. J., & Mishra, P. (2009). What is technological pedagogical content knowledge (TPACK)? *Contemporary Issues in Technology & Teacher Education*, 9(1), 60–70.

Koehler, M. J., Mishra, P., & Cain, W. (2013). What is Technological Pedagogical Content Knowledge (TPACK)? *Journal of Education*, 193(3), 13–19. DOI: 10.1177/002205741319300303

Koehler, M. J., Mishra, P., & Yahya, K. (2007). Tracing the development of teacher knowledge in a design seminar: Integrating content, pedagogy and technology. *Computers & Education*, 49(3), 740–762. DOI: 10.1016/j.compedu.2005.11.012

Kokotsaki, D., Menzies, V., & Wiggins, A. (2016). Project-based learning: A review of the literature. *Improving Schools*, 19(3), 267–277. DOI: 10.1177/1365480216659733

Kolb, D. A. (2014). *Experiential learning: Experience as the source of learning and development*. FT press.

Kolb, D. (1984). *Experiential Learning*. Prentice Hall.

Kolher, W. (1992). *Gestalt Psychology: An Introduction to New Concepts in Modern Psychology*. Liveright Publishing Corporation.

Kolleck, N., Schuster, J., Hartmann, U., & Gräsel, C. (2021). Teachers' professional collaboration and trust relationships: An inferential social network analysis of teacher teams. *Research in Education*, 111(1), 89–107. DOI: 10.1177/00345237211031585

Koller, J. M. (2018). *Asian philosophies*. Routledge. DOI: 10.4324/9781315210254

Komerath, N. M., & Smith, M. J. (2001). Integrated knowledge resources for cross-disciplinary learning. *Session D-7, Proceedings of ICEE.*

Kovach, M. (2009). *Indigenous Methodologies: Characteristics, Conversations, and Contexts*. University of Toronto Press.

Kovach, M. (2021). *Indigenous methodologies: Characteristics, conversations, and contexts*. University of Toronto press.

Kraft, M. A., & Papay, J. P. (2021). Developing teacher expertise through collaborative practice. *Education Policy Analysis Archives*, 29(46), 1–24. DOI: 10.14507/epaa.29.6815

Krall, R., Lott, K. H., & Wymer, C. L. (2009). Inservice elementary and middle school teachers' conceptions of photosynthesis and respiration. *Journal of Science Teacher Education*, 20(1), 41–55. DOI: 10.1007/s10972-008-9117-4

Kranjc Horvat, A., Wiener, J., Schmeling, S., & Borowski, A. (2021). Learning goals of professional development programs at science research institutions: A Delphi study with different stakeholder groups. *Journal of Science Teacher Education*, 33(1), 32–54. DOI: 10.1080/1046560X.2021.1905330

Krishnamoorthy, V., Chandra, S., Rajesha, S., Bhattacharjee, S., Murugan, G., & Sampath, B. (2024). Emerging Startups in the Evolving Industry Landscape by Empowering Entrepreneur Growth: An Agile Marketing Practice. In *Digital Transformation Initiatives for Agile Marketing* (pp. 455–484). IGI Global. DOI: 10.4018/979-8-3693-4466-8.ch017

Kuhn, T. (2012). *The Structure of Scientific Revolutions*. University of Chicago Press. DOI: 10.7208/chicago/9780226458144.001.0001

Kumar, D. D., & Morris, J. D. (2005). Predicting scientific understanding of prospective elementary teachers: Role of gender, education level, courses in science, and attitudes toward science and mathematics. *Journal of Science Education and Technology*, 14(4), 387–391. DOI: 10.1007/s10956-005-8083-2

Kuswandono, P. (2012). Reflective practices for teacher education. LLT Journal: A Journal on Language and Language Teaching, 15(01), 149–162. https://doi.org/ DOI: 10.24071/llt.2012.150102

Kyi, W. W., Errabo, D. D., & Isozaki, T. (2023). A Comparison of Pre-Service Science Teacher Education in Myanmar, the Philippines and Japan. *Education Sciences*, 13(7), 706. DOI: 10.3390/educsci13070706

Kyriakides, L., Christoforou, C., & Charalambous, C. Y. (2013). What matters for student learning outcomes: A meta-analysis of studies exploring factors of effective teaching. *Teaching and Teacher Education*, 36, 143–152. DOI: 10.1016/j.tate.2013.07.010

Laal, M., & Laal, M. (2012). Collaborative learning: What is it? *Procedia: Social and Behavioral Sciences*, 31, 491–495. DOI: 10.1016/j.sbspro.2011.12.092

Laneve, C. (2003). *La didattica tra teoria e pratica*. La Scuola.

Langacker, R. W. (2008). *Cognitive Grammar: A Basic Introduction*. Oxford University Press. DOI: 10.1093/acprof:oso/9780195331967.001.0001

Langelaan, B. N., Gaikhorst, L., Smets, W., & Oostdam, R. J. (2024). Differentiating instruction: Understanding the key elements for successful teacher preparation and development. *Teaching and Teacher Education*, 140, 104464. DOI: 10.1016/j.tate.2023.104464

Laseinde, P. T., & Dada, D. (2023). Enhancing teaching and learning in STEM labs: The development of an Android-based virtual reality platform. *Materials Today: Proceedings*. Advance online publication. DOI: 10.1016/j.matpr.2023.09.020

Laurillard, D. (2014). *Insegnamento come scienza della progettazione. Costruire modelli pedagogici per apprendere con le tecnologie*. Franco Angeli.

Lave, J., & Wenger, E. (1991). *Situated learning: Legitimate peripheral participation*. Cambridge University Press. DOI: 10.1017/CBO9780511815355

Lave, J., & Wenger, E. (2006). *L'apprendimento situato, Dall'osservazione alla partecipazione attiva nei contesti sociali*. Erickson.

Learning, S. T. E. M. (2020). STEM Learning Impact Report 2020. Retrieved July 10, 2020, from https://www.stem.org.uk/impact-and-evaluation/impact

Lee, E. S., & Liu, U. L. (2009). Assessing learning progression of energy concepts across middle school grades: The knowledge integration perspective. *Science Education*, ●●●, 665–688.

Lee, E., Brown, M., Luft, J., & Roehrig, G. (2007). Assessing beginning secondary science teachers' pck: Pilot year results. *School Science and Mathematics*, 107(2), 52–60. DOI: 10.1111/j.1949-8594.2007.tb17768.x

Lee, L. K., Cheung, S. K. S., & Kwok, L. F. (2020). Learning analytics: Current trends and innovative practices. *Journal of Computers in Education*, 7(1), 1–6. DOI: 10.1007/s40692-020-00155-8

Lee, M., & Tsai, C. (2008). Exploring teachers' perceived self efficacy and technological pedagogical content knowledge with respect to educational use of the world wide web. *Instructional Science*, 38(1), 1–21. DOI: 10.1007/s11251-008-9075-4

Lee, O., Luykx, A., Buxton, C., & Shaver, A. (2007). The challenge of altering elementary school teachers' beliefs and practices regarding linguistic and cultural diversity in science education. *Journal of Research in Science Teaching*, 44(9), 1269–1291. DOI: 10.1002/tea.20198

Levin, M., & Greenwood, D. (2011). Revitalizing universities by reinventing the social sciences. *Handbook of Qualitative Inquiry*, 27-42.

Levy, A. J., Pasquale, M. M., & Marco, L. (2008). Models of providing science instruction in the elementary grades: A research agenda to inform decision makers. *Science Educator*, 17(2), 1–18.

Lewis, M. (2002). *The English Verb*. Heinle Cengage Learning.

Li, G. X. W. (2016). An empirical study on college english teacher's tpack: theory and application. IOSR Journal of Engineering, 06(04), 01-04. https://doi.org/DOI: 10.9790/3021-06410104

Li, L., & Ruppar, A. (2021). Conceptualizing teacher agency for inclusive education: A systematic and international review. *Teacher Education and Special Education*, 44(1), 42–59. DOI: 10.1177/0888406420926976

Lin, S., & Wang, J. (2024). Development and application of an instrument for assessing upper-secondary school biology teachers' pedagogical content knowledge of scientific thinking. *Journal of Baltic Science Education*, 23(3), 495–517. Advance online publication. DOI: 10.33225/jbse/24.23.495

Liu, M., Hedges, H., & Cooper, M. (2023). Effective collaborative learning for early childhood teachers: Structural, motivational and sustainable features. *Professional Development in Education*, 50(2), 420–438. DOI: 10.1080/19415257.2023.2235578

Locke, J. (1847). An Essay Concerning Human Understanding. (Original work published 1690).

Lortie, D. (2002). *Schoolteacher: a sociological study*. University of Chicago Press. DOI: 10.7208/chicago/9780226773230.001.0001

Lotter, C., Singer, J., & Godley, J. (2009). The influence of repeated teaching and reflection on preservice teachers' views of inquiry and nature of science. *Journal of Science Teacher Education*, 20(6), 553–582. DOI: 10.1007/s10972-009-9144-9

Loughran, J. J., Berry, A. K., & Mulhall, P. J. (2006). *Understanding and developing science teachers' pedagogical content knowledge*. Sense. DOI: 10.1163/9789087903657

Loughran, J. J., Berry, A. K., & Mulhall, P. J. (2012). *Understanding and developing science teachers pedagogical content knowledge* (2nd ed.). Sense Publishers. DOI: 10.1007/978-94-6091-821-6

Loughran, J. J., Mulhall, P., & Berry, A. (2004). In search of pedagogical content knowledge in science: Developing ways of articulating and documenting professional practice. *Journal of Research in Science Teaching*, 41(4), 370–391. DOI: 10.1002/tea.20007

Loughran, J., & Berry, A. (2005). Modelling by teacher educators. *Teaching and Teacher Education*, 21(2), 193–203. DOI: 10.1016/j.tate.2004.12.005

Lowery, N. V. (2002). Construction of teacher knowledge in context: Preparing elementary teachers to teach mathematics and science. *School Science and Mathematics*, 102(2), 68–83. DOI: 10.1111/j.1949-8594.2002.tb17896.x

Lucenario, J., Yangco, R., Punzalan, A., & Espinosa, A. (2016). Pedagogical content knowledge-guided lesson study: Effects on teacher competence and students' achievement in chemistry. *Education Research International*, 2016, 1–9. DOI: 10.1155/2016/6068930

Luera, G. R., Moyer, R. H., & Everett, S. A. (2005). What type and level of science content knowledge of elementary education students affect their ability to construct an inquiry- based science lesson? *Journal of Elementary Science Education*, 17(1), 12–25. DOI: 10.1007/BF03174670

Lumpkin, A., & Favor, J. (2012). Comparing the academic performance of high school athletes and non-athletes in Kansas in 2008-2009. *Journal of Sport Administration & Supervision*, 4(1), 41–62.

Lundy, S. E. (2014). *Leveraging digital technology in social studies education* (Doctoral dissertation, Portland State University).

MacIntyre, A. (1984). *After Virtue: A Study in Moral Theory*. University of Notre Dame Press.

MacKenzie, M. (2022). *Buddhist Philosophy and the Embodied Mind: A Constructive Engagement*. Rowman & Littlefield. DOI: 10.5771/9781538160138

Maiorana, F. P. (2023). Perspectives on Computer Science Education.

Maiorana, F., & Cristaldi, G. (2023) From Data to Coding and responsible digital citizenship: the design of a learning journey. VI Seminar "INVALSI data: a tool for teaching and scientific research"

Maiorana, F., Altieri, S., Colli, A., Labbri, M., Nicolini, M., Nazzaro, L., Porta, M., Severi, A., & Guida, M. (2020b). "Scientix teacher ambassadors: A passionate and creative professional community linking research and practice." In *ICERI2020 Proceedings*, pp. 7461-7470. IATED, 2020. DOI: 10.21125/iceri.2020.1610

Maiorana, F., Csizmadia, A., & Richards, G. (2020). P12 Computing in Italy, England and Alabama, USA. Proceedings of the 21st Annual Conference on IT Education (SIGITE).

Maiorana, F. (2019). Interdisciplinary Computing for STE(A)M: A low Floor high ceiling curriculum. Innovations. *Technologies and Research in Education*, 37, 37–52. Advance online publication. DOI: 10.22364/atee.2019.itre.03

Maiorana, F., Nazzaro, L., Severi, A., Colli, A., Porta, M., Cristaldi, G., & Labbri, M. (2022). Reflections on inclusive leadership education: From professional communities of practices to students. *IUL Research*, 3(5), 324–337.

Maiorana, F., Richards, G., Lucarelli, C., Berry, M., & Ericson, B. (2019, July). Interdisciplinary Computer Science Pre-service Teacher Preparation: Panel. In *Proceedings of the 2019 ACM Conference on Innovation and Technology in Computer Science Education* (pp. 332-333). DOI: 10.1145/3304221.3325543

Mandrioli, D., Torrebruno, A., & Marini, L. (2010, April). Computers Foster Education and Education Fosters Computer Science-The Politecnico's Approach. In CSEDU (2) (pp. 289-296).

Mangiatordi, A. (2017). *Didattica senza barriere. Universal Design, tecnologie e risorse sostenibili*. ETS.

Mangione, G. R., Pettenati, M. C., & Rosa, A. (2016). Anno di formazione e prova: analisi del modello italiano alla luce della letteratura scientifica e delle esperienze internazionali. Form@ re, 16(2), 47-64.

Mansor, R., Halim, L., & Osman, K. (2010). Teachers' knowledge that promote students' conceptual understanding. *Procedia: Social and Behavioral Sciences*, 9, 1835–1839. DOI: 10.1016/j.sbspro.2010.12.410

Mapulanga, T., Nshogoza, G., & Ameyaw, Y. (2022). Teachers' perceived enacted pedagogical content knowledge in biology at selected secondary schools in lusaka. International Journal of Learning. *Teaching and Educational Research*, 21(10), 418–435. DOI: 10.26803/ijlter.21.10.23

Margiotta, U. (2007). *Insegnare nella società della conoscenza*. Pensa Multimedia.

Margiotta, U. (2014). Insegnare oggi all'Università. Un master per la didattica universitaria, Formazione e insegnamento. *XII*, 1, 89–106.

Mariani, A. (2021). *La relazione educativa. Prospettive contemporanee*. Carocci.

Marzano, A. (2013). *L'azione d'insegnamento per lo sviluppo di competenze*. Pensa Multimedia.

Matilal, B. K. (2017). *Epistemology, logic, and grammar in Indian philosophical analysis*. De Gruyter Mouton.

Mavhunga, E. (2020). Revealing the structural complexity of component interactions of topic- specific PCK when planning to teach. *Research in Science Education*, 50(3), 965–986. DOI: 10.1007/s11165-018-9719-6

Max, A.-L., Weitzel, H., & Lukas, S. (2023). Factors influencing the development of pre-service science teachers' technological pedagogical content knowledge in a pedagogical makerspace. *Frontiers in Education*, 8, 1166018. DOI: 10.3389/feduc.2023.1166018

Mazibe, E. N., Gaigher, E., & Coetzee, C. (2023). Exploring dynamic pedagogical content knowledge across fundamental concepts of electrostatics. *Eurasia Journal of Mathematics, Science and Technology Education*, 19(3), em2241. Advance online publication. DOI: 10.29333/ejmste/13023

McCrea, N., Meade, R. R., & Shaw, M. (2017). Solidarity, organising and tactics of resistance in the 21st century: Social movements and community development praxis in dialogue. *Community Development Journal: An International Forum*, 52(3), 385–404. DOI: 10.1093/cdj/bsx029

McDonald Connor, C., Piasta, S. B., Fishman, B., Glasney, S., Schatschneider, C., Crowe, E., Underwood, P., & Morrison, F. J. (2009). Individualizing student instruction precisely: Effects of child× instruction interactions on first graders' literacy development. *Child Development*, 80(1), 77–100. DOI: 10.1111/j.1467-8624.2008.01247.x PMID: 19236394

McGaw, M. A. D. (2024). Professional Content Knowledge: Increasing Instructional Quality. In *Cases on Economics Education and Tools for Educators* (pp. 121–135). IGI Global.

Mecoli, S. (2013). The influence of the pedagogical content knowledge theoretical framework on research on preservice teacher education. *Journal of Education*, 193(3), 21–27. DOI: 10.1177/002205741319300304

Meghji, A. (2022). Towards a theoretical synergy: Critical race theory and decolonial thought in Trumpamerica and Brexit Britain. *Current Sociology*, 70(5), 647–664. DOI: 10.1177/0011392120969764

Melka, Y., & Jatta, I. (2022). High school students' perceptions towards efl teachers' differentiated instructional practices at higher 23 secondary school, addis ababa, ethiopia. *Education Journal*, 11(2), 75. DOI: 10.11648/j.edu.20221102.14

Mensch, J. (2018). *Race and Racism in Continental Philosophy*. Indiana University Press.

Mensch, R. J. (2000). Kant and Blumenbach on the Bildungstrieb: A historical misunderstanding. *Studies in History and Philosophy of Science Part C Studies in History and Philosophy of Biological and Biomedical Sciences*, 31(1), 11–32. DOI: 10.1016/S1369-8486(99)00042-4

Merriam-Webster (2022). "Gnoseology." *Merriam-Webster.com Dictionary*, Merriam-Webster, https://www.merriam-webster.com/dictionary/gnoseology. Accessed 12 Jul. 2022.

Merriam-Webster. (2022). Gnoseology. In Merriam-Webster.com dictionary. Retrieved from https://www.merriam-webster.com

Merritt, J., & Krajcik, J. (2013). Learning progression developed to support students in building a particle model of matter. In Tsaparlis, G., & Sevian, H. (Eds.), *Concepts of matter in science education* (pp. 11–45). Springer., DOI: 10.1007/978-94-007-5914-5_2

Meyer, A., Rose, D. H., & Gordon, D. (2014). *Universal Design for Learning: theory and practice*. CAST.

Mickelson, R. A., & Bottia, M. (2009). Integrated education and mathematics outcomes: A synthesis of social science research. *North Carolina Law Review*, 88, 993.

Mignolo, W. D. (2012). *The Darker Side of Western Modernity: Global Futures, Decolonial Options*. Duke University Press.

Miller, D. I., Pinerua, I., Margolin, J., & Gerdeman, D. (2022). *Teachers' Pedagogical Content Knowledge in Mathematics and Science: A Cross-Disciplinary Synthesis of Recent DRK-12 Projects*. American Institutes for Research.

Mills, S. (2016). Conceptual understanding: A concept analysis. *The Qualitative Report*, 21(3), 546–557. DOI: 10.46743/2160-3715/2016.2308

Ministerial Decree 214 of 12 June 2020 - Modes and contents of the single-cycle degree tests in Primary Education Sciences A.A. 2020/2021Retrived July 10, 2020 from https://www.miur.gov.it/web/guest/-/decreto-ministeriale-n-214-del-12-giugno-2020-modalita-e-contenuti-delle-prove-di-ammissione-al-corso-di-laurea-a-ciclo-unico-in-scienze-della-formazione

Minner, D. D., Levy, A. J., & Century, J. (2010). Inquiry-based science instruction—What is it and does it matter? *Journal of Research in Science Teaching*, 47(4), 474–496. DOI: 10.1002/tea.20347

Mishra, P., & Koehler, M. J. (2006). Technological Pedagogical Content. Knowledge: A Framework for Teacher Knowledge. *Teachers College Record*, 108(6), 1017–1054. DOI: 10.1111/j.1467-9620.2006.00684.x

Mishra, P., Koehler, M. J., & Henriksen, D. (2011). The Seven Trans-Disciplinary Habits of Mind: Extending the TPACK Framework towards 21st Century Learning. *Educational Technology*, 51(2), 22–28.

Mishra, P., Koehler, M. J., & Henriksen, D. (2020). The role of technological pedagogical content knowledge in the 21st century classroom. *Educational Technology*, 60(1), 3–12. DOI: 10.1007/s11423-020-09701-x

Mitchell, S. (2006). Socratic dialogue, the humanities and the art of the question. *Arts and Humanities in Higher Education*, 5(2), 181–197. DOI: 10.1177/1474022206063653

Mizuno, K. (2020). *Explorations of cultural and educational values of Graded Readers in English education in Japan*. Tokyo: Kuroshio-shupan Ministry of Education, Culture, Sports, Science and Technology. (2017). *Course of Study for Junior High Schools: Foreign Languages – English.* https://www.mext.go.jp/component/a_menu/education/micro_detail/__icsFiles/afieldfile/2019/03/18/1387018_010.pdf (Date of Viewing: October 25, 2023)

Moats, L. C. (2020). *Speech to print: Language essentials for teachers*. Brookes Publishing.

Moore, B., Boardman, A. G., Smith, C., & Ferrell, A. (2019). Enhancing collaborative group processes to promote academic literacy and content learning for diverse learners through video reflection. *SAGE Open*, 9(3), 2158244019861480. Advance online publication. DOI: 10.1177/2158244019861480

Moosavi, L. (2020). The decolonial bandwagon and the dangers of intellectual decolonisation. *International Review of Sociology*, 30(2), 332–354. DOI: 10.1080/03906701.2020.1776919

Mora-Flores, E., & Kaplan, S. N. (2022). Interdisciplinary learning: Connecting language and literacy across the curriculum. *Gifted Child Today*, 45(2), 110–112. DOI: 10.1177/10762175211070845

Morin, E. (2001). *I sette saperi necessari all'educazione del futuro*. Raffaello Cortina.

Morrell, P. D., & Carroll, J. B. (2003). An extended examination of preservice elementary teachers' science teaching self-efficacy. *School Science and Mathematics*, 103(5), 246–251. DOI: 10.1111/j.1949-8594.2003.tb18205.x

Morrison, K. M. (2014). Animism and a proposal for a post-Cartesian anthropology. In *The handbook of contemporary animism* (pp. 38–52). Routledge.

Moscovici, H., & Osisioma, I. (2008). Designing the best urban preservice elementary science methods course: Dilemmas and considerations. *Journal of Elementary Science Education*, 20(4), 15–28. DOI: 10.1007/BF03173674

Mullis, I., & Jenkins, L. (1988).

National Center for Science and Engineering Statistics. (2019). https://ncses.nsf.gov/

National Council for the Social Studies. (2017). College, Career, and Civic Life (C3) Framework for Social Studies State Standards. National Council for the Social Studies. https://www.socialstudies.org/c3

National Research Council (NRC). (2012). *Framework for K-12 Science Education.* National Academies Press.

National Standards. (2019). Retrieved May 24, 2019, from https://www.educationworld.com/standards/

National Survey of Science and Mathematics Education. (2018). *Report of the 2018 NSSME+.* https://horizon-research.com/NSSME/2018-nssme/research-products/reports

Ndukwe, I. G., & Daniel, B. K. (2020). Teaching analytics, value, and tools for teacher data literacy: A systematic and tripartite approach. *International Journal of Educational Technology in Higher Education*, 17(1), 22. DOI: 10.1186/s41239-020-00201-6

Nesta (2014). Fix the pipeline for STEAM talent in the creative economy. Retrieved July 10, 2020, from https://www.nesta.org.uk/blog/fix-the-pipeline-for-steam-talent-in-the-creative-economy/

Newton, D. P., & Newton, L. D. (2001). Subject content knowledge and teacher talk in the primary science classroom. *European Journal of Teacher Education*, 24(3), 369–379. DOI: 10.1080/02619760220128914

Ngoasong, M. Z. (2022). Curriculum adaptation for blended learning in resource-scarce contexts. *Journal of Management Education*, 46(4), 622–655. DOI: 10.1177/10525629211047168

Ngubane, T. (2024). Influence of Teacher Training Programs on Quality of Education in South Africa. *African Journal of Education and Practice*, 9(2), 46–55. DOI: 10.47604/ajep.2524

Nguyen, L. C., Thuan, H. T., & Giang, T. T. H. (2023). Application of G. Polya's problem-solving process in teaching high-school physics. *Journal of Law and Society*, 4(1), 26–33. DOI: 10.37899/journal-la-sociale.v4i1.761

Niess, M. L. (2005). Preparing teachers to teach science and mathematics with technology: Developing a technology pedagogical content knowledge. *Teaching and Teacher Education*, 21(5), 509–523. DOI: 10.1016/j.tate.2005.03.006

Nilsson, P. (2008). Teaching for understanding; The complex nature of pedagogical content knowledge in pre-service education. *International Journal of Science Education*, 30(10), 1281–1299. DOI: 10.1080/09500690802186993

Nilsson, P., & Karlsson, G. (2018). Capturing student teachers' pedagogical content knowledge (PCK) using CoRes and digital technology. *International Journal of Science Education*, 41(4), 419–447. DOI: 10.1080/09500693.2018.1551642

Nilsson, P., & Loughran, J. (2011). Exploring the development of pre-service science elementary teachers' pedagogical content knowledge. *Journal of Science Teacher Education*, 23(7), 669–721. DOI: 10.1007/s10972-011-9239-y

Nind, M. (2020). A new application for the concept of pedagogical content knowledge: Teaching advanced social science research methods. *Oxford Review of Education*, 46(2), 185–2020. DOI: 10.1080/03054985.2019.1644996

Nowicki, B. L., Sullivan-Watts, B., Shim, M. K., Young, B., & Pockalny, R. (2012). Factors influencing science content accuracy in elementary inquiry science lessons. *Research in Science Education*, 43(3), 1135–1154. DOI: 10.1007/s11165-012-9303-4

Nowicki, J., & Bernstein, L. (1994). *Psychometric theory* (3rd ed.). McGraw-Hill.

Nyisztor, D., & Marcus, B. (2008). Concepts and content belong in early childhood education. *Canadian Children*, 33(2), 16–19.

O'Dwyer, A., & Childs, P. (2014). Organic chemistry in action! Developing an intervention program for introductory chemistry to improve learners' understanding, interest, and attitudes. *Journal of Chemical Education*, 91(7), 987–993. DOI: 10.1021/ed400538p

Oberdörfer, S., Birnstiel, S., Latoschik, M., & Grafe, S. (2021). Mutual benefits: Interdisciplinary education of pre-service teachers and hci students in vr/ar learning environment design. *Frontiers in Education*, 6, 693012. Advance online publication. DOI: 10.3389/feduc.2021.693012

Odonkor, T. N., Eziamaka, N. V., & Akinsulire, A. A. (2024). *Strategic mentorship programs in fintech software engineering for developing industry leaders.*

OECD. (2019b). Teachers' Professional Learning (TPL) Study. https://doi.org/DOI: 10.1787/888934026677

OECD. (2021b). OECD SCHOOLING, TEACHERS AND TEACHING PROJECT. https://www.oecd.org/education/school-resources-review/Schooling,%20Teachers%20and%20Teaching%20Project%20Description.pdf

OECD/OPSI global trend 2020 Upskilling and investing in people—Google Search. (n.d.). Retrieved 4 June 2023, from https://trends.oecd-opsi.org/trend-reports/upskilling-and-investing-in-people/

Orosco, J. S. (2014). *Examination of gamification: Understanding performance as it relates to motivation and engagement*. Colorado Technical University.

Ozden, M. (2008). The effect of content knowledge on pedagogical content knowledge: The case of teaching phases of matters. *Kuram ve Uygulamada Egitim Bilimleri*, 8, 611–645.

Özel, Z., Yılmaz, A., Işıksal-Bostan, M., & Özkan, B. (2022). Investigation of the Specialized Content Knowledge of the Pre-service Primary School Teachers about Multiplication. *International Journal for Mathematics Teaching and Learning*, 23(2), 115–143. DOI: 10.4256/ijmtl.v23i2.464

Oztay, E. S., & Boz, Y. (2021). Interaction between pre-service chemistry teachers' pedagogical content knowledge and content knowledge in electrochemistry. *Journal of Pedagogical Research*, 6(1), 1. Advance online publication. DOI: 10.33902/JPR.2022.165

Pak, K., Polikoff, M. S., Desimone, L. M., & Saldívar García, E. (2020). The adaptive challenges of curriculum implementation: Insights for educational leaders driving standards-based reform. *AERA Open*, 6(2), 2332858420932828. Advance online publication. DOI: 10.1177/2332858420932828

Pamintuan, C. F. (2024). Investigating the classroom implementation of Mandarin teachers' pedagogical content knowledge (PCK): Exploring effective strategies and practices for teaching Chinese as a foreign language in the Philippines. *International Journal of Language Education*, 8(1), 112–126. DOI: 10.26858/ijole.v8i1.60912

Panizzon, D., Pegg, J., Arthur, D., & McCloughan, G. (2021). Designing a developmental progression to assess students' conceptual understandings by focusing on the language demands in science. *Australian Journal of Education*, 65(3), 265–279. DOI: 10.1177/00049441211036518

Panke, S. (2019). Design thinking in education: Perspectives, opportunities, and challenges. *Open Education Studies*, 1(1), 281–306. DOI: 10.1515/edu-2019-0022

Papadouris, N., Hadjigeorgiou, A., & Constantinou, C. P. (2014). Pre-service elementary school teachers' ability to account for the operation of simple physical systems using the energy conservation law. *Journal of Science Teacher Education*, 25(8), 911–933. DOI: 10.1007/s10972-014-9407-y

Papantonis Stajcic, M., & Nilsson, P. (2023). Teachers' considerations for a digitalised learning context of preschool science. *Research in Science Education*, 54(3), 499–521. DOI: 10.1007/s11165-023-10150-5

Paparella, N. (2011). *Insegnare per competenze in università. Modelli, procedure, metodi*. Pensa Multimedia.

Park, S., & Chen, Y. C. (2012). Mapping out the integration of the components of pedagogical content knowledge (PCK): Examples from high school biology classrooms. *Journal of Research in Science Teaching*, 49(7), 922–941. DOI: 10.1002/tea.21022

Park, S., & Oliver, J. S. (2008). Revisiting the conceptualization of pedagogical content knowledge (PCK): PCK as a conceptual tool to understand teachers as professionals. *Research in Science Education*, 38(3), 261–284. DOI: 10.1007/s11165-007-9049-6

Park, S., & Oliver, J. S. (2008). Revisiting the conceptualization of pedagogical content knowledge. *Journal of Science Teacher Education*, 19(3), 257–277. DOI: 10.1007/s10972-008-9103-7

Parricchi, M. (2021). *Tempi e spazi della vita e dell'educazione. Cesare Scurati. Sguardi sull'educazione*. FrancoAngeli.

Peers, C. E., Diezmann, C. M., & Watters, J. J. (2003). Supports and concerns for teacher professional growth during the implantation of a science curriculum innovation. *Research in Science Education*, 33(1), 89–110. DOI: 10.1023/A:1023685113218

Pels, P. (1997). The anthropology of colonialism: Culture, history, and the emergence of western governmentality. *Annual Review of Anthropology*, 26(1), 163–183. DOI: 10.1146/annurev.anthro.26.1.163

Pels, P. (2008). What has anthropology learned from the anthropology of colonialism? *Social Anthropology*, 16(3), 280–299. DOI: 10.1111/j.1469-8676.2008.00046.x

Perla, L. (2010). *Didattica dell'implicito. Ciò che l'insegnante non sa*. La Scuola.

Perla, L. (2014). *I nuovi Licei alla prova delle competenze. Guida alla progettazione nel primo biennio*. Pensa Multimedia.

Perpignan, C., Baouch, Y., Robin, V., & Eynard, B. (2020). Engineering education perspective for sustainable development: A maturity assessment of cross-disciplinary and advanced technical skills in eco-design. *Procedia CIRP*, 90, 748–753. DOI: 10.1016/j.procir.2020.02.051

Perrenoud, P. (1994). *La formation des enseignants entre theorie et pratique*. L'Harmattan.

Perrett, R. W. (1998). *Hindu ethics: A philosophical study* (Vol. 17). University of Hawaii Press. DOI: 10.1515/9780824847043

Petticrew, M., & Roberts, H. (2008). *Systematic reviews in the social sciences: A practical guide.* John Wiley & Sons.

Piaget, J. (1936). *Origins of intelligence in the child.* Routledge & Kegan Paul.

Piaget, J. (1964). Cognitive development in children: Development and learning. *Journal of Research in Science Teaching,* 2(3), 176–186. DOI: 10.1002/tea.3660020306

Pierce, R., & Stacey, K. (2010). Mapping the landscape of teachers' professional development and technology integration. *Educational Studies in Mathematics,* 73(2), 245–262. DOI: 10.1007/s10649-010-9255-4

Pitsia, V., Karakolidis, A., & Lehane, P. (2021). Investigating the use of assessment data by primary school teachers: Insights from a large-scale survey in Ireland. *Educational Assessment,* 26(3), 145–162. DOI: 10.1080/10627197.2021.1917358

Pongsanon, K., Akerson, V., & Rogers, M. (2011). *Exploring the use of lesson study to develop elementary preservice teachers' pedagogical content knowledge for teaching nature of science.* Paper presented at the National Association for Research in Science Teaching, Orlando, Fl.: NARST.

Popa, N. (2022). Operationalizing historical consciousness: A review and synthesis of the literature on meaning making in historical learning. *Review of Educational Research,* 92(2), 171–208. DOI: 10.3102/00346543211052333

Posner, G. J., Strike, K. A., Hewson, P. W., & Gertzog, W. A. (1982). Accommodation of scientific conception: Toward a theory of conceptual change. *Science Education,* 66(2), 211–227. DOI: 10.1002/sce.3730660207

Potvin, P., & Cyr, G. (2017). Toward a durable prevalence of scientific conceptions: Tracking the effects of two interfering misconceptions about buoyancy from preschoolers to science teachers. *Journal of Research in Science Teaching,* 54(9), 1121–1142. Advance online publication. DOI: 10.1002/tea.21396

Poulou, M. S., Reddy, L. A., & Dudek, C. M. (2023). Teachers and school administrators' experiences with professional development feedback: The classroom strategies assessment system implementation. *Frontiers in Psychology,* 14, 1074278. DOI: 10.3389/fpsyg.2023.1074278 PMID: 36910749

Poulton, P. (2020). Teacher agency in curriculum reform: The role of assessment in enabling and constraining primary teachers' agency. *Curriculum Perspectives,* 40(1), 35–48. DOI: 10.1007/s41297-020-00100-w

Prabhuswamy, M., Tripathi, R., Vijayakumar, M., Thulasimani, T., Sundharesalingam, P., & Sampath, B. (2024). A Study on the Complex Nature of Higher Education Leadership: An Innovative Approach. In *Challenges of Globalization and Inclusivity in Academic Research* (pp. 202–223). IGI Global. DOI: 10.4018/979-8-3693-1371-8.ch013

Programme for International Student Assessment. PISA (2015). *Results, excellence and equity in education, 1* OECD Publishing.

Pyrialakou, V. D., Dey, K., Martinelli, D., Deskins, J., Fraustino, J. D., Plein, C., Rahman, M. T., Rambo-Hernandez, K. E., & Roy, A. (2020). Holistic engineering: A concept exploration in a cross-disciplinary project course experience. *2020 ASEE North Central Section Conference*. DOI: 10.18260/1-2--35736

Rahal, M., Alsharif, N. Z., Younes, S., Sakr, F., Mourad, N., Halat, D. H., Akel, M., & Jomha, I. (2023). The assessment of mentorship programs on pharmacy students' leadership roles and performance in experiential education. *Pharmacy Practice*, 21(3), 21. DOI: 10.18549/PharmPract.2023.3.2853

Ranz, R. (2021). Developing Social Work Students' Awareness of their Spiritual/Religious Identity and Integrating It into Their Professional Identity: Evaluation of a Pilot Course. *British Journal of Social Work*, 51(4), 1. DOI: 10.1093/bjsw/bcab046

Ratnaningsih, N., Solihat, A., & Santika, S. (2019). The1analysis of2pre- service teachers' pedagogical content knowledge (pck) in terms of grade point average (gpa).. https://doi.org/DOI: 10.2991/iclick-18.2019.85

Recchiuti, J. L. (2007). *Civic engagement: Social science and progressive-era reform in New York City*. University of Pennsylvania Press.

Redecker, C. European Framework for the Digital Competence of Educators: DigCompEdu. Punie, Y. (ed). EUR 28775 EN. Publications Office of the European Union, Luxembourg, 2017, ISBN 978-92-79-73494-6, , JRC107466DOI: 10.2760/159770

Reis, S. M., Renzulli, S. J., & Renzulli, J. S. (2021). Enrichment and gifted education pedagogy to develop talents, gifts, and creative productivity. *Education Sciences*, 11(10), 615. DOI: 10.3390/educsci11100615

Reza Adel, S. M., & Azari Noughabi, M. (2023). Developing Pedagogical Content Knowledge (PCK) through an enriched teacher education program: Cases of four Iranian pre-service EFL teachers. *Pedagogies*, 18(3), 352–373. DOI: 10.1080/1554480X.2022.2061976

Rice, D. C., & Kaya, S. (2012). Exploring relations among preservice elementary teachers' ideas about evolution, understanding of relevant science concepts, and college science coursework. *Research in Science Education*, 42(2), 165–179. DOI: 10.1007/s11165-010-9193-2

Richards, G., & Turner, T. E. (2019). Infusing Cybersecurity Concepts into PK-12 Education: The Complexity of Integrating Multiple Standards. Retrieved from https://www.nist.gov/itl/applied-cybersecurity/nice/nice-2019-spring-enewsletter #Academic Spotlight 2019

Riske, A. K. (2022). Teacher Professional Knowledge and Pedagogical Practices for Data-Driven Decision-Making (Doctoral dissertation, Arizona State University, USA).

Rivoltella, P. C. & Ross,i P. G. (2017). L'agire didattico. Manuale per l'insegnante. La Scuola.

Rivoltella, P. C. (2013). Fare didattica con gli EAS.

Ruben, B. D., De Lisi, R., & Gigliotti, R. A. (2023). *A guide for leaders in higher education: Concepts, competencies, and tools*. Taylor & Francis.

Russell, B. (1945). *A History of Western Philosophy*. Simon and Schuster.

Rutten, N., van Joolingen, W. R., & van der Veen, J. T. (2012). The learning effects of computer simulations in science education. *Computers & Education*, 58(1), 136–153. DOI: 10.1016/j.compedu.2011.07.017

Sachau, E. C. (2013). *Alberuni's India: An Account of the Religion, Philosophy, Literature, Geography, Chronology, Astronomy, Customs, Laws and Astrology of India* (Vol. I). Routledge.

Saeleset, J., & Friedrichsen, P. (2021). Pre-service science teachers' pedagogical content knowledge integration of students' understanding in science and instructional strategies. *Eurasia Journal of Mathematics, Science and Technology Education*, 17(5), em1965. DOI: 10.29333/ejmste/10859

Said, E. (1993). *Culture and Imperialism*. Vintage Books.

Said, E. W. (1978). *Orientalism*. Pantheon Books.

Sancar, R., Atal, D., & Deryakulu, D. (2021). A new framework for teachers' professional development. *Teaching and Teacher Education*, 101, 103305. DOI: 10.1016/j.tate.2021.103305

Sancar-Tokmak, H., & Yelken, T. Y. (2015). Effects of creating digital stories on foreign language education pre-service teachers' tpack self-confidence. *Educational Studies*, 41(4), 444–461. DOI: 10.1080/03055698.2015.1043978

Sánchez Utgé, M., Mazzer, M., Pagliara, S. M. & de Anna, L. (2017). La formazione degli insegnanti di sostegno sulle TIC. Italian Journal of Special Education for Inclusion, anno V, n.1, 133-146.

Sandford, M. (2018). *Kant, Cosmopolitanism, and Human History*. Oxford University Press.

Sanguineti, J. J. (1988). Epistemology and Methodology: A Research Program.

Sanguineti, J. J. (1988). *Logic and gnoseology* (Vol. 9). Pontifical Urban University.

Santau, A. O., Maerten-Rivera, J. L., Bovis, S., & Orend, J. (2014). Preservice teachers' science content knowledge within the context of a science methods course. *Journal of Science Teachers'. Education*, 25, 953–976. DOI: 10.1007/s10972-014-9402-3

Santoni Rugiu, A. (2006). *Maestre e maestri. La difficile storia degli insegnanti elementari*. Carocci.

Saravanan, S., Chandrasekar, J., Satheesh Kumar, S., Patel, P., Maria Shanthi, J., & Boopathi, S. (2024). The Impact of NBA Implementation Across Engineering Disciplines: Innovative Approaches. In *Advances in Higher Education and Professional Development* (pp. 229–252). IGI Global. DOI: 10.4018/979-8-3693-1666-5.ch010

Sarkar, M., Gutierrez-Bucheli, L., Yip, S. Y., Lazarus, M., Wright, C., White, P. J., Ilic, D., Hiscox, T. J., & Berry, A. (2024). Pedagogical content knowledge (PCK) in higher education: A systematic scoping review. *Teaching and Teacher Education*, 144, 104608. DOI: 10.1016/j.tate.2024.104608

Sato M, Akita K, Iwakawa N, & Yoshimura T. (1991). Practical Thinking Styles of Teachers: A Lesson of Descriptive Inquiry on Thought Processes. *Bulletin of the faculty of education, the University of Tokyo*.31: 183-200.

Sato M, Iwakawa N, Akita K. (1990). Practical Thinking Styles of Teachers: Comparing Expert's Monitoring Processes with Novices. *Bulletin of the faculty of education, the University of Tokyo*.30: 177-198.

Sato, M. (2015). *Educating Teachers as Professionals*. Iwanami-shoten.

Scheler, M. (2009). The Phenomenology of Knowledge. Northwestern University Press.Battiste, M., & Henderson, J. Y. (2000). Protecting Indigenous Knowledge and Heritage: A Global Challenge. Purich Publishing.

Scheper-Hughes, N. (1995). The Primacy of the Ethical: Propositions for a Militant Anthropology.

Schiering, D., Sorge, S., Keller, M., & Neumann, K. (2022). A proficiency model for pre-service physics teachers' pedagogical content knowledge (pck)—What constitutes high-level pck? *Journal of Research in Science Teaching*, 60(1), 136–163. DOI: 10.1002/tea.21793

Schildkamp, K., van der Kleij, F. M., Heitink, M. C., Kippers, W. B., & Veldkamp, B. P. (2020). Formative assessment: A systematic review of critical teacher prerequisites for classroom practice. *International Journal of Educational Research*, 103, 101602. DOI: 10.1016/j.ijer.2020.101602

Schipper, T. M., Goei, S. L., & de Vries, S. (2023). Dealing with the complexity of adaptive teaching through collaborative teacher professional development. In Maulana, R., Helms-Lorenz, M., & Klassen, R. M. (Eds.), *Effective teaching around the world* (pp. 707–722). Springer., DOI: 10.1007/978-3-031-31678-4_32

Schneider, R. M. (2015). Pedagogical content knowledge reconsidered: A teacher educator's perspective. In Berry, A., Friedrichsen, P., & Loughran, J. (Eds.), *Re-examining pedagogical content knowledge in science education* (pp. 162–177). Routledge.

Schneider, R. M., & Plasman, K. (2011). Science teacher learning progressions: A review of science teachers' pedagogical content knowledge development. *Review of Educational Research*, 81(4), 530–565. DOI: 10.3102/0034654311423382

Schneider, R. M., & Plasman, K. (2021). Science teacher learning progressions for pedagogical content knowledge. *Journal of Research in Science Teaching*, 58(1), 5–35. DOI: 10.1002/tea.21647

Schoenfeld, A. H. (2013). Reflections on problem solving theory and practice. *The Montana Math Enthusiast*, 10(1), 9–34. DOI: 10.54870/1551-3440.1258

Schön, D. (1998). Learning to teach during the practicum experience. *Revista Electrónica de Investigación Educativa*, 21, e27.

Schon, D. A. (1993). *Il professionista riflessivo. Per una nuova epistemologia della pratica professionale*. Dedalo.

Schön, D. A. (2017). *The reflective practitioner: How professionals think in action*. Routledge. DOI: 10.4324/9781315237473

Schuck, S., Aubusson, P., Kearney, M., & Burden, K. (2013). Mobilising teacher education: A study of a professional learning community. *Teacher Development*, 17(1), 1–18. DOI: 10.1080/13664530.2012.752671

Sengeh, D., & Winthrop, R. (2022). *Transforming Education Systems: Why, What, and How. Policy Brief*. Center for Universal Education at The Brookings Institution.

Sen, M., & Demirdöğen, B. (2023). Seeking traces of filters and amplifiers as preservice teachers perform their pedagogical content knowledge. *Science Education International*, 34(1), 58–68. DOI: 10.33828/sei.v34.i1.8

Sevian, H., & Talanquer, V. (2014). Rethinking chemistry: A learning progression on chemical thinking. *Chemistry Education Research and Practice*, 15(1), 10–23. DOI: 10.1039/C3RP00111C

Shabani, K., Khatib, M., & Ebadi, S. (2010). Vygotsky's Zone of Proximal Development: Instructional implications and teachers' professional development. *English Language Teaching*, 3(4), 237–248. DOI: 10.5539/elt.v3n4p237

Shallcross, T., Spink, E., Stephenon, P., & Warwick, P. (2002). How primary trainee teachers perceive the development of their own scientific knowledge: Links between confidence, content and competence? *International Journal of Science Education*, 24(12), 1293–1312. DOI: 10.1080/09500690110110106

Shaposhnikova, Y. V., & Shipovalova, L. V. (2018). The demarcation problem in the history of Science, or what historical epistemology has to say about cultural identification. *Epistemology & Philosophy of Science*, 55(1), 52–66. DOI: 10.5840/eps20185518

Sharma, D. M., Ramana, K. V., Jothilakshmi, R., Verma, R., Maheswari, B. U., & Boopathi, S. (2024). Integrating Generative AI Into K-12 Curriculums and Pedagogies in India: Opportunities and Challenges. *Facilitating Global Collaboration and Knowledge Sharing in Higher Education With Generative AI*, 133–161.

Shaver, J. P. (2020). *Handbook of research on social studies teaching and learning*. Macmillan.

Shepard, L. A. (2018). Learning progressions as tools for assessment and learning. *Applied Measurement in Education*, 31(2), 165–174. DOI: 10.1080/08957347.2017.1408628

Shepard, L. A. (2019). Classroom assessment to support teaching and learning. *The Annals of the American Academy of Political and Social Science*, 683(1), 183–200. DOI: 10.1177/0002716219843818

Shimura, T. (2017). An Educational Study on PCK (Pedagogical Content Knowledge) Theory from the Perspective of Social Studies/ Geography Education. *Bulletin of Joetsu University of Education*, 37(1), 139–148.

Shinana, E., Ngcoza, K. M., & Mavhunga, E. (2021). Development of teachers' PCK for a scientific inquiry-based teaching approach in Namibia's rural schools. African Journal of Research in Mathematics. *Science and Technology Education*, 25(1), 1–11. DOI: 10.1080/18117295.2021.1913375

Shing, C. L., Saat, R. M., & Like, S. H. (2015). The knowledge of Teaching – Pedagogical Content Knowledge (PCK). *The Malaysian Online Journal of Educational Science, 3*(3). www.moj-es.netwoo

Shing, C. L., Saat, R. M., & Loke, S. H. (2018). The knowledge of teaching â€"pedagogical content knowledge (PCK). *MOJES: Malaysian Online Journal of Educational Sciences*, 3(3), 40–55.

Shulman, L. S. (1986). Paradigms and research programs for the study of teaching. In Wittrock, M. C. (Ed.), *Handbook of Research on Teaching* (3rd ed., pp. 3–36). Macmilla.

Shulman, L. S. (1986). Those who understand: Knowledge growth in teaching. *Educational Researcher*, 15(4), 4–14. DOI: 10.3102/0013189X015002004

Shulman, L. S. (1987). Knowledge and teaching: Foundations of the new reform. *Harvard Educational Review*, 57(1), 1–22. DOI: 10.17763/haer.57.1.j463w79r56455411

Sidekerskienė, T., & Damaševičius, R. (2023). Out-of-the-Box Learning: Digital Escape Rooms as a Metaphor for Breaking Down Barriers in STEM Education. *Sustainability (Basel)*, 15(9), 7393. DOI: 10.3390/su15097393

Sikorski, T. R. (2019). Context-dependent "upper anchors" for learning progressions. *Science & Education*, 28(6), 957–981. DOI: 10.1007/s11191-019-00074-w

Simpson, L. B. (2014). *Dancing on Our Turtle's Back: Stories of Nishnaabeg Re-Creation, Resurgence, and a New Emergence.* Arbeiter Ring Publishing.

Sims, S., Fletcher-Wood, H., O'Mara-Eves, A., Cottingham, S., Stansfield, C., Goodrich, J., Van Herwegen, J., & Anders, J. (2023). Effective teacher professional development: New theory and a meta-analytic test. *Review of Educational Research*, 0(0), 00346543231217480. Advance online publication. DOI: 10.3102/00346543231217480

Singh Madan, B., Najma, U., Pande Rana, D., & Kumar, P. K. J., S., S., & Boopathi, S. (2024). Empowering Leadership in Higher Education: Driving Student Performance, Faculty Development, and Institutional Progress. In *Advances in Educational Technologies and Instructional Design* (pp. 191–221). IGI Global. DOI: 10.4018/979-8-3693-0583-6.ch009

Smith, D. C., & Neale, D. C. (1991). The construction of subject matter knowledge in primary science teaching. *Advances in Research on Teaching*, 2, 187–243. DOI: 10.1016/0742-051X(89)90015-2

Smith, L. T. (2021). *Decolonising methodologies: Research and indigenous peoples.* Zed Books Ltd. (Original work published 1999) DOI: 10.5040/9781350225282

Smith, L. T. (2023). *Indigenous Storywork: Educating the Heart, Mind, Body, and Spirit.* UBC Press.

Smith, T. (Ed.). (2023). *Animism and Philosophy of Religion.* Springer Nature. DOI: 10.1007/978-3-030-94170-3

Speed, C., Kleiner, A., & Macaulay, J. (2014). Broadening student learning experiences via a novel cross-disciplinary art and anatomy education program - a case study. *International Journal of Higher Education*, 4(1). Advance online publication. DOI: 10.5430/ijhe.v4n1p86

Spivak, G. C. (1988). Can the Subaltern Speak? In C. Nelson & L. Grossberg (Eds.), Marxism and the Interpretation of Culture. Macmillan.

Spivak, G. C. (2004). *Critique of Postcolonial Reason: Toward a History of the Vanishing Present*. Harvard University Press.

Stains, M., Harshman, J., Barker, M. K., Chasteen, S. V., Cole, R., DeChenne-Peters, S. E., Eagan, M. K.Jr, Esson, J. M., Knight, J. K., Laski, F. A., Levis-Fitzgerald, M., Lee, C. J., Lo, S. M., McDonnell, L. M., McKay, T. A., Michelotti, N., Musgrove, A., Palmer, M. S., Plank, K. M., & Young, A. M. (2018). Anatomy of STEM teaching in North American universities. *Science*, 359(6383), 1468–1470. DOI: 10.1126/science.aap8892 PMID: 29599232

Stansberry, S. L. (2017). Authentic teaching with technology through situated learning. *Journal of Formative Design in Learning*, 1(1), 16–30. DOI: 10.1007/s41686-017-0004-2

Star, J. R. (2023). Revisiting the origin of, and reflections on the future of, pedagogical content knowledge. *Asian Journal for Mathematics Education*, 2(2), 147–160. DOI: 10.1177/27527263231175885

Steinberg, M. P., & Garrett, R. (2016). Classroom composition and measured teacher performance: What do teacher observation scores really measure? *Educational Evaluation and Policy Analysis*, 38(2), 293–317. DOI: 10.3102/0162373715616249

Stein, M., Larrabee, T., & Barman, C. (2018). A study of common beliefs and misconceptions in physical science. *Journal of Elementary Science Education*, 20(2), 1–11. DOI: 10.1007/BF03173666

Steinmetz, G. (2013). A child of the empire: British sociology and colonialism, 1940s–1960s. *Journal of the History of the Behavioral Sciences*, 49(4), 353–378. DOI: 10.1002/jhbs.21628 PMID: 24037899

Stein, P. (2014). Multimodal instructional practices. In *Handbook of Research on New Literacies* (pp. 871–898). Routledge.

Stek, K. (2023). *A Challenge-Based Experiment Aiming to Develop Strategic Thinking an Inquiry into the Role of Stimulating Creativity for out-of-the-Box Thinking*. EasyChair.

Stenberg, E., Milosavljevic, A., Götrick, B., & Lundegren, N. (2024). Continuing professional development in general dentistry—Experiences of an online flipped classroom. *European Journal of Dental Education*, 28(3), 825–832. DOI: 10.1111/eje.13013 PMID: 38654701

Studley, J., & Horsley, P. (2018). Spiritual governance as an indigenous behavioural practice. *Cultural and spiritual significance of nature in protected areas: Governance, management and policy.*

Suh, J. K., & Park, S. (2017). Exploring the relationship between pedagogical content knowledge (PCK) and sustainability of an innovative science teaching approach. *Teaching and Teacher Education*, 64, 246–259. DOI: 10.1016/j.tate.2017.01.021

Sümer, M., & Vaněček, D. (2024). A systematic review of virtual and augmented realities in higher education: Trends and issues. *Innovations in Education and Teaching International*, •••, 1–12. DOI: 10.1080/14703297.2024.2382854

Sunzuma, G. Z., Zezekwa, N., Chagwiza, C., & Mutambara, T. L. (2024). Examining pre-service mathematics teachers' pedagogical content knowledge (PCK) during a professional development course: A case study. *Mathematics Teaching Research Journal, 16*(1). https://files.eric.ed.gov/fulltext/EJ1427380.pdf

Suzuki, D. T. (1953). The Natural Law in the Buddhist Tradition. *Nat. L. Inst. Proc.*, 5, 89.

Sweller, J. (1988). Cognitive load during problem solving: Effects on learning. *Cognitive Science*, 12(2), 257–285. DOI: 10.1207/s15516709cog1202_4

Taber, K. S. (2013). Revisiting the chemistry triplet: Drawing upon the nature of chemical knowledge and the psychology of learning to inform chemistry education. *Chemistry Education Research and Practice*, 14(2), 156–168. DOI: 10.1039/C3RP00012E

Tai, Y., & Ting, Y.-L. (2020). English-learning mobile app designing for engineering students' cross-disciplinary learning and collaboration. *Australasian Journal of Educational Technology*, 36(2), 120–136.

Tanaka T & Tanaka. (2014). *Designing of English Classrooms and Grammar Teaching*. Tokyo: Taishukan-shoten.

Tardif, M. (2010). *Los Saberes de los Docentes y su Desarrollo Profesional*. Narcea.

Thacker, B., Hart, S., Wipfli, K., & Wang, J. (2023). The development of free-response questions to assess learning assistants PCK in the context of questioning. *ArXiv Preprint ArXiv:2304.14285.*

The Big Draw. (2020). *The Big Draw Festival*. Retrieved July 9, 2020, from https://thebigdraw.org/

The Guardian. (2021b, 25 May, 2021). 'Horrific' cuts in pipeline for English universities and students, by Richard Adams Education editorhttps://https://www.theguardian.com/education/2021/may/24/horrific-cuts-in-pipeline-for-english-universities-and-students

The Guardinn. (2021a, 29 March, 2021). war against humanities at Britain's universities, https://www.theguardian.com/education/2015/mar/29/war-against-humanities-at-britains-universities

Todd, Z. (2016). An Indigenous feminist's take on the ontological turn: 'Ontology' is just another word for colonialism. *Journal of Historical Sociology*, 29(1), 4–22. DOI: 10.1111/johs.12124

Tokuhama-Espinosa, T. (2023). A New Science of Teaching. In *New Science of Learning* (pp. 175–209). Brill. DOI: 10.1163/9789004540767_010

Tokuoka, K. (1995). A Study on the Features of Pedagogical Content Knowledge and its Implications. *Journal of Educational Methodology*, 21, 67–75.

Tomasello, M. (2003). *Constructing a Language: A Usage-Based Theory of Language Acquisition*. Harvard University Press.

Tombolato, M. (2021). *La conoscenza della conoscenza scientifica. Problemi didattici*. Franco Angeli.

Tomlinson, C. A. (2014). *The differentiated classroom: Responding to the needs of all learners* (2nd ed.). ASCD.

Tomlinson, C. A. (2017). *How to differentiate instruction in academically diverse classrooms*. ASCD.

Tosun, T. (2000). The beliefs of pre-service elementary teachers toward science and science teaching. *School Science and Mathematics*, 100(7), 374–379. DOI: 10.1111/j.1949-8594.2000.tb18179.x

Trinchero, R. (2002). *Manuale di ricerca educativa*. Franco Angeli.

Tröbst, S., Kleickmann, T., Heinze, A., Bernholt, A., Rink, R., & Kunter, M. (2018). Teacher knowledge experiment: Testing mechanisms underlying the formation of preservice elementary school teachers' pedagogical content knowledge concerning fractions and fractional arithmetic. *Journal of Educational Psychology*, 110(8), 1049–1065. DOI: 10.1037/edu0000260

Trumper, R. (2003). The need for change in elementary school teacher training – a cross-college age study of future teachers' conceptions of basic astronomy concepts. *Teaching and Teacher Education*, 19(3), 309–323. DOI: 10.1016/S0742-051X(03)00017-9

Trygstad, P. J. (2013). *2012 National Survey of Science and Mathematics Education: Status of elementary school science*. Horizon Research. https://eric.ed.gov/?id=ED541798

Tuck, E., & McKenzie, M. (2015). Relational validity and the "where" of inquiry: Place and land in qualitative research. *Qualitative Inquiry*, 21(7), 633–638. DOI: 10.1177/1077800414563809

Tuck, E., & Yang, K. W. (2012). Decolonization is not a metaphor. *Decolonization*, 1(1), 1–40.

Turner, E. (2008). Exploring the work of Victor Turner: Liminality and its later implications. *Suomen Antropologi. Journal of the Finnish Anthropological Society*, 33(4).

Turner, M., & Hicks, T. (2017). *The new literacy: Technology and learning in the classroom*. Teachers College Press.

Turner, S., & Ireson, G. (2014). Fifteen pupils' positive approach to primary school science: When does it decline? *Educational Studies*, 36(2), 119–141. DOI: 10.1080/03055690903148662

Uchida, T. (2009). *Children with No Ambition, Youths Who Don't Study, and Unemployed Young People*. Kodansha.

United States. National Commission on Excellence in Education (1983). A nation at risk: The imperative for educational reform: A report to the nation and the secretary of education, *United States Department of Education*. https://edreform.com/wp-content/uploads/2013/02/A_Nation_At_Risk_1983.pdf

Upahi, J. E., & Ramnarain, U. (2022). Evidence of foundational knowledge and conjectural pathways in science learning progressions. *Science & Education*, 31(1), 55–92. DOI: 10.1007/s11191-021-00226-x

Usak, M. (2009). Preservice science and technology teachers' pedagogical content knowledge on cell topics. *Kuram ve Uygulamada Egitim Bilimlerim*, 9(4), 2033–2046.

Vaithianathan, V., Subbulakshmi, N., Boopathi, S., & Mohanraj, M. (2024). Integrating Project-Based and Skills-Based Learning for Enhanced Student Engagement and Success: Transforming Higher Education. In *Adaptive Learning Technologies for Higher Education* (pp. 345–372). IGI Global. DOI: 10.4018/979-8-3693-3641-0.ch015

Vaithianathan, V., Shastri, D. S., Nandakumar, V., Misba, M., Kumar, P. S. V. V. S. R., & Boopathi, S. (2024). NEP Policy Implementation Strategies in Education in India. In *Educational Philosophy and Sociological Foundation of Education* (pp. 325–356). IGI Global., DOI: 10.4018/979-8-3693-3587-1.ch013

Valentine, K. A., Truckenmiller, A. J., Troia, G. A., & Aldridge, S. (2021). What is the nature of change in late elementary writing and are curriculum-based measures sensitive to that change? *Assessing Writing*, 50, 100567. DOI: 10.1016/j.asw.2021.100567

Valnides, N. (2000). Primary student teachers' understanding of the particulate nature of matter and its transformations during dissolving. *Chemistry Education Research and Practice*, 1(2), 355–364. DOI: 10.1039/A9RP90026H

Valtonen, T. (2011). *An insight into collaborative learning with ICT: Teachers' and students' perspectives*. Itä-Suomen yliopisto.

van der Steen, J., van Schilt-Mol, T., van der Vleuten, C., & Joosten-ten Brinke, D. (2023). Designing formative assessment that improves teaching and learning: What can be learned from the design stories of experienced teachers? *Journal of Formative Design in Learning*, 7(2), 182–194. DOI: 10.1007/s41686-023-00080-w

van Dijk, E. E., van Tartwijk, J., van der Schaaf, M. F., & Kluijtmans, M. (2020). What makes an expert university teacher? A systematic review and synthesis of frameworks for teacher expertise in higher education. *Educational Research Review*, 31, 100365. DOI: 10.1016/j.edurev.2020.100365

van Dijk, E. M., & Kattmann, U. (2007). A research model for the study of science teachers' PCK and improving teacher education. *Teaching and Teacher Education*, 23(6), 885–897. DOI: 10.1016/j.tate.2006.05.002

Van Driel, J. H., & Berry, A. (2012). Teacher professional development focusing on PCK: The role of teachers' beliefs and knowledge. *Educational Researcher*, 41(1), 26–28. DOI: 10.3102/0013189X11431010

Van Driel, J. H., Berry, A., & Meirink, J. (2014). Research on teachers' professional development and its impact on educational practice. *European Journal of Education*, 49(2), 218–232. DOI: 10.1111/ejed.12064 van Driel, J. H., Jong, O. D., & Verloop, N. (2002). The development of preservice chemistry teachers' pedagogical content knowledge. *Science Education*, 86(4), 572–590. DOI: 10.1002/sce.10010

Van Meijl, T. (2019). Doing indigenous epistemology: Internal debates about inside knowledge in Māori society. *Current Anthropology*, 60(2), 155–173. DOI: 10.1086/702538

Van Meijl, T. (2019). *Indigenous Movements and Spirituality: Struggles for Cultural Survival and Self-Determination*. Berghahn Books.

Vangrieken, K., Meredith, C., Packer, T., & Kyndt, E. (2017). Teacher collaboration and professional development: A systematic review. *Educational Research Review*, 21, 15–32. DOI: 10.1016/j.edurev.2017.05.002

VanSledright, B. (2013). *The challenge of rethinking history education: On practices, theories, and policy*. Routledge.

Vavrus, M. (2008). Culturally responsive teaching. In T. L. Good (Ed.), *21st Century Education: A Reference Handbook* (Vol. 1, pp. 519–527), Sage Publications. DOI: 10.4135/9781412964012.n56

Velliaris, D. M., & Pierce, J. M. (2016). Cultural diversity: Misconceptions, misinterpretations, and misunderstandings in the classroom. In Jones, K., & Mixon, J. R. (Eds.), *Intercultural responsiveness in the second language learning classroom* (pp. 85–105). IGI Global., DOI: 10.4018/978-1-5225-2069-6.ch006

Venkatasubramanian, V., Chitra, M., Sudha, R., Singh, V. P., Jefferson, K., & Boopathi, S. (2024). Examining the Impacts of Course Outcome Analysis in Indian Higher Education: Enhancing Educational Quality. In *Challenges of Globalization and Inclusivity in Academic Research* (pp. 124–145). IGI Global.

Ventista, O. M., & Brown, C. (2023). Teachers' professional learning and its impact on students' learning outcomes: Findings from a systematic review. *Social Sciences & Humanities Open*, 8(1), 100565. DOI: 10.1016/j.ssaho.2023.100565

Verma, R., Christiana, M. B. V., Maheswari, M., Srinivasan, V., Patro, P., Dari, S. S., & Boopathi, S. (2024). Intelligent Physarum Solver for Profit Maximization in Oligopolistic Supply Chain Networks. In *AI and Machine Learning Impacts in Intelligent Supply Chain* (pp. 156–179). IGI Global. DOI: 10.4018/979-8-3693-1347-3.ch011

Vijaya Lakshmi, V., Mishra, M., Kushwah, J. S., Shajahan, U. S., Mohanasundari, M., & Boopathi, S. (2024). Circular Economy Digital Practices for Ethical Dimensions and Policies for Digital Waste Management. In *Harnessing High-Performance Computing and AI for Environmental Sustainability* (pp. 166–193). IGI Global., DOI: 10.4018/979-8-3693-1794-5.ch008

Vinodhen, V. (2020). The development of science education during the ability-driven phase in Singapore, 1997–2011. *Asia-Pacific Science Education*, 6(1), 207–227. DOI: 10.1163/23641177-BJA00007

Vygotskij, L. (2006). *Psicologia Pedagogica*. Erickson.

Vygotsky, L. S. (1978). Interaction between learning and development. In Cole, M., John-Steiner, V., Scribner, S., & Souberman, E. (Eds.), *Mind in Society: The Development of Higher Psychological Processes* (pp. 79–91). Harvard University Press.

Wakabayashi, S. (1990). *36 chapters that answer simple English questions*. Japan Times.

Wakamatsu, D. (2020). Rethinking Schulman's Theory of Teacher Knowledge: Process of Theory Development. *Bulletin of the Graduate School of Education. Kyoto University Research Information Repository*, 66, 43–56.

Wang, C., Chen, X., Yu, T., & Wang, Y. (2024). Education reform and change driven by digital technology: A bibliometric study from a global perspective. *Humanities & Social Sciences Communications*, 11(1), 256. Advance online publication. DOI: 10.1057/s41599-024-02717-y

Weaver, C. (2018). *Grammar to enrich and enhance writing*. Heinemann.

Weinberg, A., & McMeeking, L. (2017). Toward meaningful interdisciplinary education: High school teachers' views of mathematics and science integration. *School Science and Mathematics*, 117(5), 204–213. DOI: 10.1111/ssm.12224

Weiss, I. R., Banilower, E. R., McMahon, K. C., & Smith, P. S. (2001). *Report of the 2000 National Survey of Science and Mathematics Education*. Horizon Research.

Wei, Y.-Y., Chen, W.-F., Xie, T., & Peng, J.-J. (2022). Cross-disciplinary curriculum integration spaces for emergency management engineering talent cultivation in higher education. *Computer Applications in Engineering Education*, 30(4), 1175–1189. DOI: 10.1002/cae.22513

Welsch, A., & Heying, C. (1999). Watershed Management and Community Building: A Case Study of Portland's Community Watershed Stewardship Programtitle. *Administrative Theory & Praxis*, 21(1), 88–102. DOI: 10.1080/10841806.1999.11643351

Wenger, E. (2006). Comunità di pratica. Apprendimento, significato e identità. Cortina.

Wenger, E. (1998). Communities of practice: Learning as a social system. *The Systems Thinker*, 9(5), 2–3.

Whitaker, A. A., Jenkins, J. M., & Duer, J. K. (2022). Standards, curriculum, and assessment in early childhood education: Examining alignment across multiple state systems. *Early Childhood Research Quarterly*, 58, 59–74. DOI: 10.1016/j.ecresq.2021.07.008

Whitlock, B. (2024). Mentorship programs in schools: Bridging the character education gap. *Journal of Moral Education*, 53(1), 89–118. DOI: 10.1080/03057240.2023.2280757

Wijngaards-de Meij, L., & Merx, S. (2018). Improving curriculum alignment and achieving learning goals by making the curriculum visible. *The International Journal for Academic Development*, 23(3), 219–231. DOI: 10.1080/1360144X.2018.1462187

Wiliam, D. (2021). *Embedded formative assessment: Insights for learning*. Hodder Education.

Wilkinson, I., & Kleinman, A. (2016). *A Passion for Society: How We Think about Human Suffering*. University of California Press. DOI: 10.1525/california/9780520287228.001.0001

Williams, A. (2020). *Engaging the disengaged: Creating responsive classrooms for all students*. Routledge.

Wilson, S. (2008). *Research is Ceremony: Indigenous Research Methods*. Fernwood Publishing.

Windschitl, M., Thompson, J., & Braaten, M. (2008). Beyond the scientific method: Model-based inquiry as a new paradigm of preference for school science investigations. *Science Education*, 92(5), 941–967. DOI: 10.1002/sce.20259

Windschitl, M., Thompson, J., & Braaten, M. (2011). Fostering ambitious pedagogy in novice teachers: The new role of tool-supported analyses of student work. *Teachers College Record*, 113(7), 1311–1360. DOI: 10.1177/016146811111300702

Wineburg, S. (2018). *Why learn history (when it's already on your phone)*. University of Chicago Press. DOI: 10.7208/chicago/9780226357355.001.0001

Wiseman, A. (2011). Interactive read alouds: Teachers and students constructing knowledge and literacy together. *Early Childhood Education Journal*, 38(6), 431–438. DOI: 10.1007/s10643-010-0426-9

Wiyarsi, A. (2018). Enhancing of preservice chemistry teachers' self-efficacy through the preparation of pedagogical content knowledge in vocational context. *Jurnal Pendidikan Sains (Jps)*, 6(1), 14. DOI: 10.26714/jps.6.1.2018.14-23

Woolfolk, A. E. (2014). *Educational psychology: Active learning edition*. Pearson.

Wu, Z. (2022). Understanding teachers' cross-disciplinary collaboration for STEAM education: Building a digital community of practice. *Thinking Skills and Creativity*, 46, 101178. DOI: 10.1016/j.tsc.2022.101178

Xu, E., Wang, W., & Wang, Q. (2023). The effectiveness of collaborative problem solving in promoting students' critical thinking: A meta-analysis based on empirical literature. *Humanities & Social Sciences Communications*, 10(1), 16. DOI: 10.1057/s41599-023-01508-1

Yadav, U., Pitchai, R., Gopal, V., Kumar, K. R. S., Talukdar, M., & Boopathi, S. (2024). Powers of Higher Education Leadership: Navigating Policy and Management in Academic Institutions. In *Navigating Leadership and Policy Management in Education* (pp. 103–136). IGI Global., DOI: 10.4018/979-8-3693-9215-7.ch004

Yager, R. E. (2015). Real-world applications of science. *Science Education International*, 26(2), 136–145. DOI: 10.33828/sei.v26.i2.6

Yang, C., Li, J., Zhao, W., Luo, L., & Shanks, D. R. (2023). Do practice tests (quizzes) reduce or provoke test anxiety? A meta-analytic review. *Educational Psychology Review*, 35(3), 87. DOI: 10.1007/s10648-023-09801-w

Yang, Y., Liu, Y. X., Song, X. H., Yao, J.-X., & Guo, Y.-Y. (2023). A tale of two progressions: Students' learning progression of the particle nature of matter and teachers' perception on the progression. *Disciplinary and Interdisciplinary Science Education Research*, 5(1), 18. DOI: 10.1186/s43031-023-00085-2

Yannakakis, Y. (2023). *Indigenous Rights and Cultural Revival in Latin America*. Cambridge University Press.

Yano, H. (1998). Review of the Studies on Teacher's Pedagogical Content Knowledge focused on Social Studies. Bulletin of Graduate School of Education. *Tokyo Univ*, 38, 287–295.

Yao, J. X., Liu, Y. X., & Guo, Y. Y. (2023). Learning progression-based design: Advancing the synergetic development of energy understanding and scientific explanation. *Instructional Science*, 51(3), 397–421. DOI: 10.1007/s11251-023-09620-0

Yazici, H. J., Zidek, L. A., & St. Hill, H. (2020). A study of critical thinking and cross-disciplinary teamwork in engineering education. *Women in Industrial and Systems Engineering: Key Advances and Perspectives on Emerging Topics*, 185–196.

Yiğit Koyunkaya, M. (2017). A teaching experiment methodology that aims to develop pre-service mathematics teachers' technological pedagogical and content knowledge. [TURCOMAT]. *Turkish Journal of Computer and Mathematics Education*, 8(2), 284–322. DOI: 10.16949/turkbilmat.293220

Yigit, M. (2014). A review of the literature: How pre-service mathematics teachers develop their technological, pedagogical, and content knowledge. *International Journal of Education in Mathematics Science and Technology*, 2(1). Advance online publication. DOI: 10.18404/ijemst.96390

Young, R. J. (2020). *Postcolonialism: A very short introduction*. Oxford University Press. DOI: 10.1093/actrade/9780198856832.001.0001

Zanniello, G. (2012). *La didattica nel corso di laurea in scienze della formazione primaria*. Armando.

Zeichner, K. M. (2003). The role of action research in teacher education. *Journal of Teacher Education*, 54(1), 24–34. DOI: 10.1177/0022487102238658

Zheng, L., Long, M., Zhong, L., & Gyasi, J. F. (2022). The effectiveness of technology-facilitated personalized learning on learning achievements and learning perceptions: A meta-analysis. *Education and Information Technologies*, 27(11), 11807–11830. DOI: 10.1007/s10639-022-11092-7

Zinger, D., Sandholtz, J. H., & Ringstaff, C. (2020). Teaching science in rural elementary schools: Affordances and constraints in the age of NGSS. *Rural Educator*, 41(2), 14–30. DOI: 10.35608/ruraled.v41i2.558

Zwiers, J. (2014). *Academic conversations: Classroom talk that fosters critical thinking and content understanding*. Stenhouse Publishers.

About the Contributors

Nazlı Ruya Taşkın Bedizel has been serving as an Assistant Professor at Balıkesir University's Necatibey Faculty of Education since October 2023, following her role as a research assistant since 2010. She earned her PhD in Biology Education from the same institution in 2018 with a dissertation titled "The Effect of Formative Assessment Design Activities on Biology Student Teachers' Modern Genetics Learning Progression-Based Content Knowledge and Pedagogical Content Knowledge." She teaches courses including General Biology, Cell Biology, Classroom Assessment, Interdisciplinary Biology Teaching, Health and Nutrition, Microteaching, Biology Curriculum, Science and Research Ethics, and Teaching Practicum. Her research primarily focuses on genetics education, learning progressions, pedagogical content knowledge, and formative assessments.

***

Nyela Ashraf is working as lecturer at University of Poonch Rawalakot, Pakistan. Dr. Nyela Ashraf has earned her Ph.D. (Management Sciences) degree from Air University, Pakistan. She has broad insight into the areas of organizational life. She has published several papers in HEC approved journals. Her research areas are emotions in workplace, cuture, employee voice, salience.

Sampath Boopathi is an accomplished individual with a strong academic background and extensive research experience. He completed his undergraduate studies in Mechanical Engineering and pursued his postgraduate studies in the field of Computer-Aided Design. Dr. Boopathi obtained his Ph.D. from Anna University, focusing his research on Manufacturing and optimization. Throughout his career, Dr. Boopathi has made significant contributions to the field of engineering. He has authored and published over 225 research articles in internationally peer-reviewed journals, highlighting his expertise and dedication to advancing knowledge in his area of specialization. His research output demonstrates his commitment to conducting rigorous and impactful research. In addition to his research publications, Dr. Boopathi has also been granted one patent and has three published patents to his name. This indicates his innovative thinking and ability to develop practical solutions to real-world engineering challenges. With 17 years of academic and research experience, Dr. Boopathi has enriched the engineering community through his teaching and mentorship roles.

Ajay Chandel is working as an Associate Professor at Mittal School of Business, Lovely Professional University, Punjab. He has 14 years of teaching and research experience. He has published papers in SCOPUS, WOS, and UGC listed Journals in areas like Social Media Marketing, E-Commerce, and Consumer Behaviour. He has published cases on SMEs and Social Entrepreneurship in The Case Centre, UK. He also reviews The Case Journal, Emerald Group Publishing, and International Journal of Business and Globalisation, Inderscience. He has authored and developed MOOCs on Tourism and Hospitality Marketing under Epg-Pathshala- A gateway to all postgraduate courses (a UGC-MHRD project under its National Mission on Education Through ICT (NME-ICT).

Jahid Siraz Chowdhury, an associate professor, teaches in the Master of Social Work Program at Lincoln University College in Malaysia. He is also associated with the Research and Training Forum (RTF). Chowdhury's academic pursuits encompass methodological contributions to the Sociology of Knowledge, and innovative applications of social theory, including the development of the Bio-Bank Model for Indigenous Knowledge. He is the author of 10 influential books, including Ubuntu Philosophy for the New Normalcy (Palgrave, 2023), Reciprocity and Its Practice in Social Science (IGI Global, 2022), Volunteering in Social Research (Routledge, 2024, in press), History and Educational Philosophy for Social Justice and Human Rights (IGI Global, 2024), and The Intersection of Faith, Culture, and Indigenous Community in Malaysia and Bangladesh (Springer nATURE). Dr. Jahid is not merely exploring these disciplines but is also reconnecting with them on a deeper, more intellectual level.

Pasquale Gallo is a professor of General Pedagogy at the Magna Grecia University in Catanzaro, and of Didactics and Special Pedagogy in the specialization courses for support activities at the University of Roma3, LUMSA, University of Calabria and University of Reggio Calabria. He has a degree in Primary Education and Applied Cognitive and Behavioral Psychology, specializing in teaching and psycho-pedagogy for pupils with autism spectrum disorders, in metacognitive teaching, teaching and psycho-pedagogy for pupils with high cognitive potential and more resources, in media education management. Research interests are related to inclusive and innovative processes, the development of digital technologies and the Backpack-Free model for a school-community. Author of numerous papers and scientific articles.

Zulkarnain A. Hatta is Dean of the Faculty of Social Science of Malaysia's Lincoln University College. He presently serves as the President of APASWE and previously served as the Asian region's vice president (2017–2021). Zulkarnain has a DSW, an MSW, and a BA in criminal justice. He belongs to both APASWE and the MASW, the Malaysian Association of Social Workers. His areas of interest are safety net issues, spirituality, and social work education. Zulkarnain is a practicing, teaching, and researching social worker. He is fluent in both English and Bahasa Malaysia.

K. Gajalakshmi working as Associate Professor, Department of Botany, PSGR Krishnammal College for women, Coimbatore have 17 years experience in PSGR Krishnammal College for women, Coimbatore obtained B.Sc, Life science at Avinasiling College, Coimbatore, M.Sc, Botany at Government Arts College, Coimbatore, M.Phil and Ph.D at Bharathiar University, Coimbatore Specialisation in Plant Breading and Genetics.

Jamila Khurshid is working as an assistant professor at University of Poonch Rawalakot, Pakistan. Dr. Jamila Khurshid earned her Ph.D. (Business Administration) degree from the Capital University of Science and Technology, Pakistan. She has broad insight into the topics of organizational sciences and has published several papers in impact factor and HEC approved journals. She has presented many national and international research conferences. She is also a trainer and delivered training various government institutions in Islamabad Pakistan. Dr. Jamila is also a reviewer of several journals. Her research areas are women entrepreneurship, organizational citizenship behavior, Human resource development, Ethical Climate and climate change

Nabila Khurshid, Associate Professor (Tenured) at the Department of Economics at COMSATS University Islamabad. Dr. Khurshid earned her PhD in Agricultural Economics with a specialization in Development Economics. She is also a Gold Medalist in her bachelor's (Agri-Economics & Rural Sociology, University of Muzaffarabad, Azad Kashmir) and master's program (Rural Development, NWFP Agriculture University Peshawar). Her teaching and research interests are in Applied microeconomics, Macroeconomics, Development Economics, International Economics, Rural Development and Tourism and Environmental and Agricultural Economics. Dr. Khurshid has numerous publications in peer reviewed journals of international repute. She is also on a reviewer panel of Higher Education Commission of Pakistan and NTS Subject Committee in Economics. In last 5 years, she has supervised research dissertations of 08 masters and 06 bachelor students. Dr. Khurshid is an n HEC approved supervisor.

Shashank Mittal has done his FPM in Organizational behavior and Human Resource from Indian Institute of Management Raipur. He holds B. Tech from I.E.T. Lucknow. His post FPM work experience includes almost five years of industry and academics exposures in multiple roles. Prior to joining FPM, he has over two years of industrial experience and three years of teaching experience in various organizations. He has published multiple papers in ABDC ranked and SSCI indexed journals of international repute such as Journal of Knowledge Management, Journal of Behavioral and Experimental Finance, International Journal of Conflict Management, Journal of Management and Organization and Current Psychology. His current research interest includes Social identity, Knowledge exchanges, Status, Proactive helping, Employer branding, Organizational justice, and Humanitarian relief management. He enjoys badminton and cycling during leisure time.

Kunitaro Mizuno is a Professor at Kobe Women's University. My research interests are creating a learning community utilizing ICT, data-driven learning, learner's dictionary, and pedagogical grammar.

Deepa Rajesh, Vice President (Academics) and Executive Director of AMET Business School, AMET University, Chennai has rich academic, research and administrative experience. She specialized in Human Resources and System and completed her Doctorate in University of Madras, Chennai. She also serve as a Director, Human Resource Development Centre, AMET University and Nodal officer for AMET University Academic and Administrative Development Centre (AADC), Association of Indian University.

R. Sakthivel, Professor & Deputy Vice Chancellor (Research & Innovation) at DMI – St. Eugene University, Zambia holds Ph.D. in Plant Biology and Plant Biotechnology from Madras University, M.Phil. & M.Sc. Degree from Madras University, B.Sc. Degree from Bharathidasan University, Master in Education from Tamil Nadu Teacher Education University and Bachelor in Education from Bharathiyar University. He has served in various capacities from Assistant Lecturer, Lecturer, Senior Lecturer, Assistant Professor, Professor, Head of the Department, Vice Principal, Principal – Academic, Registrar and Deputy Vice Chancellor (Research & Innovation) in Colleges such as DMI – St. Eugene University, Zambia - Central Africa, St. Joseph University College of Agricultural Sciences and Technology, Songea, Tanzania, East Africa and St. Joseph University in Tanzania,

Arusha Campus, Arusha, Tanzania, East Africa. Presently he is working as Deputy Vice Chancellor (Research & Innovation) for DMI – St. Eugene University, Zambia, Central Africa. His outstanding work has been widely recognized as he has won the Best Researcher Award, Top 50 International Distinguished Academic Leaders 2020, Academic Excellence Awards - 2019 for Distinguished Principal, Outstanding Contribution in Leadership - 2019, Young Scientist Award - 2018, the Bharat Ratna Dr. A. P. J. Abdul Kalam award - 2011 and he was awarded Senior Research Fellow by the Defence Research and Development Organization (DRDO). As a researcher, he has published 47 research articles in both International and National peer reviewed journals with Impact factor, NCBI – Genbank publications 30, Blog Publications 1, Patent 1 and he has published 6 books.

R. Vettriselvan is working as an Associate Professor, AMET University, specialised in HRM and Marketing. He is acting as Mentor, Saraswathi Institute of Medical Sciences, Hapur. He served as Review Board member, National Council for Higher Education, Malawi, Head of the Department, School of Commerce and Management Studies, St. Eugene University, Zambia, and Director, Research and Publication, St. John the Baptist University, Malawi. He has published 25 books and 86 articles in peer reviewed journals and edited book chapters. Under his guidance two have completed and five are pursuing their PhD.

Subhashini S. working as Assistant Professor, Department of Botany, PSGR Krishnammal College for women, Coimbatore from 2021 and served as Assistant Professor, Department of Botany, SDNB Vaishnav College for women, Chennai from 2016 to 2021, LNG Arts and Science College, Ponneri. Specialisation in Pharmacognosy

Parth Sharma, Associate Professor at the School of Law, University of Petroleum and Energy Studies, brings a wealth of expertise to his role. With a PhD in India-China relations from Aligarh Muslim University and a gold medal in his undergraduate studies, he has established himself as a leading scholar in the field of international politics. His research, published in highly regarded journals both nationally and internationally, has made significant contributions to the understanding of strategic affairs, political theory, and the politics of development. Dr. Sharma's qualifications extend beyond his academic achievements; he is a UGC (JRF-NET) qualified scholar in Political Science and has actively participated in workshops and conferences organized by prestigious institutions like the UGC, British High Commission, and Centre for Policy Research. His diverse interests encompass international politics, strategic affairs, political theory, the politics of development, and issues related to higher education, making him a valuable asset to the academic community.

Sneha Singh is a PhD Candidate in the Department of Sociology at Waipapa Taumata Rau | University of Auckland. She is dedicated to decolonizing feminist thought and actively engages in social advocacy, impacting her community and nation with a focus on equality and social justice.

Sandy Watson is an Associate Professor of Curriculum & Instruction at the University of Louisiana Monroe where she teaches undergraduate and graduate courses in multiculturalism and curriculum. Her research interests include science education, curriculum studies, multiculturalism and diversity, and teacher education. An educator for 26+ years, Dr. Watson has published many articles and has presented at multiple conferences across her research areas.

Mohit Yadav is an Associate Professor in the area of Human Resource Management at Jindal Global Business School (JGBS). He has a rich blend of work experience from both Academics as well as Industry. Prof. Mohit holds a Ph.D. from Department of Management Studies, Indian Institute of Technology Roorkee (IIT Roorkee) and has completed Master of Human Resource and Organizational Development (MHROD) from prestigious Delhi School of Economics, University of Delhi. He also holds a B.Com (Hons.) degree from University of Delhi and UGC-JRF scholarship. He has published various research papers and book chapters with reputed publishers like Springer, Sage, Emerald, Elsevier, Inderscience etc. and presented research papers in national and International conferences both in India and abroad. He has many best paper awards on his credit too. He is reviewer of various international journals like Computers in Human Behavior, Policing etc. His areas of interest are Organizational Behavior, HRM, Recruitment and Selection, Organizational Citizenship Behavior, Quality of work life and role.

Index

A

Advanced Technology 213, 228, 231
Anthropology 90, 91, 95, 99, 105, 109, 110, 112, 114, 115, 116, 117, 268, 270
Aristotle 89, 90, 92, 93, 94, 100, 102, 108, 111
Assessment Practices 49, 61, 66, 69, 76, 80, 267, 296, 345, 346, 347, 348, 349, 350, 351, 352, 353, 354, 355, 356, 357, 358, 359, 360, 361, 362, 363, 364, 365
Assessment Strategies 4, 7, 198, 280, 347, 351, 352, 356, 358, 362, 363, 364

B

Best Practices 1, 2, 8, 9, 10, 18, 22, 42, 45, 53, 68, 74, 141, 173, 193, 213, 214, 217, 223, 229, 264, 265, 282, 357, 362

C

Classroom Experiences 32, 34, 38, 39, 55, 158
Classroom Practice 36, 41, 84, 167, 258, 360
Cognitive Development 41, 49, 51, 53, 55, 56, 57, 72, 75, 83
content knowledge 1, 2, 3, 4, 5, 6, 8, 9, 11, 12, 13, 14, 15, 16, 17, 19, 21, 22, 23, 24, 25, 31, 32, 33, 34, 35, 36, 37, 38, 39, 40, 41, 42, 44, 45, 46, 48, 50, 51, 53, 61, 63, 70, 73, 74, 76, 78, 79, 80, 81, 83, 84, 85, 89, 91, 92, 93, 106, 119, 120, 122, 123, 124, 125, 127, 132, 133, 134, 136, 139, 140, 141, 145, 148, 151, 153, 154, 155, 156, 158, 161, 162, 165, 168, 169, 171, 172, 173, 177, 178, 180, 182, 183, 184, 185, 186, 187, 188, 191, 192, 194, 200, 201, 202, 203, 204, 205, 206, 207, 208, 209, 210, 211, 212, 213, 216, 220, 221, 223, 224, 225, 228, 231, 233, 234, 237, 238, 239, 246, 257, 259, 260, 264, 265, 272, 273, 275, 276, 281, 285, 291, 292, 293, 294, 295, 296, 297, 298, 299, 300, 301, 302, 304, 307, 308, 310, 312, 313, 315, 316, 317, 319, 320, 323, 325, 326, 327, 331, 332, 334, 337, 339, 343, 345, 346, 348, 349, 352, 354, 355, 356, 357, 358, 360, 364, 366, 367, 368
Cross-Disciplinary Innovation 119, 120, 121, 122, 123, 145
culturally responsive teaching 3, 22, 165, 216, 217, 219, 235, 291, 307, 308, 309, 313
Curriculum Design 44, 49, 64, 65, 66, 124, 126, 145, 158, 265, 366

D

Descartes 92, 94, 95, 96, 110, 112
differentiated instruction 11, 15, 18, 47, 64, 73, 75, 79, 170, 175, 216, 218, 220, 291, 306, 307, 308, 313, 357, 366
Diverse Sources 31, 37

E

EAS MODEL 325
Educational Challenges 153, 169, 177
educational contexts 4, 46, 48, 58, 82, 140, 152, 153, 154, 160, 164, 167, 171, 173, 239, 295, 348, 353, 358, 363, 364
Educational Equity 361
elementary teachers 183, 185, 186, 188, 192, 193, 194, 195, 196, 197, 198, 201, 202, 203, 204, 206, 207, 208, 210, 211
Engineering Education 38, 120, 121, 122, 123, 124, 125, 128, 129, 132, 141, 142, 143, 144, 145, 147, 148, 149, 179, 180, 182, 285
English Teacher Education 237, 238

F

Flipped Classroom 40, 220, 221, 226, 227, 233

Formative Assessment 5, 7, 21, 22, 26, 49, 52, 57, 69, 76, 80, 84, 86, 165, 218, 233, 348, 350, 351, 357, 359, 361

G

Grammar Instruction 237, 253, 254, 255, 256

H

Hegel 100, 101, 112

I

Indigenous Gnoseology 89, 91, 92, 93, 95, 96, 97, 98, 99, 100, 101, 103, 104, 105, 106, 118
Innovative Problem-Solving 132
Interdisciplinary Collaboration 120, 122, 123, 129, 130, 131, 142

L

Language Arts 1, 2, 3, 11, 12, 13, 15, 16, 21, 47, 185, 222, 305, 306, 307, 308, 309, 352
Learning Progressions 25, 41, 42, 43, 44, 48, 49, 50, 51, 52, 53, 54, 55, 56, 57, 58, 59, 60, 61, 62, 63, 64, 66, 67, 68, 69, 70, 71, 72, 73, 74, 75, 76, 78, 79, 84, 85

M

Mathematics Education 2, 4, 6, 7, 8, 23, 38, 39, 46, 77, 79, 85, 185, 202, 204, 208, 211, 212, 316, 317
mentorship 14, 32, 35, 36, 39, 40, 159, 160, 161, 172, 174, 216, 291, 297, 299, 301, 306, 307, 309, 313

P

PCK models 188
Pedagogical Content Knowledge (PCK) 1, 2, 3, 4, 5, 6, 8, 9, 11, 12, 13, 14, 15, 16, 19, 21, 22, 23, 24, 25, 31, 32, 33, 34, 35, 36, 37, 38, 39, 40, 41, 42, 44, 46, 48, 50, 51, 61, 63, 70, 73, 74, 76, 78, 79, 80, 81, 83, 84, 85, 89, 91, 92, 106, 119, 120, 122, 123, 125, 132, 136, 139, 141, 145, 148, 151, 154, 155, 161, 168, 171, 172, 177, 178, 180, 182, 183, 185, 187, 188, 191, 194, 200, 201, 202, 203, 204, 205, 206, 207, 208, 209, 210, 211, 212, 213, 216, 223, 228, 231, 233, 234, 237, 238, 246, 257, 259, 260, 264, 265, 272, 285, 291, 292, 294, 307, 308, 310, 315, 316, 317, 319, 320, 323, 325, 326, 327, 331, 332, 334, 337, 339, 343, 345, 346, 349, 352, 355, 356, 358, 366, 367, 368
pedagogical knowledge 4, 5, 6, 37, 123, 155, 160, 185, 186, 187, 191, 200, 238, 275, 280, 281, 295, 297, 298, 322, 323, 324, 337, 348
Phronesis 89, 92, 93, 94, 102
pre-service teachers 38, 157, 163, 183, 185, 192, 193, 194, 195, 197, 198, 263, 282, 291, 292, 293, 294, 296, 297, 298, 299, 300, 301, 302, 303, 304, 305, 306, 307, 308, 309, 310, 311, 312, 313, 314, 315, 316, 368
Professional Development 3, 8, 9, 10, 12, 13, 14, 16, 19, 21, 22, 23, 25, 26, 32, 35, 37, 40, 44, 45, 49, 53, 56, 58, 65, 66, 68, 69, 70, 73, 74, 75, 78, 81, 82, 84, 85, 122, 125, 139, 140, 152, 153, 154, 155, 157, 158, 159, 160, 161, 162, 165, 166, 167, 168, 169, 170, 171, 172, 173, 174, 175, 176, 177, 178, 181, 182, 196, 211, 213, 214, 223, 229, 230, 231, 232, 282, 310, 311, 313, 327, 328, 330, 331, 346, 347, 351, 352, 359, 360, 361, 362, 363, 364, 366, 367
Professional Development Workshops 32, 35, 69, 161
professional growth 4, 14, 49, 68, 152, 155, 161, 209, 214, 216, 258, 308, 312, 316, 337, 359, 360
Project-Based Learning 53, 65, 67, 124,

126, 130, 141, 144, 213, 220, 223, 226, 227, 231, 234

R

reflective practice 3, 10, 13, 14, 17, 45, 152, 157, 163, 165, 169, 170, 171, 172, 173, 174, 175, 176, 177, 186, 197, 214, 216, 241, 292, 293, 295, 296, 301, 304, 308, 309, 313, 327, 362

S

Scaffolding 41, 49, 52, 61, 63, 64, 69, 73, 75, 196, 199
Science Instruction 25, 61, 74, 183, 185, 187, 192, 197, 206
science pedagogical content knowledge 183, 201
Service Learning 213, 222, 223
Shulman 2, 4, 12, 26, 44, 92, 93, 116, 120, 122, 123, 152, 154, 155, 156, 171, 185, 186, 187, 188, 210, 237, 238, 239, 241, 243, 259, 260, 261, 292, 294, 295, 319, 320, 322, 323, 325, 327, 331, 332, 333, 334, 337, 342, 346, 348, 349, 350, 360, 368
Social sciences 1, 2, 3, 9, 10, 15, 76, 80, 82, 86, 87, 90, 94, 105, 112, 130, 131, 213, 214, 215, 216, 217, 218, 219, 220, 221, 222, 223, 224, 226, 227, 228, 229, 230, 231, 232, 234, 285
Social Sciences 1, 2, 3, 9, 10, 15, 76, 80, 82, 86, 87, 90, 94, 105, 112, 130, 131, 213, 214, 215, 216, 217, 218, 219, 220, 221, 222, 223, 224, 226, 227, 228, 229, 230, 231, 232, 234, 285
Student Learning Outcomes 3, 32, 72, 81, 171, 241, 314, 345, 347, 349, 351, 352, 353, 359, 360
Summative Assessment 165, 198, 348, 350, 356, 359, 360, 364
System Thinking 263, 264, 265, 270, 271, 282

T

teacher development 202, 235, 257, 258, 351, 362
Teacher Education Programs 3, 32, 34, 36, 154, 176, 192, 193, 195, 257, 258, 294, 296, 297, 301, 302, 303, 361
teacher preparation 14, 38, 80, 81, 172, 185, 203, 224, 277, 287, 292, 312, 339, 343, 361
Teacher Professional Development 22, 26, 84, 85, 347, 366, 367
teaching expertise 152
Technological Pedagogical Content Knowledge 12, 16, 23, 24, 25, 39, 81, 191, 259, 264, 265, 272, 285, 315, 325, 326, 366, 367
technology integration 3, 23, 25, 32, 35, 36, 37, 164, 173, 177, 277, 300, 308, 312, 313

U

Universal Design for Learning 321, 326, 328, 339, 340, 341, 344